Trevor Watt

Salter
Broadway
NYC. 27

Union Real Sem.
3041 Broadway
New York 27.

June 1, 1959

Types of Religious Philosophy

Types of
Religious Philosophy

Revised Edition

BY

EDWIN A. BURTT

Susan Linn Sage Professor
of Philosophy
Cornell University

HARPER & BROTHERS
PUBLISHERS
NEW YORK

Contents

Preface to the First Edition

While an author should be appropriately modest regarding the achievements of his book, he owes it to his readers to be frankly immodest with regard to its intent. Here, then, so far as its purpose goes, is a volume which would have been very helpful to me had I met with it when I first began to struggle seriously with the problems of religious thought. Not that it solves these problems or even attempts to do so. Its aim is the more limited one of providing, in a form as undistorted as possible by partisan bias, the historical materials and comparative analyses on which as a foundation the contemporary student may make reflective progress toward his own solutions. Avoiding evangelism as far as I could, I have tried to contribute toward a fundamental clarification of religious philosophy. This is what I once desperately needed; there must be others who feel that need today.

The bulk of the book consists in an exposition of the main points of view in religious philosophy which now compete for acceptance among Western thinkers, together with an analysis of the major issues on which they differ. Some will think that such an enterprise can be carried out successfully only by the coöperative method, each philosophy being presented by one of its own convinced champions. While I recognize the danger which threatens if this method be rejected, I am disposed to think that in case a reasonable impartiality is attained there are great advantages in the unity of treatment which can be secured only if the entire task is performed by a single author. The danger in question has been constantly before me; I can only hope that I have measurably succeeded in the effort to be not only objectively fair but even generously sympathetic in my portrayal of these proposed solutions of the most insistently haunting problem of human life. In this connection I wish to express appreciation of the aid given by Father Donald M. Cleary of the Cornell United Religious Work, and certain of his

philosopher friends, in the chapter on Catholicism. This is the one
influential standpoint in Western religious philosophy through
which I have never myself passed, and I was especially fearful of
failure in treating it. They should not, of course, be held responsible
for the final result.

I cannot hope for universal approval on matters of selection
and emphasis. Many readers, especially, will feel that some of the
tendencies briefly described in Chapter X should have been expounded on the same scale as that used in earlier chapters. Some
will feel that the significance of agnosticism, or humanism, as
religious philosophies has been exaggerated, or that important and
sufficiently distinctive points of view have been omitted.[1] More
than a few will hold that the historical background of Western
religious thought has been treated at greater length than is justifiable in a book whose main purpose is not historical. The book
must take its chances with the various possible objections on these
points.

My indebtednesses are so numerous that with three further
exceptions besides the one already noted I can offer only a
wholesale acknowledgment—almost every serious treatment of
religion that I have read has contributed something to my reflections on the present theme.

A debt is owed to the students in my classes in the philosophy
of religion at Cornell University, especially for their aid in discriminating between issues that appeal to an academic philosopher
and those vital to young people today who are unspoiled by
philosophy.

Another special obligation which it is a pleasure to record
concerns Chapters VIII, X, and XI. Much of the material in these
chapters was used in three lectures at the University of Cincinnati
in March, 1938, under the auspices of the Charles Phelps Taft
Memorial Fund. The title of the lecture series was "The Influence
of Empiricism on Modern Philosophies of Religion." I wish to
express here my appreciation of the thoughtfulness of Dean Louis
T. More of the Graduate School of the University, and of the members of the Department of Philosophy on the occasion of that visit.

[1] Such as the points of view of Anglo-Catholicism, the Society of Friends,
Christian Science, and the Oxford Movement.

Finally, I owe thanks to the following publishers for permission to use quotations from volumes under their copyright: Burns, Oates, and Washbourne, Ltd.; the Yale University Press; G. Bell and Sons, Ltd.; John Murray; the Cambridge University Press; Harper & Brothers; The Humanist Press Association; the Abingdon Press; Charles Scribner's Sons; Henry Holt and Company; The Macmillan Company; the D. Appleton-Century Company; and Random House, Inc.

E. A. BURTT

Ithaca, N. Y.
June, 1938

Preface to the Revised Edition

I still believe, as I did more than a decade ago, that there is a useful place for a volume whose primary purpose is to describe the most influential positions in Western religious philosophy, and to analyze the basic issues that they disclose, with the maximum impartiality that can be attained. Hence the present revision involves no change in this central aim.

The major differences from the first edition are four. First, the material on modernism and humanism is radically condensed and the two viewpoints are treated together, although, to avoid a chapter of excessive length, two chapters are still devoted to them. Second, a full-length chapter is given to the new supernaturalism that is such a vigorous movement today, especially as it is exhibited in the "dialectical theology" abroad and the philosophy of Reinhold Niebuhr in America. Third, a section is added in the final part of the book on the issue of whether man is a helpless sinner or not. And fourth, most of the material in the chapter on "Some Individual Philosophies and Current Trends" is omitted.

There are numerous minor differences, aiming at clarity, or simplicity, or a closer approximation to the impartiality which I had sought. The chapter organization is changed, to bring out more adequately the essential structure of the book.

E. A. BURTT

Ithaca, N. Y.
April, 1951

PART I

Our Problem and Its
Historical Setting

❧ ❧

Chapter I

INTRODUCTION

The Study of Religion

GENERALLY speaking, there are two different ways of studying religion. The primary purpose of one is to help us become more religious. It wishes not so much to enlighten our minds as to edify and warm our hearts. Such study has its appropriate method; this consists in the interweaving of appealing images and illustrative analogies drawn from sacred writings or from other inspirational literature, calculated by their emotional associations to deepen our zeal and encourage a fuller exemplification in conduct of our religious ideals. The primary purpose of the other is to achieve an accurate understanding of religion. It may, and often does, further edification indirectly, but this forms no part of its essential intent. Increased knowledge, with or without increased piety, is its goal. And this way of studying religion likewise has its appropriate method, which is very different from that just described. What this method requires in detail we need not here ask, but its general principles are the same as those by which we guide our reflection when endeavoring to understand correctly other subjects than religion.

The present volume adopts the latter of these two aims. It recognizes the value of persons whose main concern is to deepen human piety, but it embodies the conviction that religion needs to be understood as well as lived, and that zeal without breadth of knowledge is at best unstable, at worst a social danger. Now, if such is to be our approach, it is important at the very beginning to

3

consider the main principles which must be respected in any pursuit of truth, and to illustrate their necessity in an inquiry concerning religion.

What are these principles? Well, true understanding, whatever its subject matter, seems to require (1) *clarity* in the meaning of the words by whose aid it is attained and in which its results are expressed. It is evident that unless we know rather definitely what we mean by such words as "God" and "faith" it is useless to try to answer the question whether God exists or to solve the problem of the relation between faith and knowledge. Only when clarity in the meaning of our terms has been gained can we profitably proceed with such reflection. Understanding also demands (2) *consistency* in the statements made about its subject. It may be emotionally stimulating to believe on one occasion that God providentially rewards the good and punishes the wicked, and to believe on another that his dealings with mankind follow natural laws of cause and effect, but an individual who holds both these beliefs is so far illogical in his reasoning on matters of religion. Either God always works in accordance with natural law, or he sometimes subordinates such law to moral purposes; for a mind in quest of religious truth both these beliefs cannot hold. Understanding involves (3) *respect for all discoverable facts* that bear upon the matters at issue. It is especially easy in dealing with religion to neglect facts which do not harmonize with convictions we are strongly moved to adopt; it is likewise easy to forget that our experience to date has been necessarily limited, and that accordingly adequate understanding of any question of religious concern would require active search for relevant facts which as yet have not come within our ken. Religious thinkers in Europe and America, for instance, have been all too prone to forget that their problems would gain illumination from a study of contrasting types of religious experience found among Oriental peoples, and that this is the case whatever conclusions about those experiences they may ultimately embrace. Finally, understanding includes (4) *impartiality* in our interpretation of the pertinent facts. To attain this in religious matters is hardest of all. Religion for most of us is so emphatically a way of meeting personal need that when we try to reflect about it our reflection is exceedingly likely to be swayed by our eager individual concern; the results are partial to our own prejudices rather than objectively fair. But this is contrary to true understanding, in religion as in anything else. To believe one doctrine as true is always to reject others as false, and the significance of the doctrine believed is in part derived from the positions rejected. This may be readily illustrated in religion. To accept, for instance, the Christian doctrine of the Trinity is to reject as false both polytheism and absolute monism in one's conception of God. Now, if such disbelief is to express true understanding rather than mere impulsive hostility, it must rest on sufficiently sympathetic appreciation of the rejected doctrines so that the disbeliever may state these doctrines and the case in their favor in a manner that seems adequate to those who believe them, and not merely in a manner obviously colored by his opposition. Otherwise he is disbelieving, not the doctrine that he seems to reject, but a verbally similar one concocted simply for the purpose of laying it low again with a triumphant flourish.

By what motives must one be controlled who proposes to be loyal to these principles in his study of religion? It would seem that two motives must be present, and perhaps these two are sufficient: intellectual honesty on the one hand, and appreciative sympathy with the religious convictions of others on the other hand. To maintain these motives steadfastly is not always easy, but let us make a strong effort to do so throughout the present study. What, now, are the important forms which religious understanding may take? What distinctive aspects of the subject may it emphasize?

THREE FORMS OF RELIGIOUS UNDERSTANDING

Broadly, there are three such forms or aspects. One is signified by the phrase "history of religion."[1] Religion, like every other human concern, is an affair of temporal change. The modes in which it now exists, in any part of the world whose past is illumined by historical record or tradition, are not exactly the same as the modes in which it has existed in any previous period that we might select. This applies to its ceremonies, its accepted principles of conduct, its

[1] As will be evident below, this phrase is intended to cover the material sometimes referred to by the phrase "sociology of religion."

social organization, its characteristic inward attitudes and sentiments, its beliefs. In some cases and at some periods these changes
are slow and almost imperceptible; at others they are swift and
revolutionary. Instances of the latter, in the Western world, are the
Hellenistic era, the time of the Protestant Reformation, and the last
two generations. Obviously, one of the important ways in which
we may seek to understand religion is set by this circumstance of
constant transformation. It suggests to us such fundamental questions as these: Just what significant religious changes have taken
place, among a particular people during a given period? What were
the causes of these changes, and to what further effects did they
lead? How are religious traits transmitted from one community to
another? What relations of comparison may we note between the
trends of change among different and separated peoples? Are there
any verifiable general laws exhibited in these changes, and if so,
what are they? At present, great difficulties haunt the effort of
students to gain adequate answers even to the first of these questions,
except perhaps in the case of a few peoples and the periods about
which their historical records are clearest. And it is evident that
acceptable answers to the other questions depend on our having
already secured the right answer to the first. All the confident gen-
eralizations on these questions which were so freely offered by
historical theorists prior to the present generation have proved
mistaken or seriously inadequate, and the need of critical and in-
tensive fact-finding before further large-scale historical generaliza-
tions are attempted is now almost universally recognized among
serious students of the subject. One interested in religion, who
enjoys an intellectual adventure where blazed trails are few and
pioneer exploration is demanded on every hand, will find plenty of
scope for his energies in this field. And a considerable part of the
work that remains to be done here—the study of religion among
so-called "primitive" peoples—will probably not be done at all
unless it is done soon. Under contemporary conditions primitive
groups are not allowed for long to remain in their accustomed ways,
and since their historical records are meager and inaccurate, we
shall in a short time have no means of ascertaining with confidence
the nature of their religion prior to the impact of the forces of
civilization, unless the required facts are accumulated now.

Another approach to the understanding of religion is indicated by the phrase "psychology of religion." Among most peoples to a considerable extent, and with peoples of advanced civilization to a very great extent, religion is an inward and personal affair. When an individual is actively religious he is in a characteristic and to some degree distinctive state of mind. He is thinking, feeling, and acting in ways that are in part different from those which characterize his behavior under other circumstances. This fact, too, poses an important problem for students eager to understand religion. The fundamental questions which it leads them to ask run noticeably parallel to those which the historian of religion asks. What *is* the state of mind of a given religious individual or group of individuals under such and such circumstances? What common factors and what distinctive differences does it reveal when compared with what we regard as secular states, and what further effects, in the individuals who exhibit it and in their relations to other persons and things, does it tend to produce? What significant comparisons may we make between the religious psychology of individuals who participate in quite different social cultures and inherit quite different religious traditions? Are there any general laws of religious psychology, and if so what are they? These questions, like those asked by the historian, are not easy to answer. One reason for the difficulty is that psychologists have as yet established no standard method of procedure and no common set of assumptions as to what constitutes a sound explanation of psychological facts. Indeed, in the field of religion, every system of doctrine has its own explicit or implicit theory of human nature. Not only do many partially irreconcilable schools of psychology compete with each other for acceptance in the modern Occident, but (with reference to the special branch of psychology which now concerns us) each Oriental religion to which intellectually developed peoples have been attached offers its own psychological theory or theories, whose presuppositions differ profoundly from all those with which we are familiar. Buddhism and Hinduism, for example, exhibit a long development of psychological experimentation and of theoretical explanation of its results, which can hardly be understood at all by a Western student without patient, sympathetic study of the characteristic interests, attitudes, and ideas of the peoples whose thinkers have contributed to that development. Here, again, is a challenging opportunity for the student of religion who is willing to undergo the severe discipline and acquire the wide information essential if he is to contribute constructively to this form of religious understanding.

We may note in passing two special themes which belong in this field of study. One is the psychology of mysticism. While the extremer forms of the mystic experience are not very common in any religious group (excepting some groups formed explicitly for its cultivation), mysticism is an affair of peculiar interest to the serious student of religion. The mystic vision of God, or ecstasy of felt union with him, is, to those who attain it, an affair of ravishing emotional intensity, of vivid intellectual illumination, and on both these accounts of supreme value. Its relations to other matters which fall within the psychologist's province are exceedingly difficult to trace with confidence. Some of them lead to phenomena which he is inclined to regard as abnormal, such as hypnotism, sexually motivated fantasies, and paranoia; others suggest that we have in mysticism an intensification of normal processes whose functioning is necessary to an individual's mastery of the tensions which all of us are called upon to face in the task of living. One who succeeds in understanding mysticism adequately will add an important chapter to our insight into what religion does for those who practice it.

The other theme is the relation between psychotherapy and religion. The psychotherapist today aims to cure individuals disturbed by inner conflict, so that they may find health and wholeness. In this process he deals in his own way with problems of sin, guilt, and mental suffering. Is psychotherapy simply a more scientific way of doing for people what religion has done for them in the past? If there are significant differences, what are they? How can we rightly understand the role of religion in relation to these new and important psychological techniques?

The third main approach to the understanding of religion is suggested by the phrase "philosophy of religion." The religious man, as religious, among other things holds certain beliefs about the universe, and especially about its impact upon his life and destiny. The historian of religion examines these beliefs, like other religious phenomena, in their temporal vicissitudes; he wants to know, if he

can, when and why they first arise, how they spread, and under
what circumstances they decline and give way to others. The
psychologist of religion studies these beliefs in their psychological
context. He is interested in the nature of believing as a mental
act; he interprets it in the light of its relations to other phenomena
of the religious mentality with which it appears to be correlated.
By neither of these inquirers are such beliefs considered from the
standpoint of their truth or falsity; they enter simply as religious
facts to be taken into account because some people, rightly or
wrongly, hold them. But from the point of view of the man anxious
to decide whether he should adopt such and such a belief or not,
the question of its truth or falsity is central. Here is the main task
of the philosophy of religion. It subjects to critical examination
the religious beliefs which in any community are live possibilities
for acceptance or rejection. Ideally it should do this for the beliefs
of all communities which have any intellectual contact with one
another. Modern philosophy of religion ought to keep in mind
perplexed Chinese as well as Europeans, doubting Hottentots as
well as Americans. But it is a rare individual who has sufficient
knowledge to deal with the varied problems which such a universal
philosophy of religion would impose upon him. And it would require
a volume in itself to provide the necessary background for discussing
them. In the main, therefore, we shall confine ourselves to the issues
set by the Western religious tradition and Western reactions against
it; these are the issues which actually challenge all but a very few
inquiring minds in our part of the world. It is indeed important to
reach beyond this limited field, by sympathetic study of religious
philosophies whose background is non-Christian, but here is plenty
of material with which to occupy ourselves at present.

   This critical examination of possible beliefs is pursued by the
philosopher of religion in the several ways indicated by the principles of reflective understanding outlined early in the present
chapter. For one thing, these beliefs need to be clarified by a careful analysis of their meaning. Such dissection reduces vagueness,
eliminates ambiguity, and makes it possible to see with assurance
what further beliefs logically follow from a belief thus analyzed.
For another, the mutual consistency or inconsistency of religious
propositions is a matter for philosophical reflection to determine,

and this can usually be done confidently as soon as the propositions in question have been clarified. Often a man can reject a
proposed belief without further consideration, as soon as he sees
its inconsistency with other positions that appear to him better
grounded. A third line of inquiry is to turn to the factual evidence
offered as support for a given religious conviction, and to consider
whether or not it is adequately assessed. And a fourth is to examine
the arguments by which we are asked to pass from apparently
innocent premises to the impartially valid conclusions supposed to
be established by them. Do these arguments reflect fairness in the
author's understanding of alternative doctrines, or a biased interpretation of them? Is he subtly assuming what he claims to be
proving? When a belief has been thoroughly tested by these four
methods we are in as favorable a position to decide whether it is
true or false as philosophy at present is able to place us.

In the modern Western world, with its distinctive religious background, the main questions upon which any philosophy of religion
will inevitably concentrate are such as the following: What kind of
being may we appropriately mean by the word "God," and does
such a being really exist or not? What is the nature of our relation
to him? To what destiny, mundane or supermundane, may we
human beings reasonably look forward—in particular, may we hope
for the continuance of personal life beyond the grave? What is the
nature of religious faith, and how is it related to scientific knowledge? Is man a link in the chain of causal law, or is he in some sense
free from causal determination? And if the latter, in what sense
are we to understand this freedom, and what is its bearing on other
religious, ethical, and psychological problems? What is the relation
of religion to moral ideals and obligations? Especially, what is the
significance of religion for the social problems that challenge every
serious thinker today—the issues of war and peace, of capitalism
versus socialism, of democracy and dictatorship? What is the
appropriate function in society of the church as the organized institution of religion? On such questions as these, varying convictions
prevail among us and compete for our acceptance. Which of them
are true, and which false? It is the business of philosophy of religion
to help us decide.

At this point, it will be well to consider whether there is any difference between philosophy of religion and theology, and if so, what it is. In the past, for many thinkers, there has been no essential difference; the reference is especially to philosophers who conceived it as their task systematically to expound a theory of the universe which included recognition of a divine being as the source of all existence. Today, also, for some thinkers there is no important difference; not only are there still philosophers of the sort just mentioned, but there are theologians whose thought has been so strongly influenced by contemporary philosophical currents that their very conception of theology and of its method has been determined by them. But by and large there is a significant difference, to which we gain a clue by noting the derivation of these two terms. Theology means literally "science of the divine," or (to expand the phrase a bit) "systematic truth about God." This implies that the task of the theologian, in general, is to take certain basic assumptions about a divine being or beings and to develop, by as accurate reasoning as he may, their detailed bearing upon all the various questions—scientific and moral as well as religious—whose solution they in any way affect. Before adopting these assumptions he may have critically examined them with any degree you please of thoroughness, but this part of his work has not ordinarily been regarded as theology. The latter will consist simply in a systematic justification of the outcome of that examination; it will not reflect the course of the examination as he actively pursued it. Philosophy of religion means literally "the love of (or, quest for) wisdom about religious matters." This implies that it is the philosopher's business to exhibit in detail precisely that part of the total reflective procedure which the theologian, as such, is apt to omit—the active critical inquiry in which different basic assumptions about religion are tentatively compared with each other and their relative claims to truth assessed. From the standpoint of this difference the theologian is essentially a teacher, presenting to others a detailed and logically persuasive defense of his major convictions after he has reached them; while the philosopher of religion, as such, is essentially an inquirer, ready to share with other inquirers the process of exploration by which he fumbles his way toward such convictions as he may ultimately reach. Of course, when he reaches them he may become a teacher of doctrine too, and proffer a theology. Whether, in doing so, his work should still be regarded as a part of his philosophy of religion is a question. Would it or would it not be wise to limit this phrase to a narrower or allow it a broader connotation? We need not dogmatize about such a matter. It is important to note, however, that certain religious philosophies naturally tend, so far as much of their content is concerned, to pass over into theology; namely, those which hold that basic religious truth is capable of systematic demonstration. In their case theology can hardly be separated from philosophy. With other philosophies no such intimate connection obtains, and theology may be entirely absent.

WAYS OF PURSUING RELIGIOUS PHILOSOPHY

How may we most fruitfully proceed with the task of religious philosophy? One way is suggested by the list of religious problems recently enumerated. We might take these up one after another, subjecting each in turn to the clarification, factual evaluation, and interpretative analysis that a quest for truth always demands. Many treatments of the philosophy of religion follow this procedure. Again, we might make use of a classification of religious issues suggested by study of the history or the psychology of religion.

The course of discussion here proposed is different from either of these, and for two main reasons. For one thing, it is difficult to carry out an analysis by a series of such selected topics without prejudice. By this is meant that one who follows this method is exceedingly apt to be unfair to religious doctrines with which he disagrees, to weight the scales unconsciously in favor of the conclusions about these topics toward which his own thinking tends. He does so simply by allowing his own preferred approach to such topics—i.e., his preliminary definitions, classifications, and emphases —without realizing that he is doing so, to make a difference in the details of his analysis and hence in the result which it appears to establish. Since this is inconsistent with the honesty and impartiality which respect for truth prescribes, it is incumbent upon us to avoid it as far as we may.

The second reason is intimated by the title of the book. There are *types* of religious philosophy—that is, basic attitudes expressed in convictions which bear in one way or another upon all the issues above mentioned. We all tend to classify our friends and associates with whom we discuss religious questions in some one of these types. After varied bits of such discussion we can predict with considerable confidence, when we learn what a man believes about God, the church, or any major theme of religion, what he is likely to believe about any of its other important problems. In other words, there are systems of religious belief, sufficiently close-knit internally so that any belief which is a member of such a system tends to be allied with, if not definitely to imply, certain beliefs about other matters of religious concern. Among those who, like all readers of this book, have been affected by the intellectual currents pervading the modern world there are at least seven of these types, which are capable of being distinguished from each other with a fair degree of clarity. We refer to them in religious discussion by such terms as: "fundamentalism," "agnosticism," "liberalism," "Catholicism," and the like.

Now, if this is the case, a study of religious philosophy by selected topics, such as God, immortality, faith, and the rest, will be apt to neglect or obscure the interrelationship which obtains between a given conviction about one of these matters and allied convictions about the others. Such a study will produce a picture of religious belief anatomized into isolated segments, rather than a canvas on which its living unity can be traced. To grasp the latter it is necessary to study, sympathetically as well as critically, these distinctive types or systems as such. This can only be done by following in each case the main lines of argument by which those who defend them endeavor to make the interconnection of their ideas persuasive to others.

In the chapters which follow there is presented an exposition, as impartial and sympathetic as the author can render it, of these seven major points of view in contemporary Western religious philosophy. The central aim is to aid the reader in reaching an impartial understanding of them. While the study is not primarily historical, being a clarification of systems of ideas now actively competing for our acceptance, the method of exposition is in part historical. A minor reason for this circumstance is that history supplies an objective basis for deciding in which order to expound these competing philosophies; we may introduce them in the sequence indicated by the dates at which they originally appeared, bearing the general character which they still exhibit. By this criterion we begin with Catholicism and end with the new supernaturalism of contemporary thought, and no suggestion is intended that either age or recency carries any special weight when questions of truth and falsity are involved. If the reader be inclined to think that hoary age implies greater trustworthiness in a philosophy, as indicating that it has been tested over a longer period and found adequate, he should remember also that the later philosophies would never have arisen had not many thinkers, at the time these new systems first appeared, found the earlier ideas inadequate. If he be tempted to suppose that recency implies greater likelihood of truth, on the ground that a new-born philosophy must have taken account of new circumstances and needs as well as those which more ancient beliefs endeavored to meet, he should remember that these older philosophies, while preserving their fundamental structure, have been continually restated in the light of more recently challenging problems, and have thus as much right to claim pertinence to the contemporary scene as any of their rivals. And in expounding them we shall try to take sufficient account of these restatements so that no holder of relatively aged doctrines will feel that his position is presented in outworn form. Religious viewpoints that have perished—such as deism —will not, except for minor references, be included at all.

Use of the historical method for this purpose, however, requires that before expounding even the earliest of these types of religious philosophy we make a brief survey of the historical background which all of them share in common. This means a study of the main stages in the development of Judaism and Christianity down to the late medieval period, when the Catholic philosophy in its now accepted form first gained systematic statement. And here the major reason both for such a study and for some use of the historical method appears. Our present reflections about religion presuppose that long development. They presuppose it in the sense that they are vitally affected, from first to last, by the deposit it has left on the present sands of time. This explains the fact, noted above, that philosophy of religion in the modern Occident is inevitably different from that of a Hindu or an Eskimo. Our problems are not his, because they arise out of discrepancies we encounter between our present experience and our past tradition, both of which are different from his. The possible solutions which we consider are not identical with his, because they consist of alternative emphases and novel combinations among our heritage of ideas, suggested by our contemporary experience. Whether we like it or no, our thinking on religion proceeds in intimate dependence on its Western context and its historical background. We cannot at will jump out of our own skins. Hence, to catch the meaning of the conclusions we are led to adopt, it is necessary to be familiar with the main features of the temporal setting out of which they emerge and which poses the problems they purport to solve.

To such a survey the three following chapters are devoted, and in each of the later chapters (except for Part III) some introductory indication will be given of the main historical forces which were uniquely influential in the rise of the particular religious philosophy there under discussion.

Chapter II

THE HEBREW BACKGROUND

WE may briefly describe the historical background of contemporary philosophy of religion in the Western world by a summary and anticipatory statement. Its original essence, so far as our knowledge goes, lies in certain forms of religious experience and attitude characteristic of the ancient Hebrews. But to the experiences themselves we must at once add the ideas by which they were interpreted and under whose influence subsequent religious experience developed. Indeed, for our purpose it is the ideas that are important rather than their roots in religious feeling and practice. The earlier of these ideas were in general indigenous to the Hebrews themselves or their Oriental neighbors, but the later ones, which contributed a unity and coherence lacking in the earlier, were due to the Greek philosophers, especially Plato and Aristotle. Characteristic emphases of the Roman mind in time played their part, and, later still, the dominant interests of modern European peoples. It will be the aim of the following survey to note the main elements and historical stages disclosed in the case of these diverse factors, and the manner in which all but the last-named came to be united into a single whole.

HEBREW RELIGION AT THE TIME OF THE PALESTINIAN CONQUEST

The earliest period in the history of Jewish religion about which we know enough so that its major details may be sketched in a manner acceptable to competent scholars,[1] is the period from about 1300

[1] At this point, as we commence the historical interpretation of Hebrew religion, a choice must be made which the author wishes were avoidable. The

to 1000 B.C., during which the Hebrew tribes were conquering the fertile plains and valleys of Palestine, and amalgamating with the earlier inhabitants. In the course of this conquest their habits were changed from those of wandering nomads to those suitable in an agricultural civilization. There was a lively tradition among them of an earlier period of captivity in Egypt, from which, according to this tradition, they had been delivered by their God Yahweh (or Jehovah) through the agency of a leader named Moses. In many respects their religious practices and ideas at this time were similar to those of neighboring peoples, but certain distinctive features are noticeable, all or most of which are connected with the conception of a voluntary covenant which their fathers had made with Yahweh under the persuasion of Moses and his successor Joshua. The main sources of our information about their religion at this time are the Old Testament books of Joshua, Judges, and Samuel.

To turn to these distinctive features first, it is apparent that prior to the time of Moses the Hebrews had cultivated relations with a large number of divine powers, each tribe, and often even each family, having its own divinity from which it sought protection and kindly aid. While they were held as captive slaves in Egypt, however, according to the tradition, Moses had a very vivid religious experience which he interpreted as the appearance of Yahweh, the God of Mount Sinai south of Palestine, commanding him to lead the Hebrews out of captivity into a land where they would find prosperity, and promising him supernatural assistance in this undertaking. The enterprise proved eventually successful, although Moses

---

interpretation demanded by the impartiality of our method would be one acceptable to historians of religion representing all the seven types of religious philosophy with which we are to deal. Unfortunately, there is no such interpretation. By and large, we face two alternatives: the traditionalist picture of Hebrew history, acceptable to fundamentalists and in general to Catholics; and the picture offered by the "higher criticism," acceptable to most historians of the other five types. The difference between these will be explained when we take up the higher criticism in chap. X. On several important points they are quite irreconcilable with each other. What we shall do is to follow the latter of these two interpretations in the main, but without insisting on any matters which would not be acceptable to those who believe in the former. Thus there is hope that, so far as concerns what the survey includes, it will be fair to both sides. It will, of course, unavoidably omit some statements which would be regarded as warranted and important by the traditionalists, especially statements concerning the period treated in the book of Genesis.

died before the promised land was reached and committed the leadership to Joshua. As a result of the stirring circumstances attending this release and migration, the Hebrews who participated in it were sufficiently loosened from their previous religious habits, and sufficiently grateful to Yahweh through whose aid the project seemed to be consummated, so that under Moses' and Joshua's insistence they entered into a voluntary pact with Yahweh, binding their descendants as well as themselves to be faithful to it. The essence of this agreement, as interpreted by their leaders, was that on their part, in thankful remembrance of Yahweh's help, they promised to worship and obey him; on his part he was to give them continued protection and guidance as his chosen people.

The two features of this convenant relation which from the very first stand out noticeably in contrast with the characteristic attitudes of neighboring peoples toward their divinities were: first, the vivid sense of responsibility, personal as well as social, which it encouraged; and second, the historical consciousness which thenceforth became likewise focal in all Jewish religious attitudes and ideas. Without these features, as will soon become apparent, it would hardly have been possible for Hebrew religion to develop, as readily as it did, in the direction required by the ideas of the great prophets. The sense of conscious responsibility was, of course, based on the conviction embedded in the covenant relation, that before they or their fathers had done anything to merit Yahweh's favor he had singled them out as recipients of his gracious attention, delivering them from bondage and providing them a prosperous homeland in which to dwell. Since they and their children all shared in the bounty thus received, there lay naturally a personal obligation on each to remain loyal to the divinity who had chosen them from all peoples as special objects of his kindly care, and to keep their religion free from all attitudes and acts which would be inconsistent with such grateful loyalty. To this sense of responsibility, however feeble at times it might be, the prophets who came later were constantly able to appeal, in their effort to deepen the understanding of the people as to what the covenant relation really involved. As for the historical consciousness, it is evident that for the Hebrews at this period Yahweh was not mainly a personification of natural powers such as sun, earth, rain, or storm, with which man must needs square himself if he is to win a secure

existence (as was the case with most of the divinities cultivated
by other peoples); he controlled these powers, but he was also
a being with a historical plan for his chosen people, to be carried
out through their active coöperation.[2] This means that Jewish
religious experience, even at this early era, was marked by a live
sense of history and of progress. It distinctly embodied a temporal
reach, extending at least from the memorable display in the past
of Yahweh's great kindness toward them to an anticipated future
in which his benefits would be still more richly revealed. This historical consciousness provided the necessary background for the
persistent attempt of the prophets to interpret the events and prospects of their own times in relation to the covenant between Yahweh
and his people and the peculiar duties which that covenant spelled
for the latter.

Aside from these features, however, and the consequence of their
impact upon other religious matters, the conceptions of the Jews
at this time were similar to those of most other peoples at their
stage of cultural development.

Yahweh, as they conceived him, displays the main characteristics of a powerful tribal chief, plus ability to control the natural
forces on which Palestine's material well-being depended. His
presence is associated especially with the storm clouds, and with
certain mountains, trees, rocks, and springs. Military glory is attributed to him as a god of armies and of battles. He is jealous of
his powers and prerogatives, punishing strictly and severely in-
fractions of the taboos under which he has placed his people. Often
such punishment takes no account of the difference between an
overt act and the intention behind it, as when Uzzah was struck
dead for reaching out to steady the ark which, on its journey home
from the city of the Philistines, was jostled by the oxen pulling
it.[3] He has little humane feeling for the enemies of the Hebrews,
sometimes ordering wholesale slaughter of their captives, including
women and children as well as men.[4] He reveals his will to his
people either by direct visions vouchsafed to their accepted leaders

[2] There is some indication that he was originally a storm god, but by the
period in question this character had already been overlaid by the qualities here
described.

[3] II Sam. 6: 6–7.

[4] Some such passages, especially in Judges, may reflect the fanaticism of a
later date.

or through simple oracles of types familiar in many early religions. Upon the Jews he is believed to have imposed a number of ritual requirements, some of which are connected with agricultural festivals or with commemoration of his deliverance of their fathers from the land of Egypt. He has also enjoined upon them certain moral duties, expressive of the demand for evenhanded justice within the nation. Whether any of the injunctions which go beyond what strict justice would require, commanding hospitality for strangers and mercy for widows, orphans, slaves, and other unfortunates, appeared as early as this is a moot question among Old Testament scholars.

THE CONTRIBUTION OF THE GREAT PROPHETS

The period of the great prophets, who gave a redirection to Hebrew thought which became exceedingly influential throughout subsequent religious history, came half a millennium later than the period we have just been considering. It extended over two centuries and a quarter, Amos preaching his gloomy prophecies at Bethel not far from 760 B.C., and Deutero-Isaiah[5] transforming suffering into hope during the Babylonian exile about 540 B.C. The main circumstance which stimulated this prophetic reinterpretation of religion was the gradual squeezing of Palestine between the pincers of surrounding military empires, ending in the complete extinction of independent political life for the Jews at the hands of Babylon in 586 B.C. Such a national calamity, among other peoples, had always, so far as our records show, spelled decay for their religion; it seemed clear proof of either impotence or hopeless hostility on the part of their tribal divinity. The significance of the Hebrew prophets whose thought we now examine lies in the fact that they so profoundly revised the fundamental conceptions and attitudes of their national religion in the face of this threatening calamity that the cult of Yahweh was able as a result of the political tragedy to win a new lease on life and embark on a novel course of historical development. The main sources for our knowledge of this reconstruction are the prophetic books of Amos,

[5] A prophet whose work is now included in the last half of the book of Isaiah, beginning with chap. 40. Isaiah lived two centuries earlier.

Hosea, Micah, Isaiah, Jeremiah, and Ezekiel; parts of the historical
books of Kings and Chronicles; and a book which is now included
among the writings attributed to Moses, the book of Deuteronomy.

The prophets were true heirs of Moses and built upon the
foundation he had laid in the idea of a special covenant binding
together Yahweh and Israel. Like him, they were men of unusual intellectual force, as is shown by the fact that they vividly
foresaw the crises to come and were moved to deep and thoroughgoing reflection by them. Like him, and perhaps more than he,
they were men of high moral sensitiveness; faced by the complex
social relationships just coming to present a serious challenge in
their day—relations of rich and poor, priest and layman, king and
subject, citizen and foreigner—they penetrated to the fundamental
problems of moral responsibility, and offered conceptions of righteousness and ethical greatness that have appealed to men of similar quality in all the centuries since. Like him, they were men
of mystic responsiveness, in whom new insights broke with sud-
denness and such apparently supernatural cogency that they could
not be taken as ordinary intellectual achievements but were inevitably regarded as revelations of divinity. They thus led to novel
interpretations of religious duty and to transformed conceptions of
Yahweh.

The central question of the prophets was: What is the meaning
of this impending tragedy to our national life? And the essence
of their answer was: As a people we have been faithless to our
convenant with Yahweh, especially with reference to the moral
and social obligations which it involves. The inroads of foreign
armies are his punishment for this faithlessness. If we turn and
repent of our sin, perhaps the fatal consequence of our disobedience
can be avoided; or if not, perhaps Yahweh will preserve the
repentant remnant of his people, even in captivity, and some day
restore them openly to his favor. It is evident that this teaching
is founded on the two distinctive features of the covenant-conscious-
ness which had been a part of Jewish religion from the time of
Moses, and to which attention has already been called. Its significance for our understanding of the history of religious thought lies
in the fact that it presupposes, and in the statements of some of
the prophets expressly embodies, a transition in both religious

conceptions and moral ideals (1) from particularism to universalism, (2) from a ritual to an ethico-social emphasis, and (3) from an attitude of externalism to one of inwardness. The contribution of the prophets will be summarized under each of these heads.

Earlier Hebrew thought (with the possible exception of Elijah) had taken it for granted that other divinities besides Yahweh existed, some of whom, like Chemosh of the Moabites, bore essentially the same relation to their people that Yahweh did to Israel. Yahweh was believed to be stronger than these other gods, and thus able, when he wished, to encroach on their territory, but in general the scope of his activity was confined to the land within which his people lived. Other regions had other gods as a matter of course. The special relation of Israel to Yahweh arose, it was believed, from Yahweh's gracious choice of her when she lay in hopeless bondage, and the deliverance and prosperous settlement which under his aid had been attained. There was no question about the existence of other divinities, and at first the covenant was perhaps not interpreted as excluding all dealings with them. But they had no special claim upon a Jew, while every Jew did have this distinctive obligation to Yahweh.

When the prophets, however, ventured to think of the invasion and conquest of Palestine by armies of Egypt, Syria, Assyria, and Babylon as Yahweh's righteous discipline of his people, a different conception is necessarily involved. Yahweh must really, whether these other nations recognize it or not, be their god too; at least they and their activities are swept within the scope of his historical plan for Israel. For Isaiah, the Assyrian invader is the rod within Yahweh's hand.[6] For Ezekiel, Nebuchadnezzar is Yahweh's agent in his various military depredations, in Judah and elsewhere.[7] Nay, even the internal economy of other nations and their historical vicissitudes are controlled by Yahweh.[8] The natural outcome of this line of thought, clearly seen at least by some of the prophets, was that other gods have no genuine existence at all. Yahweh is the sole God of the whole earth, and embraces all men within his providential care. This conception is given

[6] 10: 5–11.
[7] Especially chaps. 23–33.
[8] Amos 9: 7; also chaps. 1 and 2.

poetic expression by Isaiah in his vision that "the whole earth is full of his glory,"[9] and as a result of the prophetic reinterpretation it found theological statement in the doctrine of creation now embodied in the book of Genesis, where the Hebrew deity is portrayed as sole maker of the universe and omnipresent controller of its history.

The moral aspect of this transition to universalism is less clearly and decisively exemplified in the thought of the prophets. It would naturally take the form of a conviction that the fundamental moral requirements of Yahweh's law are to be practiced by the Jews in their relations with individuals outside the nation in exactly the same way as in their relations with fellow Jews. While at times this conception appears to be implicit in the prophets it does not quite gain explicit expression. So far as we find in them an anticipation of true moral universalism, it took its most definite form in a reinterpretation of the convenant relation between Yahweh and Israel, appearing in the suggestion of the later prophets that to be the chosen people means primarily an obligation for Israel to become a mediator of religious truth to the other nations; the Jews were selected by Yahweh not primarily to enjoy unusual material prosperity but to serve as a light to the Gentiles.[10] The most appealing statement of this transformation of a preferential convenant into a moral and religious responsibility to all mankind is made by Deutero-Isaiah in the fifty-third chapter of the book of Isaiah. According to this prophet (as most students interpret him), the very sufferings of the Jews, incurred as a result of their faithlessness to Yahweh, will be, if nobly borne, a means of winning the other nations to appreciate the spiritual values of Yahweh's religion.[11] Thus these painful experiences can be transmuted from evil into good, through the realization that they spell a positive and hopeful promise for the religious life of all peoples.

Consider now the change brought about by the prophets from an emphasis on ritual to an insistence on the ethico-social requirements of the covenant.

Prior to the work of the great prophets the prevailing notion,

[9] 6: 3. The same theme is at least equally prominent in Deutero-Isaiah.
[10] Zech. 8: 20–23.
[11] Note especially verse 11.

generally speaking, was that the various prescriptions which Yahweh had imposed upon the Jews for scrupulous observance are all on the same level of importance. The obligation to respect the taboos connected with ritual cleanliness and to bring periodic sacrifices to the altar demand at least the same degree of careful attention as the obligation to social justice and to kindness toward those in special need of protection. The prophets vigorously challenged this conception. According to them, the essence of obedience to Yahweh lies in fulfilling a man's duty toward his neighbor; in comparison with this, ceremony and sacrifice take an entirely subordinate place. Nay, these rituals even become sinful if attention to them stands in the way of conscientious fulfillment of social obligations or encourages the thought that the latter can be safely neglected. Amos cries: "Thus saith Yahweh: For three crimes of Israel, or for four, I will not turn back; because they have sold the righteous for silver and the needy for a pair of shoes; they trample the head of the poor and tread down the meek."[12] Those whose obligation it is to administer justice turn it to wormwood; they accept bribes, and hate the man who ventures to rebuke them for their iniquity.[13] To bring sacrifices to the shrines, at least under such circumstances, is a sin against Yahweh rather than a fulfillment of duty toward him. "Come to Bethel and transgress! To Gilgal and multiply transgressions! Bring your sacrifices in the morning and your tithes the third day!"[14] "I hate, I despise your feasts, and I take no delight in your solemn assemblies; though you offer me your burnt-offerings and sacrifices I will not accept them, neither will I regard the peace-offerings of your fed beasts."[15] But "let justice flow like a river, and righteousness like a mighty stream."[16] In the case of Jeremiah, indeed, the prophet goes so far as apparently to maintain that Yahweh had never imposed ritual requirements upon Israel at all.[17] The outcome of this line of prophetic teaching was that beyond the obligation of love and devotion to Yahweh himself, the essence of the covenant law is exhausted in the duty of love

[12] 2: 6–8.
[13] 5: 7–12.
[14] 4: 4.
[15] 5: 21.
[16] 5: 24.
[17] 7: 21–23.

toward one's neighbor, expressed in just dealing toward all and in mercy toward those who need special care. This thought is best summarized in a frequently quoted passage from Micah: "Wherewith shall I come before Yahweh, and bow myself before the high God? Shall I come before him with burnt-offerings, with calves of a year old? Will Yahweh be pleased with thousands of rams, with ten thousands of rivers of oil? Shall I give my first-born for my transgression, the fruit of my body for the sin of my soul? He hath shewed thee, O man, what is good; and what doth Yahweh require of thee but to do justly, and to love mercy, and to walk humbly with thy God?"[18]

By the transition from externalism to inwardness is meant the replacement of a state of mind in which overt deeds are the prime object of religious concern by one in which the spirit or attitude behind the deed is the matter of central importance. Before the time of the great prophets Hebrew religion had, in general, like early religion among other peoples, taken for granted the first of these standpoints. The inner life as such, and its varied religious possibilities, had not as yet been clearly discovered. No religious or moral distinction was drawn between what a man does and the intention expressed in what he does;[19] to violate a divine injunction by accident is just as serious an offense as to violate it deliberately. Obedience to Yahweh is complete if one's external acts have all conformed to his behests. The main feature of Hebrew religion at this time that pointed toward the later transcendence of such externalism was the vivid sense of personal responsibility toward Yahweh felt by the leaders as a consequence of the voluntary nature of the covenant with him. This encouraged the desire to be gratefully loyal, so to speak, to Yahweh himself and not merely to respect in action his specific commands; it fostered a characteristic attitude of the whole personality, not to be entirely exhausted in this or that series of obedient deeds. But the distinction here intimated was, during the preprophetic period, a vague one, awaiting conscious emphasis and development. The distinction would no doubt sooner or later have been made irrespective of the historical vicissitudes which occurred. It is really implied by the transition

[18] 6: 6–8.
[19] Cf. the episode of Uzzah above mentioned.

which has just been noted from an emphasis on ritual requirements to an emphasis on ethico-social responsibilities. Ceremonial duties can be minutely prescribed in advance, and so far as a person aims merely at fulfilling them his conduct becomes an affair of mechanical routine. But no such detailed direction can be a sufficient guide when one conceives himself obligated to express the law of justice or of mercy, for these are not matters of routine behavior—these are general principles, to be expressed in whatever varied ways are appropriate on each occasion as it arises. They reflect a constant inner attitude or purpose, a commitment to the ideal embodied in these virtues, which cannot be exhausted in any particular set of acts because it signifies a readiness to act according to this ideal in any situation, actual or possible. Now as soon as men become conscious of such a general purpose, and of its moral and religious importance, they cannot help distinguishing it from the attitude which is focused simply upon ceremonial correctness. And they cannot help noting that while the nature of the latter attitude is fully revealed in the observable ritual acts which express it, the former is not thus observable—it exists in the recesses of one's personality as a morally responsible individual. It is precisely this distinction between the outward and the inward, between the external act and the inward intention, with which we are now dealing.

In fact, it is this distinction which gives meaning to the concepts "spirit" and "spiritual," which hereafter gain central importance in Western religion. For primitive thought, almost universally, spirit is a physical entity or process within the body, usually identified with the breath which appears to animate the body while it is alive and to cease when it dies. When religion underwent the transformation it did at the hands of the Hebrew prophets, this physical conception of spirit was left behind; it now became identified with that capacity in a human being to realize himself as an ethically responsible individual—to express in his relations to other men and to God the general ideals of sincerity, justice, and love.

Naturally, awareness of this distinction could not fail to affect the prophetic conception of God. And in the work of some of the prophets, especially Hosea, Jeremiah, and Deutero-Isaiah, we see quite clearly the transformed conception of God and of his relation

THE HEBREW BACKGROUND   27

to the individual that is naturally bound up with this emphasis on
the value of inwardness and is later so beautifully expressed in the
Psalms. Formerly, of course, Yahweh had been conceived as a personal divinity; he was the kind of being with whom men could
make a covenant, involving reciprocal historical duties and con-
tractual obligations. But his relation was more with the nation as
a whole than with its individual members, and when the latter felt
his presence the attributes of which they were apt to be conscious
were mystery, power, jealousy, and august sternness; although, to
be sure, an element of gracious kindliness was not absent. As a result
of the prophetic insistence on the primary worth of inwardness,
however, Yahweh naturally came to be conceived not only as
requiring such a spiritual attitude in his people, but as exemplifying
it himself, and responding appropriately to it when expressed in
their devotional life. When the repentant Israelite turns toward his
divinity in earnest sincerity and inner loyalty he finds that Yahweh
is already welcoming him in an attitude of generous forgiveness and
fatherly love. A reverent, yet intimate, fellowship becomes possible
between the individual soul and its God. Hosea speaks of Yahweh
yearning for his people as a husband for an erring wife whose
affection he longs to regain.[20] Jeremiah, amid the upheavals of his
day and the misunderstanding and persecution to which he was
personally subjected, discovers in inward communion with Yahweh
a satisfying support and compensation.[21] And Deutero-Isaiah, endowed with poetic sensitiveness to the rich possibilities of this
emphasis in religion, implicitly attributes to Yahweh in his songs
the infinite wisdom, unfailing tenderness, commanding greatness,
and elusive wonder of an ideal personality, in whose comforting
presence hope is ever reborn so that suffering loses its poignancy
and tragedy its sting.[22] As a result of this change Hebrew religion
gained a new dimension, and became in the hands of these pioneers
the essential expression toward God and one's fellow men of an
inner spirit, a controlling attitude of trustful and joyous love.

But the catastrophic event of captivity at the hands of Babylon,
and the conditions under which life in the Babylonian exile was

[20] Chap 11; also 2: 14–3: 5.
[21] Notice the language of his prayers in chaps. 14–16.
[22] Consider from this standpoint especially chaps. 49, 55.

alone possible, sharpened this distinction and gave new value to the emphasis on inwardness. The conquest of Jerusalem involved the destruction of the Temple and suppression of most of the customary religious ceremonies; captivity in a foreign land radically reduced the number of ritual laws which could still be obeyed by an earnest Jew. Under these circumstances, if religion were to continue to have value for him as solace and guide, it had to become essentially an inward affair, a matter of the heart and soul rather than of the outward life as such. In repentance for his share of the sins of the nation which had been responsible for the exile, he could, even in captivity, maintain a sincere attitude of loyalty toward the God of his fathers; he could read and study the law with inward devotion while unable to obey many of its prescriptions in daily life; especially, he could love and praise Yahweh with all his heart and mind and strength. In its essence Hebrew religion thus became for those capable of it a spiritual experience, not dependent upon any specific form of outward expression. Its fundamental obligations became those of inwardness, and of social morality as interpreted and controlled by the ideals to which a vivid experience of inwardness gave meaning—sincerity, purity of heart, mercy, loving-kindness.

The devotional Psalms, most of which were written after the exile, indicate very clearly the result of this transformation. They express, with a wealth of appealing and beautiful imagery, the essence of this spiritual conception of religion as it was now practiced by Jews who were responsive to the prophetic ideals and influenced by the various forces which have above been sketched.

FROM THE EXILE TO JESUS

Between the time of the exile and that of Jesus of Nazareth a Hebrew community was re-established in Palestine, and maintained till after Jesus' day a troubled existence, usually under foreign political rule. During this half-millennium the story of Jewish religion is in large part that of the gradual assimilation of these prophetic ideas. They found detailed expression in the form of poetry, they guided a revision of the Mosaic law in accordance with their emphases, and they inspired theological attack on baffling problems which had come to the fore in their wake, such as the problem why evil often befalls the righteous.

The systematic revision of ceremonial and social law, so as to embody in it as far as possible the moral ideals of the prophets, was of great importance. Much of the old law was now discredited, appearing incompatible with the best insights of the new religious leaders. Hence the revision of law in terms of high moral principles gave assurance that for the future one important strand in both Judaism and Christianity—often the dominant strand—would be a legalistic conception of religion. By this is meant a conception in which God is viewed primarily as a Supreme Lawgiver, mankind being obligated dutifully to obey the system of rules promulgated on his authority.

It is during this period, however, that we must also place the growth of the so-called Messianic hope, which became especially important in early Christian ideas. It has been noted that since the beginning of their religious life the Jews as a people had been characterized by an unusually vivid historical consciousness, involving cherished memories of the past and ambitious expectations for the future. This consciousness, with special reference to its hope for blessings to come, was intensified during the exile and the partial restorations which followed it, the change being encouraged by an element in the thought of the prophets. With the possible exception of Amos, these men had not taught that the calamity of whole-sale national punishment was the last word in Yahweh's dealing with his people. A "remnant" would be preserved through the period of defeat and tragedy, to become the nucleus of a re-established kingdom, in which the divine favor would once more be made evident to the world. This re-establishment was to be carried out—so many thought—by a scion of the house of David, who might also be equipped with supernatural powers which no earthly force could resist. In the later literature and the expectant conversation of the populace this awaited deliverer was spoken of as the "Messiah," that is, the "Anointed One." As to the nature of the coming kingdom and the work of the Messiah there were varied conceptions. Many pictured the kingdom as essentially a renewed epoch of material prosperity for Israel, accompanied by severe

punishment of her oppressors.[23] Those few who were most profoundly influenced by prophetic ideas conceived it as fundamentally
a moral achievement, inaugurating a period in which the resettle-
ment of Palestine and the rebuilding of the Temple would make
possible the mediation by Israel of the worship and love of Yahweh
to all peoples.

As the preceding statement indicates, the Messianic hope was
significant mainly to the Jewish nation as a nation; it possessed value
to the individual only through the anticipated re-establishment of
the kingdom of which he was a member and his imaginative
participation in that new national life. But the development of a
satisfying personal religion after the exile naturally affected the
doctrine of a future hope. For some it led to a conception of
individual immortality, ghostly Sheol as the underground abode
of the dead becoming replaced, for them, by the ideas of hell and
heaven with which the Christian world is now familiar. Hell was
pictured as a place of everlasting torment for the persistently dis-
obedient; heaven as the perfect fulfillment of the blessings of filial
intimacy with Yahweh, of which his faithful worshiper has gained a
foretaste in this life.[24] Some added a doctrine of the resurrection of
those who had died in the past.[25] The conception of a last judgment was usually connected with this teaching; at the arrival of
the Messiah all the dead will arise from their graves and be judged
according to their deeds in the flesh along with those then living,
the righteous entering into the full joy of the kingdom and the
wicked being consigned to outer perdition.

During the period now under consideration certain ideas entered
Hebrew religion, or a redirection and new prominence was given
to old ideas, which many scholars trace to the influence of Zoroas-
trianism, the religion of the Persians at the time they conquered
Babylon and occupied the position of foremost world power. Among
such ideas are those of a final judgment and of the resurrection of the
dead, above mentioned; the conception of a host of angels and
archangels attending Yahweh and serving as his agents or messengers; and the notion of a personal devil, leader of the powers
of evil, who wars against Yahweh and tempts men into sin. Ac-

[23] Zech. 12–14.
[24] Enoch, especially chaps. 24–27, 91.
[25] Dan. 12: 2.

cording to the Hebrew interpretation, this devil had originally been an angel in heaven who became the instigator of a rebellion against God. He and his demonic cohorts had been cast out to the lower regions where they now carry on their nefarious activities; they are destined in time to be reduced to impotence by Yahweh's power and consigned to eternal punishment for their wickedness. All these ideas entered Christian thought and became part of the background of Western philosophy of religion.

It was into the religious situation prepared by the varied circumstances thus far portrayed that Jesus of Nazareth came. And at his coming there is no break with the past. Viewed in the setting in which his life is described in the synoptic gospels (Matthew, Mark, and Luke), he was essentially another Hebrew prophet, calling upon his contemporaries to repent of their sins as a preparation for the establishment of the Messianic kingdom, and we must consider him first from that standpoint. So approached, his significance for our study lies in the fact that he deepened and expanded just those elements in the teaching of the great Old Testament prophets which had proved most challenging and spiritually fertile. We shall consider later the distinctive features that appear in the Gospel of John.

While Jesus, like the prophets, recognized the special relation of Israel to Yahweh and conceived that his mission was primarily to his own racial brethren, yet on occasion he shows in clearer form than they (excepting possibly Deutero-Isaiah) the universalism implicit in their fundamental conceptions. The familiar parable of the good Samaritan is the best illustration of this. The prophets had summarized religious duty under the two heads of wholehearted love toward Yahweh and sincere love for one's neighbor on the same terms as oneself. But who is my neighbor—another Jew, or anybody that I may meet? The prophetic answer is not clear nor unqualified; that of Jesus, at least on the occasion of this parable, is. My neighbor is any human being in need, whether he belong to my race or to another.[26] And the hero of the story is, surely intentionally, not a Jew. In this parable moral and religious universalism appears with a distinctness which leaves little to be desired.

Jesus likewise carried forward the prophetic insistence that matters of ritual and ceremony must be entirely subordinated to

[26] Luke 10: 25–37.

the ethico-social requirements of justice, honesty, and mercy. His
scathing diatribes against the scribes and the Pharisees were mainly
concerned with this point. They are exceedingly meticulous (as he
describes them) in paying their tithes, bringing their sacrifices, and
fulfilling the ceremonial obligations of the law, but this only fosters
the vices of pride and self-righteousness. So far as concerns social
obligations they are guilty of every evil in the calendar—of fraud,
bribery, extortion, even ruthless violence upon the poor and unpro-
tected.[27] Unless they renounce these sins, they shall have no part
in the Messianic community but be consigned to the outer darkness
prepared for the devil and his angels. Not that the ritual duties are
to be quite neglected. It is a matter of emphasis; justice, mercy,
and kindness are the foremost obligations to be fulfilled, while the
others are not to be left undone.[28]

Jesus' deepening of the prophetic transition from externalism to
inwardness in religion is particularly notable. He interprets the
fundamental significance of all religious ideas in such wise as to
focus them directly upon the inward experience of the individual.
In the moral life it is the intention that counts, not the mere deed;
lustful desire is just as guilty as adultery, and is so judged by
him who sees the inner thoughts of the heart as easily as any outward act.[29] The kingdom for which all longed is not an affair of
external conquest and material prosperity; in the essential quality
of life which it spells it is something that comes within the heart of
each individual, and the significance of its external manifestations
lies in their enlivening and implementing the great judgment which
is passed upon each man in accordance with the true state of his
inward self.[30] The basic virtues for him are the virtues of inwardness—sincerity, truthfulness, earnestness, wholehearted filial devotion to God; and the prophetic social virtues as controlled by the
sense of unfailing personal responsibility which the attitude of
inwardness fosters—justice, mercy, friendliness, love. And love,
expressed in appropriate conduct as well as in attitude, must include
even those who harm us. No significant spiritual achievement is
reflected in merely responding with affection to those who are

[27] Matt. 23.
[28] Matt. 23: 23–24.
[29] Matt. 5: 27, 28.
[30] Luke 12: 29–33; 17: 20, 21. Matt. 25: 31–46.

friendly toward us; "if you love only those who love you . . . what is there remarkable in that? But . . . love your enemies and pray for your persecutors, so that you may show yourselves true sons of your Father in heaven, for he makes his sun rise on bad and good alike, and makes the rain fall on both upright and wrongdoers."[31] Now Jesus' doctrine of God reflects the full influence of these ideas; his own prayerful relation to God perhaps still more than his teaching. While to the wicked God is a terrifying, avenging power, to the penitent who earnestly seeks to live aright he is a loving father, with whom a heartfelt trustful communion is possible. Reverence, awe, and unquestioning submission to his will are, of course, appropriate in his children, but these may be, and in Jesus' own case were, combined with a deeply satisfying inward companionship. For Jesus, external acts and events are but the natural expression or outward symbol of religious reality; that reality itself is wholly spiritual.

But, for Christianity, Jesus became much more than one of the Hebrew prophets. And in his own conception of himself and his mission as revealed in the synoptic gospels there is some justification for this belief, though that conception is exceedingly difficult confidently to interpret.[32] He thought of himself and encouraged his disciples to think of him as the long-awaited Messiah, at least during the fateful last journey to Jerusalem. Also, at that same period of his career, he seems to have reconciled his expected suffering with his consciousness of Messiahship by applying to himself as the Messiah the lesson taught by Deutero-Isaiah about the Hebrew people. Just as purification through suffering was necessary if the Jewish people were to become capable of fulfilling the universal mission to which they were called, so he must undergo purification through suffering in order to become worthy of the great task of the Messiah. At any rate, he believed that the humiliation and death of which he had forebodings were somehow necessary to the fulfillment of his mission, and that by accepting them in trustful dependence on God's will they would become a positive factor in

[31] Matt. 5: 44–47.
[32] The difficulty arises primarily from the circumstance that our present records of Jesus' teaching were written half a century after his death, and may to a large extent reflect the typical convictions and problems of Christians at that later time.

34 TYPES OF RELIGIOUS PHILOSOPHY

leading to the early establishment of the kingdom.[33] It is also important to note that, as the Messiah, Jesus expected his disciples to show a devoted loyalty to him as well as an obedient acceptance of his message.

After Jesus' death these ideas gained a new emphasis and development. By his crucifixion his followers were at first frightened and scattered. According to ancient taboo, "cursed be everyone that hangeth upon a tree,"[34] and this dire event seemed quite inconsistent with the assumption that Jesus was the Messiah. But the appeal of his personality and its impress upon them were so profound that they could not entirely lose faith in his mission. And some of them remembered his own teaching about his death, with increased understanding of its possible significance. There early arose the belief that he had risen from the grave and ascended into heaven, thence soon to come as the Messiah in clouds of glory, surrounded by the angels of God. Accordingly, the most loyal of them came together again for fellowship and mutual encouragement, and began to carry on anew his preaching. The burden of their message was: "Repent and prepare yourselves for the early coming of the promised kingdom. He whom you lately crucified, Jesus of Nazareth, has risen from the dead and ascended to the right hand of God. He is the Messiah who was sent by God in love for his sinful people, and who will quickly return to establish the kingdom. Be baptized in his name and receive the gift of the Holy Spirit."[35] In this simple form they took the first step in a transition from teaching the religion that Jesus himself had taught to teaching a religion which was in large part a doctrine *about* Jesus, involving belief in his special divine mission and supernatural status.

THE RELIGIOUS TEACHING OF THE APOSTLE PAUL

Even with this change, however, we have in these disciples but a Jewish sect whose main tenet was a serious stumbling block to other Jews; namely, the identification of the divinely appointed

[33] Luke 18: 31–33. Matt. 20: 27, 28.
[34] Deut. 21: 23.
[35] Acts 2 and 3.

Messiah with a crucified prophet. The man who reinterpreted this religion in such form as to give it moving appeal to large numbers of non-Jews as well as Jews, throughout the whole Hellenistic Roman world, was the Apostle Paul.[36] This task Paul accomplished by blending the fundamentally Jewish ideas with which we have thus far been occupied with conceptions dominant among the Hellenistic peoples of his day—conceptions of a religion of salvation, by which the individual can be emancipated from the forces of decay and corruption and enter upon a new, immortal existence.

Paul was born into a Jewish family residing in Tarsus of Cilicia, and he was educated at the feet of Jewish teachers at Jerusalem. From the intellectual atmosphere betokened by these circumstances he absorbed a typically Jewish viewpoint as far as concerns certain basic religious ideas. His God was the Hebrew Yahweh, with his special historical relation to the people of Israel and his comprehensive purpose for the human race as a whole—Yahweh as the great prophets had portrayed his character. Jewish was his conception of sin and of law; Jewish the almost fanatical conscientiousness which led him to idealize and exalt the law so highly that it seemed impossible for any mortal really to fulfill its demands. Essentially Jewish, too, was his doctrine of the coming kingdom and of the Messiah through whose supernatural agency it would be ushered in. And, finally, his ideals of personal and social morality—of love as the perfect embodiment of the spirit of righteousness—were entirely Jewish in their origin and meaning.

But Paul also absorbed from his Hellenistic environment, at Tarsus and elsewhere in the east Mediterranean region, religious ideas which dominated the non-Hebraic world of his day, and for which he felt a deep personal need. Graeco-Roman culture at this time was swept by a host of so-called "mystery cults," promising personal immortality to their converts through mystic identification with a savior-god who had died and then triumphed over death by resurrection to a renewed divine life. This identification was achieved through a highly moving ceremony, such as a blood-bath or participation in a sacrificial feast, which gave the initiate a vivid sense that he was purged of his former corruptible nature and had

---

[36] Paul was not the only contributor to this reinterpretation, but he was one of the earliest and by far the most important.

assumed the immortal nature of the god who was present, at least symbolically, in the blood or consecrated food. The gods of these cults were of varied historical origin, some having appeared first in Egypt, some in ancient Greece, some in Persia. The fundamental character which they shared in common had probably gained its earliest significance in connection with a cult of the sun or of the vegetative life so important for agriculture. In the northern climate the former recedes and the latter dies in the winter, while both are resurrected to new warmth, energy, and fertility in the spring.

It was Paul's conversion while on the road to Damascus that precipitated these diverse elements into a unity in his subsequent thought and gave the Nazarene teacher a central place among them. However in detail we interpret that experience of the great apostle, it involved an intensely moving vision of the Jesus whose followers he had just been persecuting. By that vision he felt his own religious quest brought to an end. He underwent a profound inward transformation, his torn and distraught fanaticism being replaced by a steady glow of joy, peace, outgoing love, and of unbounded vigor and enthusiasm. He felt himself saved from sin, corruption, and death, in the sense in which his Hellenistic contemporaries who pursued the mystery cults felt themselves saved, if their zeal had achieved its desired end. And the insight, confidence, and power which this experience gave Paul remained with him through the balance of his energetic life.

Naturally the apostle, in the theological formulations later offered in his letters, which were written during the sixth decade of the first century A.D., explained this transformation and tried to make something analogous available to his contemporaries. And, of course, the explanation was couched in terms of the background of ideas, both Jewish and Hellenistic, which has just been sketched. The outcome of his reflection may be briefly described as a remolding of the moralized cult of Yahweh, developed by the Hebrew prophets, into a mystery religion of personal salvation, in which the crucified Jesus of Nazareth appears not merely as the promised Messiah but also as a savior-god. Through identification with his death and resurrection, according to Paul, we may be redeemed from sin and mortality, becoming heirs and joyous possessors of an indwelling principle of righteousness and immortal life. Our old sinful nature is crucified with Jesus, and in rising with Christ we really no longer live but Christ liveth in us.[37] The basic features of this reinterpretation may be summarized as follows:

God created the world as portrayed in the book of Genesis, and Adam as the progenitor of the human race; Adam was given the power both of obedience and of disobedience to God's commands. As a result of Adam's sin under the temptation of the devil, all his descendants fell under the control of sin too; all inherited a fleshly, corrupt, and hence mortal nature. When, therefore, God revealed the details of his law to the world, selecting the Hebrew people as a special medium of the revelation, man was unable to be faithful to it. Dominated by his sinful nature, he continued to disobey and to merit still more deeply God's displeasure; all that the law could really do in view of his corrupt inheritance from Adam was to tantalize him with an unattainable pattern of righteousness and thus make him poignantly conscious of his impotence to conform to it.

But God had foreseen this tragic result, and being moved by mercy and love as well as by justice, he had prepared a way of salvation for those whom his grace should elect. In the fullness of time Christ Jesus, a divine being and God's agent in the original creation of the world, was destined to appear in human form and carry out this plan of salvation through his death and resurrection. When he did so appear, he gave as wondrous an example of humility and obedience as Adam had given of pride and disobedience; "he was obedient unto death, even the death of the cross."[38] Just, then, as in Adam all men sinned and fell under the bondage of corruption and death, so in Christ can all be made alive, replacing their fleshly and mortal nature by a holy, spiritual, and immortal one. To be sure, not all persons are impelled to turn to Jesus in saving faith; only those whom God has foreordained to salvation become actual beneficiaries of his redeeming work. But these are drawn from Gentiles as well as Jews, from the poor as well as the wealthy, from slaves as well as free men. There are no distinctions of privilege in Christ Jesus.

Faith is the inward act of submission to the transforming power

[37] Gal. 2: 20.
[38] Phil. 2: 8.

of Christ; baptism is the external sign of sharing in his death and his resurrection to eternal glory; and participation in the divine nature is often symbolically reenacted in eating the bread and drinking the wine of the Eucharist. Strictly speaking, the Christian no longer lives, himself, at all. It is Christ that lives in him, and his presence is made evident in daily life by the fruits of joy, patience, purity, hope, and especially love toward God and man. To the one who thus lives in Christ all things work together for good here below, and he is blessed with the assurance of immortality in the life to come.

Though the Messianic aspect of Jewish thought and of Jesus' gospel seems quite irrelevant to this transformation of Christianity into a mystery religion of present personal salvation, Paul needs it to complete the historical setting of God's relation to the world into which, as a good Jew, he has embedded his novel theme. Accordingly, he teaches in quite orthodox fashion the early coming of Jesus as the Messiah, the last judgment, and the establishment of the divine kingdom.[39]

In this Pauline form, capable of appealing to the dispossessed and discouraged multitudes of the Roman Empire who were turning to the mystery cults for solacing hope, a new religion began its career of widespread conquest, and its main ideas became embedded in the heritage of the modern Occident.

DISTINCTIVE IDEAS IN THE GOSPEL OF JOHN

Thus far, we have omitted from our account of early Christianity the very important and rather distinctive portrayal of Jesus' life and teaching in the Gospel of John. Our assumption has been that although the synoptic gospels were not written till after Paul's death they were not greatly influenced by his ideas, being based upon older materials. The Gospel of John gives a quite different picture and reveals a quite different conception of religion, which has become a vital factor in subsequent Christian thought and feeling. It definitely reflects at least one major element in Paul's theology— the idea that conversion is essentially a new birth, in which the

[39] Most of these points are contained in Rom. 1–8. For the apocalyptical element (i.e., concerning the second coming) see I Thess. 4.

believer puts off the corruption and mortality that are inherent in bodily existence and rises to a new, spiritual life which is incorruptible and eternal. And the conception of mystical union with Christ, which was central in Paul's portrayal of the state of the redeemed Christian, assumes in this fourth gospel a still more significant and radical place. According to the higher critics John was presumably written early in the second century A.D., and reflects philosophical ideas current at that time, especially in Alexandria and Antioch.

The author of this gospel does not mean to question or deny the traditional Jewish concept of God as a person, with whom we men may have personal relations. But while retaining the atmosphere and language appropriate to this concept, his central idea is rather that God is an infinite cosmic substance of which we are parts. Through sin we have somehow become sundered from the cosmic being to which we really belong, and salvation consists in transcending this separation and regaining unity with the divine whole. To remain separate is spiritual death; to find this unity with the divine is spiritual life—and eternal life, because God with whom we become one is eternal.

But this mystic idea, very common in India and elsewhere in the East, assumes a distinctive form in its Christian interpretation as given in the fourth gospel. Earlier Jewish and Christian theology had culminated in the thought that the essence of God's nature is love toward his creation, and that the supreme mark of spiritual perfection in man is also love, toward God and his fellow men. This love had been conceived in strictly personal terms, as the attitude of a kindly father toward his children and of brothers toward their father and one another. The Gospel of John, while retaining this conception, adds the mystic idea that divine love is a substantial entity in the universe—the dynamic source of love in us—and that only so far as we respond to the creative self-giving which is its essence and become one with it, so that a similar power of self-giving is realized in us, do we escape spiritual death and attain spiritual life. The love of God is, so to speak, an expansive, life-giving medium pervading the universe; it reaches out to seek and win us even while we are lost in our self-caused separation from God—even while we are shrinking in upon our petty finite selves

in the fear, anxiety, and hate that spell death to the soul. So far as
we respond to the divine love this process is reversed and we pass
from death into life—we reach out beyond our separate, finite,
self-centered selves and expand into oneness with the infinite spirit
of love as it expresses itself everywhere in the universe. The analogue
in the physical world of that divine spirit is light, which by its very
nature actively penetrates the surrounding darkness and which the
darkness is unable to quench.[40] The oneness does not have to wait to
be realized after death; it is possible here and now for those who
have been reborn in the spirit and have thus become heirs of eternal
life. Hence they do not need to come up for judgment on their sins;
they have already passed from sin to righteousness, from death to
life.[41] They are one with God in Christ.

For, on this interpretation, Jesus Christ is not just the Messiah
who is destined to come to judge the world and establish the new
kingdom. He is the savior of the world, but the savior in the distinctive sense of being the cosmic and historic intermediary of God's
love toward man and man's responding love toward God. He is the
son of God in a unique sense, sharer eternally of the divine nature.
He is the "logos"—i.e., the metaphysical wisdom through whom
the world was created.[42] This son of God became incarnate in Jesus
of Nazareth, to share man's sorrows and sufferings even to death on
the cross, and thus to demonstrate in dramatic and appealing form
the eternal, divine, self-giving to men. Through him men become
one with God and with each other, as the branches find a shared
life through oneness with the vine. The branches need their union
with the vine to remain alive and to possess creative power; the vine
needs the branches through which to bear fruit.[43] This union is
physically symbolized by the Christian in the holy rite of the Lord's
supper, when he eats Christ's flesh in the form of the consecrated
bread and drinks his blood in the consecrated wine.[44]

In the Gospel of John this mystic conception of God, Christ, and
salvation became a very influential alternative in Christian history
to the predominantly legal conception which had prevailed before
it appeared.

[40] Ch. 1: 4, 5; 8: 12.
[41] 5: 24.
[42] 1: 1–3.
[43] 15: 1–8.
[44] 6: 51.

THE NEED FOR GREEK PHILOSOPHY

When the fourth gospel used the "logos" concept, and when Paul interpreted Christianity through the aid of notions drawn from the Hellenistic mystery religions, they were initiating a lengthy process which we must now trace in further detail. The leaders of these religions were not philosophers, but as, in course of time, intellectually trained men were attracted by the cults, it was natural that the latter should come to be more and more explained by conceptions with which such men were familiar. This meant conceptions derived from the great Greek philosophers. Thus it came about that although Paul, too, was only incidentally a philosopher, he unconsciously used explanatory ideas which had been first clearly formulated by these thinkers. The yawning dualism which he took for granted in human experience between the carnal and the spiritual is a conspicuous case in point. This dualism, first emphasized in the West by the Orphic religion, had been given philosophic clarity in the work of Plato.

Now as Christianity came to appeal to intellectuals in the Roman Empire, whose thinking was molded from beginning to end by the philosophers of Greece, it was inevitable that the process of formulating its doctrines and rendering rationally persuasive its claims should make greater and greater use of ideas derived from these eminent men. There were, in fact, three relatively independent reasons for this gradual translation of the Christian faith into philosophical terms.

The first was that the thinking of intellectual leaders throughout the empire, on all important matters, already moved in the current of ideas that the philosophers had expressed and defined. Their religious and moral, as well as scientific and metaphysical, problems were conceived in terms of these ideas. Well, Christianity offered itself as a solution of such problems. Obviously, in order that the solution be understood and its significance clarified, it was necessary that it be explained in the same concepts by whose aid the problems themselves were formulated. Otherwise, at best, it would have a vague emotional appeal, incapable of reflective statement and therefore of thoughtful understanding beyond the limits of the Jewish community.

The second reason lay in the nature of the written materials in the possession of Christianity at the time these intellectuals began to inquire seriously into its validity. These materials had originated at different periods extending over a thousand years; not only their emphases but their definite statements of doctrine varied enormously. Even in fundamental matters, such as the picture of God, there were profound differences—in Judges he is often portrayed as a ruthless, avenging fury, while in certain chapters of Paul and the writings of John he is the spirit of suffering and redeeming love. Now, the Jews were not philosophically minded in comparison with the Greeks; their genius was essentially practical and moral. Hence no one among them had given a high degree of unity and coherence to this vast array of varied material.[45] Paul himself had partially met this need, but at the heart of his doctrine lay a set of Jewish ideas quite unfamiliar to most Greek and Roman thinkers. Such men demanded a logically systematic formulation of the Christian faith, and the only available concepts sufficiently comprehensive, and defined with sufficient clarity to perform this service, were the concepts central in the thought of the Greek philosophers.

The third reason is found in the ideas of these philosophers themselves. Those among them who had already risen to a dominant position in the intellectual world by the time Christianity began to spread throughout the empire were, in general, deeply religious men. Their philosophy was thus, in the main, harmonious with a religious interest and hospitable to interpretations of the universe in religious terms. And in several major details their religious thinking followed lines quite congenial to those of Hebrew prophetism. They demanded an essentially ethical conception of the divine. They championed monotheism as against the prevailing polytheism of their contemporaries. They believed that purposiveness is embedded in the structure of the world, a notion into which could easily be fitted the Jewish doctrine that God has a comprehensive historical plan for the human race and that all events, local as well as cosmic, are under his superintendence. In the deposit left by these thinkers Christianity found a great ally, an ally which in turn

[45] For Philo of Alexandria, see below, pp. 65 f.

became a powerful force for its own intellectual transformation and unification.

As a result of this philosophical reinterpretation of Christianity, which occupied many centuries, subsequent philosophy of religion in the western half of the world has been unable to state either its problems or its alternative solutions without making large use of ideas which we owe to the great philosophers of Greece. The main features of their contribution to the background of European and American religious thought must now be considered.

Chapter III

THE BACKGROUND IN GREEK PHILOSOPHY

THE PHILOSOPHY OF PLATO

THE first of the great Greek thinkers whose thought will be briefly examined, in the form in which it was subsequently understood by religious interpreters, is Plato, who lived early in the fourth century before Christ. To appreciate the central features of his philosophy, however, it is necessary to glance at the general cultural and intellectual situation prevailing at Athens in his day. This situation, summarily portrayed, was one of increasing individualism and of rapid erosion, under the stress of relatively free criticism, of traditional beliefs. An urbane skepticism about the maxims handed down by the ancients was becoming widespread in intellectual circles, and a fundamental doubt whether any objective standards, in matters moral and religious, could be set up in their place. In the younger and hotter minds this skepticism frequently took the socially disruptive form of supposing that the only measure of truth and right for any individual is self-interest—the appeal of an idea or a proposed act to him at the time it presents itself.

Now Plato's teacher Socrates, and under his influence Plato himself, worked out their philosophy in a conscious attempt to meet this threatening intellectual and social anarchy. They both believed that human reason, by a process of critical and comparative analysis, can establish objective standards in morals and religion, and many of the Platonic dialogues are occupied with the quest for such standards. In fact, for both these thinkers only the grasp of such a rational standard or fixed principle can be dignified by the name

44

"knowledge"; any less stable or demonstrable belief accorded mental acceptance is to be branded as "opinion" rather than knowledge. And Plato, at least, developed a general theory of the universe in which the same contrast became focal, constancy and flux characterizing two diverse realms which between them exhaust the world as disclosed to the human mind.

On the one hand—so this philosopher taught—we have the realm of ordinary everyday experience, consisting of the objects and events revealed in the perceptions of eye, ear, touch, and the other senses. The outstanding feature of this realm of sense experience is its instability. Everything it contains is in constant change. Each object comes into being, it undergoes continual transformation while it exists; and sooner or later it perishes. Now the ubiquitous presence of this feature sufficiently indicates that the realm in question is not genuinely real, for reality, according to Plato's basic assumption, is that which in its distinctive character eternally exists; it stays put, not varying with every shifting puff of circumstance. On the other hand, there is the realm of what Plato calls "forms" or "ideas," which intrinsically possess just the character lacking in the first realm, namely, absolute fixity and changelessness. The forms are eternal by their very nature, and hence constitute the world of true reality. They are sharply distinguished from the transitory things of sense which in contrast with them become mere phenomena— that is, appearances of reality, empty of substance and with no power of self-maintenance. These forms are not revealed to sense perception, for the latter process, being adapted to the realm of change, is unable to apprehend them. They are visible only to the inward eye of reason, which is the faculty capable of grasping the changeless. Moreover, since they are the reality of which phenomena are deceitful appearances, the forms are the source of what small measure of substantiality the latter possess. These "participate" in the forms (to use the preferred word in the dialogues for expressing the relation between the two types of entity)—that is, they shadow forth in the flux enough of the stability of the forms so that in their presence reason can penetrate to the changeless reality beyond. And the relation of participation is in part teleological.[1]

---

[1] This word means "purposive," but without the implication that the purpose must be conscious.

By this is meant that the forms are not only rational ideas or principles—they are also ideals at which perceptual appearance more or
less ineffectively aims. It strives to embody them, but always to a
greater or less extent falls short of doing so.

To clarify these features of the philosophy under consideration,
and to show more exactly what the forms are, we may take a simple
illustration. Suppose we examine two sticks, which to the eye or
touch, aided if you will by a yardstick, appear equal in length.
But we realize perfectly well that they are not exactly equal; a
sufficiently refined measure, if available, would show slight inequalities even where a cruder observation had been unable to note
any difference. And we could never bring together two sticks which
would dependably exhibit absolute equality, for this reason if for
no other—that the sticks as bits of perceptual material are undergoing continual change, so that even if perfect equality should at
some happy moment be attained it could not possibly be retained
a moment later. But the form or idea of equality (that is, its meaning, as we might be apt today to express Plato's thought) is clearly
different from the equality of the sticks in each of the two respects
mentioned. It is not a mere approximation to equality, not a case
of greater or less inequality; it is just equality itself and nothing else.
And for the same reason it does not fluctuate from one degree of
inequality to another; it eternally preserves its essential character
as equality, superior to the vicissitudes of change to which its
perceptual exemplifications are subject.

Now perception through the physical senses, being a bodily act,
is affected by all the changes in which any perceptible body shares.
Accordingly, it can only perceive the approximate equality (that is,
the relative inequality) of such entities as the sticks; it can never
perceive true equality itself. Such apprehension is only attained
by the inner eye of the soul, which is the faculty of reason; it is
weakened rather than aided by the presence of the body and its
organs.[2] The relation which Plato calls participation appears in our
illustration in the circumstance that we should not describe the two
sticks as a case of equality in length if we did not recognize them
as embodying, so far as they are capable (though, of course, not
perfectly), the idea of equality. It is possible to refer to the changing

_____

[2] At least, so Plato sometimes insists. See the *Phaedo*, 65–67.

only in terms of the changeless which it haltingly exemplifies. And the teleological aspect of this relation is exhibited in the fact that the idea of equality plays in such an act of perception the role of norm or standard, by which the varying degrees of approximation to it, in the case of any pair of objects, are judged and compared. When we perceive an instance of equality in sense experience we perceive it as a closer or rougher approximation to true equality, and this means that when we use the concept "equality" we implicitly think of it as a goal at which the different instances aim with varying degrees of success.

This illustration reveals both the basic distinction and the fundamental relation between the realm of forms, in their eternal nature, and the realm of perceptual existence in its instability. The latter, because everything in it is so transitory and evasive, is unreal—that is, it has no fixed and dependable properties. Whatever stability and truth it possesses are derived from the absolute ideas which dimly shine through it.

As has been intimated, there corresponds to this twofold distinction in the world an equally basic distinction in our apprehension of it. Appropriation by the senses of the fickle objects in the realm of flux is not knowledge but opinion, and the latter necessarily shares the slipperiness of the entities with which it is concerned. It is itself undependable, changing from moment to moment and from individual to individual, and it can accordingly make no pretense of certainty. True knowledge means grasp by reason of the eternal forms, and since this faculty intuits changeless objects it is itself constant in nature. Most men most of the time, according to Plato, are lost in the shifting play of opinion; the philosopher is the one who, at least at times, succeeds in gaining a vision of the reality underlying appearance and thus attains true knowledge.

The above survey has discussed the forms as though in Plato's thought they were all on the same level and equally, if we may so put it, absolute. But in fact they compose a hierarchy, in which certain forms occupy a privileged position in relation to the rest. At the top of the hierarchy stands the form of the Good. Just as the objects of sense experience gain what measure of constancy and substantiality they possess through participation in the various eternal forms, so the lower forms themselves ultimately possess reality and intelligibility through the illumination that radiates upon them from the Idea of the Good. The latter thus appears to be the transcendent source of all reality as well as of all knowledge; Plato compares its relation to the other forms with the relation of the sun to the objects of the perceptual world, which not only require her light to become visible but her energy for their very existence.[3]

Coming now to Plato's theory of the nature of God and his relation to man, we do not find what from the foregoing we might naturally expect. God is not identified with the supreme Idea of the Good, but is portrayed as an intermediary being who, inspired by the eternal forms which he apprehends, constructs and regulates as far as possible the details of the visible world under the guidance of that inspiration.[4] Three basic conceptions provide the key to Plato's reasoning, both on this problem and on that of human immortality. One is the conception of causality. Plato regards this conception as validly applicable to all that exists and happens in the visible realm pervaded by change. In one sense only does it apply to the realm of forms; they are causes of the stable qualities exhibited by perceptible objects, but not of their coming into existence nor of the changes which they undergo. These must be accounted for otherwise. And he interprets causality in a distinctive sense, according to which every occurrence must be traced to a creative source or controlling principle which is responsible for the fact that one kind of result is reached rather than another. The second is the conception of soul. Plato draws a sharp distinction between inanimate objects, which move only when impelled by motion in some other object, and animate beings, which are capable of spontaneous motion. The difference between the two kinds lies in the fact that animate things are endowed with an "anima" (that is, "soul"),[5] which may accordingly be defined as the principle of spontaneous motion. In man soul includes three faculties, two of which, impulse and passion, are common to him and to the lower

---

[3] The classic statement of this phase of Plato's thought is in Book VI of the *Republic*.

[4] In some dialogues the divine mind appears to occupy a more ultimate cosmic position, but it is not clear whether there is definite inconsistency with the doctrine here summarized.

[5] This linguistic identity between "living" and "ensouled" obtains in Greek as well as in the Latin from which our "animate" is derived.

animals, while the other—reason—is his unique possession among
the inhabitants of earth. Now reason is the rightful authority in
the soul as a whole, imposing (in the case of those who are
rationally competent) law and orderly control upon the other
faculties; soul in turn, being the principle of life, is the source of
the distinctive kind of order (or disorder) which characterizes the
behavior of living things in contrast with that of inanimate objects.
The third is the conception of order or harmony as being ultimately
good, while its opposite, disorder, is viewed as essentially evil.
This is an evaluational judgment which plays a determinative part
in Plato's philosophy from beginning to end.[6] Let us see how the
major details of the Platonic religious creed are worked out on the
foundation provided by these conceptions.

The principle of causality implies to Plato's mind not only that
every particular thing or process belonging to the visible world had
a beginning, under the creative activity of a cause, but also that that
entire realm must have had a beginning in time. In the dialogue
which sketches his thought on the origin and structure of this world
in some detail, the *Timaeus,* God appears as the good Demiurge[7]
who, with his eye on the pattern which he envisions in the realm of
the ideas, creates the visible entities composing the cosmos out of a
pre-existing indeterminate matter. He appears to be conceived as a
quite personal agent—is even called the "father of all things"[8]—
and the principle by which his activity is guided is that of the
attainment of a maximum of good in and for the entire creation.
His first creature is a being called by Plato the "World-Soul,"
which then becomes his agent in the creation of other things. The
rational soul in man is, however, also created directly by the
Demiurge.[9]

How do we know that a God so portrayed exists? In Book X
of the *Laws* Plato offers a demonstration of the existence of a divine
mind as architect and providential ruler of the world. Three argu-

---

[6] These basic conceptions are most clearly explained in the *Timaeus,* 28–30A,
and the *Phaedrus,* 245–246. A systematic defense of the doctrine that order and
harmony constitute the supreme good is given in the *Philebus.*

[7] That is, Constructor.

[8] *Timaeus,* 28c.

[9] It is worth remembering that prior to the twelfth century the *Timaeus* was
the Platonic dialogue best known to Christian theologians.

ments may be distinguished. For one, Plato appeals to the universality of the belief in gods as offering some warrant for its truth, but this argument is not elaborated. The second and major argument seeks a sufficient cause for the occurrence of motion in the perceptible world. An ultimate ground of this phenomenon evidently must not be a being which derives its activity from something outside itself, for then we should have to make the same inquiry about the latter; it must be something capable of spontaneously moving itself as well as of initiating motion in other things. Now, physical bodies do not have this capacity, but soul does. By its essential nature it possesses energy of self-action, and is the source and governor of motion in the body to which it is attached. We may, then, confidently infer that the cosmic principle finally responsible for motion in the world is akin to soul in us and may be properly conceived as a divine soul. A third argument, which Plato connects closely with the preceding proof but which in subsequent thought has usually been formulated independently, appeals to the remarkable order displayed in the motions of the heavenly bodies. Such perfect simplicity and regularity of motion can hardly be adequately accounted for through the operation of physical causes; still less through chance, which brings disorder and erratic behavior wherever it appears. But since all motion has been shown to be ultimately due to the spontaneous activity of soul, the reasonable explanation of motions exhibiting such complete harmony is evident; they are the effect of a perfect soul—a soul fully controlled by wisdom and supreme in power. And this, of course, is identified with a divine mind.[10]

In the dialogue entitled *Philebus* a somewhat different argument is offered, although it rests on the same presuppositions.[11] Here the guiding question is: How are we to explain the presence of soul and mind in man? And the answer given is that just as the physical elements in man's make-up—fire, air, water, earth—are derived from the vast store of similar elements in the surrounding universe, so his endowment of soul and mind demands for its source a cosmic soul informed by intelligence. Moreover, as mind is the principle of

[10] In the last book of the *Laws* (966) Plato himself separates these two arguments and regards them as distinct.
[11] 28–30.

order in the behavior of its body, so this cosmic mind may be inferred to be the wise governor of the entire physical world.

Plato's method of completing the list of God's attributes is indicated in a discussion which follows his main argument for the divine existence. God has been proved to be a supremely perfect soul and an intelligent governor of the world. Whatever, now, can be clearly deduced from these descriptive terms may likewise confidently be attributed to him. Among other things it may be concluded that his providence extends even to the minor concerns of human life. Only an indolent, careless, or ignorant governor would fail to care for matters of detail, and surely such adjectives are inconsistent with the perfect goodness which God has been demonstrated to possess.[12] In the same context and elsewhere Plato insists that God's primary concern in his relation to man is moral rectitude on the latter's part. Moreover, God must be regarded as providing the supreme standard for imitation by men in their quest for apprehension of the Good and their endeavor appropriately to express it in conduct.[13]

At least equally influential with this doctrine of God in subsequent theological thought is Plato's main argument for the immortality of the soul. In the *Phaedrus* this conviction is briefly deduced from the essential nature of soul as the principle of life. The same argument is, however, in a dialogue named the *Phaedo*, embedded in a much larger context, and treated with a consummate artistry not approached in either the *Timaeus* or the *Laws*. Six specific steps can be distinguished in Plato's reasoning as reported in this dialogue, the first five of which apparently establish in each case a part of the needed proof. The last of the six—whose outcome is the same as that of the argument in the *Phaedrus*—appears to be presented as conclusive in its own right, affording an irrefutable demonstration of immortality. This crucial step begins by reaffirming the Platonic doctrine of participation—it is by participating in the form of beauty that beautiful things become beautiful; it is by participating in greatness that things become great; and so in every other case. Now, when anything participates in beauty it obviously cannot at the same time participate in ugliness, the opposite of

[12] *Laws*, Book X, 900–903.
[13] *Ibid.*, Book IV, 716.

beauty; moreover, since it must participate also in all other forms which are involved in the nature of beauty—harmony, for instance —it is clear that whatever participates in beauty necessarily repels along with ugliness the opposites of these other forms—e.g., discord. For another instance of the same principle, whatever participates in threeness must necessarily participate in oddness too, for · it is of the essence of three to be an odd number; it is impossible, therefore, for it to participate in evenness, which is the opposite of oddness. In the light of these considerations the reader is asked to examine the relations between soul, life, and death. The last two are opposite, just as oddness and evenness are opposites. But life is of the essence of the soul, which it brings with it wherever it goes; the difference between a living and a lifeless body is just that soul is present in the former and absent from the latter. The soul is by nature, then, the life-bearing principle, and by analogy with the other cases it must be irreconcilable with the opposite of life, namely, death. But to be intrinsically irreconcilable with death is to be immortal.

From the standpoint of a modern reader, familiar with post-Platonic trends in the science of psychology, the weakness of this reasoning lies in its assumption that the soul is a substantial and separable entity, only loosely attached to the body while the latter exhibits the properties of a living organism. Now in other dialogues, especially the *Timaeus* and *Philebus,* the soul is described by Plato himself as more intimately related to the body than the argument in the *Phaedo* would seem to allow. Although it appears to be affirmed there that life is an inseparable character of the entire soul, it is explicitly indicated in the *Timaeus* that only the rational part of the soul is immortal, the other faculties perishing with the body.[14] How is such a difference to be reconciled? This question is difficult to answer. We can be fairly sure of certain convictions, at least, as being quite deep-seated in Plato's thinking: that above and beyond the realm of temporal changes there is a world that is eternal and therefore by its very nature immune to the gnawing of time, that the intellectual part of our souls seeks attachment to that world as its natural home, and that in the attainment of knowledge such union is actually realized. Perhaps it was his belief that other

14 *Timaeus,* 69, 70. *Philebus,* 33, 34.

parts of the soul gain immortality so far as they come to be controlled and ordered by the rational part, as happens in the true philosopher and in those who follow his guidance.

Two further features of Plato's thought are of concern to the subsequent history of religious philosophy. One is a conflict between two corollaries of his conception of the Idea of the Good in its relation to the world of changing experience. On the one hand, since the Good, and the other ideas under its control, have the character of stable forms rather than that of shifting physical objects, and since their energy is the energy of an ideal rather than the impact of a physical force, it would seem that their influence in human life must be that of persuasion, not at all the pressure of compulsion or of a fear-provoking threat. The ethical consequence of such a conception is clear. Plato believes, when following the implications of this phase of his doctrine, that men are moved to live according to the light of the ideal through an allurement generated by a consuming vision of the Good, or through persuasive guidance by those who have attained such a vision; not through commands invoking fear of penalties for disobedience.[15] This conception readily expressed itself later in the thought that God appeals to man by enshrining before him an ideal of goodness, with the promise of friendly aid in its pursuit; he does not cow him by a display of superior power. And from this point of view love of the Good as perfectly embodied in the divine nature becomes the basic religious virtue rather than submissive obedience. As we know, however, this idea has never reigned quite without qualification, and this circumstance is also in part due to Plato. For there is another corollary of Plato's doctrine of the Good in its relation to human experience which leads in quite a different direction. Since men vary greatly in their capacity to apprehend the forms which constitute true reality, most of them being lost in the vacillations of opinion, it is clear (so he held) that the only way rationally to organize human society is to place it under the control of those who are specially competent in knowledge of the Good and the ultimately Real. The rest of mankind are to obey the rules promulgated by these metaphysical experts. Persuasion is not omitted, but it is backed by uncompromising force. In the *Republic*, Plato's greatest

[15] See in this connection the *Laws*, 718–724.

dialogue, this proposal takes a rather simple form; the state is to be governed by philosophers under whose dictatorial authority others in the community are to be taught how to live the good life, the philosophers alone being directly moved by the enticing vision of the Good. In his last dialogue, however, the *Laws*, this belief in minute political regulation by experts takes a more extreme form— that of a systematic defense of religious persecution.[16] Private worship is proscribed; only priests appointed by the state are to be allowed to conduct religious rites, and only in temples publicly assigned for this purpose. Moreover, an official orthodoxy is defined, and heretical believers who do not respond to rational exhortation are to be punished by imprisonment—in the worst cases by death. The essense of heresy is atheism, which Plato interprets as meaning not merely denial of the existence of God, but also skepticism as to his concern for moral conduct in man and confidence that he can be easily placated by a shrewd sinner.

Neither of these pregnant suggestions was lost in the later development of European religion. The one set of ideas coöperated with other forces in fostering a conception of God's relation to man that accòrds with a high valuation of human dignity and of free moral intelligence. The other proposals supported contrary trends which issued in the authoritative hierarchy of the Catholic Church with a submissive, dependent status for the Christian layman, and in belief in the necessity of political control of religion.

The other feature is that which the *Republic* was written in part to expound. This is the doctrine that it is better to suffer injustice than to perpetrate it. Man's soul—so the argument runs— is composed of passion, impulse, and reason, normally functioning under the control of the last-named faculty; when they so function, their state is one of harmonious equilibrium, which suffuses life with a pervasive happiness not at the mercy of external circumstance. Now the suffering of injustice does not destroy this equilibrium nor the inner peace of which it is the source, but to commit injustice tears the soul asunder, replacing harmony by wild discord and self-control by the abdication of reason before barbaric passion. Later theology found it possible not only to ally this doctrine with Deutero-Isaiah's vision of the constructive spiritual and

[16] In Book X.

social possibilities of suffering, but also to reconcile by its aid, on rational and moral grounds, the suffering of Christ with his divinity. Only moral evil is irreconcilable with divinity, not suffering—especially not the suffering involved in sharing the finitude of human nature and its tragic sorrows.

Aristotle

Aristotle was a younger contemporary of Plato and spent twenty years as a student in Plato's Academy. Although the impress of Plato's thought upon him was deep and lasting, he exemplified a very different type of personality from that of his master. His main interests were not moral or religious but scientific. He was consumed by eagerness to find an explanation for the puzzling details of the world that caught his attention, and to work out the essentials of a sound scientific method. Yet at certain fundamental points his philosophy, like that of Plato, was in harmony with the major convictions of Judaism and Christianity, and it proved a significant aid in their clarification and reinterpretation after the period of Platonic dominance of Christian thought.[17]

The first major difference between Plato and Aristotle, so far as concerns their main doctrines, is that for the latter the world of sense experience may not be impugned as deceitful and shadowy; it is real and substantial as such. The changes which obviously go on in it are to be seriously accepted and adequately explained, rather than, as in general with Plato, branded as evil and unreal. The changeless forms, in his view, are not to be contemplated instead of the changing entities of perception, as the true reality behind the flux; they are to be conceived as immanent principles guiding the changes that occur and as providing an explanation of their occurrence. And this causal efficacy of form in accounting for change is the second major difference. Plato, at least in many of his assertions about the forms, portrays them as patterns existing in a transcendent realm separate from the objects of sense experience. These objects more or less vainly imitate the forms, but that participation is not a temporal process—still less is it identical with the observable changes which take place in the objects—and

[17] See below, chap. V, p. 96 ff.

hence the forms do not account for those changes./Aristotle wishes
to avoid such a dualism of two separate realms in the universe, one
real but impotent, the other unreal but undergoing interesting alterations. He thinks of the forms as embedded in the experienced
objects and actively controlling the changes which can be observed
in them.

Corresponding to these differences in Aristotle's general conception of the world is an equally important difference in his theory of
knowledge. His ideal of science, to be sure, is determined mainly
by the Greek mathematicians who had been a profound influence
in his master's thinking; it is the systematic demonstration of
detailed truths about the world as flowing from first principles
whose truth has already been clearly apprehended. But Aristotle
held, in opposition to Plato, that the first steps toward knowledge
are not to be taken by turning away from sense perception, in
disgust at the instability of its disclosures. Knowledge is won,
rather, by building upon perception itself. This humble activity,
aided by memory and by what Aristotle calls the "common sense,"
produces experience, which already partially reveals the embedded
forms, at least as habitual rules of action which we follow in dealing with objects that have become familiar as a result of these
processes. Experience, thus won, provides a necessary foundation for
the activity of reason. This faculty grasps the universal principle
exhibited in any case of repeated change, and thus carries the quest
for knowledge to completion. Aristotle gives the name "induction" to
such operations as these when they coöperate in eliciting clear apprehension of truths which may later be used as principles of scientific demonstration. Induction is not itself a part of science, but since
it starts from the material of sense perception and keeps in intimate
touch with the changes which the latter undergoes, the principles
established permit explanation of change rather than, as with Plato,
requiring denial of it as unreal.[18]

A brief illustration will give concreteness to this summary statement of Aristotle's theory as to how knowledge is gained. Consider

---

[18] The *Posterior Analytics* and the *De anima* are the most important sources
of these Aristotelian doctrines. It should be noted that for Aristotle change is
explained only so far as it exhibits some regular type, not so far as it contains
an accidental element.

the growth of a plant from its seed. Perception discloses to us the various stages of this process. Through the common sense the revelations of the different senses about each of these stages— those of sight, touch, smell—are unified into the perception of the plant as a single object. These perceptions are retained in memory. Accumulation of many memories of the process of growth brings experience, by which Aristotle means habitual competence in meeting the problems which a gardener might face in raising the plant. The rules which he has learned to follow in solving those problems implicitly assume an apprehension of the form which guides and determines the growth of the plant, but an apprehension belonging to the level of successful practical experience, not to that of clear rational intuition. This latter achievement is due to reason, which abstracts the form essentially exhibited in that process of growth from its accidental attendants, and expresses it as the principle explaining the perceptual facts and changes with which we began.

Now, in elaborating Aristotle's significance for our special theme, we shall need to center on three points: first, his clarification of the basic concepts needed to explain the world in the manner just summarized; second, the general picture of the world which results from their employment; and third, the main theological doctrines which he attempts to demonstrate on this foundation.

The foremost service which Aristotle rendered subsequent thought in general and all later discussion of religious problems in particular was contributed by his success in systematizing the central ideas involved in the various branches of philosophic and scientific investigation. All but a few of these ideas, in the form which they took after passing through the crucible of his mind, dominated medieval science and theology, and the most general of them are still presupposed by serious intellectual discussion in any field of inquiry. Aristotle clarified, for example, the fundamental conception of "substance," which refers to any entity capable of independent existence, and the conception of "essence," which means the attributes included in the true definition of any object of investigation. We shall only consider certain concepts which seemed to Aristotle indispensable in the scientific explanation of nature. The most comprehensive of these are matter, form, potentiality, and actuality. Matter and form, considered alone, are principles by which a struc-

tural analysis of nature is established; considered in connection with
the other two ideas they become instruments for explaining the
varied types of change under which nature's activity falls. Let us see
how our philosopher employs these ideas.

Any physical substance, according to Aristotle, is a union of matter
with form. Matter is the passive element, while form is the active
role which that matter is organized to fill. This union of matter
with form may be illustrated most clearly in a work of art, such as
a statue. Here the marble is the matter, while the form is the artist's
conception which is expressed in it when it becomes the statue. In
the case of an organ in a living body, the tissues of which it is
composed are the matter, while the function which the organ performs in the economy of the animal or plant is the form. Aristotle
thinks of both these concepts as applicable quite universally except
in the case of certain entities capable of existing as pure form,
without any admixture of matter. These are God, the rational beings
believed by Aristotle to guide the revolutions of the celestial
spheres, and the creative reason which is the highest faculty in the
human soul. There exists, however, no pure matter; some form is
always combined with it.

Since, now, matter does not exist by itself and plays a quite
passive role, when Aristotle considers the processes of change which
go on in the world he thinks of it as the principle of potentiality.
In its own nature it is nothing actual but is simply that pervasive
receptivity in the universe which, worked upon by the activity of
form, is capable of becoming the various entities which do actually
exist. Potentiality means merely capability as such. Form, on the
other hand, since it sometimes exists apart from matter, is obviously
actual. Moreover, as has been remarked, it is a dynamic cause, the
principle by which, either alone or embodied in matter, all actualization of potentiality takes place in the universe. And it is evident
from this phase of the philosopher's doctrine that all actualization
of potentiality presupposes the prior existence of an actuality capable of producing such a change. Without a sculptor no block of
marble turns into a statue. Potentiality cannot of itself take on any
form.

The general picture of the world which results from Aristotle's
use of these concepts, interrelated in this way, is that of a hier-

archy of substances at various levels, ranging from the pure forms
at the top to those species of formed matter which approximate
most closely the passivity of matter. This means that, below the
level of pure form, form and matter are relative to their position
in the hierarchy; what is formed matter when we are thinking of
one kind of existent object appears when we turn to entities of a
more complex structure as matter upon which a higher form is
imposed. A slab of marble is not without form, but through the
activity of the sculptor a form of another sort is actualized in it; the
organic parts which enter into an animal's eye are not formless, but
the actualization in them of the function of vision gives them a new
form of a different type. The lowest level in this graded series is
composed of the inorganic material with which we are familiar on
the surface of the earth; the next level is the vegetable realm, which
in addition to inorganic characteristics has the capacity for nutrition
and reproduction; above that are the animals, which besides these
features have the power of sensitivity and (in most cases) locomo-
tion; higher still is man, whose essential form not only includes all
these powers but also the faculty of reason which therefore constitutes his unique and crowning function. The entities that exist
at any of these levels are used by those existing at higher levels in
the pursuit of their own ends, i.e., the actualization of their own
forms, while they in turn employ, as their material, entities belonging
to still lower levels. Thus the horse is used by man in the realization
of his typically human ends, while the horse uses the vegetable
world for his nutriment and the inorganic realm to supply the
theater for his activity. But above all these levels are the pure
forms; why they must be postulated we shall see when we come to
Aristotle's argument for the existence of God.

Turning now to Aristotle's systematic treatment of religious
problems, it may be observed in passing that his most elaborate
discussion was contained in a youthful dialogue entitled *On Philosophy* which is now lost. It exercised, however, considerable influence
in ancient times, especially upon the Stoic philosophers. From
fragments quoted or referred to by other writers it is evident that
Aristotle's position in it was not widely different from that of Plato
in the *Laws*, although he added further arguments for God's
existence besides those offered by Plato. His more mature position

is, fortunately, preserved in its main features; it is contained in his
Metaphysics, his *De anima,* and certain of his physical treatises.
We may turn at once to his doctrine of God. From the basic principles of his philosophy which have just been sketched, certain
corollaries followed in Aristotle's mind which show that there must
be an ultimate being on whom everything else in the universe except
sheer matter depends, and which indicate the essential nature of that
being.

First, why must there be certain pure forms, existing without any
admixture of matter but active in relation to the lower levels of
formed matter? And what must they be like?[19] On the one hand
we need a way of explaining, in terms of the above concepts and
assumptions, the typical processes that take place at the highest
levels of formed matter. What explains, for example, the characteristic activity of reason in man, which is different from anything
that happens at any of the lower levels of existence? On the other
hand we must explain these processes in a way which takes account
of their distinctive nature. Now the characteristic function of reason
is the apprehension and contemplation of form in its eternal and
changeless essence. This function can be accounted for if we
assume that there is some pure form which, though changeless, yet
causes reason in man to seek after its apprehension and contemplation. Since this form has no admixture of matter it could not act
directly as an efficient (that is, impelling) cause, but it might act as
a final cause or desired end. It could lure reason by the attractive
beauty of its eternal perfection.

We have noted above that the various levels of Aristotle's hierarchy of existence are bound together by their teleological structure,
and that every form is conceived also as an end—it guides the
process of its own realization in the appropriate matter, as the form
of a full-grown oak guides the process by which an acorn grows
toward its actualization. Hence this explanation of the function of
reason fits harmoniously into the teleological pattern in terms of
which our philosopher-scientist interprets the cosmos as a whole.
There must, he is sure, be a pure and eternal actuality which
constitutes an ultimate end for other processes in the universe, an

[19] Aristotle's own way of answering these questions is rather technical. The
account which follows tries to give a simpler statement of his basic reasons.

end characterized by the supreme excellence which the highest subordinate entities, such as the rational soul of man and the intelligences which move the celestial bodies, are desiring and seeking to realize. This ultimate and supreme being he calls God.[20]

Moreover, certain specific considerations arising mainly in the field of astronomy pointed in Aristotle's mind toward the same conclusion and indicated more fully the nature of God's relation to the physical world. At least it seemed necessary to assume, as enclosing the physical universe, an eternal source of the motion which we observe in the heavenly bodies. It is well to remember, at this juncture, that down to the scientific revolution of the seventeenth century all those who influenced the formation of European religious philosophy took for granted a geocentric cosmology. The celestial bodies were believed to be composed of a purer and lighter essence than the earth, round which they move in regular orbits. Most distant is the revolving sphere of the fixed stars which, as seen from the earth, exhibits the most rapid motion. Aristotle's doctrine of God was supported by such an astronomical picture and developed in close relation to it. Although he is immaterial, God in some sense surrounds the cosmic spheres and maintains them in motion by his eternal activity. He is the immediate cause of the rapid motion in the outermost sphere by being the object of desire to the pure intelligences which guide the stars fixed in that sphere. This motion is communicated inward to the bodies nearer the earth, some of its velocity being dissipated in the process; it finally reaches the lower heavens and the earth and is the cause of the changes which there take place.[21]

As pure form, God is necessarily immaterial; and since he has no admixture of potentiality he is himself unmoved, subsisting eternally in changeless perfection. His activity is solely that of a final cause. He stirs the world into motion as the object of love or desire awakens action in the being consumed with longing for it. He does not himself love the world, and he has no providential concern for what happens in it.[22] And, of course, God's unchanging life

[20] *Metaphysics*, Book XII.
[21] *Physics*, Book VIII.
[22] There are passages in Aristotle in which purposive governance of events by God is implied. But some, if not all, of them are to be taken metaphorically.

consists in blessed enjoyment of the highest excellence. How are we to conceive this divine happiness? Well, as has above been noted, rationality is the highest of all forms active in the material world; it is least infected by the potentiality of matter and approximates most closely to the unchanging activity of pure form. God is naturally conceived, therefore, as completely actualizing the distinctive excellence of rationality. Aristotle's ideal of rational perfection is in this connection interestingly disclosed. He holds that God is cognizant neither of change nor of any other sort of imperfection. God's life is a "thinking of thinking," that is, deity is pure reason eternally and joyously contemplating its own supreme nature.[23]

In the second place, Aristotle, like Plato, offered a doctrine of the immortality of the soul, but here, as with his conception of God, the theory presented is highly philosophical rather than popularly appealing. All the subrational faculties of the soul—sense perception, memory, desire, even reason itself in its passive aspect —are as mortal as the body. But the active or creative reason, through whose energizing light passive reason apprehends the essence of things, is, according to Aristotle, immortal. This faculty comes into the soul from without, is independent of the lower psychic functions, and being pure form unmixed with matter it does not perish with the body but is eternal. Aristotle's description of this active reason in the soul is meager and vague, but there is considerable evidence that he does not think of it as sharing in the unique personality of the individual thinker. It appears to be only universal reason realizing its characteristic excellence in the soul of each human being, but not modified by the individuality of the latter. In that case, what is preserved after death is not our personality as a whole nor even any distinctive part of it; the immortal element in us is simply the rational function which we share with all other beings possessed of intelligence.

STOICISM AND NEO-PLATONISM

Besides these great individual thinkers, two schools of ancient philosophers likewise supplied ideas of which Christian theology

---

[23] See Book XII of the *Metaphysics*, chaps. VII, IX, for this phase of Aristotle's theory.

made considerable use. These ideas will be sketched briefly. From the later of the two schools, the Neo-Platonists, only one thinker exercised a decisive influence on Christianity, but in the case of the earlier, the Stoics, a succession of philosophers extending from 300 B.C. to A.D. 200, and including such well-known Romans as Seneca and the emperor Marcus Aurelius, contributed to the heritage upon which the new religion drew.

Outside of the fact that in their logical writings the Stoics carried forward Aristotle's work of clarifying fundamental concepts of analysis and explanation, the contribution which they made to Christian thinking may be summarized under four heads. First, their rationalistic pantheism. The universe as they conceived it is an organic whole, a vast body informed and controlled by a rational spirit. This spirit they regarded as a subtle kind of matter, so that in strict logic their doctrine was a thoroughgoing materialism; nevertheless, they attributed to spirit also the essential characteristics that theologians later understood to be implied by this term. The universe thus spiritualized they called indifferently nature or God. Human beings are parts of this all-embracing nature and dependent on it for their existence and for all that they enjoy or suffer; their souls are emanations from the divine World-Soul, or "Logos," as the Stoics frequently called it, and return ultimately to be re-absorbed in it.

Secondly, God's relation to the detailed events of the world's history was described by the Stoics both in terms of necessary law and in terms of providential care. Since God is rational, all things that happen must fall into an intelligible order and be conceived as necessary parts of it; nothing occurs by chance. But since all God's doings are also controlled by spirit, they are teleological, the fulfillment of a unified plan. They thus secure the good of the world, and indeed the good of everything in it when viewed as a part in organic connection with the whole. Of course, if any part—a man, for instance—declines to subordinate his individual desires to the welfare of the universe, much that happens to him might seem to be evil rather than good. But if he be ready in humble submission to identify his own good with the good of the whole, what otherwise might appear as inexorable law or dire fate will be seen as purposive providence, as God's care that every particular life and event con-

64 TYPES OF RELIGIOUS PHILOSOPHY

tribute to the ultimate good of all. In expressing this thought the Stoics used language very similar to that of Christian divines when portraying the relation of God as a personal father to his children. He is spoken of as caring for men and desiring their good.[24] And the appropriate attitude of men toward God is one of reverent obedience and of willing acceptance of everything that happens as part of an all-controlling divine purpose. In support of this doctrine of providential teleology the Stoics pointed to the varied adaptations in nature, which seemed to indicate the presence of design in the cosmic scheme; horses, they held, are adapted for riding, and the peacock was made for the sake of its beautiful tail. This line of thought was later systematically developed into the so-called "argument from design" for the existence of God as a creative and purposive mind.

Thirdly, one feature of the famous Stoic ethics proved of constructive value to later religious philosophy. While its denunciation of indulgence in pleasure and of succumbing to emotion was often carried to an extreme which Christian thought, with its contrary emphasis on the release and guidance of emotion through an overmastering love toward God, could not follow, yet the insistence on loyal performance of duty as against the pursuit of pleasure, and on eager obedience to the will of the cosmic spirit in place of pushing one's individual designs, was quite harmonious with the Christian doctrine of sin as rebellion against God and with its mood of heroic renunciation and wholehearted devotion in response to the divine law.

Finally, the Stoics, living in a period marked by disintegration of civic ties and obligations, developed explicitly the social universalism which was implied in their conception of God's rational care over human life. The divine interest is limited to no group or nation but embraces all men; here lay the germ of a doctrine of human brotherhood. For the Stoics, we are men first and foremost, not Greeks or Romans, or members of any particular family; what is important in us is what we have in common with men everywhere. "My nature," says Emperor Marcus Aurelius, "is rational and social, and my city and my country, so far as I am Antoninus, is Rome; but so far as I am a man, it is the world."[25] This cosmopolitanism

24 Seneca, *De beneficiis*, I, 1(9); VII, 34(4).
25 *Thoughts*, VI, 44.

encouraged a somewhat unenthusiastic love toward other men, but no very definite social obligation, especially toward those distant in space or time. It did provide none the less a philosophical foundation for the Christian belief in God's equal care for all men without distinction of race or social status, as well as for the missionary zeal and the demand for abolition of outrageous social injustices which this belief fostered.

The philosophical conception of an immanent Logos or rational principle in the universe came, after some transformation, to play a vital role in Christian thought, especially after it was employed in the Gospel of John. The form it took there was largely due to Philo, a Hellenized Jew contemporary with Jesus who was deeply influenced by Plato. God, as this thinker conceives him, is identified neither with a subordinate Demiurge nor with the World-Soul of the Stoics. In place of the pantheism of the latter, a doctrine of divine transcendence is taught. God, for Philo, being supremely perfect, must transcend all limitations and cannot be described by qualities derived from imperfect human experience. Every such attribution must be inadequate in the nature of the case. Hence God is not immanent in the world but lies above and beyond it. There cannot even be any direct contact between him and the corrupt realm of cosmic existence; such contact would derogate from his absolute perfection. There must, accordingly, be intermediaries between God and the world, agents through which his creative and controlling activity determines the course of mundane events.[26] The highest of these is the idea of reason or of intelligible unity. Philo applies the term "Logos" to this supreme mediator between God and the world. He speaks of it on occasion as the "firstborn son of God,"[27] through whose agency God enters into relation with the inferior portions of the cosmos. In the Gospel of John, as we have seen, Jesus' relation to God and the world is interpreted in terms of this conception of the Logos.

This doctrine of transcendence, however, does not prevent Philo from deepening the message of the Hebrew prophets and the

[26] This idea, as suggested on p. 30, had played some part in Persian thought and had influenced Judaism after the exile.

[27] *De confusione linguarum,* chap. 146. Cf. Plato's conception of the World-Soul, above, p. 49.

Stoics with respect to the tender interest of God in the welfare of mankind. He portrays God as moved by a bountiful and unfailing love for men, expressed especially in a gracious yearning for their redemption.[28] This conception also became a central theme in the Johannine writings, since the mission of Jesus is there described as the supreme illustration of this divine self-giving to man.

As for the Neo-Platonists,[29] we may confine ourselves to a brief exposition of the philosophy of Plotinus, the founder of the school, who was born in A.D. 204 and died in 269.

Though Plotinus' main foundations are derived from Plato, he radically transforms Plato's conception of God. On the one hand he deprives the divinity of the personal traits which the good Demiurge possessed, while on the other he makes him a transcendent absolute principle, after the fashion of Philo. Instead of being inferior in cosmic status to the realm of eternal forms, God, for Plotinus, transcends and includes them. He is the ultimate, timeless source of all existence and of all good. His transcendence is brought out most forcibly by Plotinus in the insistence that no positive attributes derived from human experience may be asserted of God except—and even the exception is not unqualified—the single attribute of unity. This exception is at times allowed because unity implies no limitation and is consistent with supreme perfection, whereas all other attributes, even the most exalted, do imply limitation and are therefore inadequate to God. The fundamental limitation which Plotinus has in mind in this doctrine of transcendence is best exhibited in his analysis of knowledge. For Plato, knowledge—that is, apprehension of the eternal forms—betokened perfection both of wisdom and of good, since he conceived knowledge as identification of the apprehending mind with its object. But for Plotinus knowledge is not identification. It involves for him an inescapable duality of subject and object, of thinker and thought, in which each member of the pair stands over against the other and limits it. Hence we may not attribute intelligence to God, and not even existence, for it, too, is a category of thought and at once implies the duality to which all thought is subject.

[28] De somniis I, 181. Quis rerum divinarum haeres sit, H31.

[29] In the broad sense of this term Philo may be called a Neo-Platonist. The latter term is commonly restricted, however, to the members of the school led by Plotinus.

But with God conceived in terms of eternal and absolute perfection, how does it come about that there is anything inferior to
him in the universe? How does the world of limitation and imperfection arise? Plotinus' answer is that it is not created, nor does it
evolve out of its own elements; it must be explained as an emanation or overflow from the divine nature. Although any symbolism
here is necessarily inadequate to our philosopher's conception, we
may adumbrate this doctrine by the aid of poetic metaphors which
Plotinus himself suggests. We may think of God as an eternal light
which by its own nature spreads illumination into the surrounding
darkness,[30] or as a scented substance from which fragrance perennially flows without ever exhausting its source. In harmony with
this theory of emanation, the world which arises from the divine
overflow falls into a hierarchy of levels, those nearest God partaking
most of his perfection while those farther removed exhibit a greater
measure of privation and finitude. Highest in the hierarchy is Plato's
realm of eternal forms, which Plotinus conceives as ideas energized
by the divine contemplation; they are the efficient causes of reality
and activity in the next lower level of existence. This is the level of
soul, a defective image of the divine intelligence from which it
emanates. Soul shares in the power of intelligence and can apprehend eternal form, but it is also turned toward matter as exhibited
in the unstable realm of sense perception; in fact, sensible objects
arise just from this degenerate activity of soul. In such perverse con-
sorting with the flux, soul forfeits its unity and rationality, and this
loss is betrayed by its appearing in the guise of a horde of conflicting
desires. Lowest of all is the level (or perhaps for Plotinus it is but a
limiting concept) of pure matter, totally without form, quality,
power, or unity. It is the principle of evil in the universe, but it is
such simply by lacking all positive character. It is pure privation,
utter darkness, empty space.

In harmony with this theory of the universe, Plotinus describes
the nature, history, and destiny of the human soul. This entity is,
of course, part of the World-Soul and exhibits the properties appropriate to its level in the cosmic hierarchy. Originally its gaze was
directed toward God and the good; its contemplation was fixed on
the eternal forms. But through weariness or self-will it shifted at-

[30] Remember analogies used in the Gospel of John, as noted above, p. 40.

tention toward the realm of matter, and thus fell from its high estate. It became steeped in the life and concerns of the body. Still, however, it retains its heritage of reason. This faculty, even while handicapped by chaotic sensuous desire, is able to turn back toward pure thought and through it to God. To achieve genuine recovery of its original vocation, however, it must be purified from the poison of sensuality so that it may again steadily contemplate the eternal ideas. But this recovery is for Plotinus not the highest attainment possible for man. That is mystic union with God, which is a super-rational exaltation of the soul. Such union is possible only in the state which Plotinus calls "ecstasy," wherein all finite limitations are left behind and the soul is ravished by full immersion in the divine unity. In his earthly life ecstasy is attainable by man only on rare occasions; Plotinus himself claimed to have experienced it four times.

The suggestive relations between this philosophy and dominant Christian emphases are so evident that they need not be labored. The form in which Neo-Platonism entered the orthodox theology will be noted shortly when we deal with Augustine. While Neo-Platonism is before us, however, it is important to remark that this philosophy provided the materials for a clear statement of two problems which have haunted Western religious philosophy throughout its history. One is the problem of evil. Other philosophies, in general, had supplied a distinctive metaphysical source for the evil in the world, or, if they were monistic, had not insisted without qualification that the ultimate cause is good. For them, then, no peculiarly harrowing problem of evil arose. But Neo-Platonism traced all reality back to a single principle and identified that principle with absolute perfection. How account in these terms for evil? The only consistent answer would seem to be that evil really does not exist. The difficulty with Plotinus' doctrine is that, if no reality genuinely exists besides absolute perfection, there seems to be no reason why its overflow should be less perfect than perfection itself. In any case, Christian theology, however Neo-Platonic it might become, could not deny the existence of evil, for that would have meant denying the reality of sin and consequently of the need for salvation. Moreover, both Greek and Christian thought, in their doctrines of creation and redemption, suggested an answer to this problem which led to another and at least equally difficult one. This answer is that God's supreme perfection required, for its own complete expression, the creation of an imperfect world and of finite creatures over whom he could exercise fatherly care; it involved, further, for Christian theologians, his leaving the absolute bliss of his celestial paradise and participating in the sufferings of those weak and dependent beings, moved by a yearning desire for their salvation. Here arises a problem which can be stated most simply in the form of a paradox. Absolute perfection, at least in part, consists in the creation of and participation in a realm of imperfection—nay, a realm in which there appear all grades of imperfection, from the lowest to the highest.[31] Certain fundamental aspects of this paradox were present in the thought of all the philosophers with whom this survey of Greek thought has been occupied. Christian theology, of course, attempted to resolve it; we shall soon note the main features of the result.

It is instructive to observe that, as we pass from Plato through Aristotle to Philo and Plotinus, God assumes a more and more exalted position in the cosmological scheme. If we read the earlier of these thinkers in the light of the conception of a hierarchy of being which is fundamental in the later, it could be said that for Plato God occupies the middle position in a structure involving five levels of perfection. Above him is the realm of the changeless forms, and transcending the other forms as the source of their reality is the supreme form of the Good. Below him is the realm of embodied soul, and under that the order of inanimate existence. Since the forms are without motion or efficacy to produce change, God is needed as a self-moving agent to account for the creation of the world of perceptible motions and for the teleological laws by which its detailed changes are to be understood. To the question why he creates at all, and why he follows these laws rather than others, there is no answer except that he is good; in his creative activity he is guided by the idea of the Good. Aristotle wished to answer this question in terms of the same principles of explanation that apply to other problems and thus to provide a systematic scientific account, embracing the interrelations of all these levels of

[31] Professor A. O. Lovejoy refers to this conception by the phrase "the Great Chain of Being." See his book under that title.

being. He does this by offering a more adequate conception of the teleological method of explanation and by showing how pure form, itself unmoved, can be a teleological cause of motion in other things. Thus Plato's Demiurge disappears, and God is identified with the highest among the pure forms—an object of desire to the intelligences next lower in the scale of existence and, through their activity thus motivated, the source of motion in the various levels that are lower still. He is promoted to the realm above that assigned him by Plato. In Philo and Plotinus even this status seems unworthy of the supreme object of religious aspiration. Form and intelligence, as such, are for them imperfect; the absolutely perfect being must transcend them and lie in a realm inaccessible to mere thought. And God's infinite perfection becomes the principle in virtue of which the entire universe is explained and the interrelations of its hierarchical levels rationalized.

Chapter IV

THE FORMATION OF ORTHODOX THEOLOGY

Major Problems and Doctrines

With such materials as these available from the thought of the great philosophers, Christian thinkers could satisfy the pressing need of giving intellectual clarity, system, and such consistency as appeared possible to the picture of the universe and its bearing on man's life and destiny which seemed to be involved in the Christian gospel. Through this process the gospel itself became a philosophical doctrine as well as a way of life. Many conflicting interpretations appeared, giving rise to controversies, but the creed subsequently hailed as orthodox was gradually distilled, and by the aid of concepts and distinctions derived from the philosophers it was given coherent logical form.

The complexity of the problems faced in this quest for systematization, and certain basic features of the outcome reached, should be briefly illustrated. For this purpose we may focus attention on the varied and partially conflicting elements that as a result of the factors above considered came to be united in the Christian conception of God; the attempt to do so will also helpfully summarize the most important matters with which the preceding chapters have dealt.

In this conception Christianity endeavored to unite two apparently rather different ideas: the idea of a strictly personal being, characterized by the qualities of a person, with whom men may stand in an essentially personal relation; and the idea of a metaphysical substance or principle, which provides an ultimate explana-

71

tion of the world with all that it contains, and especially provides the ground of its pervasive unity. The basic need to which the former idea responded is the need of popular religion in all ages and countries for a God with whom the human heart can feel in intimate touch when meeting the practical troubles and emotional crises of daily life. The essential need which the latter idea met is the intellectual need felt by every systematic thinker for an ultimate entity in terms of which the manifold phenomena of the universe can be explained. In its all-pervading unity it also responds to the religious need of those whose piety takes a mystic or contemplative turn, leading them to seek salvation from what they regard as the intolerable limitations of separate individual existence by gaining absorption in the superpersonal substance which binds all things together. Christian theology found it impossible to deny either of these important needs, and consequently could not abandon (nor even definitely subordinate) either of these ideas, no matter how difficult their reconciliation might prove to be.

But each of these ideas is itself no single or simple thing. In fact, there lurked within both of them, as they became clarified in the history of thought, a fundamental duality which has been the source of continued perplexity and repeated efforts to overcome apparent inconsistency. The idea of God as a person took, as we have seen, two major forms and expressed two contrasting ideals. One, whose historical source lay primarily in a pervasive strand of Hebrew religion, pictures God as essentially a monarchical ruler of men and author of the law which they are obligated to obey. They are his subjects, ultimately dependent on him and owing him unquestioning fealty. The other, supported by a different strand in Hebrew religion, but whose main source for Christian thought lay in the Hellenistic mystery cults, interpreted by the aid of Stoic ideas and the crucifixion of Jesus, pictures God as the loving and suffering redeemer of men from sin and mortality. He is the God who so cared for the world as to become incarnate in human form and to die an agonizing death for man's sake. Again, Christianity could not give up either of these ideals of a personal God—the ideal of kingly supremacy and the ideal of perfect love—although it has never been easy to reconcile them. The difficulty is twofold. On the one hand, the God of kingly majesty is self-sufficient; his creatures are entirely dependent on him, but he is not dependent on them for his perfection and happiness. They might never have existed, and yet his perfection would be complete. But the God of self-giving love needs creatures on whom he can bestow his affection, and he is happier when they respond by sharing in his love than when they fail to do so. He is thus not sufficient unto himself. On the other hand, in some sense the God of love must be regarded as saving men *from* the God of monarchical law, since it is the just judgment of the latter upon their trespasses which makes some way of redemption necessary if they are not to perish eternally. God the Royal Judge condemns them for their sins; God the Savior reconciles them to the offended majesty. And yet the two Gods must be identical, or at least not working at cross-purposes with each other.

The metaphysical idea of God also took two major forms. Both are clearly present in Platonic and Neo-Platonic philosophy; in Aristotle a serious effort to reconcile them is evident. One is the idea of God as a universal substance in which the mystic quest for a unity transcending all divisiveness can attain its goal; the same idea provides the principle needed for cosmological explanation, in the form of an ultimate ground out of which all things emerge and to which in time they return. The original historical source of this conception is probably to be found in Hindu thought. The other is the idea of God as furnishing a causal account of why certain particular things exist in the world rather than others which can be imagined, and why they behave in the special way that they do. This idea is the major origin of the intellectual enterprise that we call science. It derives from the conception of both Plato and Hebrew thinkers that the world is the creation of God and in its historical changes is carrying toward completion a purposive plan. In the *Timaeus* a detailed scheme of scientific explanation on this basis is offered, and out of such beginnings European science as we know it gradually developed.[1] From the standpoint of the former of these two ideas God is the culmination of the way up for human thought and aspiration from the unsatisfying particularities of ordinary experience to the unity which overcomes and resolves them. From the standpoint of the latter he is the guiding principle of the way down from the one eternal cause to its manifold transitory

[1] There were other sources, of course; e.g., the atomism of Democritus.

effects in their varied modes of behavior. Theology could not renounce either of the needs expressed in these two conceptions, but
again their reconciliation has always been a challenging problem.
The former principle, when made fully consistent, seems to require
the denial of genuine reality to the particular objects of experience
with which our quest for unity begins; the only being that really
exists is the one all-pervading substance in which our thought finds
rest. But if this is the case, how was the beginning of the quest
possible? The latter principle assumes that particular objects are
entirely real, and it involves the serious difficulty of explaining how,
given the existence of absolute unity—especially if the latter be also
regarded as absolute perfection—a world of specific, imperfect entities should arise. It is hard to see how the former can really account
for the latter. Why and how does goodness create evil, unity gen-
erate difference? In modern times theology has strongly tended to
abandon this problem, surrendering it to a quite secularized science
which makes no use of the idea of a divine First Cause at all.

The orthodox Christian solution of these perplexities took form
in the doctrine of the Trinity. God the Ruler and Lawgiver was
identified with the creative power which is the source of the
detailed phenomena of the world; he also had to be identified,
whatever the philosophical difficulties, with the ultimate substance
of the mystic and the metaphysician. Thus appears the Father of
the Christian Trinity. God the Loving Redeemer was identified
with the Logos or mediating principle which it seemed necessary
to postulate to account for the specific forms created by divine
power at the lower level of phenomenal existence. Thus appears
the Son, a distinct person of the Godhead, though consubstantial
with the Father. The Holy Spirit, proceeding from both the Father
and the Son,[2] personified the continued presence of Christ in the
life of the individual Christian, and the special providence of God
as exhibited in the historical career of the church. Most of the
theologians would not seriously have missed the third member
of the Trinity, but his inclusion with the Father and the Son in
the earliest baptismal formulae made it necessary to provide a
place in the Godhead for him. It is worth noting that this trinitarian
doctrine in effect makes God a superpersonal being. Each of the

[2] The Greek Catholic Church teaches that he proceeds from the Father only.

members of the Trinity is a person, but the Godhead in which they are united can hardly be a person in the same sense. We shall soon observe the form taken by these various conceptions in the system of Augustine. The one major idea he subordinated to a degree which does not reflect the dominant temper of Christian history is that of God as Loving Redeemer of men.

During this exploratory period in which the main content of Christian doctrine was being established, acceptable methods of expounding it and arguing for its validity were likewise taking definitive form. Here the most important figure was Origen of Alexandria, who wrote, about A.D. 250, the first systematic treatise of Christian theology. Origen shared the Hebrew and the Neo-Platonic conviction that God is the source of all reality, and he adopted the prevailing Greek conception of science. We recall that, according to the latter, science consists in the deductive exposition of detailed truths as flowing from first principles which are prior by nature to the things of experience to be explained by their aid.[3] By conforming his treatment to these conceptions Origen set the fashion of theological method which prevailed till the twelfth century, and in many fundamental respects till the time of Schleiermacher early in the nineteenth century. Origen begins his system with the doctrine of God and his essential attributes. God is defined as "spirit," which concept is then analyzed to yield the attributes of the divine nature, such as simplicity, omnipresence, intelligence, and incomprehensibility by finite thought. From this beginning Origen builds up his treatment of Christ, the Holy Spirit, angels, demons, the physical world, man, and the plan of salvation.[4] In each case his premises are taken on the authority of the Bible or apostolic tradition; his conclusions are reached by developing the bearing of these premises on problems current in his day. The conclusions are often confirmed by further appeal to scripture, and in expounding it Origen makes free use of allegorical interpretations. The mental faculty active in this whole procedure is reason, operating by the aid of metaphysical and moral concepts which had been clarified in the work of the great philosophers. The adoption of this

[3] See above, p. 56.
[4] The Greek title of Origen's treatise is περὶ ἀρχῶν; it is usually referred to by the Latin translation, *De principiis*.

analytic-deductive mode of demonstration, resting on authority and formal logic, instead of a more empirical procedure such as was appearing at this time in a few branches of knowledge, notably medicine, proved exceedingly important for the entire subsequent history of Western theology. Had the contrary choice been made by Origen and his successors, the modern conflict between science and theology might have been a matter of secondary details rather than an issue which cut to the very roots.

Among the important social changes occurring during the same centuries was the rise of a unified organization and administration of the Western churches under the authority of Rome. The early Christians, for the most part at least, believed that entrance into the church community through baptism was necessary for salvation,[5] but they did not think of complete submission to ecclesiastical control as required of the individual. To the Roman mind, however, demand for a thoroughgoing administrative order was almost instinctive. And historical events gave it support. As disturbing heresies continued to raise their heads, even after the great councils had defined the orthodox creed, and as the decay of the Roman Empire made obvious the need for some center of social integration and control, this demand became more insistent and more widely shared. The outcome of the tendency thus indicated was the gradual establishment of the Roman Catholic Church in the position of authority in western Europe which it continued to occupy till the rise of Protestantism, and the gradual acceptance of the doctrine that only by submission to its rites and discipline can an individual receive the saving grace of God. Cyprian of Carthage (a contemporary of Origen) was one of the influential thinkers who expressed this tendency and provided intellectual justification for it. He called emphatic attention to the special responsibility and authority given by Christ in the gospels to the apostle Peter, reputedly the founder and the first overseer of the Church of Rome.[6] For him a dissenting Christian community lacks the divine life which is necessary for its spiritual nourishment. "No one can have God for his Father who has not the Church for his Mother."[7]

[5] Cf. John 3: 5; 6: 53.
[6] He later quarreled with the Bishop of Rome and modified this phase of his position.
[7] De catholicae ecclesiae unitate, 6.

THE THEOLOGICAL SYNTHESIS OF AUGUSTINE

It is in Augustine of Hippo (A.D. 354–430), however, that all the varied tendencies which were destined to dominate Western religious thought for a millennium and longer gain systematic unity and come to clear, coherent, and persuasive formulation. Through his creative genius and power of synthetic organization of ideas, the foundations of Christian reflection on all major problems were definitely laid, and the main answers to those problems which seemed cogent to most thinkers throughout the subsequent history of Catholicism were provided. Indeed, with respect to many doctrines the Protestant revolution meant no break with Augustine, and some of its emphases mark a return to him from divergent conceptions which had come to the fore during the intervening period, especially in the thirteenth century.

To understand Augustine it is essential to note first that the manifold tendencies which he systematized stem from three major roots in his thought. As a result of his molding and harmonizing power these three diverse factors were wrought into an enduring unity. He never succeeded in rendering them entirely consistent with each other; hence it is easy to find apparently discordant statements in his treatment of every doctrine. But the principles by which he wished to resolve such inconsistencies when they broke into open conflict are quite clear, at least in his later writings. One of these is the historical precipitate of Greek metaphysical speculation which was most congenial to Christian aspiration, namely, Neo- 1. Platonism. Another is the predominantly moral element derived from the teaching and religious example of the Hebrew prophets; 2. it also is rooted in Augustine's personal religious struggles. The third is the element of social dependence, of need for authority and order, which we may view as the distinctively Roman contribution 3. to this man's theological synthesis. We shall examine Augustine's use of each of these elements in some detail.

It is to be expected that a man of Augustine's keen intellect would be attracted by many philosophical currents and would attempt to square himself with their claims. Such is the case. Prior to his conversion he passed successively through periods in which he was deeply affected by Cicero's half-Stoical eclecticism, by Manichean dualism, by skepticism, and by Neo-Platonism. Manicheanism he came decisively to reject, and his ultimate answer to skepticism was the supernatural illumination of the mind through the ministrations of the Catholic Church. Stoicism and Neo-Platonism remained an influence, and in the case of the latter it was very profound. The Neo-Platonic strain is unmistakable in his treatment of every major theological theme, and in the form which it takes in his system it became an enduring factor in subsequent Christian thought.

The Neo-Platonic deposit in Augustine's theology consists of one central idea—the idea of God as the source of all reality and of every good. The Bishop of Hippo does not follow Plotinus in ascribing to God such complete transcendence as would remove him from contact with human experience and render theology impotent to assign his attributes. But God remains the sole ultimate ground of all things, the absolute cause through whose creative energy existence and goodness everywhere in the universe come into being. Nor, apart from constant dependence on him, can anything continue to exist or remain good. This implies, of course, the underlying assumption that being is essentially good, and that evil is nothing positive but simply the absence of good. God is thus the only real being, the only true substance, the only genuine good. All else—that is, everything in the universe when considered apart from God—is evil and unreal. God is immanent and energizing actuality throughout space and time; he is wholly everywhere and yet nothing contains him, because he is the source of all that is positive in it. To dwell in him, cleave to him, is to live; to be away from him is to die.[8]

This thought of the absoluteness of God—with its corollary, the essential impotence and dependence of nature and of man—entered into Augustine's treatment of every religious theme. It affected his doctrine of creation, making it necessary for him to hold that God created the world out of nothing, since apart from God's activity nothing exists. It gave an ultimacy to his doctrine of providence, for without God's preserving care and power not only can nothing new happen but nothing can even retain its existence. It con-

[8] *Confessions,* I, 2, 3; VII, 12(18). *Soliloquies,* I, 1(3).

trolled his theory of grace and of predestination. Since apart from God man is nothing, the very first germ of faith which leads him toward salvation, as well as every further nourishment of his soul, must be due to God.[9] This means that the reason why some have saving faith and some never attain it must lie in a humanly inscrutable choice of God. God predestines to be saved those who attain salvation. He is, of course, just to all men, in that he treats all as well as they deserve, and sinners deserve only what comes to them. But, to some, God is also gracious and merciful, planting and watering in them this additional germ of goodness through which they become heirs of eternal joy.[10] It determined his conception of Christian love and of the nature of salvation. Love is not primarily good will for man but reverent devotion to God. It is the fullness of grateful and obedient response by the human soul toward the source of its life and of the good in which it comes to participate.[11] And salvation consists in the unutterable blessedness of the vision of God, which marks the final purging of the soul from all unreality and evil; it is the mystic union with divine being, of which we gain a foretaste in moments of rapture in our present life, but which can become perfect only in the life beyond.

It is evident that a systematic theology could have been developed under the guidance of this Neo-Platonic note alone, and it would have been a more logically consistent theology than the one which actually came from the hand of this religious genius. But Augustine was not only nor primarily a metaphysician, seeking the unity of a comprehensive explanation of things by referring them all to a single principle. He was the heir of Hebrew prophetic religion as well as of Greek speculation, and his own moral struggle and religious conversion pointed toward a theology more harmonious with the characteristically Jewish emphasis than with the Neo-Platonic metaphysics. At certain points—and they emerge in connection with each of the major doctrines—these two theologies break into open conflict with each other, and Augustine has to choose between them. It is clear that at these threatened contra-

[9] *Enchiridion*, 32, 98. *De corruptione et gratia*, XIV, 45. *De spiritu et littera*, XXXIV, 60.
[10] *Enchiridion*, 100. *De dono perseverantiae*, XVII, 34; VIII, 17.
[11] *De moralibus ecclesiae catholicae*, I, 20(37).

dictions the personal-moral emphasis of Hebrew religion is triumphant; the metaphysical monism of Greek thought, especially in his later works, is made subordinate to it.

Augustine's Christian mother had from his childhood sought his conversion, but for many years he had rebelled against her God and her church. Pride of learning combined with the quest for sensual pleasure to prevent his submission to an authority which his deeper nature felt all along to be good and right. This struggle suggested to his mind a conception of God and of man framed ultimately in terms of personal will. What is capable of rebellion, of proud self-assertion against rightful control, is obviously more than a metaphysical nonentity. It is just that which we call "will," the controlling spring of motivation and of action in each individual.[12] And as Augustine interpreted the history of Hebrew religion, this seemed to him to be the essential key to its understanding. God appeared there as a purposive and authoritative will, with a chosen plan for his people and through them for mankind at large. They responded to him either by willful disobedience, bewailed and flayed by the prophets, or by willing and humble submission to his law. From this standpoint a quite different theology from that just summarized emerges. The Neo-Platonic conception of God as a cosmic ground of all existence is replaced by the thought of him as strictly a person, with whom we as individual persons may commune, be enemies or friends, who can guide and love us, being obeyed and loved in return.[13] And Augustine's pastoral labors undoubtedly supported this emphasis. Metaphysicians among his flock must have been few, while those who were attracted by the possibilities of an intimate relation with a personal God, and found it a support in the exigencies of life, must have been many.

The fundamental point of inconsistency between this conception and the other concerns the nature of evil and the problems mentioned when Neo-Platonism was examined above. Here, evil is not nonexistent but is a real and active force; or rather, it proliferates into an indefinite number of real and active forces, namely,

---

[12] See the reference in *Enchiridion*, 100.

[13] *De trinitate*, especially X, XIV, XV. His prayers also uniformly reflect this conception.

all those individual wills which are capable of setting themselves up in proud opposition to the divine will. The Neo-Platonic monism is lost, and the central guide to our understanding now is not metaphysical contemplation of the universe through its ultimate dependence on a unitary principle, but the historical and psychological emergence of obedient reconciliation out of rebellious conflict. And Augustine wishes to make clear this story of human redemption from inward struggle through divine grace more than he wishes to respond to the panorama of existence in its metaphysical unity; hence the triumph of this theology over the other wherever they come into serious clash.

Just as every major doctrine was affected by the Neo-Platonism, so it was affected, and if necessary dominated, by this emphasis on the ultimacy in the universe of personal will. When separated from God, man now does not fall into nothing but becomes a disturbing rebel; he does not depend upon God for metaphysical existence but he does depend on him for moral transformation. Without God he can will evil but he cannot will the good.[14] Divine grace is needed, not for the maintenance of his existence but to conquer pride, the root of all sin. And grace is irresistible, not because man is nothing but because God's will is infinite in power.[15] In terms of this approach the prime expression of Christian love is not cleaving to God in abandonment of self, but submission and obedience to his will. Man is subject to God as his sovereign. And the essence of salvation is not union with the divine substance but perfect harmony of our will with the divine will.[16] Heaven thus becomes not mere passive blessedness of ecstasy, but active coöperation with the divine purpose in the world. We may see an intimate blending of the Neo-Platonic and Hebrew notes in the prayer so frequently quoted from Augustine: "Thou awakest us to delight in thy praise; for thou hast made us for thyself, and our heart is restless till it rests in thee."[17]

Augustine's primary achievement as a Christian philosopher was the welding together of these two conceptions under the final con-

---

[14] De dono perseverantiae, VIII (19). De gratia et libero arbitrio, VI (15).
[15] De corruptione et gratia, XIV (45).
[16] Confessions, VIII, 10, 22; IX, 1; X, 37. City of God, XXII, 30.
[17] Confessions, I, 1.

trol of the latter. This integration he carried out with systematic thoroughness, and with a profound appreciation of both the theoretical and practical religious needs of the Western world. One interesting corollary of the dominance of the moral over the theoretical in his philosophy appears in his theory of knowledge; we find here also the explanation why, prior to his conversion, Neo-Platonism could offer no final answer to skepticism. Since God is the supreme good for man, his intellect is the ultimate standard of truth for human thought. But apart from God's grace man cannot sincerely seek truth, for his will is poisoned by sin; he wanders from error to error and no certainty is attainable. Only when his will is turned by divine grace, so that it forsakes pride of self-learning along with all other forms of pride, can he know the truth, because only then can his mind be guided and illumined by the light that streams from the divine wisdom.[18] Knowledge is a moral, not merely an intellectual, matter; insight into truth depends upon that obedience of will through which alone a pure love of truth can arise. Certainty is not born of intellectual contemplation alone, but of moral transformation. This insistence became a central note in later Protestantism.

But there is a third essential element in Augustine's philosophy to which, in the end, the two elements thus far discussed are both subordinated. When he was converted he accepted not only Christianity but also the Catholic Church. He believed its claims and threw himself on its authority. Like Cardinal Newman's pilgrimage many centuries later, his spiritual journey was distinctively Catholic. The Roman genius for unity, order, and discipline was a part of his very nature, and the sense of ultimate social dependence which the effectiveness of Roman administrative organization had bred in the men and women whom it knit together had become a vital motive in his feeling and thinking. He needed the support of a great institution which had existed before him and would continue to exist after him, and he was convinced that the spiritual growth of most Christians demands a living historical mediator between God and the individual. Their personal faith, unaided by established modes of social guidance, is inadequate. Amid the dissolving ties of the empire he felt the responsible function which the Church had to

[18] *Confessions*, VI, 5–8. *Liber* LXXXIII *quaestiones,* 966.

discharge in preserving secular as well as spiritual unity throughout the far-flung Christian community. Moreover, when in his later years he faced what seemed to him the destructive menace of dissentient sects such as the Donatists, it was clear to his mind that no individual or limited group as such could justly be confident that what appears to be an illumination from the Eternal Light is really such.[19] There are no intrinsic marks of divine revelation which are quite unmistakable in the experience of an isolated individual or group; were that the case all who have inner assurance that they are right must be right. There is needed, then, a socially objective criterion of truth and duty, and this means an authoritative organization to interpret God's will for man and mediate his saving grace. Augustine is sure, of course, that the Bible is infallible, but the authority of the Church is superior to the Bible, since it is ultimately the Church which decides what books are to be regarded as belonging to the Bible and how they are to be interpreted.[20] The Church is the living body of Christ and his representative on earth; it is infallible, both intellectually and morally. Christians must accept its authority as to what beliefs they are to hold and what rules of conduct, both as general principles and in their bearing on particular cases, express God's will for them. Our philosopher attributes political authority to it also, in that the Church, as the "City of God," is ultimately supreme over the worldly city, the Empire, and is destined in time to witness its complete destruction and everlasting punishment.

Naturally, this conception, too, affected his formulation and interpretation of all the major Christian doctrines. Each of them was viewed not only from the standpoint of unified metaphysical explanation and from that of personal conflict and reconciliation, but also from the standpoint of the historic career of the Church as the living mediator of divine truth and grace to the individual, the "ark of salvation." And when this conception promised to clash with the others they were the ones to yield. Hence the systematic unity which pervades Augustine's theology, as it actually passed to his successors, is the unity given by Augustine the Catholic churchman rather than by Augustine the speculative mystic or Augustine

[19] *De baptismo*, II, 3 (4).
[20] *Contra epistulam quam vocant fundamenti*, 5.

the reconciled personal will. From this point of view God is essentially the founder, through Christ, of the Church, who commits to it living responsibility for the souls of men and accepts none who remain outside it.[21] His grace is made available to men through the sacraments, which are in the possession of the Church and are invalid except when administered by its officers.[22] These sacraments, of which baptism and the Eucharist are most important for the layman, are mysterious external symbols of divine activity in the soul, "visible signs of divine things."[23] But they are more than mere symbols. As officially used by the authorized representatives of the Church, they are vehicles of saving power to men, in the absence of which salvation is impossible. The doctrine of Christian virtue is likewise transformed. Love of God is expressed in submission to the Church as his vice-regent, and love of the brethren involves maintaining the unity of the Church through acceptance of its authority.[24]

Augustine's second great achievement[25] as a Christian theologian was the welding of his interpretation of personal religion, through the two principles previously discussed, with his theory of its social dependence on a divinely commissioned, authoritative Church. And, as already noted, his picture of the world and of human destiny was in the last analysis integrated around the third of these conceptions.

We may conclude this survey of the Augustinian synthesis by a brief summary of those features of his system which most clearly reveal how these three diverse principles were bound together and handed down as a body of ideas in terms of which later Western religious thought couched its problems and sought its solutions for many centuries. The summary will be mainly historical rather than metaphysical or psychological, because it is in the form of Augustine's philosophy of history that his comprehensive unification of doctrines under the dominance of his theory of the Church was attained.

We begin, of course, with God, who is ultimate reality and

---

[21] *De baptismo*, I, 1.

[22] This doctrine is qualified in the case of baptism and ordination.

[23] *De catechizandis rudibus*, XXVI, 50.

[24] *De baptismo*, III, 16, 19. *Contra litteras Petiliani*, II, 78, 79.

[25] It is not intended, of course, that the two phases of Augustine's synthesis were temporally separated in his thought, although it is true that the Catholic emphasis is most prominent in his later writings.

absolute good. His basic attributes are unity, simplicity, eternity, perfection, infinity—attributes which, while possessing positive meaning, yet indicate God's transcendence of the categories of human knowledge and show that his inner nature is incomprehensible by man. Through his will he is omnipotent; through his providence he is omnipresent throughout the entire creation; as the standard of all truth for finite thought he is omniscient; he is the source of all good in the universe. How do we prove his existence? Augustine offers, and states with remarkable clarity, all the basic types of argument which have loomed large in subsequent theological speculation, with the exception of the Kantian argument.[26] He realizes, however, that those whose minds are not illumined by the light of divine grace may not accept these arguments or agree with their implications; natural reason has no final answer to skepticism. Apart from God man is impotent, intellectually and morally.

For the sake of his own glory God created the finite universe. It was created out of nothing, and in time, which came into being in virtue of the exercise of his creative activity. Divine providence is eternally active in preserving the creation; without it all would lapse into nothing.

Among the various finite entities man was created, possessing a material body and an immortal spiritual substance as a soul. The central and controlling faculty in this soul is will. As originally disposed, man's will was turned toward God and the good. But he was free to choose evil if he so wished, and in the exercise of this freedom Adam, the first man, chose sin and fell from his high original estate. The essence of Adam's sin was not carnal desire, but pride; he ate the apple proffered by Eve not because he was hungry, but because he arrogantly set himself up as superior to the need of obeying God's command. He chose himself instead of God. As a result of this sin he lost the divine grace and was impotent any longer to will the good. Thus he could not avoid falling into further sin and corruption. Being, then, dominated by sin and burdened with continually increasing guilt, instead of upheld by grace, he lost his natural immortality and became the prey of death.

An evil nature now controls Adam which reveals itself in the form of fleshly lust. And all his descendants inherit from him as original

[26] Since these are later discussed in detail they are not stated here.

sin a lustful and rebellious urge, which renders them so susceptible
to temptation that all likewise fall into positive individual sin.
The tempter, of course, is the Biblical devil, who had been created
an angel but who had himself, with his followers, rebelled against
God and had lost his heavenly prerogatives; he expresses his continued hatred and enmity of God by luring weak mortals into sin.
God, being just, must punish sin, and considered from the standpoint of his justice alone, man's plight is hopeless. But, on the other
hand, God cannot allow his original purpose in creation to be
frustrated by rebellious and sinful beings. He cannot forgive the
devil and his cohorts, for there is no way of palliating their sin
and persistent hostility, but he must fill up the places in heaven
which have remained empty since their rebellion. This provides an
opportunity to elect for salvation enough mortals to replace the
number of angels that are lost. To the mortals thus chosen by
inscrutable divine decree he extends mercy in the form of saving
grace, arousing first faith in their souls, then the assurance of
forgiveness for original as well as actual sin. Gradually his grace
transforms them from evil to good creatures. This transformation
is manifested in loving obedience to God's will, as the supreme and
all-embracing virtue, without which other virtues are nothing. Each
step in this process of salvation is due to God's activity, man being
throughout but a passive and helpless recipient. Such extreme predestination, and the accompanying total impotence of man, intellectual and moral, were the most important features of Augustinianism that proved unacceptable to orthodox Catholic theology as
later developed; they reappeared, however, in Protestantism.

But this plan of salvation is not simply an affair of individual
psychology. God does not ordinarily work through the individual
directly, but through his social dependencies; moreover, since
Adam's fall has had inevitable historical and social effects, the purpose of grace must embed itself in a historical process and a social
institution. God thus chose a special nation, the Jews, to whom
progressively to commit the oracles of his will; and he proposed to
incarnate himself, in due time, in one of their members to complete
the historical foundations of salvation for the elect. The significance
of the incarnation of Christ in human form is that it made possible
the renewed participation of humanity, by adoption, in the divine

nature which Adam had forfeited by his sin. God became man that men might become divine. The significance of the atonement by Christ's death on the cross is that it propitiated God's justice and reconciled men to him; it gave a supreme example of humility, patience, and obedience to the will of God; and it revealed God's gracious love to the world. The chief accomplishment of Christ's mission, however, is that he became the founder and head of the Church, which is his body and his living representative on earth throughout subsequent time. The Jews rejected Christ and their special historical function is over; a new dispensation began with the establishment and universal spread of the Church. To the Church Christ committed authority to bind and loose the souls of men, and he entrusted to it administration of the sacraments which are the necessary vehicles of saving grace. The Church is thus the sole ark of salvation, and the subsequent history of the world is the story of its progressive triumph over the secular concerns of men.

In relation to the Empire, which is the city of the world and the devil, the Church is the City of God, holding rightful supremacy over it. But the great task of the Church is of course supertemporal. All temporal history pales in importance before the supreme issues of eternal salvation or condemnation. Finite life is but a prologue to eternity. The essential function of the Church is through history to express an eternal idea; to pilot the elect through the vicissitudes of earthly existence and the purifying discipline of purgatory to ultimate glorification in heaven, which consists in the rapturous vision of God and the blessedness of perfect harmony with the divine will. Those who reject Christ and his Church are condemned to a hell of everlasting fire, where they are kept in pain without dying, and their bodies burn without being consumed. In the face of these immense issues all human interests besides the interest in salvation fade into insignificance, including the interest in scientific knowledge. For Augustine, knowledge of the physical universe is not important except so far as it may promote salvation, and the prime source of such knowledge is not factual observation but the statements of the Bible.

Measured by its subsequent influence as well as by the range of ideas which it unified, the theology of Augustine is one of the most impressive products of the human mind. Almost in its entirety it guided religious reflection in the Western world for eight hundred years, especially as refracted through the popular and widely used *Moralia* of Gregory the Great.[27] And in many of its doctrines, as we shall see, it has controlled orthodox theological formulation, both Catholic and Protestant, ever since.

SELECTED BIBLIOGRAPHY TO PART I

SOURCES

The Bible (especially Joshua, Judges, Samuel, the great prophets, the Gospels, and Paul's Epistles).
The Dialogues of Plato (especially the *Phaedo, Republic, Timaeus* and *Laws*), Jowett trans.
The Enneads of Plotinus (translated by Stephen MacKenna). 5 vols. London, The Medici Society, Ltd., 1917–1930.
St. Augustine (especially *The City of God*, the *Confessions*, the *Enchiridion*, and the *Anti-Donatist Writings*). The two first named are available in many editions; for the others, see the *Nicene and Post-Nicene Fathers* (edited by Philip Schaff), Vols. III and IV.
The Works of Aristotle (especially the *De anima* and the *Metaphysics*), Oxford edition.

SECONDARY

Caird, E., *The Evolution of Theology in the Greek Philosophies*, Maclehose, 1904, 2 vols.
Edman, Irwin, *The Mind of Paul*, Holt, 1935.
Fuller, B. A. G., *The Problem of Evil in Plotinus*, Cambridge University Press, 1912.
Goodspeed, E. J., *A Life of Jesus*, Harper, 1950.
Hicks, R. D., *Stoic and Epicurean*, Scribner, 1910.
McGiffert, A. C., *The God of the Early Christians*, Scribner, 1924.
McGiffert, A. C., *History of Christian Thought*, Scribner, 1932–1933, Vol. I, chaps. i, ii, xi; Vol. II, chaps. ii, iv.
More, P. E., *The Religion of Plato*, Princeton University Press, 1921.
Ross, W. D., *Aristotle*, Scribner, 1924.
Smith, H. P., *The Religion of Israel*, Scribner, 1914.
Smith, J. M. P., *The Prophets and Their Times*, The University of Chicago Press, 1925.
Tolley, W. P., *The Idea of God in the Philosophy of St. Augustine*, R. R. Smith, 1930.

[27] This energetic administrator and statesman was Bishop of Rome from A.D. 590 to 604. He was a close student and follower of Augustine.

PART II

The Major Western

Philosophies of Religion

Chapter V

THE CATHOLIC PHILOSOPHY OF RELIGION

INTRODUCTION

SHORTLY after Augustine's time intellectual darkness settled over western Europe. Though broken occasionally by the rise of a few notable luminaries, it reigned in general for half a millennium. By the eleventh century, however, renewed intellectual activity was everywhere manifest, which in the thirteenth century burst into a brilliant display of philosophical power. It was during this period of bold speculative advance that the first of the major types of religious philosophy which actively compete for acceptance at the present day was initially created in its essential structure and given definitive formulation. The man most responsible for this long influential achievement was Thomas Aquinas, who was born near Naples in 1225 and died while on a journey to Lyons in 1274. His systematic exposition of the Christian faith, which now in general supplies the standard of orthodox interpretation for the Catholic Church—the *Summa theologica*—was written during the last few years of his life, while his almost equally famous *Summa contra gentiles*, a defense of Catholicism against Mohammedans, Jews, and pagan philosophers, appeared a decade earlier.

In order to understand the Catholic philosophy of religion today it is necessary to see it in relation to the historical circumstances which Thomas attempted to meet. And the first step toward this end is to note the main novel features in the intellectual atmosphere of the thirteenth century as compared with the period of darkness following Augustine.

Foremost among these, and supplying the ground for all the

others, was a greater interest in philosophical inquiry and a greater confidence in the powers of human reason. During the half-millennium from A.D. 600 to 1100 such interest and confidence were at a very low ebb. This situation was to a considerable degree encouraged by Augustine's theological emphasis. Though the great African himself used reason freely, yet his doctrine, making God all and man nothing but a blindly rebellious will, completely subordinated human reason to a divinely engendered faith. Craving for intellectual activity appeared again, however, on a widespread scale late in the eleventh century, and it naturally sought justification for itself in a higher estimate of the powers of the human mind apart from the aids of grace than Augustine had been willing to allow. Anselm of Canterbury, who was active during the last quarter of that century, gave the first clear token of the impending transition. His motto "I believe in order to understand" breathes a new spirit. The Christian capable of understanding the great articles of faith should not remain content in belief without understanding; his act of faith should be the doorway to vigorous rational inquiry into the meaning of what he believes and into the discovery of proof such as would make it persuasive to those who accept the standard of reason alone.

In Abélard, a younger contemporary of Anselm, this program gained considerably in boldness. According to him, it is illegitimate for one to believe unless he does understand, at least to the extent of grasping clearly the meaning of what he believes and making sure that it is consistent with the dictates of natural reason. This philosopher even went so far as to denounce all authoritative compulsion in matters of belief, and to praise the value of systematic doubt as a necessary incitement to the earnest inquiry through which alone it is possible for truth to be discovered. Such insistence shows quite clearly his full confidence in the capacity of reason. In Hugo of St. Victor, who was eighteeen years younger than Abélard, this rationalistic eagerness began to change the very structure of systematic theology. Hugo distinguished propositions into four classes: those which are from reason, those according to reason, those above reason, and those contrary to reason.[1] The first

---

[1] The distinction between the first and second of these classes is that the first depends merely on data derived from reason (e.g., logical truths), while the second requires data which reason by itself cannot supply.

and the last of these classes do not admit of faith; the first because it is fully known without the aid of faith, and the last because what is contrary to reason cannot be believed. Faith therefore concerns only the second and third of the four types. In accordance with this scheme Hugo divided theology into two parts called "mundane" and "divine" theology respectively. The former of these, which he expounded first, includes what is from reason and what is according to reason; it covers, in general, the doctrine of God and of his creation of the world. In this part of his treatment Hugo's method was mainly that of rational demonstration, without appeal to revelation. Divine theology, on the other hand, deals with matters which are above reason and which can therefore be known only through revelation. This part includes the statement of God's plan of redemption for men, as embodied in the doctrines concerning incarnation, atonement, the sacraments, and all that has to do with the supernatural office of the Church. This division of Hugo's was accepted by Thomas, at least for apologetic purposes, and has been recognized since as the legitimate mode of formulating the basic argument for the Catholic point of view in religion. So far as concerns recognition of the appropriateness of such a division (and in one other respect soon to be mentioned) Origen's theological method was at this period modified. Natural reason first establishes what it can in its own way, then it sees the need of revelation and allows its own demonstrations to be supplemented by a deductive exposition of the latter.

As this intellectualism developed, two problems in particular which Catholic thinkers found themselves compelled to face seemed to warrant the trust in reason that the age was adopting, and the admission that mundane, or natural, theology must logically precede faith and provide its rational foundation.

One was the problem arising from the fact that the early fathers, whose writings were accepted as authoritative, disagreed on many vital matters of Christian belief. The extent of this disagreement was forcibly displayed in Abélard's famous work entitled *Sic et non,* in which one hundred and fifty-eight propositions were listed on each of which contradictory statements of the fathers were cited. Now since, according to the Church, the time of supernatural revelation had long since ended, so that a new disclosure from God could not settle the matter, there was apparently no way of solving the contradictions and overcoming the disagreement except by rational analysis of the disputed propositions and systematic criticism of the various positions taken. Realization of this need led to a new and high appraisal of logical rigor, since only by its aid could such analysis and criticism hope to reach results on which opposing thinkers would unite. The effort to give adequate room to this way of determining the true content of Christian faith led to a further change in the prevailing method of theological reflection. This was the second modification of Origen's procedure to gain general recognition at this time. The thinker who followed this conception of what demonstration required would proceed systematically from a statement of diverse positions on the great articles of faith to a conclusion so related to them that it would appear to embody an adequate answer to the objections of those with whom it disagreed. We find this mode of exposition carried to its highest level of thoroughness and precision in the *Summa theologica* of Thomas. The outcome was to transfer, over a wide area of theological interpretation, the ultimate appeal from historical authority to those principles of analysis and demonstration which are common to all rational minds.

The other problem arose from the fact that during the period of philosophical activity now under consideration Christian thinkers were thrown for the first time since the patristic era into live intellectual commerce with non-Christians. In Sicily, and even more in Spain, controlled at this time by the Moslems, there was a common meeting-ground for Christians, Mohammedans, Jews, and pagan philosophers. From these areas an influence radiated to all active minds in western Europe which reflected the challenge to thought thus engendered. The essence of the challenge to Christian thinkers was: how to find a way of presenting Christian faith which would render it persuasive (or at least have a genuine chance of doing so) to these non-Christian philosophers? In this situation it was obvious that the ultimate appeal cannot be to faith in revelation nor to authority. For the seat of Christian authority was not accepted by Moslems, Jews, or pagans, nor was the Christian revelation accepted either, at least not in its entirety. In this situation it seemed necessary to assign a fundamental role in apologetics to natural reason, which was common to Christians and non-Christians alike. Reason must be the primary court of appeal; it must be regarded as competent to establish, by its own resources, the foundations of faith and to provide them logical proof. This is the main explanation of the fact that the distinction between natural and revealed theology (following Hugo's division of the subject into mundane and divine) came to be generally recognized as legitimate. To the former was assigned the task of demonstrating the basic and primary articles of Christian belief, up to the point where it could be seen, on rational grounds, that reason demands supplementation by revelation. And the criteria by which one could tell which among the various scriptures is the true revelation were also to be determined by reason.

This meant that even such central themes of theology as the existence of God and the nature and immortality of the soul must be held capable of demonstration by natural reason. Prior to the twelfth century the most influential trends in Christian theology had regarded the existence of God either as self-evident or as totally beyond the reach of reason. Thomas decisively rejects both these doctrines. As for the first, he remarks that any idea which has become familiar to us through custom, "especially if it date from our childhood, acquires the force of nature, the result being that the mind holds those things with which it was imbued from childhood as firmly as though they were self-evident."[2] The implication is that apparent self-evidence is no indication that the doctrine thus supported rests on satisfactory grounds; even if all people, on this basis, accept as real a being whom they call God, the kind of being meant by the word will not necessarily be the same. For pantheists this reality might be identified with the world of nature; for others, with a being very different from this. But true belief is in God's reality, not merely in his name. As for the second, Thomas's answer is to offer a rational proof which he is confident will be conclusive to any mind willing to grant the principle which he assumes as necessary to any demonstration, namely, that the existence and nature of a cause may be deduced from an examination of its effect.

The new method of establishing religious doctrine meant also that the sphere allotted to revelation and faith must be carefully

[2] *Summa contra gentiles,* I, 11.

circumscribed, lest theology be brought into disrepute through asserting as a dogmatic truth what natural reason, operating by its own appropriate method, can disprove. To be sure, "nothing may be asserted as true that is opposed to the truth of faith, to revealed dogma. But neither is it permissible to take whatever we hold to be true, and present it as an article of faith. For the truth of our faith becomes a matter of ridicule among the infidels if any Catholic, not gifted with the necessary scientific learning, presents as a dogma what scientific scrutiny shows to be false."[3] This insistence led Thomas strenuously to oppose Augustine's convictions—shared by many during the long centuries preceding the rise of modern science —that accurate knowledge of the world of nature is unimportant, and that such acquaintance with it as we insist on attaining should be based on the Bible rather than on scientific observation. Since we reach our knowledge of God by causal demonstration from effects spread before our eyes in the great universe of things, error in our views about the latter will be exceedingly likely to lead to error in our views about their ultimate cause.[4] And the way to avoid error in our scientific study of these effects is not to follow revelation (whose main concern is with the supernatural plan of salvation, not with cosmology); it is, rather, to apply that method in the examination of nature which is acceptable on logical grounds alone and can therefore be employed in common as between Christian scientists and those of Moslem or Jewish persuasion. Thomas identified this with the method originally developed by the philosopher Aristotle, who, through the aid of Mohammedan thinkers, was coming to be widely known in southern Europe at this time. Starting from observations by the senses, one proceeds under the guidance of causal axioms to universal and final explanations of the facts with which he began.

We must pause briefly over the circumstance that in the thirteenth century—and largely through the powerful influence of Thomas—a generally Aristotelian approach came to displace, for Christian theology, the Platonic and Neo-Platonic conceptions which had previously dominated Catholic thought. In the Greek

[3] De potentia, 4, 1 (trans. by M. Grabmann in his Thomas Aquinas, His Personality and Thought).
[4] Summa contra gentiles, II, 3.

Church this transformation had taken place five centuries earlier, though along somewhat different lines, mainly through the work of John of Damascus. But in the West, previous to the twelfth century, only certain of Aristotle's logical works were theologically influential. Moslem and Jewish thinkers, however, especially in Spain, were already making extensive use of his metaphysical and psychological writings. During the twelfth century these parts of the Aristotelian philosophy were rapidly becoming accessible to thinkers in France and Italy. They aroused a storm of discussion and naturally much opposition, since a reinterpretation of the Christian faith in terms of the foundations they provided involved radical changes from the assumptions and procedures previously prevailing among theologians. Thomas was one of those who championed the Aristotelian cause with a deep conviction that it was essentially right. He did not, of course, follow the Greek genius where the latter conflicted with items central in established Christian belief, such as the creation of the world in time and the personal immortality of the soul. But in other matters he embraced the philosopher almost entire, and especially in those methodological principles on which Aristotle had disagreed with Plato. His great achievement was to Christianize Aristotle and to Aristotelianize Christian theology, and he performed this task with such logical acumen, precision, system, and completeness that he supplied the main foundation and norm for the development of Catholic theology ever since.

Before expounding the major steps of the Catholic argument, which was first given its standard form in the writings of Thomas, it is worth our while to note the connection between this shift to an Aristotelian foundation and the main problems in face of which, as above outlined, the theologians had found justification for their increasing confidence in reason. The ultimate appeal of Neo-Platonic thought, which had in general supplied the philosophical basis for Christian theology prior to this time, was to a yearning for perfection and a mystic experience rather than to the familiar facts of ordinary life. God is the reality in which all things find their unity, and God is a transcendent, supremely perfect being. Man gains positive knowledge of him through spiritual intuition, a faculty which raises one above the world of everyday experience and gives direct insight into the supersensible and the eternal. This faculty might be called reason, to be sure, but it was rather different from reason as the Aristotelians conceived it. The trouble with this intuition was that it reached different results in different thinkers and provided no common court by which these differences could be adjudicated. By its exercise Moslems discovered Allah and the truths of the Koran; Christians found the Christian deity and the truths of the Bible. Hence, as long as Christian theology appeared to rest in the main on the metaphysics and methodology of Neo-Platonism, it could give no rational answer to those who raised critical objection against its primary propositions. It could only reiterate that the conceptions in question were intuitively self-evident (which an honest objection to them seemed to disprove) or that they were to be accepted on faith (which was unconvincing to those who did not see the validity of faith as Christians understood it).

The virtue of shifting, in this situation, to an Aristotelian foundation lay in the fact that Aristotle's ultimate appeal was empirical, i.e., to objects and events as disclosed in the daily perceptual experience of everyone, whether housewife or mystic philosopher, whether Jew, Moslem, or Christian. All knowledge was held to rest on this basis of everyday observation, which supplied the ultimate content, and provided the concrete meaning, for all our conceptions, however abstract and general. In building it we start with universally familiar experiences, and our scaffolding consists of structural principles which rational explanation everywhere seems to warrant. Theology when Aristotelianized thus appeared to be securely grounded in the common sense of all mankind. Thomas adopts as a guiding principle that "our knowledge, even of things which transcend the senses, originates from the senses,"[5] and is to be understood in terms of its derivation from sense perceptions that are available to all men. God, from this standpoint, is not a translogical idea, nor one supported by the inner visions of some limited sect. He is the First Cause of effects open to the observation of everyone every waking hour of his life. And his existence and attributes are to be demonstrated by appeal to just such universally accepted facts, explained by axioms of reason which are believed to be equally universal. The strength of the Catholic philosophy of re-

[5] *Ibid.*, I, 12.

ligion, at the time of its first systematic formulation in the writings of Thomas, lay primarily in this circumstance.

We are now ready to survey the main steps of the argument by which a typical Catholic thinker attempts to render logically persuasive the essential foundations of his point of view. This argument divides into four major steps: first, the demonstration by natural reason of the existence and nature of God; second, the establishment, also by natural reason, of the freedom and immortality of the human soul; third, the transition from reason to faith in revelation; and fourth, the proof of the authority of the Church to interpret the true revelation. In expounding the argument our discussion will follow the formulation of Thomas except on points where contemporary Catholic thinkers usually prefer to rest their case otherwise than on the considerations he emphasized. And when following Thomas we shall use his statement in the *Summa contra gentiles* except in the case of his argument for the existence of God, where the *Summa theologica* gives a more succinct and more widely influential statement.

1 God for Catholicism

The first step is to prove the existence of God, as an unchangeable, primary, necessary, perfect, and intelligent cause of the world of experienced fact. Thomas's famous proof is as follows:

I answer that, The existence of God can be proved in five ways.

The first and more manifest way is the argument from motion. It is certain and evident to our senses that some things are in motion. Whatever is in motion is moved by another, for nothing can be in motion except it have a potentiality for that towards which it is being moved; whereas a thing moves inasmuch as it is in act. By "motion" we mean nothing else than the reduction of something from a state of potentiality into a state of actuality. Nothing, however, can be reduced from a state of potentiality into a state of actuality, unless by something already in a state of actuality. Thus that which is actually hot, as fire, makes wood, which is potentially hot, to be actually hot, and thereby moves and changes it. It is not possible that the same thing should be at once in a state of actuality and potentiality from the same point of view, but only from different points of view. What is actually hot cannot simultaneously be only potentially hot; still, it is simultaneously potentially cold. It is therefore impossible that from the same point of view and in the same

MOTION

way anything should be both moved and mover, or that it should move itself. Therefore, whatever is in motion must be put in motion by another. If that by which it is put in motion be itself in motion, then this also must needs be put in motion by another, and that by another again. This cannot go on to infinity, because then there would be no first mover, and consequently, no other mover—seeing that subsequent movers only move inasmuch as they are put in motion by the first mover; as the staff only moves because it is put in motion by the hand. Therefore, it is necessary to arrive at a First Mover, put in motion by no other; and this everyone understands to be God.

(2)   The second way is from the formality of efficient causation. In the world of sense we find there is an order of efficient causation. There is no case known (neither is it, indeed, possible) in which a thing is found to be the efficient cause of itself; for so it would be prior to itself, which is impossible. In efficient causes it is not possible to go on to infinity, because in all efficient causes following in order, the first is the cause of the intermediate cause, and the intermediate is the cause of the ultimate cause, whether the intermediate cause be several, or one only. To take away the cause is to take away the effect. Therefore, if there be no first cause among efficient causes, there will be no ultimate cause, nor any intermediate. If in efficient causes it is possible to go on to infinity, there will be no first efficient cause, neither will there be an ultimate effect, nor any intermediate causes; all of which is plainly false. Therefore it is necessary to put forward a First Efficient Cause, to which everyone gives the name of God.

(3)   The third way is taken from possibility and necessity, and runs thus. We find in nature things that could either exist or not exist, since they are found to be generated, and then to corrupt; and, consequently, they can exist, and then not exist. It is impossible for these always to exist, for that which can one day cease to exist must at some time have not existed. Therefore, if everything could cease to exist, then at one time there could have been nothing in existence. If this were true, even now there would be nothing in existence, because that which does not exist only begins to exist by something already existing. Therefore, if at one time nothing was in existence, it would have been impossible for anything to have begun to exist; and thus even now nothing would be in existence—which is absurd. Therefore, not all beings are merely possible, but there must exist something the existence of which is necessary. Every necessary thing either has its necessity caused by another or not. It is impossible to go on to infinity in necessary things which have their necessity caused by another, as has been already proved in regard to efficient causes. Therefore we cannot but postulate the existence of some being having of itself its own necessity, and not receiving it from another, but rather causing in others their necessity. This all men speak of as God.

(4)   The fourth way is taken from the gradation to be found in things.

Among beings there are some more and some less good, true, noble, and the like. But "more" or "less" are predicated of different things, according as they resemble in their different ways something which is in the degree of "most," as a thing is said to be hotter according as it more nearly resembles that which is hottest; so that there is something which is truest, something best, something noblest, and, consequently, something which is uttermost being; for the truer things are, the more truly they exist. What is most complete in any genus is the cause of all in that genus; as fire, which is the most complete form of heat, is the cause whereby all things are made hot. Therefore there must also be something which is to all beings the cause of their being, goodness, and every other perfection; and this we call God.

The fifth way is taken from the governance of the world; for we see ⟨5⟩ that things which lack intelligence, such as natural bodies, act for some purpose, which fact is evident from their acting always, or nearly always, in the same way, so as to obtain the best result. Hence it is plain that not fortuitously, but designedly, do they achieve their purpose. Whatever lacks intelligence cannot fulfil some purpose, unless it be directed by some being endowed with intelligence and knowledge; as the arrow is shot to its mark by the archer. Therefore some intelligent being exists by whom all natural things are ordained towards a definite purpose; and this being we call God.⟨6⟩

Let us examine these five arguments, clarifying their major assumptions.

The first is the least intelligible and the least conclusive to modern minds, and although for Thomas it was the clearest and most convincing of all, Catholic theologians today are apt to give it a subordinate place and to reinterpret it with care. The essence of the argument seems to be as follows: We perceive things in motion. Now no body moves itself; the cause of its motion must lie in something else. If that something else is another moving body, we must in turn seek the explanation of its motion in a third thing different from these two. But this series of explanations cannot be infinite. There must be a first mover, who, himself unmoved, is the ultimate source of all motion in the world. Otherwise there would be no actual production of any motion and no motion could anywhere take place. Since we see that it does take place it is necessary to posit such a first mover. The reasons why this argument

⟨6⟩*Summa theologica*, I, qu. 2, art. 3. Translated by the British Dominican Fathers. Reprinted by permission of the publishers, Burns, Oates, and Washbourne, Ltd.

often appears unconvincing to modern minds are two: its assumption that the occurrence of motion needs to be accounted for, and the further assumption that an infinite series of motions, each accounting for the motion that follows it, is irrational.

(♦) The first of these assumptions poses a difficulty because modern science is built on a dynamic rather than a static foundation. It assumes that the things which make up the world are by their very nature in process rather than at rest; one of its basic principles is Newton's first law of motion, according to which every moving body continues to move in the same direction and with the same velocity unless external forces prevent. This means that motion as such needs no explanation; it is only change in the velocity or direction of motion that must be accounted for. The same assumption is implied in the more recent theory of evolution. As a matter of fact, Thomas means by motion something much more general than modern thought does; he includes under it any change by which an entity tends toward its specific end. None the less, when the argument is sufficiently transformed to become plausible to modern dynamic conceptions, it is apt to lose all features that clearly distinguish its postulates from those of the second argument, which proceeds not from the nature of motion but from that of efficient causality. The same is true of the other assumption which may occasion difficulty to the contemporary mind, namely, that an infinite series of motions, with no first member, is irrational. The Catholic philosopher's answer to this objection rests on considerations which are expressed in clearer and more persuasive form in his defense of the argument on efficient causality. To this argument we may therefore turn at once.

(2) The proof from the nature of efficient causality, second in Thomas's presentation of the five arguments, may be briefly summarized in a form parallel to that of the argument about motion. We perceive in our world sequences of cause and effect, one thing causing a second, that in turn a third, and so on. No such thing can cause itself, because to do that it would have to exist before it came into existence. Its cause therefore must lie in some other thing. But the causal series which we thus begin to trace cannot be infinite, because if there were no first cause none of the intermediate causes could have come into existence and the present effects which we

observe could therefore not exist. Hence we must posit a first efficient cause, on which all the various chains of cause and effect ultimately hang.

The chief objection which the modern mind is apt to raise against this reasoning is the one already noted: Why may there not be an infinite series of causes and effects, with no first cause at all? Moreover, it will wonder whether the very notion of first cause is a defensible one; if it is legitimate and necessary to ask for the cause of other things and to find it in God, is it not just as legitimate and necessary to ask for the cause of God's existence? This objection seems to many modern thinkers a strong one because of their familiarity with modern mechanical science, which in general rejects the notion of ultimate causality and assumes the validity of unending series of causal relationships. It generalizes from such cases as the motion of a billiard ball across a table, which has been caused by the preceding motion of another ball, that by a tap from the cue, and the latter in turn by some equally specific motion. In such a situation each cause and each effect is a definitely localized occurrence in space and time, and no matter how far we trace back the sequence science assumes that we shall remain within the sphere of particular, spatio-temporally localized events. Hence the earliest cause that we find ourselves able to reach in any such series cannot be regarded as ultimate and self-explanatory; it, like the rest, must be the effect of some equally particular and localized occurrence, or set of occurrences, which we might be able to determine by further investigation. This theory of causality will be elucidated in the chapter dealing with agnosticism.[7] Suffice it to note here that nothing more than such a conception of causality appears required to satisfy the need of confidently predicting the future on the basis of dependable connections observed in the past, and the assumptions of modern science, in general, express just this interest in confident prediction.

The Catholic answer to such an objection is that the true conception of causal explanation involves more than mechanical science assumes; it demands as a logical necessity the notion of a first or ultimate cause. In Thomas's argument this answer is intimated in the assertion that if there were no first cause none of the intermediary

[7] See below, chap. VIII, p. 210 ff., 226 f.

causes or effects could ever have come into existence. This shows—
and the point is elaborated in contemporary Catholic treatises—that
Thomas does not think of a cause simply as an event regularly connected in time with its effect and thus enabling confident prediction
of that effect. He thinks of it as the productive agent which makes
the effect arise and possess the essential characteristics that it reveals. Before clarifying this theory of causal explanation it will be
well for us to have in mind typical illustrations of the process which
it assumes to be universal. Such are found in the relation between
a sculptor and the clay which he is molding into artistic form, or in
the relation between a mind and an idea which is being shaped so as
to solve a problem by which that mind is challenged. In these
situations we observe two important features.

First, it is evident that the cause is not just an occurrence antecedent in time to the effect, which is over when the effect takes
place, and to which the effect merely stands in the relation of
dependable sequence. It is an active operation which continues
during the emergence of the effect, and is productively responsible
for every property exhibited in the nature of the completed effect.
Without such an operative and continuously controlling agency the
effect could not conceivably arise, nor could it be the kind of thing
that it is. Whereas, if motion may be explained as modern mechanical science usually assumes that it can, we may investigate by the
postulates of the latter a sequence of motions without feeling under
any need to discover a cause which holds to the effect such a complex relation as this.

Now, the fundamental assumption of the Catholic philosopher at
this juncture is that every observable effect must be, and can be,
explained by some productive efficiency in the sense just described.
Every true causal relation involves this active operational bringing
of the effect into being. Other, and more limited, conceptions of
causality, such as that of mechanics, may be sufficient for certain
branches of science considered by themselves, but no fully adequate
or complete causal explanation is reached until it conforms to the
above conception. And, reasoning on this basis, he finds himself led
to a first or ultimate efficient cause of all the effects which the
world discloses. No infinite regress is consistent with this conception of causal explanation. The decisive reason for this conclusion

is the one above noted: unless a first cause exists, no productive efficiency is actually at work by which the effect immediately dependent on it can come into being; no subsequent effects can then arise; thus, in this event, nothing can exist at all. The supposition of an infinite regress might permit prediction of later events in terms of earlier ones, but it would provide no real explanation of the actual production of any event nor of its having the nature that it does, for nowhere in such a regress do we come upon a cause which we can be sure is really engaged in making its effect arise. All in that case is hypothetical; each effect would exist *if* its own cause, about which we do not yet know, should have really existed and been able to produce it.

The second important feature in the Catholic illustrations is this. *(ii)* It is evident that the full cause of such effects as we have here in mind is an affair which is necessarily either equally comprehensive in nature and enduring in time as its effect, or else more so. It is equally comprehensive, because it must possess all the perfections[8] which it imparts to the effect in producing the latter, and it may possess more. It is equally extended in time because only through its continued operation does the effect gradually assume the character that it comes to exhibit and it may be active over a longer period than the emergence of this particular effect requires. Our illustrative cases exemplify this possibility. A mind usually engages in concentration on a given problem longer than the time required to engender any particular idea as a possible solution of that problem. Thus, as we trace our way back from present effects to more and more remote causes, we seem compelled to reach agents which are more and more comprehensive, both with respect to the types of perfection they possess and with respect to the period throughout which they are active. Before long in this regress, of course, we reach causes which can no longer be observed by the senses but which must be conceived by the intellect alone. The productive cause of a human soul with all its faculties is, for instance, not thus observable. This does not, however, cast doubt upon the validity or reality of such causes, so long as we arrive at them by pursuing a self-evident metaphysical principle, and the Catholic philosophers

[8] That is, *qualities*. This is the most nearly corresponding term in modern thought. See, however, p. 107 f.

hold the above-described conception of causality to be an axiom of this kind. By such a route it is obvious that our thought will reach bottom in a cause which is self-active, productive directly or mediately of all other effects but not itself an effect. And it cannot be an effect because it gathers up in its nature all possible types of perfection and is active throughout all time. When, in our quest for causal explanations, we reach an entity so conceived we need not and cannot go further. On these assumptions it is self-explanatory. It contains its own reason for existence, and is a first efficient cause of everything else.

⟨3⟩   Thomas's third argument consists in an examination of the conceptions of necessity and contingency as bearing on the causal explanation of the world. We perceive about us contingent objects, that is, objects capable either of being or of not being. Anything that arises and later disappears is obviously of this sort. Now, if everything in the universe were capable of not being, it must sometime have been nonexistent, and there must have been a time when nothing actual existed at all. But in that case nothing ever could have become actual, since entities come into existence only through the activity of something already actual. So, since some things do exist, we must suppose that not everything is capable of not existing; there must be something which necessarily exists. Is the ground of its necessity in itself or in some other necessary being? Perhaps the latter, but we cannot fall into an infinite regress here, for the same reasons that applied in the preceding arguments. Hence we must posit some being which is necessary in itself and is the ultimate ground both of necessity elsewhere and of contingent being wherever the latter appears.

(1)   One link in this reasoning is felt by many Catholic authors to be insecure, namely, that in which Thomas asserts that if all things without exception were merely contingent, there must have been some time at which nothing existed. They are disposed to admit that even though no one contingent thing exists forever, there might be an unending succession of contingent existences, with no period at which nothing contingent exists. So they prefer to state the argument in a form which does not depend on this link. Their central contention is this: Even though it be admitted that there may have been no time at which nothing existed, if anything is capable of

nonexistence it is evidently not self-explanatory; the ground of its
existence must lie in something other than itself. And Thomas elsewhere makes it clear that, allowing such an admission, this is his
position.[9] Hence even with this concession we find ourselves forced
back to some being which is not merely contingent but necessarily
exists. The essential assumption underlying this argument is simply
that implication of the causal principle which asserts that something
cannot come from nothing, nor can it pass away into nothing. If this
is the case there must be some necessarily unending form of
existence out of which all contingent things arise.[10]

The fourth argument brings explicitly into prominence another
feature of the conception of causality which the Catholic position
involves—a feature referred to briefly when we considered the
second argument. Not only can nothing come into existence except
through the activity of something already existent; none of the
perfections or excellences it exhibits can come into being unless the
cause contains those perfections either in the same or in higher
degree. Otherwise we may have an explanation for the existence of
the effect but not for the specific properties which it reveals. On this
basis the reasoning proceeds as follows: We perceive in the world
characters which vary in degree; there is the better and also the
worse, the more and the less noble, etc. Such comparative distinctions, however, rest on a relation to the superlative in each of these
qualities, without which they cannot be understood; we mean by the
better that which is more like the best, by the worse that which is
less like the best, and similarly with the other qualities. Moreover,
the cause of anything so far as it is good must be a being equally
good, or better, i.e., something whose goodness is imparted to it
either wholly or partially. The ultimate cause, then, of the various
grades of goodness in the universe must be the Best—a being possessing supreme or infinite goodness. Now, the same reasoning
applies to every other quality which is capable of degrees, such as

---

[9] Cf. his statement of the argument from contingency in the *Summa contra
gentiles,* II, 15; and his discussion of the eternal existence of matter as philosophically possible in *Summa theologica,* I, qu. 46, art. 2.

[10] Modern science seems to have held some such assumption in its doctrine of
the conservation of matter and energy. Any particular material existent is a
selective concretion from the sum total of matter and energy which is constant
and eternal.

nobility, beauty, heat, and the like. Hence we must posit as the ultimate cause of all things a being uniting in his nature all types of perfection in their superlative form.

Modern Catholics are not in agreement as to how far this argument may be properly applied to purely physical attributes such as heat. As regards metaphysical and moral attributes, however, they are agreed that its application is demanded by the axiom of causality. If existence cannot arise from nothing, for the same reason a higher grade of perfection in such attributes as goodness, truth, beauty, intelligence, power, and being itself, cannot arise from a lower. Wisdom and love in man point toward at least equal wisdom and love in his creator. Moreover, it is a part of man's essence that he feel an urge toward a higher excellence in these respects than any he has yet attained. Such an urge implies a superlative excellence as the end toward which he is striving. In the face of these considerations our explanation must evidently take us finally to a cause which is not merely equal to the highest excellence we can glimpse; a being is required who is infinitely perfect in all these attributes.

A common feature of these four arguments is that the proof may start from any object whatever that ordinary experience might disclose to us. We need only open our eyes to see something that moves, has come into being, is contingent, and reveals some degree of the excellence which is typical of the species to which it belongs. And with any such object our demonstration may commence. The fifth argument is different in this respect. It takes its start, not from a universal feature of all perceived objects as such, but from a feature frequently exhibited in their relations to each other. Moreover, the preceding inferences have not explicitly proved that the ultimate cause is personal, and this omission is made good by the present argument. In expounding it we shall depart from Thomas's brief formulation, which is as clear as it could be made by a paraphrase, and shall provide an expanded statement.

The behavior of many things clearly exhibits adaptation toward the attainment of some end. This is shown by the circumstance that, though most of them do not consciously aim at any goal, they act regularly (i.e., when accidental factors do not intervene) in ways whose normal effect is to realize an end which is either of value to the thing itself or to some other creature in its environment. Now, these orderly adaptations, in the view of Catholic thinkers, cannot be accounted for by blind mechanism, but point toward a controlling intelligence as their cause, since the characteristic mark of intelligence is the introduction of purposive order in the materials with which it deals. An illustration especially well calculated to reveal the force of this argument is the growth of wings on a bird, through which it is equipped to fly.[11] Here, selection and adjustment of many varied materials in just the right way are necessary if the full-grown bird is to be able to fly. The bony structure of the forelimbs must be long enough. The skin must be webbed, and the muscles must be very powerful. The limb must be sheathed with an exceedingly light coat, capable of shedding water, and yet strong enough to support the body's weight. The creature's instinctive reactions to the pressure and currents of the air must be such as to enable it to make appropriate use of all these adaptations. Now, obviously, the young bird does not foresee the goal of flying and consciously direct his own growth so as to attain that goal, as did the human beings who invented airplanes. Can this remarkably complex adaptation be accounted for mechanically, by the principle of gradual natural selection, for example?[12] No, the Catholic philosopher replies, because the first rudiments of a wing would hardly enable their possessor to fly; they would not only bring no positive advantage in the struggle for existence, but would be a useless burden and therefore a handicap. Their possessors would be less adapted to the needs of life rather than more. Yet, according to the Darwinian theory of natural selection, such adaptations are acquired through the accumulation of specific variations of structure, each of which when it occurs is preserved because it provides its possessor with a distinct advantage over others who compete with it for the privileges of existence. There is no such advantage in a quarter or half of a wing; to explain the gradual growth of a complete wing enabling its possessor actually to fly, we must leave natural selection and suppose an intelligent cause directing the entire process toward the attainment of its appropriate end. There are many such adapta-

[11] See G. H. Joyce, *Principles of Natural Theology* (3d ed.), pp. 125 ff.
[12] This principle will be discussed in greater detail later. See chap. X, pp. 301–304.

110   TYPES OF RELIGIOUS PHILOSOPHY

tions in all areas of nature, and they can only be accounted for by referring them to a controlling purpose or providential wisdom operative throughout the entire world. Let us survey these arguments in retrospect and see just what each, if valid, establishes. The first leads to an unchangeable origin of all change, the second to a primary cause of all productive efficiency in the world, the third to a necessary ground of contingent events, the fourth to a supremely perfect source of all varieties and grades of perfection in finite things, and the fifth to an intelligent governor of the adaptive order in nature. Catholic philosophers sometimes add other arguments to these, one of which will be best considered in connection with their theory of the human soul.[13] Another, which may be briefly mentioned here, is the moral argument from the witness of conscience; our sense of right and wrong, so it is contended, points for its explanation to a lawgiver whose commands conscience recognizes itself as bound to obey.

Now, do these lines of reasoning point toward one and the same being as the ultimate cause of all things? At first sight it might not be evident that such is necessarily the case. But on examination of the arguments it becomes obvious that they are all closely interrelated; it might be said with justice that each brings into prominence a single phase of the same underlying argument, and that the being toward which each points is therefore clearly the same entity. The ultimate source of motion must be the same as the primary efficient cause, for all effects come to be what they are through a process of change. This primary cause must possess all the perfections exhibited in its various effects in order to make them attain their distinctive excellence, hence it must be identical with the most perfect being from which the infinite grades and types of perfection come. The necessary ground of all contingency must, because its existence is necessary, be pure actuality without any admixture of potency; a being possessing potentiality is by that very circumstance capable of growth and decay, and is hence contingent. But pure actuality must also be identical with supreme perfection, since an imperfect being is capable of change in the direction of fuller perfection, or of loss of some quality which it has attained. And the supremely perfect being must include infinite

[13] See below, p. 123 f.

intelligence among his attributes because intelligence is one of the irreducible modes of perfection which the world exhibits. The creative ultimate established by these reasonings is therefore one entity, not a plurality of beings.[14] If the arguments are sound, we have proved a single original, unchangeable, intelligent, supremely perfect being as the necessary ground of everything in the cosmos, and such a being is what we mean by the word "God."

From the attributes of God established by these arguments several others may be deduced by logical analysis. We shall note, however, merely the deduction of goodness in God, since that is not specifically established by any of the above proofs. Thomas proves this attribute directly from the divine perfection.[15] We see from experience that the goodness of anything is measured by the degree to which it attains the perfection proper to its species; a man is good, for instance, in so far as he achieves the sort of excellence of which human nature is intrinsically capable. Now, since God possesses superlative perfection, he is not only good but supremely good; inasmuch as his nature sums up in itself all types of perfection, he contains what every particular excellence, no matter of what sort or how high in degree, needs for its supplementation. Considered from both these standpoints he embodies that which every other good in the universe lacks. From God's goodness, together with his intelligence, Thomas proves the attribute of will and through this in turn God's love for his creatures.[16] The divine intelligence apprehends the essence of all things, including goodness; now, to understand anything as good is to tend toward it also, i.e., to will it, hence God must be will. And since he understands and tends toward good as such, without any limitation, he not only wills his own good but the good of all creatures who in one way and degree or another participate in his perfections. But to will the good of anyone is to love him. Therefore God loves all finite beings in the world, and he especially loves man as being capable of a higher mode of perfection than any other species of his creatures.

[14] The Catholic philosophers also demonstrate the unity of God in other ways than this, but in the present context this way appears to best advantage.
[15] *Summa contra gentiles,* I, 37 ff.
[16] *Ibid.,* I, 72, 91.

At this juncture it will be well to clarify certain assumptions in the preceding arguments which we have not so far explicitly examined. One assumption concerns the metaphysical status of goodness; it is that good is a positive reality and an effective cause in the world, while evil is not a positive reality and is only accidentally a cause. This conviction rests on the teleological theory of the universe which had been systematically worked out by Aristotle and is now harmonized by Thomas with Christian emphases. Everything that happens is a striving toward an end; it is a process in which a material entity realizes some form, the latter effectively guiding that process as a final cause. When an acorn grows into an oak tree the form controlling that occurrence is the nature of the mature oak which appears at its completion. Now, an end presents itself subjectively as good to the creature striving toward its realization, as being the goal of its desire; considered objectively, it is the characteristic perfection of the species to which the creature belongs. And from the objective standpoint any creature is itself pronounced good in so far as it succeeds in embodying the perfection appropriate to it. A good oak tree is one which succeeds in fully realizing the essential nature of an oak, while a bad oak is one which is prevented, by whatever external or internal factors, from completely attaining the typical excellence of the species. Well, in the case of subhuman creatures, the typical good striven toward is a limited one; it is the form which, for knowledge, distinguishes that particular species from others. Thus the good or perfection of an oak tree is specifically different from that of any other kind of tree, and generically different from the good of all things that are not trees. In man's case, however, the possession of intelligence enables him to transcend the limitations of this or that particular good.[17] The characteristic function of intelligence is to apprehend form as such, abstracting from the individuality and the material content of the objects which awaken the apprehension. This applies to the form of good as well as to any other form. In other words, man is not merely able to

[17] This point will be developed more fully in another context. See below, pp. 119–122.

grasp the common essence of oaks and other species of physical things; he can grasp the essential nature of such all-inclusive forms as those of goodness, truth, beauty, unity. This indicates that the good of man as an intelligent being is not any specific or finite good —it is good as such, universal and absolute good. But this is the same as the good of God himself, the perfection which the divine nature eternally embodies. One important corollary of this inference is that when we apply the term "goodness" to God we use it in strictly the same sense as we do when we apply it to man.

If, now, we view the universe in terms of this teleological conception, it is evident that goodness must be conceived as a positive and effective reality. Specific goods or excellences guide what happens in specific types of process which aim at their realization, while the ultimate end and controlling cause of all processes is the universal good or absolute perfection envisioned by intelligence. What, then, from this standpoint, is evil? Well, nothing strives toward badness, hence the latter is no positive reality or effective cause of any event. Evil is accidental in the universe. It is so sub- (3) jectively (i.e., from the standpoint of one who falls into it) in the sense that it happens to him because, in his striving to realize his typical excellence, he cannot foresee all the contingencies into which he may run, or avoid everything which may prevent his successful attainment of what is good. Such contingencies then become for him evil, but since it is not a law of his nature that he fail to escape them, as it is that he pursue his appropriate good, evil is clearly accidental, (3) while goodness is an intrinsic and essential factor. It is so objectively (i.e., from the standpoint of one who examines any instance of it from the outside) in the sense that it appears always as due to conflict between two teleological processes, as a result of which one or both are prevented from realizing their end. When a hunter is attacked and killed by a hungry grizzly, each of these two agents is pursuing an end appropriate to his species; the evil happens because the attainment of one end precludes the attainment of the other, and in this case the representative of a higher grade of perfection is overwhelmed and reduced to a means for the attainment of a lower perfection. But such an outcome is not required by the essence of man or hunter, hence it must be pronounced accidental.

In all this reasoning the Aristotelian conception of natural law (4) is assumed rather than the conception characteristic of modern science. Stated in more familiar terms a law, on this assumption, is a *tendency* rather than an unexceptional relation; an acorn may be prevented by many circumstances from growing into an oak, but it *tends* to do so—i.e., wherever possible it utilizes environing factors toward the realization of that end. Modern science, eager to predict and control natural events in terms of their dependable relations, could find no virtue in this notion of law. Its idea of law is such a connection between two events as makes possible the confident prediction of one on the occurrence of the other. And when no quite dependable connection appears to be discoverable, it seeks probable connections rather than tendencies, the former being for its aims the best substitute for unexceptional regularities whereas tendencies, implying a certain purposiveness in what happens, do not fit into its basic scheme of explanation at all.

Another assumption which we may appropriately consider at this point concerns man's knowledge of God. The Catholic position on this matter implies, in the first place, that this knowledge, when reached by applying the self-evident axioms of reason which guide the above arguments, is true and certain as far as it goes, while yet it is in the nature of the case far inferior to God's knowledge of himself. Human reason is metaphysically competent, in other words, to attain absolute truth concerning God's existence and certain of his attributes—those at least which we need to understand in order to see where our true good lies and how it may be secured. But some of these attributes indicate, when we examine them, that God's nature in itself far transcends human comprehension. We know him, for instance, as eternal and as infinite in perfection, and one of the implications of these attributes is his incomprehensibility by such a finite creature as man. The same consequence may also be seen in another way. Everything known is known after the mode of the knower—this Aristotelian principle is taken by Thomas and other Catholic theologians as essentially sound. But since man is obviously an imperfect being, whose intelligence is limited, the manner in which he understands anything must reflect his limitations, especially when the thing understood is infinitely greater than he. In the case of man's knowledge of God the clearest illustration of this circumstance appears in connection with the divine attribute of simplicity.[18] We see that God, considered in himself, must be a simple being, because whatever is compound possesses potentiality—at least the potentiality of dissolution into its component parts. God, being pure actuality with no admixture of potentiality, must hence be absolutely simple. This means that his attributes are merged in a perfect unity; his essence, existence, eternity, goodness, truth, etc., are all one and the same. But since these attributes as grasped by human minds are different from each other, we cannot comprehend this ultimate identity into which they dissolve in God. When, accordingly, we apprehend the divine nature and try as best we may to describe it, the only way in which we can proceed is to add these various attributes to each other as though they were distinct; although we know that God is simple, we have to think and talk about him as if he were a composite being, possessing such characters as distinguishable aspects of his nature.

These considerations pose a serious problem about man's knowledge of God, and we need, in the second place, to observe the Catholic answer to it. This affirmation of divine simplicity, in spite of the fact that our thought must appear to contradict it, suggests that perhaps we were too hasty in assuming that human reason is metaphysically competent at all. If our knowledge is everywhere affected by the limitations of finite intelligence, how can we affirm anything whatever of a perfect being with confidence that it truly and certainly applies to him, that its meaning is not perverted by our finitude? If God is really simple, how can we venture to assert of him attributes which to our thinking are clearly distinct from each other? And if we do so—if we say that God is good or intelligent—how can we be sure that these attributes, as pertaining to God, mean anything even remotely similar to what they mean when we apply them to creatures familiar to our finite experience? But if we cannot be sure of this, the ascription of these attributes to God gives no genuine knowledge of him; they are words and nothing more; God becomes at best a mysterious unknown, whose existence we may vaguely affirm but about whom we may make no assertion that conveys positive significance.

The Catholic solution of this problem is that we must make two distinctions when dealing with the nature of the Divine Being. First,

---

[18] *Summa contra gentiles,* I, 18.

we must distinguish the attributes whose meaning is essentially negative from those which carry positive implications. Among the former belong such aspects of God's nature as eternity and infinity; these mean simply that in God certain limitations which are evident in the case of finite creatures are removed. The ascription of such attributes to God is clearly justifiable, and in their case the difficulty in question does not arise, since we can derive no affirmative knowledge from them. They simply express the divine transcendence of finite conditions as such. The problem arises only with the positive attributes. These are all applied to God by "analogy" with their application to finite things; the meaning in the two cases is similar though not absolutely identical.[19] But we must here make a second distinction, that between two degrees of analogy.[20] Some attributes imply imperfection in their very definition; such, for instance, are all those which involve dependence on material conditions or on transitory emotions. If these are asserted of God—as when the Bible tells us that on a certain occasion God was angry—the application is metaphorical merely. No true knowledge of him is expressed by them; the analogy is simply one of "proportion," to use the technical terminology of the theologians. But other attributes imply no imperfection in their essential nature. Such are the famous transcendentals (as they were called by medieval thinkers)—unity, being, goodness, truth. Since the meaning of these is clearly not limited by any conceivable conditions, they may be applied to God in the same basic sense as to other entities. The same principle applies to such attributes as intelligence, will, life. Intelligence is just the power to apprehend being and truth as such—that is, wherever they are found and whatever form they take. In this, its essence, no limitation or imperfection is implied. These attributes, therefore, do express positive and true knowledge of God. There is still analogy rather than identity of meaning, since God, being infinite, must possess these attributes in a far higher manner than we do. But their essential meaning remains the same. Therefore we truly know God's nature through them and can be confident that whatever is logically deducible from them must hold of him as well as of any finite mind that possesses them. Here we have, in technical

[19] Ibid., I, 31–36.
[20] G. H. Joyce, Principles of Natural Theology (3d ed.), pp. 242–253.

parlance, analogy of "attribution" rather than analogy of mere proportion.

These distinctions, and the result reached by their aid, are vital to the Catholic philosophy. Its whole point of view, so far as concerns man's knowledge of God, rests on the threefold conviction that (1) human reason is metaphysically competent up to a certain point but (2) incompetent beyond it, and that (3) the determination of that point is one of the matters that lie within its competence. Without the first conviction the ultimate appeal would have to rest on revelation and authority rather than reason, and there would be no answer to the questions of those who are not moved to accept the authority of revelation. Without the second conviction nothing lying above reason could logically be allowed; God, being fully knowable by man, would possess no transcendent nature, and there would be no need or place for a divine revelation to supplement human knowledge. Without the third conviction the first would go by the board. If reason cannot tell with assurance how far it is competent and where its competence ends, then it cannot be sure of its competence anywhere. It would not know in what matters it could reach truth; in what, not. [21]

So much for the Catholic arguments concerning the existence and nature of God.

II   THE HUMAN SOUL

The second main step is to establish the spirituality, freedom, and immortality of the human soul. This is likewise done by the aid of fundamental ideas derived from Aristotle; in this case it is the psychology of the Greek thinker that provides the required foundations. Aristotle had recognized several different faculties as entering into the composition of the human soul, ranging from the sensitive and nutritive principles which man shares with the lower organisms to the creative intellect whose function elevates him far beyond them. Thomas and his followers emphasize very sharply the line of demarcation that separates intellect from the

[21] A challenging difficulty arising from these convictions is discussed below. See chap. XIII, p. 402 ff.

lower faculties and the extent to which it dominates them in the soul as a whole.

According to their analysis there are two basic differences between intellect and such faculties as sense perception, imagination, and memory, which indicate the essential immateriality and incorruptibility of the former. These differences are that the lower powers are immersed in matter and dependent on physical organs for their exercise, while the intellect is restricted in neither of these ways. What is given to the mind in perception, imagination, and memory is the image of a particular material object such as a mountain or a tree; these faculties can deal with nothing which does not present itself in individualized sensuous form and whose material nature is not, therefore, fully evident. Moreover, as experience amply teaches, their exercise is dependent on bodily organs, especially the senses and the nervous system. But what is the case with intellect in these respects? Well, on the one hand, when objects are apprehended by the intellect their individual and sensuous character is transcended. The universal pattern which they exemplify is abstracted from the sensuous clothing and grasped in its nature as pure form. Perceiving an individual human being, we apprehend by the intellect the essence of man as a common type; observing an instance of causal connection, we envision the nature and essential validity of the universal principle of causality. Now, that such a common essence or principle is pure form without any admixture of matter is evident in the fact that it abstracts from everything individual and sensuous in its object. According to Aristotle, matter is the source of particularity and individuality in things. The faculty which transcends these and apprehends pure form is therefore shown to be essentially independent of matter in its existence and exercise. On the other hand, we find that this apprehension is independent of our bodily organs. Introspection tells us that it is a simple, indivisible act of the mind. But all our organs are composite affairs, divisible into various parts. Hence if such an act were dependent on any physical organ it would be likewise a composite affair, reflecting the distinguishable parts of the organ involved. The way it occurs is, to be sure, correlated with changes in those organic parts, but its essential nature is not determined by them.

The intellect and everything that follows from it or is bound up with it is thus proved to be independent of matter and of the physical organism to which its activity at present is attached. Being immaterial, it is spiritual in character, for freedom from matter is the primary attribute of spirit. Being simple instead of composite, the intellectual principle is shown to be incorruptible, for only what is composite can disintegrate or perish. This simplicity is proved by our consciousness of the unity of selfhood and by our inner identity through the changes continually taking place in the matter of which our bodies consist.[22] Activity of the lower faculties, accordingly, for Thomas, ends with the dissolution of our bodies, but our intelligence continues to exist and to act.[23] It could, of course, be annihilated by a special act of God, but no reason can be given for expecting such destruction at his hands.

From intellect, and in intimate dependence on it, arises the activity of will, which our theologians define as "rational appetency." Appetency of a less rational sort is exhibited at the sensuous level, where it appears in the form of craving or desire for particular satisfactions and the material possessions through which the gratification of such desire can be assured. But, as we have seen, intellect apprehends what is good in its universal essence—goodness as such—and from such apprehension arises an active tendency toward the realization and enjoyment of this rational good. Such appetency, guided by intellect, is will.[24] Now will asserts itself as rightfully dominant over all lower desires. The latter are focused upon this, that, or the other specific object which at some particular time appeals to us as good, but will is focused upon universal good —upon what is intrinsically and unqualifiedly excellent. And while the lower animals, in virtue of their limited nature, are satisfied with particular goods, a being whose distinctive faculty is intelligence can be satisfied with nothing less than goodness as such. He is capable of apprehending such an absolute perfection, abstracted from the limitations of this or that particular embodiment of goodness, and the ideal thus apprehended is proposed as an

[22] *Summa contra gentiles,* II, 50, 55.
[23] *Ibid.,* II, 79, 80, and 81. Other faculties bound up with intelligence, such as will and love, are, of course, also immortal.
[24] *Ibid.,* II, 47.

object to his will. Obviously, good as such—good in its universal character—is greater than any specific good; it transcends it as the infinite transcends the finite and as the eternal surpasses the transitory; it is the sovereign good, rightfully supreme over every more limited good in the universe. As rational beings we are necessarily lured onward in the pursuit of this absolute good; conscious of intrinsic capacity to attain it, we can find no final satisfaction in any lower appetency, even if completely gratified.[25]

Tending thus toward an infinite, rational end, the will proves itself further to be morally free.[26] By freedom of the will the Catholic philosophers do not mean a complete absence of causality in its choices and volitions, which would make its action the prey of mere chance; they mean that it is self-determined. When, after deliberation, it makes a decision, that decision is neither a pure accident nor is it completely controlled by the motive which prior to reflective consideration was strongest. The cause that determines the decision is just the intelligent self of the individual who makes it, in his quest for the universal good. Thus in such situations we are free both from mere spontaneity and from fate; our will neither swings in a moral vacuum, undetermined by anything, nor is it mastered by causes which have been fully formed in the past so that they are immune to present reassessment or redirection.

This conclusion is established, in part, by deduction from the nature of the will as above explained. If there is such a thing as rational appetency at all, it must, in the judgment of Catholic thinkers, be free in this sense. For the essential difference between this kind of appetency and the lower desires is just that the former is guided by an intelligent vision of the good in its universal nature. It is, of course, influenced by sensuous appetite and played upon by the urge of passion, but if it were wholly determined by such forces it would be indistinguishable from them; nothing that we could describe as rational appetency would be discoverable in the situation. Wherever there is will, the true cause of its action is just the faculty of intelligence in its quest for an absolute and supersensuous excellence. In part, the same conclusion is reached

---

[25] Ibid., II, 47.

[26] For a good summary of this Catholic doctrine see M. Maher, Psychology (4th ed.), chap. 19. Cf. Summa contra gentiles, II, 48.

by examining the implications of conscience. Through conscience we are aware of a moral law, whose commands are recognized as binding upon us, although they bid us turn away from the pull of transitory desire in obedience to an eternal principle of right. Now, whatever we ought to do we can do; otherwise the sense of moral obligation is illusory and meaningless. Hence we must assume that our actions are in the end determined neither by chance nor by passion. They are due to that faculty through which we perceive and respond to the conception of universal law —the faculty of intelligence. Finally, this conclusion is directly confirmed by psychological observation. When we watch ourselves choose and act we see that while much of our conduct is controlled by some irrational urge or other, and while such motives are never without influence upon it, yet when the intellect is alert and operative these lower forces do not tell the whole story. In such cases intelligence shows itself to be the crucial factor in the result that emerges. In the first place, it determines the course of our attention, drawing the latter away from the limited ends posed by particular desires and fixing it upon a universal, and hence infinite, good. In the second place, it sustains and controls the process of deliberation, in which the motives present as effective factors are not allowed to issue at once into conduct in accordance with their original strength or weakness, but are weighed, compared, criticized, and finally accepted or rejected in the light of their bearing upon our rational vision of the true good. Unless introspection is to be trusted on this point, deliberation must be pronounced an entirely futile and meaningless performance; without it, the same result would appear that is attained with it. In the third place, our consciousness that the decision reached is *our* decision, not that of some limited part of us, and that we are responsible for the ensuing action, attests the fact that our total self in its distinctive nature, that of reason, is the cause of what has happened. The lower animals are doubtless determined in all that they do by particular desires for transitory objects; only man is free to will an eternal and infinite good.

Where, now, do we find this transcendent good? Clearly, only in God, who, as the most perfect being, sums up all the excellences of the universe at their highest pitch of actualization. He is not only supremely good; he is goodness itself, the very essence of good. He is therefore the final end which lures toward its attainment all creatures possessed of will. And the manner in which we must conceive that satisfying attainment of God is also obvious. Since intellect is our unique excellence, and the faculty in virtue of which we are lifted above matter and its corruptions, it must be the characteristic activity of the intellect, operating upon God as its object, in which that ultimate good for us is realized. But the proper activity of the intellect is clear understanding of the essence of things, a direct vision of their true and universal nature. The vision of God, then, in which he is immediately apprehended in his essence, is the ultimate good and last end of the human will.[27]

In the present life, however, we are incapable of attaining such a vision. Here only two modes of apprehending God are possible. We may have a demonstrative knowledge of his existence and of certain of his attributes, after the mode of a created intellect and under its finite limitations. Such knowledge, even though it attain a First Cause of all things, does so by gradually abstracting from the sensuous matter with which it begins. It is never purified from all particularizing imagery nor from the analytic distinctions with which, owing to the circumstance that it must be gained by adding one limited idea to another in a process of temporal learning, it must perforce be content. We may also know him by faith, which because of its supernatural guidance brings us into more confident touch with his true nature, but which lacks the characteristic virtue of intelligence. Only in the life beyond, when we are freed from the limitations of bodily existence, may we win a rational vision of God as he truly is, and only then by a ray of illumination from the divine light which bridges the still infinite gap between creature and creator, and endows us with the intellectual perfection enabling our minds to endure the brightness of absolute being. In that supreme happiness every desire of man as man is completely fulfilled.[28]

With the considerations just emphasized in mind, we see the possibility of another proof of human immortality in addition to

[27] *Summa contra gentiles*, III, 25, 37.
[28] *Ibid.*, III, 47, 52, 53, 63.

that based on the Aristotelian psychology; by a slight extension it becomes a further proof of the existence of God. Man, in virtue of his very essence, craves a good which cannot be attained in this present life, and which indeed, because it is infinite, requires eternity for its complete realization. Now God has been proved to exist as a most perfect being, supreme in goodness and characterized by unbounded love for his creatures, especially for man. It is inconsistent to suppose that such a God would endow his creatures with a desire for infinite good unless he also rendered available the necessary means for the fulfillment of that desire. But this implies that he creates them with the natural capacity, under his conserving power, for an immortal existence, since nothing less is required for such fulfillment.[29] Moreover, if we had not already proved God's existence by other arguments, we should have in man's natural longing for an infinite good an adequate proof of this great truth, provided that we add a justifiable further assumption. This assumption is that experience reveals no natural and normal desire which appears to be intrinsically incapable of adequate satisfaction. Teleology is pervasive throughout the world; everywhere we see adaptation of organs to their functions, adjustment of creatures to their environment. To be sure, this adaptation is not perfect nor is it apparent in every detail; hence we may not hastily assume a guarantee that every desire for this, that, or the other particular object or goal will be satisfied. We observe in fact that many such desires meet defeat, but we nowhere observe any essential (or even general) type of desire for which no satisfaction is available. Living things desire food. Now, there is no warrant that any particular living creature will not starve; none the less, food exists in the universe, and such creatures are in general adapted to find it. Roots instinctively seek moisture. And even though some roots do not find the water they need, yet there is moisture in the earth, and the growth of roots takes place in such a way that if it is available they usually secure it. Generalizing from such cases, we must hold it inconceivable that man should be equipped, through his essential and distinctive power of intelligent will, with longing for an infinite good, unless there exists in the universe that which is needed to satisfy it. Some men may fail

[29] M. Maher, *Psychology* (4th ed.), pp. 525–533.

to attain it, but failure cannot be regarded as inevitable in the nature of things. And this good, to be infinite, must possess in supreme degree all the perfections which man can conceive. We have here, hence, an independent proof of the real existence of God.

THE TRANSITION FROM REASON TO FAITH

Let us now take the third main step in the development of the Catholic position. The existence and essence of God have been established; likewise the moral freedom and essential imperishability of the human soul. And in treating both these themes, especially the latter, it has become evident that man, although a limited and imperfect being, seeks through his rational appetency an unlimited and perfect good—a good which is strictly supernatural, since its full attainment depends on conditions which lie beyond this life and surpass what the unaided exercise of his natural faculties can hope to gain.[30] Here we face the basic consideration which, according to the Catholic philosopher, points toward the necessity of supplementing what reason can apprehend by a knowledge above reason. Natural understanding itself, at this point, bids us seek a supernatural revelation of truth which, while not conflicting with what natural reason can establish, yet supplements it and also confirms by a new mode of assurance the results reason has thus far reached.[31] It is still the function of our natural faculties, of course, to determine the tests by which we can tell whether any assertion of truth claiming to be divinely revealed is really so, but that there should be such supernatural additions to its own discoveries it recognizes as implied by those discoveries themselves.

Consider this step first in the form which it naturally takes when deduced from the above results alone, without any appeal to history or to existing institutions. We men are finite creatures, of limited and imperfect intelligence, engaging in the quest for a good which our reason shows to be supernatural and transcendent; its attainment depends on conditions which we cannot at present anticipate, let alone confidently apprehend. Obviously, without

[30] *Summa contra gentiles*, III, 147. *Summa theologica*, II, Part I, qu. 2, art. 5.
[31] *Summa theologica*, II, Part II, qu. 2, arts. 3, 4.

supernatural help we cannot know with assurance how to reach this supreme good. The most competent exercise of our natural faculties must in the nature of the case provide inadequate guidance in face of such a problem as this. At best they could only show us how and where to find the highest possible happiness in this present life; they could not hope to point the way with confidence toward an otherworldly and eternal bliss. For salvation, therefore, we need instruction which lies beyond the power of our own reason to attain; were such assistance absent, the probabilities are very great that we should somewhere make a fatal mistake and miss the great goal of human life. Now, only God can give us the needed instruction and assurance, for in him alone is absolute power conjoined with perfect knowledge. And since he has also been proved to be infinite in goodness and in love, we know that he must have provided that supernatural guidance for mankind.[32] A God in whom mercy and loving-kindness are demonstrable properties would not create a race stirred to seek him and find their good in him without so supplementing their inadequate natural powers that they may, if they will, attain the fulfillment of the urge implanted in them by his own act.

Moreover, the truths which natural reason is competent to establish likewise need to be supernaturally revealed.[33] It is evident that most men have neither the training nor the logical acuteness requisite to follow with complete confidence the demonstration of God's existence and attributes by the aid of the metaphysical axioms to which natural reason appeals. And all but a few are so constantly harassed by the practical duties of life that even if they were equipped to attain such a demonstration the necessary leisure is lacking. The consequence of these handicaps is especially evident in the sphere of desire and volition. Were all men possessed of the highest intellectual advantages, all would by their own resources come to see the necessary existence of an infinitely perfect being and would find him the supreme object toward which a rational will naturally tends. But we see in fact that most men fail by their own powers even to apprehend those ends which promise the most rational happiness attainable in the present life; they

[32] *Catechism of the Council of Trent,* Preface, qu. 1, 2.
[33] *Summa theologica,* I, qu. 1, art. 1.

remain under the control of sensuous desire, passion, and ambition, flitting from the dominance of one such irrational urge to that of another. That such a situation should remain unremedied cannot be intended by a God whose infinite love flows out equally toward all men, the ignorant and heavily encumbered as well as the leisured and sagacious. He must have made available all the great truths necessary for salvation in another form than that of arduous rational demonstration—a form readily understandable by and capable of appealing directly to the humblest mind, provided it be earnest and sincere.[34] There must, in short, be a supernatural revelation, suited to awaken assured faith in place of logical apprehension where the latter is weak, and confirming it where it is strong.

Now when, having in mind these anticipations drawn from the truths thus far established, we look about for the expected revelation, Catholic thinkers are sure that we cannot long remain in doubt as to where it is actually to be found. Here before us lie the Christian Scriptures. Reading them, we find a spirit of purity, nobility, and hopeful idealism that directly appeals to the best impulses of our nature. The authors of these sublime sayings agree in denying that the ideas they proclaim with such assurance originated in their minds; they claim that these truths come from God, who disclosed them by a supernatural illumination and instilled the courage to teach them in face of skepticism, persecution, and ridicule. This claim is confirmed by many and marvelous accompanying circumstances. The prophets and apostles who proclaimed these momentous truths announced the coming of future events which were to carry forward the divine plan of which their own work was a part, and these prophecies were wondrously fulfilled, especially in the life and work of Christ. Further to attest before a skeptical world their divine mission, they performed miracles— arresting manifestations of God's presence directly revealing the power of him who created and ordered the world of nature to supersede for good ends the laws which he had imposed.[35] The sick and infirm were instantly healed by a spoken word; the dead were raised from their graves; the course of inanimate nature and the

[34] *Catechism of the Council of Trent*, I, chap. 2, qu. 6.
[35] G. H. Joyce, *Principles of Natural Theology* (3d ed.), pp. 426–433.

normal instincts of animals were changed. Christ's virgin birth and resurrection from the grave were miracles especially important for establishing his divine status and mission. Such wondrous events, especially those of healing, still continue in the life of the Christian Church as well-attested present proof of the supernatural origin of the whole historical enterprise in which they play their part.

To the contemporary mind, profoundly influenced as it is by the assumptions of modern science, miracles have become such a serious problem [36] that it will be well to consider more fully just why Catholicism is confident that by appeal to them natural reason can with assurance supplement its knowledge by supernaturally authenticated truth. The Catholic attitude toward miracles frankly depends on the prior demonstration of a God who is personal and good in the same fundamental sense that is implied when we speak of men as persons and as good. If we were not thoroughly convinced of this truth, Catholic philosophers agree that we might easily take a quite different attitude toward events which are claimed to be miraculous from that taken in the doctrine of the Church. But with this conviction in mind we approach such events with certain definite expectations. First, there is the expectation that the God whose intelligent will is responsible for the laws of nature will sometimes override those laws for moral ends—not that he prefers disorder to order or indulges in irrational spontaneities, but that physical laws are subordinate to beneficent spiritual purposes in the economy of the universe, so that when the two conflict the latter will be determinative. Second, there is the more specific expectation that God will somewhere have provided a supernatural revelation in the interest of man's salvation. This would presumably be done by selecting certain men as the media for such a revelation, and by communicating to them, through a miraculous control of their intellectual powers, truths that they otherwise could not have discovered. Since man's intellect is intrinsically competent to apprehend truth, this operation merely involves removing certain limitations, such as the dependence of finite mind on material objects to provide the content of its ideas. Third, there is the expectation that the genuineness of such revela-

[36] The precise nature of this problem is taken up in chap. VIII. See below, p. 212 ff.

tions would be attested by other striking manifestations of God's presence. Since, except for their moral appeal, these illuminations are not distinctively different from speculative and erroneous exuberances of the human imagination, God would naturally accompany their bestowal by vivid indications that they are truly his gift to men, indications apt to persuade the earnest and humble inquirer that he is not deceived when he accords them his faith. To be sure, since history presents many counterfeit miracles, reason must be allowed the right to judge their evidence and to determine the criteria of genuineness by which they are to be tested. However, when it does so it is guided by the above anticipations, i.e., it does not admit as a possibility that the evidence for *all* miracles might be inadequate, but assumes that some such marvels will prove to be due to genuine interventions of God. Thus the often puzzling similarities between true and counterfeit miracles will at worst pose a difficulty to our reason in its attempt to decide which are genuine; they can never justify it in rejecting the miraculous entirely.

Should we, however, question the authenticity of the miracles and prophecy-fulfillments recorded in the Bible, on the ground that the evidence for their actual occurrence is insufficient to satisfy the demands of scientific criticism, the Catholic answer is that the greatest miracle of all lies open before any man's eyes, and cannot be honestly doubted. This is the miracle of the growth and expansion of the Christian Church itself. The disciples of the Master were but a handful of weak, poor, unlettered men, drawn from the humblest ranks of society. They faced the most powerful opposition that can well be conceived, and with none of the advantages that natural reason would pronounce essential to their success. They were completely lacking in wealth, learning, and political position. They were required to meet, not only the misunderstanding and ridicule of people from their own class of society, but the utter scorn of the wise and the most ruthless, merciless efforts at suppression by those in administrative power. Appalling torture and agonizing death were their lot. Moreover, their gospel proclaimed no promise of sensuous bliss or worldly prestige; it won its converts by calling them to forsake the prizes of this life and to welcome poverty and suffering in the quest for spiritual perfection—for a deeper purity, humility, patience, and love. Judged by all the expectations of natural reason, such a movement should have perished before it had been fully born. Instead of this, it steadily grew, expanding its influence from generation to generation. Its ignorant teachers confounded the wisdom of the philosophers; its patient determination overcame all persecution; the purity and nobility of character which it instilled conquered the depravity and corruption into which a senile empire was steadily sinking. "How," asks Cardinal Newman, "without the Hand of God, could a new idea, one and the same, enter at once into myriads of men, women, and children of all ranks, especially the lower, and have power to wean them from their indulgences and sins, and to nerve them against the most cruel tortures, and to last in vigour as a sustaining influence for seven or eight generations, till it founded an extended polity, broke the obstinacy of the strongest and wisest government which the world has ever seen, and forced its way from its first caves and catacombs to the fulness of imperial power?"[37] This is the miracle on which the Catholic philosopher would prefer in the end to place his main reliance.

THE PLACE AND AUTHORITY OF THE CHURCH

If, now, one be moved by these considerations to accept the Christian revelation as divinely authenticated, and thus to supplement reason by a rationally justified faith, he finds one Christian community which offers many distinctive claims for his consideration. And here the fourth, and last, main step in the Catholic argument is taken. The Catholic Church traces its historical continuity back through the centuries to Christ himself in an unbroken line of succession, and it is more universal in its spread than any other Christian sect. Its life expresses the accumulated experience of this long period, and one who embraces it may expect to find all his spiritual needs and longings fully met. At least such is the promise which it confidently extends. If one be moved by unusual ardor, a life of worldly sacrifice may be his; he may take the vows of monastic chastity, poverty, and obedience, or share the adven-

[37] *The Grammar of Assent* (2d ed.), p. 459.

turous hardships of a missionary career. If he be willing to abandon for God's sake the joys of family life, and if he reveal capacity for spiritual guidance of others, he may serve the Church and his fellow Christians as a parish priest. If he be endowed with intellectual power he may become a teacher of the young, and contribute by his pen to the never ending task of rendering his faith persuasive to those who doubt and inquire. If he be content to live as a humble layman, the Church has the instruments by which to bless, comfort, and guide him in the great emergencies of life, as well as to suffuse with poetry its daily routine.[38] By the sacraments it brings in visible form the wonder of divine love and the hope of ultimate salvation close to his present experience; they are concrete remedies by which he can feel the mystery of Christ's redeeming death applied to vivify and enrich the life of his soul.[39] When he passes from this world to the life beyond, it is as though he were held in the arms of a reassuring mother who quiets his fears and encourages his confidence that having placed his full trust in her he will not miss the joys of eternal life which constitute the supreme good for man.

Especially in the intellectual authority and the moral guidance exercised by the Church, a universal human need is, according to its claim, satisfied. No man can be certain of his own judgment when he comes to interpret the divine revelation in the Scriptures, and particularly when he tries to derive from it the rules by which he ought to live. Any of us, no matter how able and earnest, is likely to make mistakes in this matter, and mistakes that may be fraught with the most disastrous consequences for our spiritual pilgrimage.[40] The Church takes from weak individuals the responsibility for such interpretation, and it does so by the express direction of Christ himself. On at least two occasions Christ is reported in the Gospels to have assigned to the apostle Peter a position of special leadership and authority. "Your name is Peter [a rock], and on this rock I will build my Church, and the powers of death shall not subdue it. I will give you the keys of the Kingdom of Heaven, and whatever you forbid on earth will be held in heaven

---

[38] K. Adam, *The Spirit of Catholicism*, pp. 167 ff., 175 ff.
[39] *Summa contra gentiles*, IV, 16.
[40] K. Adam, *The Spirit of Catholicism*, pp. 24 f., 32 f., 42 ff.

to be forbidden, and whatever you permit on earth will be held in heaven to be permitted." [41] Now, according to Catholic tradition, Peter became the founder and first head of the Church at Rome, and transmitted this special function to his successors in that post, just as the other apostles handed on their subordinate responsibility to the bishops who in course of time took their places. By Catholic theory this lodges in the present pope the same authority that was originally given to Peter, and in the present bishops the same subsidiary overseership that the other apostles exercised. [42] The organization of the Church is thus entirely aristocratic. No power or control is lodged in the laymen or the lower priesthood; all authority derives through apostolic succession from Peter and the original disciples, who received it in turn from Christ, and Christ from God. Its ground is solely historical continuity with a divine right bestowed in the distant past, not in any sense the religious need of men in the present. [43]

This authority residing in the pope and the bishops is not, however, according to Catholic thinkers, exercised arbitrarily or hastily. On every issue of importance final decision awaits the clarification which the experience and thought of the entire Church can contribute to it. While the foundations of Catholic faith rest on the Scriptures and the early fathers, and are believed to have remained unchanged through all subsequent time, yet there is room for continued progress, both in the direction of a deeper appreciation of particular elements in those foundations than had earlier been evident, and in the direction of squaring the foundations with philosophical and social issues which from time to time newly emerge. [44] The

[41] Matt. 16: 13–19 (Goodspeed trans.). See also John 21: 15–18.
[42] Summa theologica, Part II b, qu. 1, art. 10. Catechism of the Council of Trent, I, chap. 10, qu. 11–17. The Vatican Council of 1870 defined this doctrine of papal authority as follows:
"The Roman Pontiff, when he speaks ex cathedra (that is, when, fulfilling his function as pastor and teacher of all Christians, in the name of his supreme apostolic authority he defines a doctrine concerning faith or morals as to be held by the universal Church), by the divine assistance promised to him in Blessed Peter possesses that infallibility with which the Divine Redeemer willed His Church to be equipped in the defining of faith or morals, and therefore, the definitions of the said Roman Pontiff are irreformable of their own nature and not owing to the consent of the Church."
[43] K. Adam, The Spirit of Catholicism, p. 22 f.
[44] Summa theologica, Part II b, qu. 1, art. 7.

former of these lines of development is illustrated by the exalted
position in the life of the Church which gradually came to be
taken by the Virgin Mary; the latter by the recent rejection on
the part of Catholic authorities of the claims of modernism and
of communism. Toward this growth the earnest experience of even
the humblest Catholic will contribute. At any period of time there
are alternative doctrines between which the Church has not yet
committed itself—doctrines inconsistent with each other, but all
alike consistent, or capable of being so interpreted, with the great
historic creeds. The life of every Catholic can help indicate which
of those doctrines shall be regarded as expressing the true bearing
of the changeless foundations upon contemporary experience.[45]
When the pope speaks *ex cathedra,* defining faith or morals for the
Church, he is in practice guided by a twofold standard of truth:
the divine revelation bestowed in the past, which determines the
essential core of saving doctrine; and the universal consent arising
from Catholic experience throughout the centuries. Final responsibility for every decision, however, lies with the pope himself as
the vicar of Christ on earth.

While God is thus the ultimate object of faith for Catholics,
the immediate object is the Church. It determines religious truth
and moral right for them, not they for themselves. And in its
exercise of this supreme responsibility the Church explicitly or
implicity recognizes three distinct roles or functions in the
historical process of rendering salvation available to men. First
and foremost, there is the role of the prophets and apostles,
who by special illumination from God first received the truths
that supplement natural reason. In performing this role they
were elevated in a manner which the rest of us cannot expect
until after death; their faculties were entirely freed, for the
purpose of understanding and communicating the revelation which
later generations owe to them, from dependence upon sensuous content and upon matter.[46] Since the canon of Scripture was
closed, however, this role has been performed no longer, for all
truth necessary for men's salvation has already been bestowed.[47]

[45] K. Adam, *The Spirit of Catholicism,* pp. 153 ff.
[46] *Summa theologica,* II, Part II, qu. 171–175.
[47] *Ibid,* I, qu. 1, art. 8.

Second, there is the function of the pope and the bishops. No new revelation comes through them, but they have the authority, resting on apostolic succession, to interpret the divine disclosure already given, in its bearing on challenging issues faced by men in the present. Third, and last, there are the lower clergy and lay-men whose main duty, so far as truth is concerned, is to accept the revelation and humbly submit to ecclesiastical control. Their earnest experience may indirectly contribute toward more precise definition of doctrines in the future, but they share neither power of prophecy nor authority to interpret the prophecy already made. Except so far as individuals among them may be chosen by the powers above to enter the bishopric, it is their business to remain humble followers. "To some it belongs to govern and to teach; to others, to be subject and to obey." [48]

From these considerations it is clear that faith, for the Catholic, is both an intellectual and a moral affair. On the intellectual side, it is firm assent to supersensible truths on the authority of divine revelation. In reliability it is superior to the demonstrations of natural reason, since it derives by supernatural illumination from God who is the source of all truth, while finite reason may at any time err. Because of the same circumstance it is likewise superior in dignity. On the moral side, it is sincere, voluntary commitment to God as the Sovereign Good for man, and to the Church as his authorized living representative. [49] Such commitment is essential, in Catholic eyes, because without it pride of learning and self-will are apt to stand in the way of readiness on the part of reason to appeal beyond itself and the humility requisite for acceptance of authority.

Before we turn to less basic features of the Catholic position, let us note an interesting point about this skeletal line of argument as a whole. As will be seen more fully as we proceed, different religious philosophies have based their conclusions ultimately either on experience, or on reason, or on some superrational in-tuition, or on the authority of church or tradition. [50] The strong and continued appeal of the Catholic philosophy lies largely in the

[48] *Catechism of the Council of Trent*, I, chap. 10, qu. 24.
[49] *Ibid*, I, chap. 10, qu. 24.
[50] Cf. below, chap. XVII, p. 448 ff.

fact that it rejects none of these four methods, but includes them all in a certain organic interrelationship. According to it, we begin our intellectual quest by resting on the facts of ordinary experience and the causal axioms of reason, and they are never forsaken. But when we complete that quest we will have also been led to recognize the right of ecclesiastical authority to interpret these facts, and the need of a supersensible intuition, available only in the life beyond, to apprehend the divine light which is absolute truth and our supreme good.

THE CATHOLIC ATTITUDE TOWARD SCIENCE

What of the relation, from the Catholic standpoint, between religious faith and scientific knowledge? The answer to this question follows consistently from the convictions already discussed. Science cannot, of course, from this point of view, contradict any doctrine of the Church; when it does so it becomes pseudo-science and has evidently mistaken its appropriate assumptions and methods. Thus any supposed findings of psychology which are inconsistent with assertion of the spirituality, incorruptibility, and freedom of the human soul must be rejected as not merely religiously, but also scientifically, unsound.[51] The divine intelligence from which all truth comes is one, and it cannot be at odds with itself. Catholic thinkers will admit that officials and congregations of the Church sometimes spoke too soon in opposition to scientific discoveries, and found it necessary later to retract their position; thus for many generations the Copernican astronomy was rejected as irreconcilable with statements of Scripture and with Aristotle's cosmology. Bruno was burned and Galileo compelled to recant. The theory of evolution, however—which marks the second great reorientation of thought due to science in modern times—it has not officially opposed, except so far as concerns its insistence on the supernatural origin of each human soul.[52] Science cannot, either, contradict the axioms of causality which natural theology uses to establish its foundations. These are assumed to be metaphysically valid and to lead, accordingly, to ultimate truths on which all other truth, including the

[51] M. Maher, *Psychology*, Preface to 4th ed.
[52] *Ibid*, p. 578.

truths established by the various branches of science, depends.[53] But in its own proper field of establishing particular causes of observable effects, and subject to the limitations above noted, science is allowed a free field within which to follow her own bent. Nay, the Church has encouraged the progress of scientific discovery so far as these conditions are not violated, both because of the practical alleviation of human suffering which such discovery often makes possible, and because of the enrichment of religious feeling which a humble contemplation of the wonders of the natural universe may inspire. Some of the outstanding leaders of science in modern times have been devout Catholics: Pascal, Descartes, Pasteur, and Mendel are perhaps the best known of these.

THE CATHOLIC SOCIAL PHILOSOPHY

It remains to consider briefly the essentials of the Catholic position with regard to the momentous social problems which challenge our time. As we enter this field, two major considerations must be kept in mind. One derives from the metaphysical and psychological foundations with which, in the main, we have thus far been occupied. The other rests on the unique position of the Church in Catholic theory and practice; that is, its claim to be the ark of salvation for the human race, outside of which and apart from whose divinely ordained sacraments it is impossible, except in extraordinary cases, for men to be saved.

As for the first of these considerations, all truth and right in social matters, including political and economic relations, is based ultimately for Catholicism on moral principles, and these in turn rest upon the fundamental doctrines about God and man which natural theology, supplemented by revelation, is believed to have established. In the light of those doctrines it is evident that every man has a unique dignity and a great responsibility. His moral and social life should accordingly be so ordered as fully to express this status. Human dignity arises from the fact that man is not only the creature, but the child of God; alone in the created world he possesses a rational nature which renders him capable of a supersensible good—the vision of God in his true essence. Every

[53] G. H. Joyce, *Principles of Natural Theology* (3d ed.), chap. II.

human being, therefore, has the moral right always to be treated in a manner which accords with this exalted prerogative. Man's responsibility arises from the fact that each individual may miss this supreme good unless his personal and social life here below is so controlled as to foster the earnest faith through which alone that good can be won. This life is essentially a prologue to eternity, and moral analysis must never forget that decisive fact.

As for the second consideration, the special position and authority of the Church as an organized social institution enter into the account, in theory and doubtless still more in practice. While, except for brief periods during the height of its power, the Church has not attempted to order in detail the internal economy and political structure of nations, it cannot help weighing, in its pronouncements on such matters, their bearing on its own growth and influence. The revolt of Spanish fascism was justified by Catholic leaders, while German fascism and communism were resisted by them as soon as they began to threaten the influence of the Church upon Catholic youth. Since the Church is the corporate body on which men depend for their eternal welfare, its power in human affairs is important; and if individual men gain dignity through possessing an intelligent and immortal soul, to the Church belongs supreme dignity as the living authoritative community by which such souls are piloted to final salvation.

This latter consideration plays little, if any, part in the Catholic position with regard to sexual morals and the family. Here the dominant factors are explicit teaching in Scripture and the general moral principles by which such teaching is interpreted. The most important of the principles applicable to this matter are: (1) that the appropriate use of any natural function is determined by its end in the economy of nature, while purposive perversion of such functions is a sin; (2) that gratification of sensuous desire must be subordinate to and controlled by the higher spiritual ends to which man in virtue of his distinctive faculties is called; and (3) that individual happiness must be found not in selfish pursuits, but in the fulfillment of dutiful obligations to the various social relationships into which men and women enter. To love and serve others is the great responsibility of each. Certain statements in the Bible, interpreted by the first and second of these principles, supply the ground on which the Church rests for its opposition to the practice of birth control. This opposition has been insistent and vigorous so far as concerns the use of contraceptives. Such use is regarded as immoral; it perverts the sexual function whose natural end is reproduction.[54] The so-called "rhythm" method of limiting offspring has, however, remained uncondemned. Other statements in the Bible, interpreted by the third of these principles, provide the basis for the Catholic refusal to sanction divorce.[55]

When we turn to the problems of capitalism, socialism, and the rights of labor, the main determinative considerations, as with the family, are the moral and social principles involved. The Catholic economic philosophy as reflected in the writings of its main contributors takes for granted the legitimacy of capitalism, in that it recognizes the established rights of private property[56] and the general structure of class relationships to which the exercise of those rights leads; it holds that in most circumstances the economic welfare of society is promoted by allowing the control of industrial processes to remain in private hands. But economics is not for it an independent discipline whose laws are self-sufficient. The economic pattern of life, affecting as it does many human relations, is ultimately a question of ethics, and is to be determined by the universal principles which the latter establishes. Laborers are men and share the moral dignity of man, hence they rightfully demand a wage sufficient for the essential needs of their families and for security against illness, unemployment, and old age. These things may not be given as charity; they are required by justice. All exploitation of labor by capital is wrong. The industrial organization of society should be such as to reduce it to a minimum.

Different schools of economic theory among Catholics vary considerably in their conclusions on specific problems here. There seems, however, a rather large degree of consensus on the following points: (1) Wide distribution in the ownership of property, especially land, should be encouraged, so that families may be effective economic units wherever possible. (2) Industrial enterprises should be organ-

---

[54] *Catechism of the Council of Trent*, II, chap. 8, qu. 13.

[55] The Church frequently annuls marriages, however, on grounds defined in canon law.

[56] The Church is itself a holder of large properties.

ized in such a way that the main groups whose lives or interests are vitally affected will have an appropriate share in determining the conditions under which they operate. These groups will include, of course, employers, workers, bankers, and consumers. (3) It is the responsibility of the state to ensure, by wise regulation, that the economic life of the community truly serves the common good. State socialization should be avoided as far as possible, however; the rights and opportunities of individuals and families are better secured by the kind of socialization that takes the form of producers' or consumers' coöperatives. Catholic thinkers have made a significant contribution toward the theory and practice of such coöperatives.

When we come to the issue of war and peace, the position and function of the Church must be kept in mind as well as the fundamental moral principles concerned. The latter, considered alone, would imply that war is justified only when necessary for self-defense. Nations are subject to the same moral laws which govern individuals. Their task is to secure the temporal welfare of mankind, as the task of the Church is to point the way toward eternal salvation. It is their duty, therefore, to promote coöperation rather than antagonism, and to eliminate all the injustices and entrenched forms of greed which naturally lead to war. Catholic citizens, in fulfilling their political responsibilities, are expected to press for the adoption of such policies. In practice, however, the leaders of the Church have often hesitated to denounce explicitly particular acts of nationalistic aggression and to use the full force of its temporal power against them. This is conditioned in part by the circumstance that clear judgment in such matters is often difficult; in part (as it seems to non-Catholics, at least) by the fact that successful wars, when waged by Catholic nations, often result in a larger opportunity for the spread of Catholic missions in the conquered countries, and the unhindered winning of souls to the true saving faith. Thus the interest of the Church, in the performance of its supernatural function, is not always or unequivocally on the side of peace.

What of the Catholic attitude regarding the increasingly threatening problem of democracy and totalitarianism? The Catholic philosophy unqualified opposes communism, on the ground that this form of government, whatever its virtues in economic matters, rests on a materialistic interpretation of history, officially encourages atheism, and proscribes or seriously handicaps the work of the Church. As for other forms of government, it does not officially favor or disfavor any one of them. Yet it champions individual and group liberty to worship God and obey the dictates of conscience, to enjoy the protection of impartial law, and to share in the rights of a free ballot, free speech, and free assembly. In democratic countries Catholicism encourages its members to fulfill intelligently their responsibilities as citizens and to use political power to further the ends which the Church approves. In countries ruled by monarchy or dictatorship it requires its members to accept their lot obediently as long as their fundamental religious rights are recognized. Where such rights are not fully protected, it encourages nonviolent resistance and uses its diplomatic power in the endeavor to secure them.

To facilitate critical comparison of the Catholic philosophy of religion with other philosophies, the exposition concludes with a summary statement, in outline form, of the assumptions vital to the main Catholic argument which have been rejected by one or more of the philosophies to be discussed in subsequent chapters.

The Major Disputed Assumptions of Catholicism

1. Assumptions Concerning Man's Moral Situation
   a. He needs certainty to attain his highest good (salvation).
   b. He cannot attain it by his own resources.
2. Assumptions Concerning Man's Metaphysical Knowledge
   a. He can attain partial certainty here, and by its aid the needed certainty in morals.
      (1) This is accomplished primarily through natural theology.
   b. The scholastic conception of the causal relation is valid.
      (1) In the sense of productive efficiency.
      (2) In its postulate that a cause must be as perfect as its effect in the scope and degree of the qualities it possesses.
   c. Teleological explanation is metaphysically valid.
      (1) Good is a positive reality and an effective cause.

(2) Evil is not a positive reality and is only accidentally a cause.

d. The faculty which knows—intelligence—is an entity independent of matter.

3. Assumptions concerning Knowledge of the Supernatural
   a. Through special divine intervention the natural limitations of human reason can be transcended and natural knowledge can be supplemented by a supernatural revelation.
   b. By appeal to miracles a true revelation can be discriminated from false ones.

4. Assumptions Concerning the Structure of Religious Authority
   a. A supernatural revelation was given to the prophets and apostles.
   b. The right of interpretation attaches by apostolic continuity to the pope and the bishops.
   c. The proper role of others is acceptance and obedient submission.

With the exception of the first two propositions, these assumptions have been clarified in the course of the preceding exposition. A word concerning those items is therefore all that is needed here.

The main Catholic argument, as we have seen, begins with (2) rather than with (1). But in the interest of ready comparison with other religious philosophies, it is best to place (1a) and (1b) at the head of the outline. That this is entirely just to the Catholic point of view a few considerations will make evident. Catholicism is not interested in the metaphysical argument primarily for its own sake. It insists upon it because only when the results of that piece of reasoning are reached do the nature of man's true good and the way to its attainment become clear. Hence when the proof of God's existence is embarked upon, two prior assumptions are really involved which have been indicated under (1). Obviously, the metaphysical argument becomes superfluous, so far as concerns its bearing on the quest for salvation, should either of these propositions be rejected. If we believe that man by his own resources can attain assured knowledge about his highest good, or if we believe that such assurance is not necessary, holding it sufficient for our ultimate welfare that we be guided by such probabilities as finite minds are competent to attain, there will be no need for God to supplement man's moral uncertainty. In a philosophy founded on such beliefs, either God will not appear at all or he will fill a different role from that which he fills in the Catholic argument.

Some criticism of the assumptions in this outline will be introduced when we consider religious philosophies which abandon them in favor of contrary assumptions, and in such a form as will facilitate sympathetic understanding of those philosophies. A more systematic critical analysis of the major issues in Western religious philosophy is offered in Part III.

SELECTED BIBLIOGRAPHY

Adam, K., *The Spirit of Catholicism*, Macmillan, rev. ed., 1935.
Catechism of the Council of Trent. Several English editions are available.
Gilson, E., *The Spirit of Mediaeval Philosophy* (Downes trans.), Scribner, 1936.
Gilson, E., *The Philosophy of St. Thomas Aquinas*, W. Heffer and Sons, 1924.
Haas, F. J., *Man and Society: An Introduction to Sociology*, Century, 1930.
Joyce, G. H., *Principles of Natural Theology*, Longmans, Green, 3rd ed., 1951.
Maher, M., *Psychology: Empirical and Rational*, Longmans, Green, 9th ed., 1949.
McGiffert, A. C., *History of Christian Thought*, Scribner, 1933, Vol. II, Book IV (especially chaps. IX, XI, XII).
Martindale, C. C., *The Faith of the Roman Church*, Methuen, 1927.
Sheen, F. J., *Philosophy of Religion*, Appleton, 1948.
Thomas Aquinas, *Summa contra gentiles* (trans. by the English Dominican Fathers), Burns, Oates, and Washbourne, 1927–1929 (Books I and II).

Chapter VI

PROTESTANT FUNDAMENTALISM

WHAT is now usually called fundamentalism in Protestant circles (at least in America) is the heritage of the contemporary world from the orthodox Protestantism established by the Reformation in the sixteenth century. Its original form has been overlaid by many accretions, most of which are of minor importance. The effects of the major accretions, so far as is vital to our understanding of present-day fundamentalism, will be noted in due time.

THE CULTURAL TRANSFORMATION IN MODERN EUROPE

The central thread to be held fast throughout the discussion which follows may best be indicated by calling attention to the general cultural transformation which took place in northern and western Europe during the four hundred years following the late fifteenth century. The essence of this transformation, measured in terms of its broad social outcome, was the rise of the so-called "middle class" to a position of dominance in the countries most concerned, displacing the landed aristocrats, the clergy, and finally the monarchs from the control they had formerly wielded. On its negative side the most characteristic and insistent demand of this movement was the demand for *liberty,* which meant freedom, in all the major spheres of life, from the shackles by which the members of the rising middle class felt themselves restrained and oppressed. On its positive side the distinctive emphasis was on *tolerance,* which quickly proved itself the necessary complement of liberty if the latter were to be safeguarded and peacefully exercised. It was natural that during the early part of this period of

four centuries the call for liberty was most vociferous, while only
during the latter part did a general recognition of the need for
tolerance become very evident. Now, the historical significance of
orthodox Protestantism is to be found in the fact that, in opposition to the characteristic emphases of the Catholic point of view,
it insisted on the validity of these principles of individual liberty
and tolerance in the sphere of religion. The intimate connection
thus indicated between the religious transformation and the accompanying general cultural change in Protestant countries is to be
explained, from the Protestant standpoint, as the gradual permea-
tion of social institutions at large by the ideals of true religion re-
discovered by the great Reformers; to non-Protestant thinkers,
it is to be accounted for as the effect of deep-lying forces affecting
all phases of modern European culture alike, including religion.

It will aid our understanding of Protestantism in its original
emergence if we first consider briefly the form which the transformation sketched above took in economic and political affairs.
The economic aspect of the change is usually described as the
rise of modern capitalism. During the Middle Ages and the early
modern period processes of industrial production and trade came
to be hedged about by a mass of detailed regulations, some of
which were imposed by the trade guilds, some by the Church, and
some by political agencies. The more aggressive members of the
growing middle class in the cities and towns of Europe found a
promising outlet for their enterprise in expanding and developing
these processes through exploration, invention, and centralized
manufacturing. But the traditional regulations imposed serious restraints on the exercise of their initiative in these ways. There arose
from them, accordingly, a more and more vigorous demand for
freedom from these hampering restrictions. In time this demand
became fairly effective in a large part of Europe and her colonies,
with the result that by the late eighteenth century most of the handicaps which irritated these business leaders had been removed. They
were free to establish new enterprises and enlarge old ones, in quest
of profit and economic success, under no major shackles except those
necessary to secure for others the same freedom. And this last consideration indicates the form in which the positive aspect of this
transformation—tolerance—appeared in the economic sphere. We

call it the maintenance of free competition. Each captain of industry sought primarily, of course, his own profit; but he could not expect a stable opportunity to pursue this end unless he recognized and respected the equal right of other business enterprisers to the same opportunity. The principle of toleration in this form accordingly proved necessary. All members of the growing community of business found it requisite to coöperate with each other to the extent of maintaining by their united force a code of fair business practice. This meant in effect freedom of competition, in which each participant rose or fell according to his measure of ingenuity or incompetence in meeting the economic needs of the public through an open market.

In the political realm the transformation with which we are concerned is known as the rise of modern democracy. The middle class, in its quest for various other forms of freedom, found a large measure of political freedom necessary as a major means of attaining and safeguarding them. Political power is the ultimate power for coercing human action in this world, hence control of government is usually essential if any fundamental cultural change is to be brought about and protected when won. The strategy of the middle class, in this aspect of its struggle, was first to support the national monarchs in their rise to power against the emperor, the pope, and the feudal barons, and then gradually to make the representative assemblies, which they dominated, supreme over the monarchs. During the early part of this political revolution tolerance was not generally regarded as a virtue, or at least was not respected in practice; each organized pressure-group sought its own advantage and maneuvered for a position of special privilege. But no one group was able to attain such a position by itself, or to hold it for long if by some lucky chance it was gained. Hence it proved necessary for such groups in the middle class to combine forces, and this was possible only on a common platform of the equal right of all members of that class to liberty and to a share in political control. The price of liberty for each, from clerical and monarchical oppression, was recognition, in political theory and practice, of the same liberty for others. Representative parliamentarianism or democracy is the concrete form of political structure to which this transformation gradually led. Through it the members of the middle class secured freedom from traditional political interferences, and expressed the recognition by each of the equal natural right of all to the pursuit of happiness through free speech, free press, free assembly, and free participation in the ballot.

The Protestant movement, in the form which now persists as fundamentalism, exhibited these same tendencies in the field of religion. And it involved, in matters of religion, the same major consequences, positive as well as negative, that appeared under another guise in the political and economic fields. On the negative side it expressed the demand for religious liberty, which meant essentially emancipation from the institutional controls over the individual to which the Catholic Church required him to submit. On the positive side it came to reveal, with increasing emphasis as time went on, an interest in religious tolerance—that is, willingness to allow for all the same liberty which each demands for himself, and a confidence that even though such freedom be seriously abused it is none the less better to maintain it as the foundation of spiritual life than to leave men and women in submissive dependence on ecclesiastical authority. And the claim of Protestantism that it is the essential source of the accompanying transformation in political and economic life is objectively sound at least to this extent, that just as in other major cultural shifts in the history of the Occident new religious insights and aspirations have played a pioneering role in the vanguard of social change, so here; Protestantism was not merely the religious expression of the transformation, but also to a large extent the anticipator and inspirational guide of the entire cultural movement in which it played a part. In virtue of this position of prophetic leadership throughout the period in question, which the foremost champions of Protestantism occupied, one notable result of the process was that the social principles of the middle class—liberty, equality, and democracy—assumed not merely the status of political ends, but also that of religious ideals. They came to symbolize a new fundamental outlook upon life and upon the nature of the divine purpose in the world. Other forces contributed, of course, to this outcome, but its initial root lay in the religious significance given to freedom by the Protestant pioneers, a significance capable of subsequent expansion and deeper emphasis.

We may observe, in passing, one inevitable result of this persistent emphasis on freedom, namely, the cleavage of the medieval unity of Christendom into a number of independent social groups, each bound together by certain common concerns. In politics this effect took form in the rise of the various national states of Europe into a position of independence from the empire, and the emergence within each of rival political factions, frequently precipitating civil war. In religion it appeared in the growth of the numerous Protestant sects, all standing in common opposition to Catholicism and each a rival of the others. The most influential of these sects are those of the Baptists, Methodists, Lutherans, Episcopalians, Presbyterians, and Congregationalists. We cannot, of course, take the space which would be necessary to treat their sectarian differences.

SALIENT POINTS IN PROTESTANT HISTORY

Before expounding the essentials of the point of view with which we are now dealing, let us make a rapid survey of certain outstanding landmarks in the history of Protestant orthodoxy. This will give some indication of the main lines of continuity between its original setting and emphasis and those which characterize it at the present day.

The original hero of this religious movement was Martin Luther, who in 1517 posted the famous ninety-five theses at Wittenberg, in which he denounced certain prevalent abuses of the Catholic sacramental system. Luther's religious experience was as profoundly moving as that of Paul or Augustine, and in one fundamental respect it was similar to theirs: at its heart was an exuberant sense of release from the tension of sin, and from the overwhelming fear of divine condemnation under which he had been quaking. Having experienced this release, he felt himself free from every sort of bondage and control except that of a grateful eagerness to make his life thenceforth pleasing to God. Especially did he feel free from the intellectual authority and penitential discipline of the Catholic Church. Such an experience, he believed, was the right and privilege of all Christians. By preaching with fervor and enthusiasm this doctrine of Christian freedom, Luther was a major factor in breaking the social power of Catholicism, convincing thousands of men and women in nothern Europe that they could attain eternal salvation apart from the sacramental system and priestly authority of the Church.

In 1536 John Calvin published the first edition of his *Institutes of the Christian Religion*. This work shared with Luther the platform of justification by faith, and it has stood through subsequent history as the outstanding systematic formulation of Protestant theology. Luther had rejected the Catholic conception of natural theology, returning in his basic theological principles to an extreme Augustinianism which denied all natural competence to human reason. "It is Satan's wisdom to tell what God is, and by doing so he will draw you into the abyss. Therefore keep to revelation and do not try to understand."[1] Now Calvin's foundations were likewise Augustinian, his central and all-controlling doctrine being that of man's complete dependence upon God as absolutely sovereign Will. None the less, under the influence in part of his older contemporary Zwingli, whose followers united with his in the Reformed Church, he assigned an important place to natural theology as one of the two main ways in which God is known by man. Protestant orthodoxy has in the main followed him here, admitting that God is disclosed in nature and history as well as in the Biblical revelation with its challenge to conscience, and that this disclosure is legitimately used for apologetic purposes in the case of those who feel the force of its appeal.

To these early Protestant Reformers tolerance was no virtue. They wanted liberty for themselves but not for others, except so far as those others agreed with them, at least on matters they accounted essential. Hence whenever they fell into possession of political power they embarked on almost as vigorous repression of nonconformists as had been the case with Catholics. Because of this intolerance, aggressively displayed in the kaleidoscopic political shifts of the time, there ensued for a hundred and fifty years or longer unparalleled religious turmoil in western Europe. As each sect rose to power it attempted to force its interpretation of Christian truth upon rival sects who refused to submit to such oppression; as it fell from posts of advantage its only recourse was to unite with other dispossessed sects in noisy protest against the

[1] Quoted in P. Smith, *Age of the Reformation*, p. 625.

oppression of others. Only two solutions of this unendurable strife were possible, in view of the inability of any single Protestant denomination to silence the others and reduce them to a position of complete impotence. One was to return to the unity of Catholicism, but this was inconsistent with the basic tenets of the Protestant faith. The authority of the pope and the necessity of the sacraments possessed by the Church had been rejected; the Bible had been made available to everyone in the vernacular languages, and all had been encouraged to study it under the direct guidance of the Holy Spirit so that they might find for themselves what truth God had there revealed. These things could not be surrendered, come what may. The other was to make tolerance an equally basic religious principle with liberty. This was not inconsistent with the genius of Protestantism; it was but applying to liberty the still more basic Christian ideal of the Golden Rule, to do unto others when one is in power what he would that they should do unto him when they hold official position.

In 1644 Roger Williams, who had more than once been hounded into exile by religious persecution, published his *Bloudy Tenent of Persecution for Cause of Conscience,* in which he argued that political power should not be used to support any religious belief or any sect. In the colony of Rhode Island this principle was actually put into practice under his leadership. In the same year appeared the *Areopagitica,* written by the great poet of Protestantism, John Milton, in which freedom of conscience and of speech was defended as necessary in the interest of religion itself; the religious wisdom which God has provided for man cannot be fully discovered otherwise, for no individual or group can be sure of possessing all of it. "Give me the liberty to know, to utter, and to argue freely according to conscience, above all other liberties." During the following half-century broad strides were made toward the practice of religious toleration, notably in Great Britain, the American colonies, and still more in Holland, while in the next century the rationalistic tendencies expressed in the so-called "Enlightenment" coöperated strongly toward the same end. The outcome was the gradual elimination in Protestant countries of civil disabilities because of nonconformity in matters of religion, and the gradual acceptance of a certain measure of religious toleration as itself a central Protestant principle. A distinction came to be drawn between "fundamental" doctrines, which practically all Protestants found taught in the Bible and acceptance of which they believed necessary to salvation, and less important matters which varied from sect to sect, on which error could be permitted without imperiling immortal souls. Within the limits set by the fundamental beliefs, every individual—so it was insisted—must be allowed freedom to study the Bible and to preach what his conscience, led by the Holy Spirit, finds to be its message. If he strayed beyond those limits he usually fell under no legal ban but was regarded by public opinion with considerable distrust and suspicion. Such a dangerous character could not in social practice be fully tolerated.

The difference between fundamental matters and those not fundamental may be illustrated by the case of baptism. Orthodox Protestants who are members of the Baptist denomination hold that the word in the Bible which is translated "baptize" means "immerse," and accordingly that immersion is the only mode of baptism recognized in the Bible. Yet, having rejected the Catholic position that any sacrament is essential to salvation,[2] they cannot regard an error on this matter as involving death to the soul. Hence, although they usually decline to admit to the Lord's Supper (the Protestant form of the Eucharist) unimmersed persons, they do not, on this ground alone, stigmatize them as non-Christian. A considerable measure of fellowship with them will be welcomed, at least on occasions when distinctive sectarian convictions do not naturally come to the fore. With people who reject the doctrine of the virgin birth of Christ, or that of his physical resurrection, the situation is different. Since these doctrines are pretty clearly taught in the Gospels and are involved in the traditional theory of the deity of Christ, such persons are not regarded as true Christians at all. They may be accorded political license but not the full tolerance requisite for religious fellowship.

In the seventeenth century the Puritan movement within Protestantism reached the peak of its influence. On the theological side it was grounded in Calvinism, but the significant stamp which it

[2] It should be noted that on this matter certain Protestant sects, notably the Episcopalians and the Lutherans, retain an attenuated Catholicism.

gave to subsequent Protestant orthodoxy was moral and social rather than theological. Fundamentalists today favor a rather rigid code of moral prohibitions; in doing so they continue an emphasis whose historical origin lies in Puritanism. And the social ideals of the Puritans were such as to fix permanently the already intimate connection between Protestantism and the capitalistic system in industry. These matters will soon be dealt with more fully.

During the eighteenth and nineteenth centuries waves of evangelistic revivalism swept over the main Protestant countries. The major outcome of these expressions of religious enthusiasm was a deepening in Protestant communities of emotional warmth and personal piety, in contrast with the formalism and ceremonialism which had crept into many of the churches. They left a permanent mark, however, on the philosophical attitude of Protestantism. The aim of the leaders of these revivals was to guide their hearers through the same kind of vivid religious experience that had been illustrated in men like Paul and Luther. A very successful revival technique was developed, which rested throughout on the ability of the evangelist, aided by songs rich in appealing imagery, to awaken in his audience a conviction of sin and of desperate need for divine forgiveness. When this conviction was well established, the promise of release from God's wrath, through faith in the cross of Christ, often came with telling effect, replacing the tension of terror and despair by a joyous sense of gratitude and peace. The impact of this emphasis on the character of traditional Protestantism, and of fundamentalism as its heir in the contemporary religious world, has been profound. For our purposes, its most significant consequence was to make more emphatically central than before the original Protestant tendency to concentrate, in proving the existence and nature of God, as well as the supernatural claims of the Bible, on the appeal to man's moral conscience. The arguments of natural theology are usually not rejected as invalid, but this appeal is accorded a distinctive place.

It is only within the present century that Protestant orthodoxy has become widely known as "fundamentalism." The reason for the prominence of this term as the main present symbol for that religious viewpoint is simple. During the late nineteenth and the early twentieth century liberalizing tendencies both in theology and in morals came rapidly to the fore in the Protestant churches.

Distrusted and checked at first, they gradually gathered momentum until they bid fair to become the dominant force in many of the Protestant communions. The religious philosophy expressed in these tendencies—liberalism—will be considered in some detail later.[3] Now, some of the champions of liberalism denied explicitly or by implication traditional Biblical doctrines which to the more orthodox seemed essential to the Christian faith, such as the virgin birth of Christ, his physical resurrection, the special creation of man, and the eternal torment of unbelievers. Reacting violently against these "dangerous" innovations, holders of the time-hallowed Protestant creed concentrated more explicitly than ever in their sermons and teaching on those articles of the traditional faith which appeared to be threatened by the insurgent attacks. In 1909 twelve volumes of essays on *The Fundamentals* were published in Los Angeles by these conservatives; millions of copies were distributed all over the Protestant world. Ten years later two aggressive inter-denominational organizations were formed to combat the rising tide of liberalism—the *Christian Fundamentals League,* on the Pacific Coast, and the *World's Christian Fundamentals Association,* with headquarters in the Middle West. By 1920 the term "fundamentalist" had come into general use as the accepted means of referring to these traditionalists. Although disliked by some among the conservatives, it is now probably the least prejudicial word for describing their religious philosophy in its contemporary guise, and we shall use it for this purpose as synonymous with present-day Protestant orthodoxy. As will be evident from these historical considerations, the major emphasis of fundamentalism today is not on liberty or tolerance—these basic features of earlier Protestantism are taken for granted—but rather on the importance of holding fast to the traditional faith now endangered by liberalism. The latter, not Catholicism, is at present its main enemy.

DIVERGENCES OF FUNDAMENTALISM FROM CATHOLICISM

What is the substance of that faith? What are the fundamentals of fundamentalism? And by what line of argument does a typical adherent of this position defend them?

With regard to the first of these questions the answer, in general,

[3] See below, chaps. X, XI.

is that the fundamentals consist of the convictions included since ancient times in the traditional Christian creeds, with the one major modification that the authority of the Church and the saving power of its sacraments are replaced by trust in the Bible, interpreted directly by the mind and conscience of the individual Christian. And the answer to the last question is that the fundamentalist argument is closely similar to that of Catholicism up to the point where the doctrine of the Church enters the account, except for a different theory of human nature and a corresponding difference in the conception of God and of his relation to man. Beyond that point, a distinctive conception of the Church and of the Christian life is affirmed, grounded in a different interpretation of God's revelation in the Bible and a different assumption as to the basic religious needs of men. We are taking no account, of course, in this brief treatment, of differences between the various fundamentalist sects[4] but only of what is common to the more influential and widespread among them. Before we plunge into the major divergences from Catholicism there are two minor ones which should be noted briefly.

One is the denial by most fundamentalists that miracles have taken place since the apostolic age. This difference is due mainly to the Protestant position regarding the Bible. Since God designed this book to be the sole supernatural revelation to man, and since miracles are needed merely to authenticate such a revelation, there has been no call for special intervention since the canon of Scripture became complete. And the Bible contains no promise that miracles would continue in the Church after the death of those living when its latest books were written. Moreover, admission of genuineness to later miracles would seem to recognize the claim of the Catholic Church to divine authority, since most of the supposed miracles in the West since the time of the apostles have taken place under the aegis of Catholicism and have been used to support its pretensions.

The other is the heightened sensitiveness to sin which has been characteristic of fundamentalism. Catholicism in its worldly wisdom, while not abandoning responsibility for the moral training of its

---

[4] Some of these differences are not unimportant. Presbyterian fundamentalists, in their rather rigid Calvinism, frequently clash seriously with Baptist fundamentalists. The former group has produced more influential theologians, hence the summary offered below mainly reflects their standpoint.

members, came to have a rather tolerant eye for the lesser peccadilloes of men, and to treat them, in its system of penance, from a quasi-commercial standpoint. Such and such a delinquency could be requited by the recital of so many prayers, or corrective discipline for it could even be replaced by a contribution in money to some religious cause. Of course, sincere penitence was expected to accompany these acts. In their revulsion against such practices Protestants emphasized the heinousness of sin as an affront to the majesty and holiness of God; they insisted on a high standard of personal purity and of unselfish service to one's fellows; and they encouraged, even to the point of morbidness, earnest self-examination to detect unsuspected shortcomings in character and conduct. When the fire of this moral awakening had begun to flicker and had given way to a complacent ritualism, the evangelical revivals to which reference has been made fanned the flame by preaching more vigorously than ever man's natural and inevitable sinfulness against the demands of the divine law. The conception of sin here involved, of course, is that distilled from the Bible by Luther, Calvin, and their early theological followers.

Let us examine now the more basic and crucial divergences of fundamentalism from Catholicism.

The first lies in a return by Protestants to Augustine in their fundamental conception of God, of man's nature, and of man's complete dependence on God for the attainment of truth and goodness. Against the devout rationalism of Thomas Aquinas and his followers, with its insistence on an exalted place for intelligence in God and in man, the Protestant Reformers followed the Bishop of Hippo in subordinating reason to will. God is Almighty Will; man in his inmost essence is also will, capable either of rebellion against the divine law or of humble and obedient submission. And without God's help man's will is so corrupted by sin that it can do absolutely nothing for itself. All this, of course, meant a renewed adoption of several important doctrines in Augustine which during the intervening period had been qualified or denied. One is the famous doctrine of "prevenient" grace: that even the first step taken by man toward justifying faith must be aroused in his soul through the grace of God. The Lutheran Formula of Concord expresses the need of such grace vividly when it says that as a result of Adam's sin "no spark of spiritual power was left him for the knowledge of truth and the accomplishment of good." Another is the doctrine of predestination, which, especially in Calvin and his followers, takes a quite uncompromising form: God by his inscrutable decree of election predestines to salvation those on whom he bestows saving grace, and likewise predestines to eternal reprobation those from whom he withholds that beneficence. In both cases he acts for the sake of his own glory. Thus, before God, man is left by Protestant theology completely and abjectly humbled. But to these humiliations of man's pride it adds a doctrine whose effect is to exalt the Christian and give him unbounded fearlessness before his fellow men. Catholicism, to protect its members from the confidence that might lead to license, and to emphasize their continued need for the ministrations of the Church, had taught that no Christian can in this life know for certain that he is destined to eternal glory. He may hope and expect the bliss of heaven, but must not allow himself full assurance of it. Luther and Calvin, partly as a result of their own religious experience, partly to free their followers from the long-instilled sense of dependence on the Catholic Church, taught that the individual who has experienced God's forgiveness may have here and now a joyous certainty of eternal salvation. This engendered, especially among the later Calvinists, an unlimited confidence before possessors of earthly power. Sure of eternal bliss, they denounced kings and magistrates in this temporal realm for abuses of power, built up constitutional guarantees of the right to be free in conscience and in speech, and became a powerful force for the establishment of representative democracy in western Europe.

The second (and last) concerns assumptions (4b) and (4c) in the outline at the end of the preceding chapter. The Protestant position is that the distinction of function in the Church marked by these two propositions is not justified. As the above discussion indicates, it fully agrees with Catholicism, though on slightly different grounds and with some difference of emphasis, on the distinct role indicated by (4a). A supernatural revelation, it holds, did historically come to man through the Hebrew prophets and Christian apostles, who were selected by God to receive and proclaim it. Since the canon of Scripture was closed, this special function of supplementing human reason by divinely bestowed and authenticated truth has been no longer performed, and indeed is no longer needed. All guidance requisite for man's salvation is provided in the inspired pages of the Bible. But God intended the other two functions to be merged in one. All Christians are on the same footing in their privilege to approach God directly with naught but the humble obedience and earnest faith of their own hearts, and in their responsibility to study the Bible for themselves under the guidance of the Holy Spirit and to reach their own understanding of its message. To the Protestant mind the authority of the pope and bishops to interpret the Bible to the individual Christian and to prescribe works of penance for his sins is a source of bondage rather than a needed support in man's quest for salvation.[5] Each Christian is to be his own bishop and priest, refusing to submit to the servitude and spiritual dependence symbolized by the Catholic ecclesiastical hierarchy.

This insistence, in its first historical appearance, was grounded mainly in the religious experience of Martin Luther. He had won the assurance of divine favor through a direct inward realization of faith in God, unmediated by the institutional apparatus of the Church, and he became profoundly convinced that that apparatus and the feeling of dependence on the officers of the Church which accompanied its use were a form of slavery rather than an aid to the true Christian life; they constituted a barrier between the individual soul and God instead of a means to their reconciliation. Accordingly, his central teaching in opposition to the Mother Church was summed up in two basic doctrines: justification by faith alone, and the universal priesthood of Christian believers.[6] All men can approach God directly, bringing nothing more than sincere faith in divine grace, and if God vouchsafes it they can win an assurance of salvation in complete freedom from ecclesiastical supervision or interference. Their authority in matters of belief is the Bible rather than the Church, or at least those portions of the Bible which in the light of Luther's experience of divine forgiveness seemed of major importance. And all Christians may freely search for truth in its pages under divine guidance, accepting what

---

[5] *Luther's Primary Works* (Wace and Buchheim ed.), p. 117.
[6] *Ibid.*, p. 268.

they find without fear of ecclesiastical censorship over mind or conscience.

These central Protestant convictions do not mean that the Reformers were blind to the fact that in religion, as in other realms of life, some men in every generation are equipped to fill positions of leadership while others must in the main depend on their guidance. What they denied was: first, that this living duality of function, attested in history and social psychology, is identical with the duality actually exhibited between ecclesiastics and laymen in the Catholic Church, and that the spiritual value of religious leadership rests essentially on its continuity, through the transmission from generation to generation of supernatural grace, with the original apostles.[7] Capacity for true leadership is proved for them simply by the urgent call in a man's own heart to preach the gospel, attested by his power actually to feed hungry souls from the pages of the Bible. These may be present in a man who remains unaccepted as a priest by the ecclesiastical powers. No magical continuity with the apostolic past, resting on the sacramental transfer of grace through the bishops, is necessary. They denied, second, that this duality of social function should be accepted and exploited, after the fashion that seemed exemplified in the Catholic hierarchy. Rather, so far as possible, it should be overcome. Christian laymen should not be kept in humiliating bondage to the priesthood; they should be encouraged to exercise the full liberty of their Christian calling and become kings and priests themselves, acknowledging servitude to no human authority. The valid ideal is that all Christians should treat each other as equal in the sight of God, recognizing their mutual interdependence in faith and service.[8] Those who lead should not lord it over Christ's flock, but should constantly recognize that even though a special responsibility has been placed in their hands they, like other men, need the support and counsel of their fellow Christians, and can learn much from the experience of those to whom they minister. The true Church is a democratic fellowship, a community of mutual friendship, not an aristocracy in which some are spiritual masters while others humbly obey.

[7] One branch of Episcopalianism holds to the Catholic position on this matter.

[8] *Luther's Primary Works* (Wace and Buchheim ed.), p. 115.

To what, ultimately, did Protestant thinkers appeal in justifying this insistence on a democratic leveling of the ecclesiastical hierarchy? Primarily and directly, of course, to the Bible, since for them, as for Catholics, it is the authoritative revelation of God. In interpreting the Bible they attempted to turn the edge of those passages to which Catholics appeal in supporting their claim to ecclesiastical authority, either by insisting that such passages are later interpolations, or that, properly understood, they do not give the Church the authoritative function deduced from them. On the positive side they emphasized all those passages, especially in the Gospel of John and in Paul's Epistles, which stress the equality, mutual helpfulness, and freedom from external control of Christian believers. Jesus is reported to have said to his disciples: "You are my friends if you do what I command you. I do not call you servants any longer, for a servant does not know what his master is doing, but now I call you friends, for I have made known to you everything that I have learned from my Father."[9] And in the context he implies that the same relationship is to extend equally to all who shall become his disciples in the future.[10] Paul writes to the Christians at Rome: "All who are guided by God's Spirit are God's sons. It is not a consciousness of servitude that has been imparted to you, to fill you again with fear, but the consciousness of adoption as sons, which makes us cry, 'Abba!' that is, Father."[11] Such passages, of which there are many, seemed to the Reformers to teach an entirely different conception of the Church and of the Christian life from that reflected in the structure of Catholicism. The Church is not itself a proper object of faith; that object is God, incarnate in the redeeming death of Christ, and revealed to men in the Bible. The Church is the community of the faithful, existing for the mutual service of Christians in faith and love. Its officers have no lordly authority or priestly prerogative over their fellows, but are simply their ministers. They owe their position not to consecration by representatives of an apostolic tradition, but to the inner summons of God, recognized by their Christian brethren who thereupon appoint them to fill the duties of the pulpit.

But while appeal to the Bible is the primary method by which

[9] John 15: 14, 15.
[10] Ibid., 17: 20–26.
[11] Rom. 8: 14, 15.

Protestants justified this democratic freedom of the Christian life, the student of Reformation literature will find plenty of evidence for the supposition that underlying this primary appeal there is a less avowed but at least equally important ground for their opposition to Catholicism. This lies in a different fundamental feeling as to what kind of affair true religion is. Having this feeling, it was easy for them to find it supported in the Bible. Their aspirations, instinctive convictions, and spiritual experiences emphasized liberty as a central religious good; they rebelled against the position of obedient humility before human ecclesiastics assigned to the religious life of laymen in the Catholic system. They were sure that God wanted free men, not slaves, as his children. This feeling and assurance led to an insight into the essence of religion which was irreconcilable with the conception occupying the status of Catholic orthodoxy. The heart of religion for them is the complete freedom of the Christian man from all priestly law, all prescribed works of penance, all bondage to human authority. Utterly prostrate before God, he is a serf to no man.

Every Christian is by faith so exalted above all things, that, in spiritual power, he is completely lord of all things, so that nothing whatever can do him any hurt; yea, all things are subject to him, and are compelled to be subservient to his salvation. . . . Not that in the sense of corporeal power anyone among Christians has been appointed to possess and rule all things, according to the mad and senseless idea of certain ecclesiastics. That is the office of kings, princes, and men upon earth. . . . This is a spiritual power, which rules in the midst of enemies, and is powerful in the midst of distresses. . . . This is a lofty and eminent dignity, a true and almighty dominion, a spiritual empire, in which there is nothing so good, nothing so bad, as not to work together for my good, if only I believe. . . . This is the inestimable power and liberty of Christians.

Nor are we only kings and the freest of all men, but also priests for ever, a dignity far higher than kingship, because by that priesthood we are worthy to appear before God, to pray for others, and to teach one another mutually the things which are of God. . . . Christ has obtained for us this favor, if we believe in Him, that, just as we are His brethren, and co-heirs and fellow-kings with Him, so we should be also fellow-priests with him, and venture with confidence, through the spirit of faith, to come into the presence of God, and cry 'Abba, Father!', and to pray for one another and to do all things which we see done and figured in the visible and corporeal office of priesthood. . . .

Who then can comprehend the loftiness of that Christian dignity which, by its royal power, rules over all things, even over death, life, and sin, and by its priestly glory, is all-powerful with God?[12] . . .

In these words there breathes an attitude toward religion which is non-Catholic through and through. At its heart lies insistence on freedom instead of dependence, individualism instead of ecclesiasticism, dignity instead of humility, equality instead of authority of some over others. And despite a certain distrust of Luther's emphasis on liberty which we note in Calvin and in some of the other Reformers—indeed, in Luther himself in relation to other branches of the reformed movement than his own—this spirit became characteristic of the whole Protestant movement. It is the distinctive and vital contribution of Protestantism to the religious philosophy of the modern Occident, and the five philosophies which remain to be discussed side on this matter with the Reformers against the emphasis on ecclesiastical authority characteristic of Catholicism.

SUMMARY STATEMENT OF THE FUNDAMENTALIST ARGUMENT

With these distinctive features in mind, and remembering the many beliefs which Protestants and Catholics hold in common, we may now summarize briefly the fundamentalist argument.

Through conscience, awakened by the preaching of the Bible, we feel ourselves in the presence of an authoritative law. Behind that law stands a holy lawgiver, against whose commands we are aware of having sinned, and whose eternal condemnation we merit. The infinite power and majesty of this lawgiver are shadowed forth in the physical world, of which, by the causal argument which Protestants accept from the Catholic theologians, we see that he is likewise the author. Now, by our own resources we can do absolutely nothing to gain release from divine punishment and forgiveness for our sins. Apart from God's grace we are impotent.[13] But happily we have from him a special revelation which tells us that he is a God of mercy and love as well as of justice. This

---

[12] "Concerning Christian Liberty" (Wace and Buchheim ed. of *Luther's Primary Works*), pp. 115 f. Reprinted by permission of the publisher, John Murray.

[13] J. G. Machen, *The Christian Faith in the Modern World*, pp. 13–26.

revelation is the Bible. How do we know that the Bible's claim to come from God is true? First and foremost, by the fact that to the law proclaimed in the Bible our moral nature directly responds; when we hear the Word expounded our conscience is pricked, and our hearts murmur, "Here is that which we ought to have done and which, alas, we have not done."[14] Second, by the fulfillments of prophecy and the miracles which are recorded in Holy Writ. Some of the more striking of these, so fundamentalists are convinced, can be attested by adequate historical evidence. How, for instance, can we explain the change in the early disciples, after Jesus' death, from despair to joy and confidence—their sudden readiness to meet persecution in proclaiming his Messiahship and divinity—unless we suppose that their testimony was correct in asserting that he had risen from the dead, had conversed with them, and had ascended into heaven?[15] Convinced that such marvelous things really happened, we find no reason to disbelieve other miracles recorded in the same wondrous book. And if to modern minds, filled with scientific notions of the uniformity of law, miracles are hard to believe, it is important to remember that without them we could not establish those attributes of the divine author of the Bible which are necessary to give us assurance of salvation. Bereft of the miracles, the Bible would be a moral teacher, stirring our hearts into conviction of sin, but there its message would end; with the miracles it reveals a Savior from sin. For these marvelous events, especially the virgin birth and resurrection of Jesus, attest the supernatural power of God, and of Christ as the incarnate son of God, both to destroy utterly those whose sins remain unforgiven, and to redeem for everlasting glory in the future life those who through faith in Jesus' death and resurrection gain release from the burden of sin.[16]

The Bible is thus justified in becoming our infallible moral guide and intellectual standard. It points the way of escape from spiritual death; it discloses the path to everlasting life. And that path consists in childlike faith in God, roused in our hearts by his supernatural grace, which brings joyous realization that our sin is

---

[14] J. G. Machen, *Christianity and Liberalism*, p. 56.
[15] J. G. Machen, *The Christian Faith in the Modern World*, chap. XVI.
[16] J. G. Machen, *Christianity and Liberalism*, p. 103.

forgiven and assurance of our eternal salvation.[17] Free from bondage to sin, and lifted above dependence on ecclesiastical law, we express our eager gratitude in a life of holiness and of brotherly kindness to our fellow men. For after all, "it is our neighbor who needs our service; God in Heaven needs it not." [18] With others who have likewise experienced the gladness of salvation we form a universal priesthood of Christian believers, and we join together with those who find the same essential message in the Bible that we do in a community of Christian fellowship. The Church thus established, looking to the Bible for its pattern of organization, sets up no authoritative hierarchy by which to reduce free men again to servitude, but expresses in its organization the principles of equality before God and mutual dependence of all Christians in meeting the spiritual challenge of daily life.

RELIGION AND SCIENCE FOR PROTESTANTISM

In considering the relation between religion and science under Protestantism we may observe that in one significant respect this conception of religion proved favorable to the growth of modern science, while in another important respect it proved exceedingly difficult to reconcile with science. It was favorable to science in its central insistence on freedom of thought, of speech, and of publication for all members of the Christian community. Such insistence opened a wide opportunity for scientists to investigate, experiment, and publish their conclusions free from all serious threat of ecclesiastical censorship with its decrees of suppression backed by secular authority. It was no accident that modern science, especially during the seventeenth and eighteenth centuries, advanced most boldly and rapidly in Protestant countries. Moreover, the interminable theological disputes between Protestantism and Catholicism, and among the Protestant sects, gave continual excuse and encouragement to those who claimed that the important lesson to be learned from such disagreements is the fundamental inadequacy of the method of reaching truth by Biblical exegesis and theological interpretation— that the true method, at least so far as knowledge of the physical

[17] J. G. Machen, *The Christian View of Man*, pp. 291 f.
[18] Luther, quoted in A. C. McGiffert, *Protestant Thought before Kant*, p. 35.

world is concerned, is the method of reason and experience. During the eighteenth century a wave of rationalism (in the sense of confidence in these two ways to truth) swept over Europe which, coming directly after the astounding successes of Newtonian astronomy, took form in a profound trust in science and its method which has never since been lost.

On the other hand, the literalism of the fundamentalist interpretation of the Bible—the conviction that it is infallibly true in all its statements when taken in their most obvious meaning—placed the reformed sects under a much more serious handicap, in face of the challenge of rapid scientific progress, than Catholicism had to overcome. Catholic interpretations of the Bible, resting as they ultimately do upon the judgment of the living head of the Church, have shown a moderate degree of flexibility; allegorical, or at least metaphorical, interpretations of many passages in the Bible have always been allowable in Catholic exegesis. This has made possible a considerable measure of adjustment to the results of scientific progress. Orthodox Protestants, however, rejecting the pretensions of ecclesiastical authority, and holding that God has given in the Bible a revelation disclosing to the humblest mind, in readily understandable language, the true way of salvation, were perforce led to champion an extreme literalism in their exposition of the Bible. God must mean everywhere in the holy book what the simplest and most direct interpretation of the words would seem to imply; otherwise only theological specialists could discover their truth. This meant that the supernatural world-view of the writers of the Bible, in all its main details, became a fixed and absolute foundation for Protestant religious thinking, permitting almost no margin of accommodation to theories of science newly arising.

In the era of Copernican and Newtonian science this circumstance did not involve as serious a conflict between Protestantism and the new world-view as might have been expected. Some of the pioneers of the Reformation (notably Luther) denounced Copernicanism, but by the time the great Protestant confessions came to be formulated, the new astronomy was so well established that the custom of interpreting metaphorically rather than literally those passages in the Bible which taught the flatness of the earth and the motion of the sun was usually taken for granted. When the theory of evolution appeared, however, such accommodation was no longer possible. The standard interpretation of the Bible, including the doctrine of God's direct creation of man in his own image, had for generations been fixed. There seemed to be a stark, irreconcilable contradiction between this dogma and the scientific conclusion that man has slowly evolved from an animal ancestry. Thus during the last century a serious cleavage has arisen between fundamentalism and science. Protestant literalists find themselves compelled to oppose the theory of evolution as well as the newer historical and psychological ideas which imply rejection of the supernatural position traditionally assigned to the Bible and to the human soul. At times (as in Tennessee during the 1920's) they have endeavored to proscribe the teaching of these theories in the schools.

Fundamentalism and Social Issues

The bearing of fundamentalism on contemporary social problems is in large measure evident from matters already discussed. So far as concerns the issue of democracy versus dictatorship, fundamentalists are strong champions of democracy, and they stand as vigorously as any in the modern world behind the rights of freedom of conscience, of speech, and of assembly. The intimate connection of this position with the distinctive emphases and the early history of Protestantism has been sufficiently portrayed above. On the matter of war and peace the attitude of fundamentalists is equivocal. They approve peace as desirable, and expect it to be established on the earth, through supernatural intervention, at the second coming of Jesus to judge the world and usher in the millenium. But in the meantime they accept as inevitable that wars and rumors of war will multiply as foretold in Holy Writ.[19] Moreover, since these dire tragedies are part of God's righteous judgment on the nations, it is impious as well as futile to assume that they can be brought to an end by human effort; hence fundamentalists rarely support organizations aiming at the goal of international peace. In practice they tend to encourage a rather aggres-

[19] For example, in Matt. 24: 5–8.

sive nationalism and strong feelings of patriotism. This tendency has been strengthened by the sectarian cleavages of Protestantism and the circumstance that these cleavages, to some extent, have coincided with national lines. The result of this situation is that Protestants have often felt their religious interests to be bound up with those of particular national states. The same tendency has also been furthered by the close connection of Protestant orthodoxy with capitalism in industry and with the economic imperialism to which capitalism naturally leads.

In treating this last-mentioned circumstance in its bearing on contemporary issues, we must turn back to Puritanism in somewhat fuller detail. Puritanism appeared originally as a natural development of Calvinism. Calvin had taught that the supreme virtue of the Christian life was holiness, and holiness as he conceived it implied not only a high standard of personal purity and self-control, but also avoidance of the luxuries and worldly frivolities which easily tempt people into sin, especially the sins of impurity, imprudence, self-indulgence, and extravagance. We are all familiar with the social product that emerged when, under the concentration of the Puritan conscience on this moral ideal, large areas of the Protestant world came actually to express such teaching in the form of accepted custom. Dancing, theatergoing, gaming, drinking, cardplaying, and unrestrained amusement of all kinds were denounced as wiles of the devil; the Sabbath was treated as a day apart, in which no unnecessary work was allowed, and when even the most wholesome forms of recreation were proscribed. On the positive side the virtues of family loyalty, of soberness and self-control, were given a high place.

At this point the close relation of Puritanism to capitalism in the economic sphere comes to the fore.[20] Holiness, for Puritan thinkers, implied not only the virtues and prohibitions just mentioned, but the entire list of qualities which the business world under expanding capitalism has regarded as desirable, qualities which in general lead to commercial success in a free competitive economy. The most important of these qualities are thrift, prudence, industry, sobriety, faithfulness in the performance of contracts, and vigorous insistence on business rights. Luther had stressed the importance of steady

[20] The classic treatment of this theme is in Max Weber, *Protestant Ethics and the Spirit of Capitalism.*

application to the duties of one's worldly calling, to the end that one might amass the means by which to aid his neighbors when they were in distress.[21] The Calvinists went much further in this direction, consecrating as religiously important the virtues of freedom of contract, of shrewdness in trading, and of business prosperity. The English divine, Richard Baxter, expressed this consecration in provocative form: "You may labor in that manner as tendeth most to your success and lawful gain, for you are bound to improve all your talents. . . . If God show you a way in which you may lawfully get more than in another way (without wrong to your soul or to any other), if you refuse this and choose the less gainful way, you cross one of the ends of your calling, and you refuse to be God's steward."[22]

As a result of these historical factors Protestant fundamentalism today finds itself committed to the support of the capitalist economic system;[23] its moral interests, so far as affairs of this world are concerned, are one with those of the business class. Hence it has little sympathy with the labor movement and it strenuously opposes all forms of socialism. It rightly feels that a socialist economy would encourage and make central a set of basic virtues quite different from those which traditional Protestantism has emphasized, virtues such as coöperation, security, acceptance of present enjoyments, and a sense of interdependence.

In family morality there is little clear difference between fundamentalism and Catholicism. Champions of the former, however, usually regard divorce as allowable where the partner of the one seeking it has committed adultery. Birth control, also, is not as uncompromisingly opposed.

Our analysis of Catholicism ended with an outline summary of those among its main assumptions which have been subject to dispute. There follows here a similar statement of the assumptions of fundamentalism. It is so couched as to emphasize the central points of agreement and difference between fundamentalism and Catholicism, as well as those on which both have been attacked by other religious philosophies.

[21] *Luther's Primary Works* (Wace and Buchhein ed.), p. 125.
[22] *Christian Directory*, I, chap. X, 1 (9).
[23] It can appeal of course, to Christ's parables for support here; cf. Matt. 20: 1–16.

The Major Disputed Assumptions of Fundamentalism

1. Assumptions Concerning Man's Moral Situation
   a. Man is conscious of sin, which prevents his attainment of salvation.
   b. By himself he is totally impotent to gain release from sin.
2. Assumptions Concerning Man's Metaphysical Knowledge
   a. He can attain valid knowledge here, which, with supernatural aid, may lead him to the needed moral transformation.
      (1) This is accomplished primarily through consciousness of an authoritative law and lawgiver, implied by conviction of sin. This consciousness attests the truth of the Bible.
      (2) It is accomplished secondarily through natural theology.
   b. The scholastic conception of causality is valid.
   c. Teleological explanation is metaphysically valid.
      (1) Goodness (in God) is a positive reality and the sole ultimate cause.
      (2) Evil is not metaphysically ultimate, but in the form of rebellious angelic or human wills it is a real secondary cause.
3. Assumptions Concerning Knowledge of the Supernatural
   a. Through our acceptance of the miraculous events recorded in the Bible the latter's claim to be a supernatural revelation, supplementing our natural knowledge, can be proved valid.
   b. The testimony of conscience, aided by miracles and fulfilled prophecy, can discriminate the true revelation from false ones.
4. Assumptions Concerning the Structure of Religious Authority
   a. A supernatural revelation was given to the prophets and apostles.
   b. Freedom to interpret that revelation, under the guidance of the Holy Spirit, belongs to every Christian.

Selected Bibliography

Bryan, W. J., *In His Image*, Revell, 1922.
Calvin, John, *Institutes of the Christian Religion*. (Many English editions available.)

Cole, S. G., *History of Fundamentalism*, R. R. Smith, 1931.

Luther, Martin, *Primary Works* (Wace and Buchheim ed.), John Murray, 1883.

McGiffert, A. C., *Martin Luther, the Man and His Work*, Century Co., 1912.

McGiffert, A. C., *Protestant Thought Before Kant*, Scribner, 1929.

Machen, J. G., *The Christian Doctrine of Man*, Macmillan, 1937.

Machen, J. G., *The Christian Faith in the Modern World*, Macmillan, 1936.

Machen, J. G., *Christianity and Liberalism*, Macmillan, 1930.

Torrey, R. A., *The Fundamental Doctrines of the Christian Faith*, Doran, 1918.

Chapter VII

THE RELIGION OF SCIENCE

THE IMPACT OF SCIENCE ON MODERN CULTURE

THE TWO religious philosophies thus far examined gained systematic formulation during the period preceding the rise of modern science. Those which are now and hereafter to be described have been developed since the scientific movement became an effective factor in Western thought, and each of them, to a greater or less degree, reflects its influence. To exaggerate the importance of this circumstance would be very difficult. Science has been the major transforming agency in modern culture. This is not only true of the intellectual aspects of that culture, in which the impact of science has been directly evident—e.g., literature and philosophy; it is true likewise of all other phases of modern life—industrial, moral, political, aesthetic, religious. As we proceed, this fact must never be forgotten.

Note that the phrase "modern science" is used rather than "science" alone. Fairness to Catholic and fundamentalist philosophies requires this qualification, for the medieval thinkers who laid the foundations of these theologies and built much of the superstructure were quite confident that their reasoning was scientific. And indeed any systematic pursuit of truth may in the broad sense of the word "science" be legitimately called a scientific enterprise. Now, from the Catholic point of view theology in this sense is not only scientific; it is itself the supreme science, all other branches of knowledge being its humble handmaidens or less important supplements. It is systematic truth about the ultimate reality in the universe, on which

168

every other reality depends. In the light of this circumstance we can understand the intimate union achieved between religion and science in medieval times, science pointing toward God as the primary cause of all things, and being inspired by religion in its quest. What happened in the late medieval and early modern centuries was that the conception of science held by intellectual leaders gradually changed. For the most part, the same scientific categories continued to be used, such as matter, form, potentiality, cause, and the rest, but they came to carry a different meaning. A novel set of underlying assumptions as to what constitutes a sound scientific explanation of any event slowly replaced the predominantly Aristotelian assumptions which had previously prevailed. This shift of assumptions in the course of time disclosed itself in somewhat different methods of scientific discovery and new ways of formulating scientific results. At first the implications of these changes were not realized. Slowly, however, the extent of the transformation came to be recognized, and then it became evident, among other things, that the medieval unity of religion and science was no more. A fundamental conflict appeared between theology as it had been conceived by the dominant schools of thought and assumptions essential to the new science, a conflict which has ever since exercised the wits of would-be reconcilers of these two great expressions of human need. Natural theology, on which Aquinas and Calvin had based the essential truths of religion, gradually lost its validity for minds committed to the novel intellectual trend, and the concepts of revelation and faith became still more suspect than those of the Aristotelian metaphysic. Such a change, of course, challenged religious philosophy to a radical readjustment. The major details of this transformation will presently occupy a central place in our discussion.

Before embarking on this survey, however, we should distinguish, as a preliminary guide to the analysis, the two major ways in which religious philosophy was reconstructed to meet the impact of modern science, during the two centuries preceding the appearance of the Critical Philosophy of Kant (1781). One of these will occupy us in the present chapter, the other in the chapter succeeding it. A general characterization of these two kinds of reconstruction will indicate how natural and almost inevitable each of them was in view of the historical situation which had arisen. Both accorded unqualified acceptance to what at the time had gained recognition as the basic assumptions of the new science. But beyond this point they differed profoundly. The first reinterpreted the major concepts and truths of religion so as to harmonize them with the presuppositions of science. It made a religion out of science, focusing upon the rational order of the universe, as conceived by modern inquirers, the pious attitudes and attachments characteristic of traditional religion, and thus finding the supreme good which men have always looked to religion to provide. This mode of reconstruction appears earliest in challenging form in the religious philosophy of Spinoza (1632–1677), which will soon be discussed in some detail. The second, in general, retained the established theological interpretations, but asked whether they are grounded on adequate evidence—applying, of course, the criteria of evidence upon which the new scientific movement, in contrast with medieval scholasticism, had come to insist. The answer given to this question was that the evidence is inadequate, that the propositions of theology remain unproved. Hence this philosophy of religion assumes the form of skepticism or agnosticism.

What accounts for the circumstance that two such different modes of adjusting religion to the new science should appear, one issuing in a religion of science, the other leading to the rejection of theology as unscientific? In part, the answer is to be found in the nature and profundity of religious interest in the two cases. Those who adopted the religion of science were, in general, men of deep and placid piety, and their piety expressed itself in the same major attitudes that had been fostered by the dominant religious currents of the past. Those who turned to skepticism were men of essentially moral and practical concerns, in whom religious motives of the traditional type were less vital and for whom contemplative detachment was relatively uncongenial. But a more important part of the answer lies in the fact that modern science itself reveals two distinctive emphases, one of which was capitalized by the religion of science to the relative exclusion of the other, while the skeptics fastened upon the latter to the subordination of the former. The first of these is the mathematical emphasis; the second is the empirical. A brief examination of these two aspects of the new science will aid our understanding of its impact upon religion.

The Twofold Emphasis of Modern Science :

In ancient and medieval times mathematics had occupied a much less central place in the scientific enterprise than it came to assume in the modern world. Arithmetic, geometry, and elementary algebra had undergone considerable development, and they had been successfully applied to certain problems in astronomy, in optics, in mechanics, and in the theory of music. But no general method of applying mathematics to the study of physical nature had been invented, and no thinker seems to have envisioned the advantages of such an application which have bulked large in the estimation of modern scientists. The Pythagorean philosophers and, later, Plato had suggested that the entire physical universe is composed of geometrical units, but the motivation behind the theory was moralistic and mystical rather than the interest in exact prediction which underlies most modern theories of science; in any case, these philosophies did not beget any practically usable way of analyzing physical processes in mathematical terms till they were resurrected to aid in just this enterprise at the beginning of the modern period. The main picture of the physical world entertained by scientific minds during late ancient and early medieval times was Neo-Platonic in its essential structure; after the thirteenth century it was Aristotelian. For both these systems, as we have seen, the fundamental principle applied to the explanation of events was the teleological idea that everything happens as the expression of, and the quest for, some typical perfection or good. Obviously, from such a standpoint mathematical analysis could only occupy a position of subordinate importance in the hierarchy of the sciences. In the form of geometry it delineated the spatial structure and relations of objects; with minor exceptions, it offered no aid in explaining the changes which they underwent. It did, however, exercise one pervasive influence upon the theory of science held by these philosophies—it supplied their general ideal of what scientific demonstration should be. Just as for Euclid geometry consisted in the detailed deduction of specific theorems from the axioms and definitions which constitute its first principles, so for Aristotle any science must consist in the deductive demonstration of particular truths from primary principles established by some method other than demonstration.

For three centuries and more prior to Spinoza a gradual change had been taking place in men's interest in and hopes for mathematical knowledge, with special reference to its further application to physical problems. Two different motives appear to have been active in this change. One motive was quite practical. The fact that influential thinkers felt it reflects an important social change; the interests of what we now call "technology" had come to be shared by intellectual leaders, as in general they had not been during Greek and medieval times. Specifically, a number of questions concerning the motion of bodies had been thrust upon the attention of inquiring minds, in which the needed solution was not an explanation in general terms of why the motion took place (which was all that a teleological account could provide), but a statement of the quantitative law of its course, so that it could be more accurately controlled. Typical problems of this sort had to do with the motion of projectiles, the navigation of ships, the pumping of water and its flow in a conduit. Such problems could be adequately met only by an exact statement, in categories of distance, time, weight, pressure, etc., of the way in which these motions ran their course, for only through such a statement could one anticipate with precision, at the commencement of a motion, what the result would be at each of its later stages, and thus control it to any desired end. The other motive was theoretical; it consisted in a strong interest in attaining certainty and demonstrative cogency in human knowledge. To appreciate this motive we must remember that in the fifteenth and sixteenth centuries such intellectual unity as had prevailed in Europe under the dominant influence of Aristotle and Thomas was rapidly slipping away. In the religious sphere the rise of Protestant theologies was the most striking indication of this disruption, but the same chorus of disagreement was evident everywhere in philosophy and in science. New branches of investigation, implying by their methods novel underlying assumptions about the world, were appearing; fantastic speculations, especially in the form of cosmological theories, were proffered in rapid succession. Intellectual authority was still vigorously claimed, but it was everywhere disputed. The printing press, recently invented, contributed greatly to the confusion by spreading these new ideas all over Europe. In this situation it was natural for some keen minds to arise whose thought was influenced mainly by the desire to find a way of ending this intellectual chaos and to establish a stable foundation on which thinkers could agree. When they cast about for materials out of which to build that foundation they were readily attracted by the promise of mathematics in this regard. Its demonstrations seemed to carry a coerciveness and an assurance that could not be equaled elsewhere in science or philosophy. Other so-called truths were being disputed and replaced, but not the truths of mathematics. Descartes says:

> I was especially delighted with the mathematics, on account of the certitude and evidence of their reasonings. . . . I was astonished that foundations, so strong and solid, should have had no loftier superstructure reared on them. . . . Of philosophy I will say nothing, except that when I saw that it had been cultivated for many ages by the most distinguished men, and that yet there is not a single matter within its sphere which is above doubt, I did not presume to anticipate that my success would be greater in it than that of others. . . . As to the other sciences, inasmuch as these borrow their principles from philosophy, I judged that no solid superstructures could be reared on foundations so infirm.[1]

These motives naturally found expression in a rapid expansion of mathematical knowledge and the discovery of methods for its application to problems arising in the other sciences. They also led a few bold thinkers of philosophic caliber to resurrect the central thought of Pythagoreanism and conceive the very structure of the universe—at least, of the physical world—in mathematical terms. If mathematics can everywhere be employed in disclosing the truth about physical objects, then (such men reasoned) those objects must be essentially mathematical in nature. But they took a still more daring step than this statement specifically implies, for they meant to include the motions of objects as well as their structure; whatever happens in physical nature should reflect a mathematical order and take place in accordance with mathematical law. The consequence

[1] *Discourse on Method*, I, Haldane and Ross translation. Reprinted by permission of the publishers, the Cambridge University Press.

of this postulate for modern science and philosophy has been exceedingly radical. The categories involved in the mathematical
description of nature were exalted to metaphysical prominence at
the expense of the categories emphasized by Aristotle and Thomas
Aquinas, and they now seemed more suited to clear rational understanding of the world. The two most fundamental of these newly
prominent categories were space (or extension) and time. The
change which came about in the case of the former of these is
especially interesting. For the entire dominant tradition in previous
philosophy space had been an affair of minor importance, possessing
only a queer and spurious sort of rationality; Plato thought of it as
a mysterious, though somehow necessary, receptacle of the eternal
forms when they assumed perceptible embodiment. Now it became
the most rational entity conceivable, being one of the two patterns
of order in terms of which exact measurement and knowledge of
motion is necessarily expressed. From being an irrational receiver of
forms it became itself the very model of formal perfection.

At present let us notice simply the main bearing of this new
orientation on religion. This is that it offered a radical alternative
to the teleological theory which Plato and Aristotle had championed,
in terms of which both Catholicism and Protestantism had justified
their conviction that the processes of the universe are guided toward
ends promising full satisfaction to the deepest needs and aspirations
of man. By the aid of this conception it had been possible for these
philosophies to hold that the ultimate cause of all things is a personal God, who in relation to his creatures is supremely good in the
same sense in which a wise and benevolent man is good. The mathematical theory of the universe, if carried through consistently and
without qualification by other notions, is squarely opposed to this
conception. It has no place for teleology nor for providence. A
mathematical deduction takes no account of human ends; whether
we regard it as good or bad, the truth remains that a three-sided
plane figure must have three angles and not two or four. There is a
necessity here which is quite indifferent to our desires. We must
simply accept it, whatever be the consequences for our good or ill.
Ultimate reality, then, when conceived in this way, may be regarded
as "perfect" (if its perfection be interpreted in terms of the completeness and rigor of its mathematical order) but not at all as "good" in

any humanly significant meaning of the word. From this standpoint goodness has no cosmic standing, but is purely relative to human wants; events happen in the world not because they are good or bad but because they are necessarily determined to happen in accordance with mathematical law.

The notion [is] commonly entertained, that all things in nature act as men themselves act, namely with an end in view. It is accepted as certain that God himself directs all things to a definite goal (for it is said that God made all things for man, and man that he might worship him). . . . Experience day by day protested and showed by infinite examples that good and evil fortunes fall to the lot of pious and impious alike; still they would not abandon their inveterate prejudice, for it was more easy for them to class such contradictions among other unknown things of whose use they were ignorant . . . than to destroy the whole fabric of their reasoning and start afresh. They therefore laid down as an axiom that God's judgments far transcend human understanding. Such a doctrine might well have sufficed to conceal the truth from the human race for all eternity, if mathematics had not furnished another standard of truth in considering solely the essence and properties of figures without regard to their final causes.[2]

As for the other emphasis, the empirical, we may at present be quite brief, since its consideration in some detail will be necessary in the next chapter. It is rooted historically in the empiricism of Aristotelian science, which modern scientists and philosophers revised in several important ways. When its method of testing the adequacy of the evidence needed to justify the claim of truth for a proposition came to be clearly formulated, the consequences for the traditional doctrines of religion were very disturbing. None of the main items in the creed could offer the empirical evidence required to meet these tests. The first result of applying this revised empiricism to religious beliefs was thus negative. It issued in the religious philosophy which is today usually called "agnosticism." Later, a broader conception of empiricism in dealing with religious experience came to the fore which led to more positive results; this constructive form of religious empiricism will be treated in the chapter on liberalism.

Now the first of these two emphases of modern science to gain

[2] Spinoza, *Ethics*, Appendix to Part I, Elwes translation. Reprinted by permission of the publishers, G. Bell and Sons, Ltd.

a position of prominence and influence, both in general and in its bearing on religion, was the mathematical emphasis. Scientists and philosophers alike, during the sixteenth and early seventeenth centuries, were concentrating their energies on the task of applying in detail the theory that the structure and go of the universe are essentially mathematical. And in the work of Spinoza, who wrote during the third quarter of the seventeenth century, a religious philosophy built squarely on this foundation was first systematically offered to the world. The empirical emphasis lagged about a century behind the mathematical. Its important place in scientific method was stated near the end of the seventeenth century by Sir Isaac Newton, who also pointed the way toward its effective union with the mathematical aspect of science. In John Locke, a contemporary and friend of Newton, some of the challenging philosophical problems involved in this empirical viewpoint first attracted serious attention. David Hume, who applied empirical criteria to an examination of religious doctrines, lived not quite a century later than Spinoza. Following our chosen historical order, therefore, we turn first to the mathematical emphasis and to the religion of science whose theological structure was erected mainly by its aid.

THE AGE OF MATHEMATICAL RATIONALISM

The general point of view dominating the intellectual movement which reached its religious culmination in the philosophy of Spinoza may be described as "mathematical rationalism." By this is meant that, on the one hand, it takes as axiomatic the principle that the universe is mathematical in structure and behavior and that, on the other, it establishes particular truths about the details of nature by rational deduction, with only a subordinate place for empirical verification of the truths thus reached. The essence of scientific and philosophical method for the men active in this movement consists in intuitive apprehension of general laws, followed by deduction of their specific implications—in both of which processes reason is the operative faculty. Except for their insistence on the mathematical character of the laws intuited, this was quite in line with the conception of scientific procedure which had prevailed in Europe since the time of the Greek philosophers; the term "rationalism" is applied to it in modern discussions to signalize its contrast with the revised empiricism which later became accepted as the sound method of physical science. That empiricism insisted, among other things, on the importance of verifying observations through the aid of the senses in addition to the processes of intuition and deduction.

It is from this standpoint that one must understand the contribution of such early modern scientists as Copernicus, Kepler, and Galileo. All of them were convinced that mathematics was the key to nature; all failed to anticipate or to emphasize features of empirical method which later science found essential. But the rationalism which in varying degree and form is exhibited in these scientific men gained its first systematic philosophical formulation in the work of René Descartes, who was a younger contemporary of Kepler and Galileo, living from 1596 to 1650. Descartes's main scientific achievement was in the field of pure mathematics—the invention of analytic geometry—but he was primarily a great philosophical genius, who devoted himself to the twofold task of constructing a general method for applying mathematics to the study of the physical universe, and developing the comprehensive picture of nature presupposed in or resulting from the application of that method. It has been observed already that his eagerness for certainty and for coercive demonstration was the main motive behind his confidence in mathematics. During the first decade of his mature career— roughly from 1619 to 1629—the first of these two problems was central in his thought. He had conceived the idea of a "universal mathematic," that is, a distillation from the mathematical sciences of the general principles of order and measurement which were common to them all. Geometry was the science which appeared most fundamental and valuable for this purpose. His task was so to formulate these principles that they would provide a method capable of attaining exact and certain knowledge in any field of inquiry.[3] Early in the 1630's we find him occupied mainly with the second problem; he is working out a picture of the physical universe such as the systematic use of this method seems to require. Its basic categories—contrasting sharply with those of Aristotle—are extension and motion. Every knowable entity—at least such appears to be

[3] This stage of his work is most fully reflected in his *Rules for the Direction of the Mind*. See the Haldane and Ross edition of his works, Vol. I.

his ideal at this time—is conceived as necessarily extended in space and movable in space and in time. Motion in a body takes place solely as a result of the impact of another moving body, hence Descartes's picture of the world is mechanical in the narrowest and strictest sense of that term. Everything happens by the same forces and in the same fashion as are exemplified in the behavior of a group of billiard balls when one of them moves toward the others. Nothing occurs for the sake of an end, but simply as a result of mechanical necessity.

This picture, which in its main features (as corrected by Newton) came in a relatively short time to dominate the thought of educated men about the astronomical universe, was an exceedingly important historical contribution. It provided a fundamental alternative to the astronomical picture which had controlled the imagination of medieval theologians and harmonized with their man- and God-centered teleology. The earth, inhabited by men, lay at the center of this picture; it was surrounded by the celestial bodies moving in circular orbits as the expression of their ordered quest for geometrical perfection; at the outer edge of astronomical space was the empyrean, seat of the deity himself, who thus enclosed the entire cosmos within his providential protection. The line of God's creative activity and loving care pointed inward toward the center, while the line of man's worshipful surrender to the divine will and quest for mystic absorption in the divine nature pointed outward toward the periphery. There was thus a basic correspondence between the main teleological dependencies of things and their geometrical structure, weaving into a profound unity the whole imaginative sketch of the world. This unity had been disrupted by the Copernican system, which removed man from the center and God from the periphery. It encouraged the notion of an infinity of solar systems revolving throughout unbounded space and expressing mathematical symmetry rather than preoccupation with human life and its need for salvation. No longer could it be made credible that man was the prime object of cosmic concern; the vast universe now seemed controlled in its behavior by mathematical principles quite divorced from any humanly satisfying implications. Descartes gave concreteness to this new conception by the use of a simple analogy with which all men were familiar, the analogy of mechanical push and pull between extended and movable balls of matter. In a world so portrayed, geometrical structure and algebraically formulable laws of motion could be conceived to reign without ulterior qualification.[4]

But Descartes's consuming interest in certainty made it impossible for him to sweep the entire universe into the net of this mechanical system, and the final development of his thought under the guidance of this interest led him to subordinate the mathematical conception of the physical world to a teleological metaphysic quite in tune with that of Thomas and the Catholic philosophers. Even at the height of his geometrical daring it had seemed to him impossible to analyze the rational intellect of man in terms of extension and motion. Thinking, at least, did not present itself as a mechanical process. And, as he considered this distinctive phenomenon from the standpoint of his demand for certainty, it came to occupy a place of special metaphysical privilege. After all, we frequently make mistakes in our geometrical deductions; what guarantee have we that any given chain of mathematical reasoning may not be erroneous, to say nothing of any warrant for the validity of applying it to the study of physical motion? Its several steps can only be held together by memory, which is not infallible; this indicates that there is no such guarantee in mathematical knowledge considered by itself. But thinking is something whose existence we cannot seriously doubt. Even when we are lost in uncertainty about everything else we cannot doubt that our own doubting is going on. Now, doubting is a kind of thinking; it is one expression of that enduring cogitative nature in us which we call our "mind" or "self."[5] And this nature seems to be a radically different affair from the physical substance which is revealed in the form of extension and motion. It fits no mathematical pattern. Its essential attribute is just thinking, which is not a kind of motion and seems to involve no spatial spread-outness whatever. We are familiar with it in such modes as perceiving, willing, doubting, feeling. All these processes betray a reality independent of and incommensurable with motion in space. Conscious activity, then, not any mathematical entity, is our ultimate certainty. Descartes's famous metaphysical

[4] Descartes, *Principles of Philosophy,* especially Part II. (Haldane and Ross, Vol. I.)

[5] *Meditations on the First Philosophy,* I and II. (Haldane and Ross, Vol. I.)

dualism between the realm of thinking mind and that of mechanical nature, which became profoundly influential in subsequent thought, was grounded in these considerations.

How, now, to extend this certainty so that it may include the more important matters which had previously proved unable to withstand skeptical doubt, such as the trustworthiness of our mathematical knowledge and the validity of applying it to the study of physical nature? Here Descartes falls back upon the Catholic theology. Starting with the indubitable certainty of the thinking self, and using arguments similar to some of those emphasized by Augustine and Thomas, he establishes the reality of a divine being supreme in goodness and perfection. But such a being surely would not place his creatures under the control of a basic deception that would render their clearest knowledge illusory. Hence mathematics and mathematical physics gain the certainty which Descartes had demanded for them, but they gain it by becoming grounded in the theological metaphysic of the Catholic tradition.[6]

An Augustinian argument for God which Descartes couches in a somewhat novel way has been a matter of such controversy throughout modern religious philosophy that we may well state its essence before leaving him. It is known as the "ontological" argument, and attempts to prove the real existence of God from considerations involved in the traditionally familiar definition of the divine being.[7] The argument runs as follows: We conceive and define God as a supremely perfect being. Now, it is evident that such a being must exist, for, if he did not exist, he would lack one important aspect of perfection. Let us suppose that he does not exist; at once we can conceive a being possessing all his other perfections and, in addition, the attribute of real existence. Obviously, the former of these two assumed entities is not unqualifiedly perfect; only the latter is. Hence a supremely perfect being must exist, by virtue of implications involved in the very notion of supreme perfection. Spinoza accepts this argument as valid, though with a different interpretation of the term "perfection"; it will be subjected to critical examination when we come to Kant.

[6] *Ibid.*, III and VI.
[7] *Ibid.*, V.

SPINOZA'S PHILOSOPHY OF RELIGION

Spinoza was a younger contemporary of Descartes, and a careful student of his writings. In stating in appropriate order the main steps of his reasoning, so far as they bear on the fundamentals of religious philosophy, it will be advisable to undertake the same twofold task that has been attempted with Catholicism and fundamentalism. On the one hand, Spinoza must be understood in his own historical setting; on the other hand, the essentials of his position need to be explained in terms that seem intelligible and valid to those who now share his major assumptions.

The major problem of life, the solution of which may properly be called salvation, is according to Spinoza set by the circumstance of disappointed desire.[8] When we human beings first begin to reflect about our lot and the possibility of its betterment we discover that we are creatures consumed by craving for various objects or goals. Because we desire them, these objects appear good to us, and they arouse in us such emotions as love, hope, fear, anxiety. For the most part, the things which thus appeal to men fall under three general classes: riches, fame, and sensual pleasure. But in our pursuit of such allurements experience teaches the bitter lesson of frustration. In some cases the object loved or end sought proves beyond our reach; we continue to long for it but never succeed in gaining possession of it. This is one of the common forms of disappointment. In other cases we succeed in gaining what we seek, but it then turns to dust and ashes in our hands. It fails to bring the continued satisfaction expected, or else it draws unwanted pains in its wake. This is an equally frequent kind of frustration. Together they pose the plight from which man needs salvation.

Now, from the standpoint of the type of philosophy which Spinoza represents, nothing more than such experience of disappointment is needed to refute the providential teleology assumed by the Catholic and fundamentalist positions. The cosmos at large is not controlled in its doings by any responsibility to satisfy human needs or further man's welfare. If it were, frustration would be the rare and easily explicable exception, not the universal rule.[9]

[8] *On the Improvement of the Understanding*, pp. 1–3. (Elwes edition of his works, Vol. I.)

[9] W. Lippmann, *A Preface to Morals*, pp. 175 ff.

To be sure, if we knew on adequate independent evidence that a personal God, guided by a benevolent purpose, were behind the stream of events, our many disappointments would not necessarily overthrow that conviction; we could always suppose that our own ideas of what is good for us are often mistaken and that God is achieving a higher good than our limited experience enables us to glimpse. But it is human experience, interpreted in terms of mathematical order, that provides all the evidence we have as to what really is the essential structure of the world in which our life is set. Consequently, the lesson suggested by constant subjection to frustration must be allowed its appropriate weight in determining our ideas about the universe. And the lesson thus taught is very simple; it is that things occur in the world not through any teleological reference to our good, but in accordance with their own necessary law. Events happen because sufficient causes are there to produce them, not because man's ultimate welfare will be furthered by their occurrence. The reason why we miss happiness, then, is failure to adjust our desires, emotions, and actions to the objective order in which we and the objects pursued are involved; when we discover a source of dependable joy, as we sometimes do, it is because we have accidentally or wisely accommodated ourselves to that necessary order.

In terms of Spinoza's context of ideas, this notion of the universe as an objective and necessary structure found its natural expression through appeal to the concepts of mathematics. Spinoza was not a modern scientist, eager for the detailed advantages that quantitative formulae might bring to physics; what he saw in mathematics was that it provided an interpretation of the universe in which this vision of impartial and fateful necessity gains adequate formulation. When we picture events that happen as flowing from the ultimate substance of reality in the same way that the various theorems about a triangle—e.g., that the sum of its angles is equal to two right angles—follow from the defined essence of the triangle, our thought is true to the basic clue that experience offers about our world. And if we dare to generalize from this clue and sweep everything without qualification under such a conception, as Thomas did under his universal teleology, we see that such a step can very plausibly be taken. Even human purposive activity fits readily into the scheme; our desires and emotions, too, can be viewed as occurring not because they are good—indeed, we quickly find that most of them are not genuinely good—but because they have fixed causes in the nature of things by which they are necessarily produced. The reason why we are so apt to be blind to this truth is that we are always conscious of our loves and longings and usually unconscious of their causes.[10]

When, now, contemplating our experiences of disappointment, and realizing that the world is not made for us but follows its own necessary laws, we soberly reflect on the problem of life, what form does that problem take? In general terms it is this: Is there anywhere a good, a normal object of desire, whose very nature is such as never to frustrate the one who loves it and devotes himself to it? Can we put in place of these futile, fickle, and transitory goods which so easily arouse our impulsive craving, an eternal and absolute good, in eager union with which we may find "continuous, supreme, and unending happiness"?[11] And if so, where is this incomparably great good to be found, and how shall we gain effective attachment to it? The answers to these questions will give meaning, from the present standpoint, to the religious idea of salvation, and will show us the way to attain it.

Our progress toward a satisfying answer begins when we consider again the experience of frustration—its cause, and the way in which we sometimes manage to avoid it. The prime reason for its occurrence is evidently our ignorance. When we yearn after and seek objects that prove beyond our reach, this is because we did not understand those objects clearly in relation to our powers; had we realized their unattainability, and the consequent hopelessness of our emotional attachment to them, our desire would have been weaned away from captivity to them, it would concentrate on goods which are more obviously within our power. When we pursue goals that, even when attained, fail to yield the enduring and unalloyed satisfaction we craved, this is again because we did not understand them and the passions in ourselves which fasten irrationally upon them; had we done so we should not have been so sadly deceived but would have sought ends less infected by these errors.[12]

[10] Spinoza, *Ethics*, Appendix to Part I. (Elwes edition, Vol. I.)
[11] *On the Improvement of the Understanding*, p. 1.
[12] *Ethics*, Part V, props. I–VI.

Knowledge, then, especially knowledge of our emotions and desires in relation to their objects, is the key to salvation if salvation be possible.

Let us pause a moment to realize the full force of this step in the argument, in relation to the Catholic and fundamentalist answers to the question: Is human reason competent to understand man and his world, or is it not? Resting on their teleological hierarchy in the cosmos, in which man occupies a high but not the highest place, and confident that the deliverances of his reason require supplementation by supernatural revelation from an omniscient mind, the Catholic authors gave a divided answer to this question. Man's reason is competent up to a certain point, and this point it can itself determine; beyond, it must recognize its incapacity and dependence. And Protestant orthodoxy was even more distrustful of human competence; apart from the redeeming activity of divine grace, man's reason is corrupt and will readily fall into error; hence submissive acceptance of divine truth is needed from the very beginning. Now Spinoza represents a bolder rationalism, which is convinced that there lurks a fundamental error in supposing that knowledge gained by human intelligence can be supplemented or replaced by knowledge communicated from a more perfect intelligence.[13] The crux of the matter, from the standpoint of such a rationalism, is this: If man's clear intuition of truth is trustworthy in its disclosures, his competence wherever it can reach is equal to that of a divine intuition; if it is not trustworthy, then it is just as likely to be mistaken in believing that there exists a superhuman intelligence, able and willing to supplement its apprehensions, as it is in any other of its beliefs. In the former case it will need no correction; in the latter it can draw no conclusions whatever, even about God, with any confidence.[14] Is it essentially trustworthy, or is it not? With the achievements and promise of mathematics before him, Spinoza was confident that the affirmative answer is right, and the detailed content of his philosophy is developed on that basis. The ultimate criterion of truth for human thought is not the revelation of a divine mind,

---

[13] See in this connection Spinoza's *Tractatus Theologico-Politicus,* chaps. I, II, VI especially. See also in his *Correspondence* the letters to Blyenbergh of 1665.

[14] This important issue will be examined further in Part III. Cf. below, pp. 402–408.

but just that standard which is successfully applied in mathematical reasoning—the clarity of man's apprehending consciousness when he is immediately certain of correctly intuiting the nature of his object.[15]

Appeal, then, to a supernatural revelation, and the ultimate subordination of human reason to faith in divine reason, are eliminated from the religious philosophy we are now examining. Not that man's wisdom is regarded as omniscient; it has its limits, which it can itself recognize and determine. But, for this philosophy, the thought of transcending those bounds by supernatural aid is entirely chimerical. Certain limits to human apprehension are ultimate, and all that we can do when we meet them is to acknowledge the finitude of man's reason. For instance, Spinoza holds that we are confined to the comprehension of phenomena which are either modes of thought or modes of extension and motion, but that there is no ground for supposing that Nature herself is confined to these two dimensions of being. Certain limits, however, are merely those of our present intellectual attainment; when these confront us our task is to find, if possible, methods for gaining a clear apprehension of the objects with which we are concerned and thus add by our own discoveries to previously established knowledge. Fortunately for the present religious philosophy (unlike Catholicism and Protestantism), the intuitions of man's reason reach far enough to give us the guidance needed in pursuing the path to salvation, so that rejection of faith in supernatural assistance is not disastrous to our quest. Knowledge which man is capable of attaining is the key to the discovery of a supreme and eternal good.

But what sort of knowledge will it need to be?

Well, a two-fold understanding is needed—understanding of ourselves in relation to particular objects that stimulate our desires, and understanding of our universe as a whole. In both cases we must be guided by the principle of causality, in its theoretical and its practical bearings. That is, we must realize that true understanding of anything—understanding of it in such a way that we can adjust ourselves effectively to its existence or occurrence—is knowledge of it in relation to its necessary causes. Suppose we see a cause in operation which we know will produce a certain effect. If we are

[15] *On the Improvement of the Understanding,* pp. 10–12.

pursuing a good whose attainment or continued enjoyment assumes that that effect will not occur, we can modify our pursuit in the light of this knowledge and devote ourselves to objects whose attainment is consistent with the causal network which we see to be operative. And this circumstance indicates that such knowledge is itself an effective cause—not, to be sure, of anything that happens outside of us, but of changes in our emotional attachments within. Clear understanding of objects as they are related to our emotions tends to transform the latter, destroying or at least weakening those which are inharmonious with it and giving rational guidance to any that remain.[16]

Hence the twofold character of the understanding that is needed. In order for this process to go on—of gaining causal knowledge and adjusting ourselves to reality by means of it—we require on the one hand a clear intuition of the nature of the universe as a whole. We need to see and accept the fact that it is not a teleological order, providentially taking care of us in our weakness, but that it is a mathematical order, in which effects flow from their causes in the way in which mathematical theorems follow from the definitions and axioms which determine them to be what they are. In this form, for Spinoza metaphysical cognition is one kind of knowledge without which salvation cannot be secured.[17] Having attained such an apprehension of the whole, and having appropriately adjusted our fundamental attitudes to it, the process of modifying our passions in the right direction is already under way and may continue, even though our detailed understanding of objects and events be very meager. How this modification takes place will shortly be described. But on the other hand we obviously require, besides this intuition of the essence of the whole, as much specific knowledge of our desires and emotions in relation to their objects as we can gain, and of the manner in which clear apprehension of such truth modifies them.

Let us now return to the major problem of life, as Spinoza formulates it, and see how the above analysis determines his answer to it.

16 *Ethics*, Part IV, props. VII–XIV; Part V, props. VII–X.
17 *On the Improvement of the Understanding*, pp. 4–16.

Our problem was to find, if possible, a good for man, an object of emotional attachment, whose nature intrinsically forbids its ever failing the one who devotes himself to its pursuit—a good such that our love of it may grow from strength to strength and which may thus become a source of continuous, supreme, and unending happiness. We saw, too, that knowledge—metaphysical and psychological knowledge especially—points the way toward this good if it can be found, for it is by such knowledge that our frustrated attachments to fickle and transitory goods are avoided or corrected by wiser desires. Pursuing further this same line of reflection, we see that this knowledge itself is the good of which we are in search. For the only sure road to conquest of an undependable, emotionally impulsive desire is found through understanding that desire and the emotion which dominates it in relation to the necessary causal order of the universe by which they are determined. By such understanding we clearly see a passion both as causally necessitated, on the one hand, and as deceptive in our quest for enduring happiness, on the other; this apprehension itself then operates as a cause whereby we are weaned away from the dominance of that desire and turn instead to some more rational attachment. But such growth brings joy and a sense of enhanced power in relation to our emotions and to the environing universe. And since it is through knowledge of the necessary causal order of the world that that growth has taken place, this knowledge becomes associated in our minds with the joy of attainment and of heightened power. Because of this association, which is repeated in every similar experience and therefore becomes riveted more and more firmly as the years go by, the knowledge which leads to such delight becomes itself increasingly prized and enjoyed. And, finally, the object which through it is known—the order of necessary mathematical law pervading the cosmos, in which both our passions and the things that incite them exist and by which they are determined to act— likewise becomes associated with this course of liberating growth. Since that inflexible order is the ultimate source of our enjoyed enhancement, it, too, becomes increasingly a prized value to us; we not only understand it, but love it. The good, then, which cannot disappoint because rendered more secure and appealing by every

experience, once it has been discovered, is knowledge of the necessary order of existence and love of truth and reality grounded upon
that knowledge.[18]

To be sure, in the early stages of our progress toward intimate
attachment to this good, the notion of finding happiness in it is apt
to seem quite incredible. Our interest in truth is pale, cold, and
weak, while the emotions and desires which the true order of events
disappoints are often vivid, hot, gripping. We rebelliously continue
sometimes to identify ourselves with those passions even after we
have seen their deceptiveness; the inexorable order that has frustrated them seems to us an enemy, not a friend, an object of hate
rather than of welcome acceptance. One is desperately in love—but
his lady rejects him for another suitor, or after a blissful period of
romantic absorption he finds a barrier in their relationship incompatible with harmonious wedlock. The easy response is not to
pursue and love truth; it is to revolt at the fate which has thus
played him false, and to plunge into some new attachment in the
hope of finding there the happiness previously denied. None the
less, as long as he finds it worth while to continue to live at all, a
man cannot really hate the true causal structure that obtains in his
world; he must rather learn his lessons by it. The ultimate irrational-
ity is to hate truth, of which no one who still faces the future is
capable. And this, for the philosophy now under examination, is
the decisive point.

This illustration reveals again, in its own way, that it is not sufficient for salvation to learn, with however great rapidity or clarity,
such particular lessons of disappointed experience as these. Metaphysical knowledge is necessary to guide the process. Without it we
will continue to hope that the cosmos must satisfy at least some of
our irrational desires. But if one has this knowledge—if he clearly apprehends, especially at an early point in his pilgrimage, that the
universe in which he lives is characterized by the necessity and inevitability of a mathematical system, and if that fundamental truth is
adhered to firmly and used to guide his adjustment in particular frus-
trations—he will find himself following the process above outlined
and capable of making significant progress in it. Emotion will be
gradually transformed by understanding, and that transformation

[18] W. Lippmann, *A Preface to Morals*, pp. 180 ff., 190 f., 326 ff.

will be experienced as a gain in freedom and strength. Each new lesson learned from a previous frustration through the aid of knowledge will lead him to prize that knowledge and the impartial order which is its object more than before; love of truth will continually grow in strength at the expense of all less stable loves. And there is no upper limit to the intensity which may come to characterize such an attachment, for once one has viewed life from this standpoint every experience feeds that affection while none undermines it. Whatever happens, knowledge increases, and the love of truth associated with it. By the same token all other emotions which are incompatible with love of truth are fighting a constantly losing battle. Every time they lead to disappointment, or are apprehended as likely to do so, they forfeit something of their heat and their power over us. Vivid and absorbing as many of them are at first, their appeal gradually fades; our energy of devotion is continually transferred from them to a more dependable source of joy.[19] Of course, no miracle is performed. The extent to which we come to find real and enduring happiness in accepting the mathematical structure of nature and our dependent place in it varies from individual to individual and is affected by many factors, themselves all causally necessary. But many persons can reach the point where a stable and satisfying life on these terms is possible.

We may thus readily conceive the power which clear and distinct knowledge, and especially that third kind of knowledge founded on the actual knowledge of God, possesses over the emotions; if it does not absolutely destroy them in so far as they are passions, at any rate it causes them to occupy a very small part of the mind. Further, it begets a love toward a thing immutable and eternal, whereof we may really enter into possession; neither can it be defiled with those faults which are inherent in ordinary love, but it may grow from strength to strength, and may engross the greater part of the mind, and deeply penetrate it.[20]

Here is a good, then, which, once we come clearly to apprehend it, can in the nature of the case never disappoint; it becomes a source of continuous and unending happiness, and a happiness which, because it is enhanced through every experience, may in time

---

[19] Spinoza, *Ethics*, Part V, props. I–XVI.
[20] *Ibid.*, Part V, prop. XX. Reprinted by permission of the publisher, G. Bell and Sons, Ltd.

become supreme. It is the good in search of which the major problem of life has led us.

What about those whose weakness of understanding and whose intense longing for security and protection make it impossible for them to see the universe in this way or to make much progress in this direction? Spinoza recognizes that there are many such and he does not forget them. His *Theologico-Political Treatise,* together with reported incidents in his biography, make clear what he hopes for in their case. This is that they will make the most of the best elements in whatever religious faith they have been taught. Sincere piety, expressed in the framework of any inherited faith, will be in their case the wise substitute for the deeper insight that lies beyond their attainment. It can bring them inner peace and the moral guidance necessary for coöperative social relationships.

We are now in a position to see more distinctly the appropriateness of describing this point of view as the "religion of science." In modern times the word "science," if we leave out of consideration its practical applications in the control of physical nature, has stood chiefly for two things: a conception of the world and an eager quest based on this conception. The conception is that of the world as an impartial order, in which all events are determined to occur in accordance with objective laws of cause and effect, such laws being ideally capable of mathematical formulation. The quest is the enthusiastic search to discover ever more of the detailed regularities which are parts of this all-embracing order—specific truths in their determinate relation to the total structure of truth. The present type of religious philosophy sees in these two things not only the essence of science but also the answer to the fundamental problem of religion. The impartial world-order is the supreme object of religion. Clear apprehension and love of its all-pervading truth constitute the highest good for man, alone capable of providing him what religion has always aimed to provide—that object in intimate devotion to which petty and corroding emotions are conquered and dependable happiness more and more fully found.

In Spinoza's case the major concepts of Catholic and Protestant theology are reinterpreted so as to become harmonious throughout with this viewpoint. On that account, in reading him we find ourselves moving in the language hallowed by traditional Christian piety. The ultimate structure of the world, from which all events flow by geometrical necessity, is God. God is absolutely infinite and absolutely perfect, but his perfection is, of course, not that of an ideal personality. It refers rather to the completeness of his power and the unqualified rigor with which all that happens is determined by his nature; it is mathematical, not personal, perfection. In knowledge of God, and love grounded in knowledge—the "intellectual love of God" in Spinoza's own phrase—is man's salvation and blessedness accordingly to be found.

Moreover, in this context of assumptions Spinoza finds room for a doctrine of individual immortality. He cannot, of course, justify the Platonic conception of the soul in the *Phaedo* as an indestructible substance, essentially independent of the body. But, on the other hand, he allows for a preservation of the individual after death in a sense in which Aristotle apparently did not. Sense perception, memory, imagination, emotion—all those processes in the mind which are passive and seem obviously to depend on bodily organs are entirely mortal, ending with death. But knowledge, so far as it is true knowledge, is in a different case. When knowing truly, the human mind transcends its otherwise hampering finitude; it apprehends its object under the form of eternity. This is so because knowledge of anything is clear intuition of its essence as contained in the eternal nature of God and its existence as necessarily determined by God. Such knowledge is a part of God's own knowledge of himself,[21] which is not subject to change or destruction. And the love of God, since it arises from true knowledge and depends solely upon it, cannot be a transitory emotion but is likewise everlasting. However, this knowledge and love, as gained by an individual mind, are not without qualification identical with God's knowledge and love of himself. They retain an element of the individuality of the thinker in whom they are realized. This circumstance arises from the fact that each human mind is intimately united to a bodily organism which occupies a particular spatio-temporal locus in existence and undergoes its own distinctive vicissitudes. Thus, while we

[21] God for Spinoza, being the source of mind in the world as well as of matter, has the attribute of thought as well as that of extension. He thus possesses infinite knowledge. But the relation of that knowledge to its parts, i.e., to human minds, is, of course, conceived in terms of mathematical determination, not in terms of purposive guidance.

may come truly to know God, and other things in their dependence on God, that knowledge still reflects the particular perspective in existence which attachment to an individual body has imposed upon it. It is apprehension of eternal truth, but apprehension from a unique focus and under specific conditions which are never the same for any two persons. The everlasting part of any mind is hence also unique, different from the everlasting part of any other finite mind.[22]

Developments Since Spinoza

Since Spinoza's day, this type of philosophy has naturally undergone detailed modification, as prevailing conceptions of science have changed and as traditional religious terms have become less indispensable to the reverent imagination. Between the time of Spinoza and the late nineteenth century the outstanding changes were three. First, the emphasis on empirical method became equally central with that on mathematical law. Second, the prevailing scientific picture of the universe became dynamic instead of geometrical; the ultimate laws of physics were expressed in terms of energy and mass rather than in terms which mere geometrical reasoning could be supposed to exhaust. Third, many of the hallowed religious concepts either came to seem unwarranted or fell sufficiently out of harmony with the prevailing climate of thought so that the essentials of the philosophic viewpoint were more naturally stated without them. The latter was the case with such concepts as salvation and blessedness; the former, with the doctrine of immortality. Spinoza had believed that thought is as fundamental in the structure of the universe as are extension and motion; nineteenth-century science, however, generally regarded it as a quite dependent by-product of changes in matter, and as such incapable of surviving death. The form of the religion of science natural in this situation is well represented by the "monistic religion" of Ernst Haeckel, which is expounded in *The Riddle of the Universe*[23] and other works. Haeckel has no serious objection to applying the term "God" to the all-embracing world-substance which he, like Spinoza, assumes,

[22] *Ethics*, Part V, props. XXI–XL.
[23] Note especially chaps. XI, XII, XV, and XVIII.

but almost all the other terms colored by traditional religious associations are abandoned. In his theory love of truth, though central, is not accorded the uniquely important function which it gained in Spinoza; aspiration toward an ideal of goodness and sensitivity to forms of beauty are given equal and coördinate religious value.[24]

More recently, the fortunes of this type of religious philosophy have become much more complicated. The general conceptions of the world held by men dominated primarily by the scientific attitude are undergoing a more radical transformation than ever before, and the bearing of this transformation upon the fundamental problems of religion, from this as from other religious standpoints, for the most part remains to be worked out. Certain basic aspects of this point of view in religious philosophy, however, which mark it off from other approaches to religion and which it would presumably exhibit in any context, stand out clearly and are occasionally expounded. Walter Lippmann, for example, in his widely read *A Preface to Morals,* found in the religion of science as above described a basic solution of the problem of individual and social adjustment in its highly complex setting after the First World War. Its distinctive features, as he views the matter, are: acceptance of reality as an objective order uncontrolled by human concerns; emancipation from dominance by desires which arc not fully adjusted to such acceptance, resulting in an attitude of disinterestedness as the foundation of moral character; and the quest for continually increasing value in the achievements of man's faculty of understanding as that part of his nature which can freely function in harmony with such an attitude.[25]

In dealing with the relation between religion and science from the standpoint of the religious philosophy now under consideration, a word of summary only is needed. Since it is taken for granted that modern science is essentially right in its main picture of the universe and in its conception of truth, there is no possible ground

[24] In this respect Haeckel's monism becomes a form of humanism. See below, chap. XI. At the present time, in fact, there is no clear borderline between the religion of science and the kind of humanism which gives a distinctive religious value to scientific knowledge and love of truth. Lippmann (cf. the following paragraph) belongs in both camps.

[25] Note particularly chaps. I, VII, XV, and the whole of Part II.

for conflict between science and religion. Since, further, it is held that the pursuit of knowledge on the basis of these assumptions is of unique religious value, religion and science for this philosophy fall into a relation of constructive, self-developing harmony. Were such a harmony fully accepted by a civilization as its basic ideal, it would experience the same perfect unity between religion and science that medieval civilization realized on the foundation provided by Aristotelian science.

THE RELIGION OF SCIENCE AND MORAL PROBLEMS

The consequence of this wholehearted acceptance of the assumptions of modern science which is most distinctive for the present religious philosophy is its radical reinterpretation of human freedom. Except for the extreme predestination of Calvinistic fundamentalism—and even here the doctrine was softened by the conviction that God's will is good—other influential philosophies of religion have made some place for a freedom which promises man emancipation from the causal determinism of nature and real scope for the fulfillment of his desires. For the religion of science, nothing in the universe happens by chance or caprice. Human thoughts, words, and deeds, like all other events, have fixed causes by which they are determined to occur when and as they do. In this position, however, it sees no encouragement to a loss of the sense of human dignity or a despairing feeling that one is a puppet of fate. For man is capable of understanding the necessary structure of things, and such understanding, when gained, becomes itself a cause leading to some degree of conquest over childish emotion and some measure of progress toward dependable happiness. No one knows beforehand how great an advance toward true blessedness may be achieved in his own case, hence this rejection of capricious freedom gives no justification for hopeless surrender to irrational impulse.

We may be almost equally brief in examining the bearing of the viewpoint just expounded on the challenging social issues of the present day. This bearing has a twofold aspect. On the one hand, it cannot be said that love of impartial truth has of itself any clear implication on the problems which have been chosen for emphasis in this connection, hence it is possible for those who share it to fall on either side of such major controversies. On the other hand, the conquest of aggressive desires and self-centered passions in favor of a detached understanding of the world shows a natural tendency to ally itself with the motives which support the (so-called) liberal side on these issues. Since social conflict arises from the impulsive push of interested ambition, the attitude of impartiality naturally prefers harmony and coöperation to competitive rivalry; since the quest for special rewards and autocratic privileges is driven by egotistic desire and is not consistent with recognition of the needs and rights of others, a high valuation of objective understanding naturally favors a fundamental equalitarianism. For these reasons, those whose personality is unified on the foundation provided by this philosophy are apt to be promoters of international peace resting on mutual understanding, and opponents of the narrow nationalism which stands in its way. They are apt, also, to prefer democracy to dictatorship, because the former allows the freedom of thought and of speech necessary for the exercise of disinterested love of truth, while the latter compels all intellectual inquiry to conform to stipulated governmental controls, and substitutes clever propaganda for recognition of objective fact. And, finally, they are apt to favor either socialism or a collectively controlled capitalism rather than the relatively unsocialized capitalistic structure which has prevailed throughout Western industry in the recent past. The profit-seeking motive and the spirit of aggressive competition bound up with capitalism would seem to have no place in a character founded on devotion to impartial truth; an economic order grounded in coöperative pursuit of the common good would, however, be the natural expression of such a character in its industrial activities.[26]

We may close, as before, with an outline summary of the basic assumptions of the philosophy with which we have just been occupied, so couched as to facilitate critical comparison with the philosophies already treated and those yet to be considered.

[26] See Lippmann, op. cit., Part III, for a rather conservative assessment of two of these issues in the light of this philosophical standpoint.

THE MAJOR DISPUTED ASSUMPTIONS OF THE RELIGION OF SCIENCE

1. Assumptions Concerning Man's Moral Situation
   a. He needs certainty to attain his highest good, whose nature is indicated by the experience of disappointed desire.
   b. He can attain the needed certainty through the power of his own reason.
2. Assumptions Concerning Metaphysical Knowledge
   a. The ultimate criterion of truth is the clarity of direct apprehension of an object's essence or the law of its behavior.
      (1) Correction of human reason by supernatural revelation is therefore superfluous and irrational.
   b. The ultimate structure of the world is mathematical in its determinate order and its unconcern for human welfare.
   c. Good and evil are relative to human desire.
3. Psychological Assumptions
   a. Knowledge of the real structure of the world on which we depend engenders love of that which is known.
   b. Love of truth and reality is capable of indefinite growth.
   c. Such love can transform desire and emotion into harmony with itself.

SELECTED BIBLIOGRAPHY

Browne, L. E., *Blessed Spinoza,* Macmillan, 1932.
Haeckel, E., *The Riddle of the Universe.* (Many editions.)
Lippmann, W., *A Preface to Morals,* Macmillan, 1934.
Maeterlinck, M., *Wisdom and Destiny.* (Various English editions.)
Roth, L., *Spinoza,* Little, Brown & Co., 1929.
Santayana, G., *Obiter Scripta,* chapter on "Ultimate Religion," Scribner, 1936.
Spinoza, *Ethics* (especially Parts I and V).
Spinoza, *On the Improvement of the Understanding.*
Spinoza, *Theologico-Political Treatise.*
   These works of Spinoza are available in many editions.

Chapter VIII

AGNOSTICISM

OUR ATTENTION is now to be centered on the second of the two emphases of modern science discussed in the preceding chapter. After mathematical order, empirical method! What is the nature of this method, and what was the outcome of its impact upon the assertions of the established theological creed?

ARISTOTELIAN VS. MODERN EMPIRICISM

The empirical theory with which European thinkers were familiar prior to the emergence of empiricism as employed in modern science was that of Aristotle. In sharp contrast with Plato, Aristotle had insisted that knowledge begins with particular objects of sense perception; as a result of our experience with them the form, i.e., the universal principle or law which they exhibit, is disclosed to the mind's apprehension. The universal truth is grasped through the presentation of some of its particular instances in perception—such is the essence of Aristotle's empiricism. Now, as Aristotle conceived this theory of cognitive method in his systematic statements about science, and as it was almost unanimously understood by his medieval followers, five important contrasts distinguish it from the later empiricism of modern science. As these are discussed it should be remembered that Aristotle himself sometimes spoke much more like modern empiricists than his avowed theory would seem to justify, and that his practice was still more akin to theirs than his words.

First, the place of this empirical process of distilling truth from what perception discloses in the total context of man's cognitive activities was vastly different to an Aristotelian from what it is to a. modern scientist. Aristotle thought of this operation as merely preparatory and ancillary to rational demonstration, that is, to the use of the knowledge thus reached as a basis for proving other truths which logically follow from it. Science proper consisted for him of such systematic demonstration of further propositions from principles already known; the passage from perception of objects to intuitive apprehension of their form was a necessary prior step but no part of science itself. If we ask what accounts for this attitude, the most general answer is that from the standpoint of the Greek, and also from that of the medieval world, there were few empirical discoveries of consequence waiting to be made. Valid basic truths, such as could be ascertained from the use of sense perception and were significant for the larger problems of human life, were supposed to be already known, at least by the wiser of mankind. Now in recognition of this situation, what naturally seemed most important in the early days of systematic logical theory was not a method of new discovery; pursuit of novel truths was far too rare to be seriously considered as constituting the essence of science. The fundamental matter was rather the way in which principles already established and accepted could be put to effective use in demonstrating, to a popular assembly, a court of law, or a group of young learners, conclusions which had not hitherto been generally seen to follow from those principles. In medieval times this orientation was, of course, even more widespread than it had been for the majority of Greek thinkers. The day of original revelation of truth was past; in the Bible and the pronouncements of the fathers was a storehouse of all the knowledge significant for human welfare. The need in theological science was not for a method of getting a larger number of truths, but for a way of proving what theological creed is the correct systematic interpretation of the revelation which all accepted. Original apprehension of the truths which supplied the basis of proof was here, at least before the general acceptance of natural theology, presupposed by the activity of the scientist; it was hardly a part of his task to show how it could be attained.

In the second place, and as a natural consequence of the intellectual setting just described, it did not occur to Aristotle and his followers to lay down detailed safeguards for guiding and controlling the process of empirical discovery. They seem to have assumed that all the guidance required was provided by the natural operation of such processes as perception, memory, and rational apprehension, without any special canons being held in mind nor any special routine followed. In particular, the advantages of careful experimentation, as a supplement to observation of what takes place in nature apart from human interference, were not emphasized, and it was not seen to be important that deductions from apprehended principles be put to the test of further observation before they and the principles from which they had been derived were accepted as fully warranted. Verification was thus not an explicitly prescribed feature of scientific method. This absence of safeguards accounts for the fact that many beliefs were handed down as a part of medieval science which did not at all accord with observed fact and whose falsity would have quickly become apparent had they been carefully tested. An interesting instance is the belief that the acceleration of a falling body is proportional to its weight.

Thirdly, and again as a consequence, in part, of the circumstances just mentioned, the Aristotelians did not, save for minor exceptions, realize that the results of empirical discovery are relative to the range of data known at the time, to the scientific tools available, and to the prevailing concepts of explanation and interpretation. Any clearly apprehended principle was believed to be unqualifiedly true; no possibility of future correction need be recognized and systematically provided for. Infallibility in the act of rational intuition was implicity assumed. This does not mean that the Aristotelians supposed that no thinker ever made mistakes. Then, as now, it was obvious that errors sometimes occurred. But it does mean that confidence in the competence of reason was so strong, and recognition of the limitations to its power that modern science has been forced to regard as inevitable was so generally absent, that errors were regarded as we should regard mathematical blunders; their correction would be secured by more concentrated attention or better scientific training. They need not, therefore, be provided for as a constant feature of man's intellectual history. Hence the results reached by any piece of scientific reflection were normally expected to be final; they were not consciously held as tentative and liable to subsequent improvement.

In the fourth place, certain psychological assumptions were involved in the Aristotelian empiricism which, as long as they were not replaced by clearly formulated alternatives, gave it support and enabled its features above listed to seem natural. The most important of these assumptions, from the present standpoint, was that while the lower cognitive functions, such as sensation, memory, and imagination, are dependent on certain organs of the thinker's body and on the matter of the object known, the active reason, which completes the cognitive process and apprehends the universal form, is independent in these respects. It comes into the mind from without and seems to be a disembodied universal function—one and the same for all thinkers, and unaffected by time. Thus, while the Aristotelians did not believe in Plato's doctrine that ideas are innate, implanted in the soul prior to the vicissitudes of the present life and apprehensible apart from sense experience, they did believe that when, as a result of perceptual activity, a form came to be apprehended through the active reason, that apprehension carried the degree of certainty with which such an exalted function would naturally endow it. This psychological theory, of course, lent support to the assumption above noted, that knowledge does not ordinarily need correction, and to the feeling that the course of empirical discovery needs no control by a system of canons or rules.

In the fifth place, this absence of anticipation that future correction might be needed involved another consequence than the one just mentioned. Modern empiricism, as a method of scientific discovery, has been vitally affected by the fact that the universal laws in nature which men seek to establish are expected to be such as will permit dependable prediction and effective control of future events by their aid. This expectation restricts the meaning of all explanatory concepts used in the process of discovering truth; in particular, it limits in a very definite way the meaning of the concept of causal connection, as will be noted in due time. But Aristotelian empiricism was not influenced by any such demand for power of prediction and control over nature. All that was implicitly asked of its results was that they should assume such a pattern as would render events rationally intelligible. This meant merely that behind the variety of particular things should be seen forms that are constant and capable of entering into systematic relation with other forms in nature. But they need not be predictive laws. In fact, the Greeks had no ambition to control physical nature, and their notions of rationality and of explanation would not naturally therefore reflect such an ambition. In medieval times such worldly interests were, by and large, condemned on principle, as substituting a transient for an eternal good; the important thing was to understand the world in terms which would illumine the career of the soul and guide it to its immortal destiny. The empirical method of Thomas obviously harmonized throughout with such a guiding interest.

Now the mathematical rationalists with whom we were occupied in the preceding chapter proposed no fundamental transformation of empirical theory in these respects. If anything, they were less empirical (as modern thinkers understand empiricism) than Aristotle himself.[1] Most of them believed that there are innate truths in the mind not derived from sense perception. They hoped that mathematical method would provide a way of discovery as well as a way of demonstration. This hope proved chimerical, so far as truths of physical nature are concerned. But there was gradually appearing, even during the epoch of Thomas Aquinas, a conviction that science could not manage successfully without assigning a larger significance to empirical method, and that the prevailing conceptions of that method were inadequate, needing criticism and correction. This conviction became especially widespread and influential in England. A long succession of thinkers arose who contributed toward the development of a new empiricism, which not only transformed the theory of science but also exerted a profound influence on philosophy and religion. This development at first was faltering and somewhat incoherent. But during the century and a half following the year 1600 a number of geniuses in science and philosophy appeared, whose combined efforts were sufficient to give definite form to the new theory. They made it an intellectually defensible and practically usable alternative both to the mathematical rationalism of the Cartesians and to the traditional empiricism of the Aristotelians.

[1] This statement should be qualified in the case of Galileo.

In general terms, the result of their work was a radical revision of the prevailing idea of the task of science. From being primarily a method of demonstration, to which original apprehension of true principles was a necessary but subordinate preliminary, science becomes primarily a method of discovering new truth, in which demonstration fills a requisite but subsidiary function. And the heart of this method of discovery consists in a technique for systematically using the facilities of sense perception, which now supplies not only the starting point but also the court of ultimate appeal in the establishment of truth about nature. Science, thus revised, came to be regarded as essentially an expanding enterprise, constantly widening the boundaries of human knowledge by the addition of new truth, empirically grounded.

MAIN CONTRIBUTORS TO THE NEW EMPIRICISM

We shall only take note of the specific contributions of the men who shaped the new empiricism so far as is necessary to clarify its essential nature and the manner of its impact upon religion.

The first thinker in this development over whom we should pause is Sir Francis Bacon, who at the year 1600 was entering a period of great influence and political influence. In many aspects of his thought Bacon reflects the character of his time, but on three of the five points above discussed he challenged the empiricism of the Aristotelians and gave clear expression to ideas that other thinkers were struggling less successfully to master. He was vividly conscious that the knowledge of nature at the disposal of men was sadly deficient; in his well-known *Advancement of Learning* he exemplified a viewpoint previously very rare by surveying the field of science in the attempt to indicate where new discovery was especially needed. He was eager, too, for knowledge on such terms as would render possible the largest measure of human control over physical nature, reducing her to the status of a subjugated empire. In this ideal he believed the proper end of science to be found. Hence he boldly demanded a new method, which he realized quite clearly must be explicitly a method of discovery, devised to correct inadequacies in the accepted Aristotelian procedure; that his interest in control affected the meaning of the concepts used in this method he did not so definitely see. The essence of the new method, in his eyes, was to go to the empirical facts in a much more humble and persistently teachable mood than had been characteristic of most previous inquirers, and to learn, by dint of systematic experiment as well as by patient observation, all the instruction that they might give. To be controlled, nature must first be carefully obeyed. The great mistake in the empirical procedure of the Aristotelians, besides their failure to recognize the true end of scientific knowledge, was in his judgment hasty and large-scale generalization. On the basis of a meager examination of a few facts they jumped to the assertion of general principles, from which deductions were blithely drawn and pronounced without more ado to be true of the objects to which they referred. One of the ways recommended by Bacon for avoiding this mistake is to follow certain canons in the inductive process of establishing universal laws on the evidence supplied by observed instances of those laws. He especially emphasized the importance of studying the event investigated under widely varying conditions, of comparing cases where the event occurs with cases otherwise similar in which it does not occur, and of noting situations in which its essential character is present in different degrees. In these discussions it is evident that Bacon's conception of causality has been mainly determined by his interest in discovering laws such as would permit prediction and control of similar events in the future by their aid, and is widely different from the conceptions present in Thomas and Spinoza; he assumes that the cause of an occurrence is the condition or complex of conditions in the presence of which the occurrence regularly takes place—and which, therefore, if artificially produced, can be counted upon to produce the effect. The bearing of this difference on the theological use of the concept of causality will soon be considered.

Sir Isaac Newton's greatest works were being published during the two decades following 1686. In him we have a scientist who, in addition to his other achievements, made important contributions to modern empirical theory. On the practical side his most significant addition consisted in showing how the mathematical and empirical emphases can be appropriately united in the process of discovery, in such a way as to secure, in the results reached, both faithfulness to

relevant facts of perception and exactitude of mathematical formulation. As regards the philosophy of empiricism, he insisted on two
important points which had escaped Bacon.
One was the necessity of predictive verification of asserted
explanations through observation or experiment. Except for an
occasional stray thinker without influence, this had not been
regarded as essential prior to Newton's time. It was usually taken
for granted that the explanation intuitively conceived, as a result
of analysis of the observations with which the scientist's thinking
began, would be adequate to all the facts which naturally fall
under its scope. Even Bacon's canons did not go beyond the
function of guiding the classification of these observations and
their analysis as guides to the formation of possible explanations.
According to Newton, the scientist has not reached the end of his
task when by such analysis he has conceived a general law and
has deduced detailed implications from that law as to what happens
in fields or under conditions not yet specifically examined. These
deductions must be verified by further observation or experiment.
It is not enough, in other words, that the formulated law be consistent with the empirical facts whose analysis had originally
led to its apprehension. One of the main scientific functions of
such a law is to guide confident prediction of future observable
facts. Surely, then, the only way to tell whether a generalization
can adequately fill this function, and to tell in how broad terms
it may properly be formulated, is to turn to some of the further
specific facts that ought to occur if the law be true and see whether
or not they do occur. In the language of subsequent discussions
of scientific method, an explanatory law, prior to such verification,
must be regarded merely as a hypothesis; experimental verification,
if successful, first gives it the status of an established law.

An illustration which brings out with special force the importance of such verification may be taken from one of Kepler's studies.
Suppose that, on the basis of certain observations of the planet
Mars which seem inconsistent with the traditional theory that the
planetary orbits are circles, we are led to the hypothesis that the
orbit is really an ellipse. Can we affirm this hypothesis as true
merely on the ground that the recorded observations already at our
disposal appear to be consistent with the supposition? No,

for these observations only record certain positions of the planet at certain times, and these positions are reconcilable, especially when lack of precision in our instruments is allowed for, with other geometrical curves besides the ellipse. But if, adopting the elliptical orbit as a hypothesis, we deduce from it the series of positions which the planet ought to occupy at various future times, and find these deductions empirically verified within the limits of experimental error, the theory stands on a much more solid footing than it had occupied before. And this is unanswerably the case if not all these verifying observations are consistent with deductions drawn from alternative theories. Newton insists that such considerations hold good universally in empirical science.

The other point emphasized by Newton was that even verified laws must be regarded as tentative, not absolute and final. They are dependent on, and relative to, the range of observations known at the time they are formulated. Accordingly, they are always liable to correction by future experience. New facts may at any time be perceived which are inconsistent with them; if so, the task of science is to attain a formulation that is true to such new experiences as well as to the facts which the older explanation had taken into account. Other scientific thinkers of Newton's day, notably Robert Boyle, also stressed the essential tentativeness of empirical truth.

If we stop to consider for a moment the implications of these changes in the theory of empirical method, it will be evident that they involve a fundamental shift in what is regarded as the central step of the process of induction. For Aristotelians the crucial and decisive step was the intuitive apprehension of the form or law of the event to be explained; everything else was preparatory and subordinate to this seizure by reason of a universal truth. For the new empiricism the decisive factor and the ultimate court of appeal is sense perception; explanation begins and ends with observation of relevant facts. The birth of rational ideas is important, but they are not self-justifying; they must submit to the test of further sense experience. Apart from such verification they are incomplete and hypothetical. Factual observation alone is final.

Now it might have been possible for a thinker familiar with this transformation to state, merely on the basis of the considerations just surveyed, the essential criterion of truth in our ideas about the world which they implied. Obviously, that criterion, simply put, is this: An idea is true if it corresponds in detail with the sense perceptions which it purports to explain. The self-evidence of rational apprehension is no adequate test of truth from this standpoint; neither is the clarity and distinctness with which an idea is conceived, as Descartes and Spinoza believed. But if its every feature is verifiable in observation, then it is shown to be true. However, as a matter of historical fact, clear formulation of this empirical criterion awaited the development of a psychological theory appropriate to the new scientific emphasis, and was first expressed in terms provided by that theory. Its initial expression was very inadequate, but did not in practice lead to serious confusion.

John Locke, a contemporary and friend of Newton, propounded an empirical psychology of cognition as an alternative to Aristotle's doctrine and other theories which reigned at the time. The decisive feature of his position lay in the fact that when it is accepted one would expect that a true idea must correspond in detail with the perceptual facts which it claims to explain, whereas in terms of those other theories no one would expect such correspondence. According to Locke, the mind has no innate ideas about the world; all ideas are nothing but sense perceptions or their copies in memory and imagination. Their origin lies either in sensation, which is the mind's immediate commerce with external physical objects, or in reflection, which is the mind's perception of its own activities and operations. The mind can combine them in new ways, but all ideas are of exclusively empirical origin. Thus any ideas which could plausibly claim to be true of what we have experienced in perception would have to be copies of those perceptions as retained in memory. To appreciate the historical force of this position it is important to recall that Aristotelianism did not, any more than Platonism or the mathematical rationalism of Spinoza, identify explanatory ideas with memory-images, which in the nature of the case are always particular and concrete entities, since they are apprehensions of a universal form or abstract essence. They are dependent on sense perception for their occurrence, but they transcend its specific and temporally limited character. As long as such theories prevailed, a radically empirical criterion of truth was not likely to be proposed, since on these terms no one would look for detailed correspondence between an explanatory idea and a perception.

Hume's Conception of Empirical Method

In the situation prepared by these various circumstances arose one of England's greatest philosophical thinkers, David Hume. Born in 1711, he challenged the reflective world by a series of important writings which appeared from the late 'thirties till after his death in 1777. He was familiar with the development of empirical science, and was a convinced follower of Locke in his radically empirical doctrine of the origin of ideas and of knowledge. From our stand-point, his most important contribution consisted in the formulation of a general criterion of truth on the foundations provided by his empiricist predecessors, and in his examination of the main doctrines of theology in the light of this criterion.

Hume used the term "impression" to denote an original perception, either of some external object or of some activity of the mind. He used the term "idea" to denote any later copy of such an impression presenting itself in memory or imagination. In view of the assumptions which he shared with Locke, idea as thus understood includes all laws and principles proposed as explanations in science, philosophy, and religion, as well as all simple recollections of earlier experience, since all alike can only arise as copies of some antecedent impression. Now Hume sees in this relation a general criterion which can be applied whenever any idea falls under our suspicion of being possibly false. His rule is: Trace it back to the impression from which it is derived. If it corresponds to that impression, then it is valid; if it does not correspond, then it must be abandoned as erroneous or corrected so that its meaning will correspond to the impression. Armed with this criterion of truth, Hume proceeds to examine some fundamental conceptions in science and religion.

Although this formulation is entirely natural, in view of Locke's and Hume's preoccupation with the problem of the origin of ideas, it is seriously defective. Strictly speaking, no one can trace an idea back to the impression *from which* it was derived. Such an impression (or collection of similar impressions) occurred in the past and is now dead and gone. What we can do and actually do where possible is to compare the idea with some present impression of the same object, or of an object belonging to the same class. If I am in doubt as to whether my idea of the location of a certain book in my library is correct or not, what I do is not to recover any original impression but to obtain a present impression of that location and compare the idea with it. Despite Hume's mode of statement, however, his actual procedure takes account of this circumstance, so far as the nature of the problems which he wishes his readers to consider allows. His results, then, are not vitally affected by this inadequacy.

Let us begin with a summary of Hume's application of this criterion to the scientific and philosophical concept of causality, for the result of this analysis has important bearings on his treatment of religious beliefs. The fundamental difficulty which he faces here concerns the *necessity* that people ordinarily suppose to characterize a causal connection: they believe that the cause exerts some kind of compulsion over the effect, dragging it into existence willy-nilly. Given the occurrence of the cause, the effect not only does happen, it must happen—so, at least, we readily believe. This "must," however, raises a serious problem from the empirical standpoint as it had now come to be conceived.

Hume's method, of course, is to ask the question: From what impression is the idea of causal necessity derived? And his answer, reached by appealing to typical experiences of causal connection, is as follows: If we examine any particular instance of a cause-effect relation, we can discover in it only two essential features. First, the cause and the effect are contiguous in time. Second, the cause precedes the effect. But neither of these relations involves any necessity that the effect should follow on the occurrence of the cause. The eating of bread, experience teaches us, brings relief to an empty stomach. In any case of this relation, what we can observe is: first, an impression of the eating; then, following closely upon it in time, an impression of the cessation of hunger and of its natural organic accompaniments. Here is temporal contiguity, here is also precedence of the effect by the cause; but where is the impression underlying our notion that the effect "must" follow the cause, our assurance that any future occurrence of the cause will be followed by the occurrence of the effect?

Suppose we expand the inquiry by taking into consideration other cases of the same causal connection. Each of them, taken alone, reveals simply the two factors just mentioned and nothing more, but by bringing together all our experiences of the same sort we may add a third important point to the analysis—namely, that every time we have eaten bread in the past our hunger has been satisfied by it. Still, however, we appear to find no impression of necessity. The circumstance that we have always experienced such an effect to follow upon such a cause contains, of itself, no warrant that the same effect will follow upon the same cause in the future. We sometimes meet exceptions to relations between events that had previously been quite regular. What has not yet taken place is therefore not certain to take place, and its occurrence is not necessary. "Eating bread has always satisfied my hunger" is one proposition; "eating bread will satisfy my hunger in the future" is another proposition, and the latter cannot logically be deduced from the former. We all believe it, of course, but that is not the point in question. What we are after is an impression to underlie and justify our idea of necessity in this causal relation.

The conclusion thus reached to Hume's primary inquiry in this matter is that we cannot find any impression which would seem to give validity to the notion of causal necessity. It would appear to be an illegitimate and perhaps even meaningless idea. We expect the same effects always to follow from the same causes, of course, but that expectation would appear to rest on no adequate empirical foundation. For aught we can tell, the course of nature may at any moment change, and entirely different effects might follow from familiar causes.

But a second, though closely connected, problem now arises. Since, according to Hume's position, an idea is always a copy of an antecedent impression, there must be some experiential foundation for the idea of causal necessity or the idea would never have been entertained by anybody. What is the impression from which this idea actually derives, and how have we come to mistake for it a different impression which does not exist?

Hume's answer to this question rests mainly on an appeal to habit. If the eating of bread had only been followed by the cessation of hunger on one single occasion in the past, and on other occasions had been associated with different occurrences, we should not expect that it would appease hunger in the future nor should we feel any necessity in the connection between those two events. But the connection has been repeated many times in our experience, and we have noticed no case in which the antecedent (bread-eating) has not been followed by the consequent (satisfaction of hunger). This unfailing repetition has built up a vivid association in our minds between the events thus regularly connected, and one aspect of that association is a strong habit of expectancy. Having an impression of the cause, our mind is inevitably carried to an idea of the effect—we confidently expect it, trustingly await it. Now, Hume holds, it is this vivid association in our minds, built up by habitual repetition of cause and effect in our past experience, that underlies our feeling of compulsion in the connection between them. The impression from which the notion of necessity is really derived is that of the smooth and easy transition in our minds from the impression or idea of the cause to the idea of the effect. The necessity is not in the external events—so far as our experience of them goes, the connection is entirely contingent and might fail at any time—it is in us, in our inevitable anticipation of the effect, given the cause.

The idea of causal necessity is thus invalid if we interpret it to mean that there is some mysterious logical bond between cause and effect which compels the latter to follow upon the former. It is only valid if it is interpreted as psychological necessity—that is, as the inevitable expectation in our minds of the effect when the cause occurs, an expectation established by the constant connection between the two in our past experience.[2]

It is well to note at this juncture that although Hume is not aware of the historical contrasts involved, he conceives the causal relation as the growing movement of empirical science had come to interpret it. The conception is quite different, both from that of Thomas and from that of Spinoza, for the context of ideas

---

[2] Hume, *Treatise on Human Nature*, Book I, Part III. *Enquiry Concerning the Human Understanding*, secs. IV–VII.

and attitudes in which it is embedded is of another order. For
Thomas, causality is the intellectual principle by which we proceed
in our quest from this or that particular object of sense experience
to the ultimate source of all reality and all good, on whose providential care our eternal welfare depends. Its meaning, as applied to
any specific connection of objects, is determined by the expectation
that the mind can pursue that quest successfully, and by the whole
network of assumptions which it involves. For Spinoza, causality
is the relation between a defined essence and the detailed theorems
which can be mathematically demonstrated from it, permitting
a fundamental adjustment, based on clear and certain knowledge,
to the necessary order whose nature is disclosed in the definition.
It is evident that in both these sets of assumptions causality is so
conceived that the notion of a primary or ultimate cause is essential—in fact, the relation between particular causes and effects only
validly holds because all alike are grounded in an absolute cause
from which all flow in a determinate sequence. But the postulates
underlying the conception of causality in modern empirical science
are very remote from the ones dominating the thought of these men.
They express the newly influential interest in predicting and controlling future events in terms of the guidance provided by past
experience of events of the same kind. From this standpoint, the
essence of causal connection is simply such a relation between two
events as permits a confident forecast (and, if possible, control)
of the later on the occurrence of the earlier. Constancy of experienced sequence between cause and effect is all that is required,
provided we assume also that future experience will be like the
past. In this context the meaning of causality seems to be such
that the notion of ultimate cause is not at all involved. All causes
and effects are particular events in time, and are in principle capable
of empirical observation, so that predictions of what is going
to take place can be tested by our future experience. Hume, in
common with most thinkers whose attitudes harmonize with those
of empirical science and whose dominant conceptions have been
molded by it, thinks of causality in these terms. This is indicated
by his favorite illustrations, and by the kind of experience to which
he turns when searching for the foundations of the idea of causal
necessity. The bearing of this transformation in the meaning of the

category of cause on religious problems is exceedingly important, as the following paragraphs will attempt to show.

We shall now follow Hume in the application of his criterion of truth to the three important religious themes which he specifically considers.[3] In each of these cases he does not formally begin, as he did in his analysis of causality, by asking from what impression the idea under discussion is derived. But it is quite clear that this is the method of analysis which he constantly has in mind, and his examination proceeds exactly as it would were it guided by this question. For reasons to be later explained, we shall regard Hume in these arguments as spokesman for the agnostic point of view, and hence shall give no separate summary of its reasoning.

His Criticism of Belief in Miracles

First, his treatment of belief in miracles.[4] In his famous discussion of this subject there are some ambiguities in his definitions, and the conclusions which he draws sometimes go beyond what his guiding principles would justify. The following analysis aims to bring out the main burden of his argument as it would stand if freed from these questionable features.

In view of what has been said about his theory of causality, it is clear that Hume cannot consistently reject belief in miracles on the ground that would have been sufficient for Spinoza—namely, that the mind clearly intuits the world as a necessary order, in which every event is inexorably determined to happen by some definite cause. Hume's discussion of causal necessity leaves no empirical support for such a contention. What he must do is to seek the impressions in terms of which belief in miracles is to be validated, if such validation is possible. Now, a miracle (as Hume defines it) is a violation of, or exception to, the laws of nature. It follows at once that no one could have any impression of a miraculous event. Nothing prevents, of course, his observing an exception to what he had previously regarded, in the light of his experience to date, as a law of nature. But if he did notice an exception he would—or should —at once reject the law as not being genuinely such, since only

---

[3] Excluding his treatment of the *Natural History of Religion*.
[4] Contained in sec. X of his *Enquiry Concerning Human Understanding*.

unexceptional regularity justifies the assertion of causal law. Its very meaning is that of a completely dependable relationship between cause and effect. Consequently, experience of an exception would remove the regularity in question from the class "laws of nature" and reduce it to the status of a high probability, to which further exceptions would naturally be expected. It is impossible, then, for us to experience a miracle directly.[5] But sometimes the reports of other people tell us of the occurrence of events which are exceptions to natural regularities hitherto, so far as our personal experience is concerned, entirely uniform. Under what conditions is it reasonable for us to accept such reports as true, i.e., to believe that those strange events actually occurred? This is the question to which the body of Hume's discussion is addressed.

Now this question, of course, for Hume, can only be properly answered by applying the empirical test. And this means, in effect, that we weigh our experience of the reliability of human testimony (and of the particular sort of testimony present in any given case) against our experience of the law of nature to which, it is claimed, there occurred an exception, and decide which of the two is the more trustworthy. When I am told, for instance, that at a certain place and time a dead man was raised to life I consider (or should, if nothing but application of the appropriate empirical test affected my judgment) which is the more likely: that such an extraordinary event, to which my previous experience offers no parallel, really happened, or that there was some mistake or deception in the sequence of testimony through which the report that it happened reached me?

[5] Hume fails to consider here the Catholic view which entirely rejects this contention. The rejection is based, of course, on the position, taken to be adequately established on other grounds, that the ultimate cause of the universe is a personal God, the so-called "laws of nature" being expressions of his orderly plan for his creation. Since, however, those laws are continually subject to his will, and since physical regularity is subordinate to his moral purpose for man, it is to be expected that physical law will occasionally be set aside in the interest of furthering such moral ends. When the devout Catholic, holding this background of ideas, witnesses an extraordinary event he has no logical difficulty in experiencing it as a miracle. A law still remains a law after he has seen miraculous exceptions to it. The issue between Hume and such a point of view depends on whether this doctrine of God and of his relation to the physical order is warranted or not. Hume's answer, therefore, to the Catholic view of miracles is really given in his treatment of the problem of God. See below, pp. 217–225.

And I believe that it really occurred only if I am persuaded, after this reflective consideration, that such a mistake or deception in the testimony would be more extraordinary than the actual return of the dead man to life. The principle to apply, as stated by Hume, is "that no testimony is sufficient to establish a miracle, unless the testimony be of such a kind that its falsehood would be more miraculous than the fact which it endeavors to establish."[6]

What general conclusions emerge regarding the legitimacy of belief in miracles when we make systematic use of this principle?

Well, first, it is evident that our experience always affords as full and complete a proof as is possible that any alleged miracle did not really occur. For (as has been noted above) it would not be a miracle unless the law to which it is an exception has been quite uniform—unless, in other words, our experience of it hitherto has been entirely constant. Judged in the light of past experience, then, the likelihood that the miracle did not occur is as great as any empirical likelihood could possibly be. On the other hand, our experience of the reliability of testimony is not by any means so uniform as our experience of such laws of nature as that dead men stay dead. We know that testimony is often mistaken, and that people frequently lie and deceive. The easy spread of spicy gossip is a case in point. Moreover, when reports of extraordinary events are concerned, love of the marvelous, a very strong human emotion, comes into play, and is apt to supersede the critical caution which we otherwise usually observe in deciding what it is plausible to believe. The net result, so far, then, would be that the balance of empirical probability is always against testimony to the occurrence of a miracle. It is more likely that the testimony was mistaken than that the extraordinary event really happened.

But other factors must not be forgotten. We know, second, that our personal experience is very limited, and that many events take place which have not heretofore come within its reach. And we often learn of such events through the testimony of others. Now, since our own experience occasionally presents us with exceptions to regularities which had previously been quite uniform, it is reasonable to expect that we shall sometimes be apprised of such

---

[6] *Enquiry Concerning Human Understanding* (Open Court ed.), p. 121. Notice that "miraculous" here means simply "strange" or "surprising."

exceptions first by other people. With this consideration in mind, we see that it is just as unreasonable to be overskeptical as to be credulous in dealing with testimony. There are times when we ought to accept reports of events even though they announce the occurrence of exceptions to our uniform past experience; the ultimate empirical court of appeal indicates that there are cases when belief in such reports would be amply justified by the sequel. There is a group of instances, in other words, to which the general comparative principle reached in the preceding paragraph does not apply. In them testimony is more likely to be trustworthy than the conclusion naturally drawn from our own previous experience. What canons ought to guide us in selecting these cases?

Hume himself gives a considerable part of the answer to this question.[7] If the testimony to an exceptional event is given by a sufficient number of men, reporting independently of each other, and agreeing in every relevant detail; if they are men of good sense, education, sober critical judgment, and unquestioned integrity; if they had nothing to gain by falsehood or deception; if the event in question occurred publicly and in a well-known part of the world so that the records describing it could be checked further; and if there are plausible analogies between it and events with which our experience has made us familiar—then it may be reasonable to accord a balance of favorable judgment to the testimony and enlarge our own experience by its aid. When these circumstances conspire together in testimony to a novel occurrence it would be foolish to refuse credence simply because our own narrow experience fails to include instances of such an event. Experience itself teaches that under these conditions testimony is usually reliable.

But there is a third important consideration. Miracles which are announced as a foundation for belief in a religious system— as warrant for the supernatural claims of a special revelation—are, Hume asserts, so patently untrustworthy that they can be confidently rejected without serious examination of the testimony supporting them. Several reasons are given for this contention. For one thing, testimony to the occurrence of such miracles is always found to fail in one or more of the characteristics just mentioned which are

[7] *Ibid.*, pp. 122, 134 f.

requisite to justifiable belief. Those wondrous events happened among ignorant and superstitious people; records about them rarely agree and were never critically checked when the evidence was fresh and readily available. For another, religious fervor is naturally allied, as experience teaches, with certain qualities whose tendency is opposed to reliability and full integrity.

A religionist may be an enthusiast, and imagine he sees what has no reality: he may know his narrative to be false, and yet persevere in it with the best intentions in the world, for the sake of promoting so holy a cause; or even where this delusion has not place, vanity, excited by so strong a temptation, operates on him more powerfully than on the rest of mankind in any other circumstances; and self-interest with equal force. His auditors may not have, and commonly have not sufficient judgment to canvass his evidence: what judgment they have, they renounce by principle in these sublime and mysterious subjects: or if they were ever so willing to employ it, passion and a heated imagination disturb the regularity of its operations. Their credulity increases his impudence: and his impudence overpowers their credulity.[8]

Still another reason lies in the fact that different religious systems, each claiming to possess the sole supernatural revelation to mankind, appeal in substantiation of their claims to the same kind of testimony. We cannot reasonably believe any of the miracles thus reported without believing them all, for the evidence is similar; but we cannot reasonably believe them all, for the revelations they authenticate contradict each other at certain vital points. Hence we have no recourse but to reject all these testimonies to extraordinary events as the product of credulity and delusion. Religious miracles, then, are shown by experience entirely to fall under the general principle first above formulated.

It is experience only, which gives authority to human testimony; and it is the same experience which assures us of the laws of nature. When, therefore, these two kinds of experience are contrary, we have nothing to do but subtract the one from the other, and embrace an opinion, either on one side or the other, with that assurance which arises from the remainder. But according to the principle here explained, this subtraction, with regard to all popular religions, amounts to an entire annihilation; and therefore we may establish it as a maxim, that no human testimony can have such force as to prove a miracle, and make it a just foundation for any such system of religion.[9]

[8] *Ibid.*, pp. 123 f.
[9] *Ibid.*, p. 134.

It might be objected, Hume observes, that in the case of religious miracles our ordinary ways of deciding what is probable or improbable do not apply, for the Being held responsible for these wondrous events possesses infinite power to do whatever he might wish.[10] His answer to this objection reveals more emphatically than ever the fundamental place that he gives to his empirical criterion of truth and his complete confidence in it. Suppose such a being does exist; still, the only way in which we learn what he does is by our experience of the effects that he produces, as the course of nature reveals them. Exceptions to what we had taken to be the laws of nature, and likewise exceptions to exact truth in the testimony of men, are due, then, ultimately to him, and we are still reduced to our past observation of such matters if we are to judge intelligently which of these two kinds of exception is most likely to be present in any given case. Since our experience shows that exceptions to truth in the testimony concerning religious miracles are far more frequent than such miracles themselves, we naturally form the appropriate general resolution for the guidance of our beliefs which such experience teaches.

His Argument Regarding Belief in God

But can we reasonably believe that there is such a being as men call God? Is the evidence from which this idea is derived adequate to prove it valid?

In Hume's day the conception of God common to all theological parties was that of the First Cause of the universe. Behind and beyond the various chains of secondary causes and effects in the observable course of nature, reason seemed to demand an original initiator and necessary ground of the whole complex of events composing the world. As each particular occurrence must be accounted for by a particular cause, so the order and sequence of things taken as an entirety must be explained as the effect of a First Cause. Hume applies his empirical principles to the examination of this contention.[11]

[10] *Ibid.*, p. 136.
[11] The works which deal systematically with this problem are his *Dialogues Concerning Natural Religion, Natural History of Religion,* and sec. XI of his *Enquiry Concerning Human Understanding.*

Two general arguments are offered, and each of these emphasizes two distinct considerations. The first argument raises the question whether the very conception of First Cause is not logically and empirically unjustifiable. The second assumes its legitimacy and deals with the question: What kind of being would a cause of the total experienced universe be?

One consideration emphasized in connection with the first argument is that the notion of a First Cause would seem to be superfluous. Take a chain of twenty events, the first being cause of the second, the second of the third, the third of the fourth, and so on. The first, of course, will be the effect of the last event in some preceding sequence. Now, in thus assigning the cause of each of these twenty events in detail, have we not provided all the causal explanation that is requisite in the case? Each event in the chain is causally accounted for—what more do we seek?

In such a chain, or succession of objects, each part is caused by that which preceded it, and causes that which succeeds it. . . . But the WHOLE, you say, wants a cause. I answer, that the uniting of these parts into a whole, like the uniting of several distinct counties into one kingdom, or several distinct members into one body, is performed merely by an arbitrary act of the mind, and has no influence on the nature of things. Did I show you the particular causes of each individual in a collection of twenty particles of matter, I should think it very unreasonable, should you afterwards ask me, what was the cause of the whole twenty. That is sufficiently explained in explaining the cause of the parts.[12]

The other consideration brought forward as part of the same general argument points toward a more radical conclusion—that the conception of First Cause is not merely superfluous but also meaningless. Here Hume wishes us to think seriously of his analysis of the empirical foundations which give meaning to the category of causality. He has there shown, he believes, that a single experience of an event affords no basis for the use of this concept. Such an event is empirically neither cause nor effect. To apply these latter terms with meaning we must have two temporally contiguous events whose conjunction has been repeated in various experiences; only then can be built up the vivid anticipation of an effect, on observa-

[12] *Dialogues Concerning Natural Religion*, Part IX.

tion of its cause, which distinguishes a case of causality from one of mere temporal succession. When, then, we experience an event otherwise than as a term in such a regularly repeated conjunction, there is no basis for calling it either a cause or an effect—it just exists. Now the universe taken as a whole is in exactly this case. There is only one cosmos; it is a unique entity. We observe it, but not its cause. Or, more fully, we have had no experience of the production of various worlds, so as to tell what antecedent experience, if any, bears a regular relation to the appearance of a universe; in the nature of the case such experience is impossible. How, then, can we significantly think of the universe as an effect at all?

Or—what comes to the same in practice—if we persist in calling such a unique entity as the universe an effect, how can we make any rational conjecture whatever as to what its cause might be? In advance of experience we cannot tell in the least what sort of event will be regularly connected with any other sort of event— who would suppose beforehand that the time of descent of a falling body would be connected with its distance from the center of the earth rather than with its weight? Well, if we have had no direct experience of a cause preceding the emergence of its effect, are we not quite helpless in trying to decide what sort of entity that cause would be?

I much doubt whether it be possible for a cause to be known only by its effect . . . or to be of so singular and particular a nature as to have no parallel and no similarity with any other cause or object that has ever fallen under our observation. It is only when two species of objects are found to be constantly conjoined, that we can infer the one from the other; and were an effect presented which was entirely singular, and could not be comprehended under any known *species,* I do not see that we could form any conjecture or inference at all concerning its cause. If experience and observation and analogy be, indeed, the only guides which we can reasonably follow in inferences of this nature; both the effect and cause must bear a similarity and resemblance to other effects and causes which we know, and which we have found, in many instances, to be conjoined with each other.[13]

Were this argument entirely sound and convincing, it would be quite conclusive and would hardly require supplementation by further discussion. Hume is aware, however, that only the few

[13] *Enquiry,* pp. 156 f.

converts to his analysis of causality would be persuaded by it and he is, perhaps, not perfectly sure in his own mind that this radical application of his principles is cogent. After all, even a very singular event will show some analogies to other events which we have experienced in conjunction with their causes, and do we not ordinarily assume the right to make constructive use of such analogies in explaining an unusual occurrence, even though we have had no opportunity to observe its cause? In Hume's day the most widely used proof of God was an analogical proof of this kind. The scientists, led by the great genius Newton and encouraged by the philosophy of Descartes, had taught the educated world to think of the physical and astronomical universe as a vast machine, like a clock in the regularity, intricacy, and mutual adjustment of its many motions. Now a clock is the effect of the intelligent activity of a clockmaker; hence, so it was reasoned, the universe so similar to it must be the effect of an intelligence greater than the clockmaker's, but likewise similar. Hume could not entirely reject this argument. He felt its force in his own thinking when the mood of radical skepticism was absent, and he was not sure that his empirical criterion required its complete abandonment. He was sure, however, of two principles which were being constantly violated in the theological discussions of this problem, and in his longest work on religion, the *Dialogues Concerning Natural Religion,* it is these principles which he is most concerned to emphasize. We turn, then, to the second main argument which he develops.

Suppose we grant that it may be legitimate to think of the whole experienced universe as an effect, and to define God as its Author or Cause. What attributes does the observed evidence permit us justifiably to assign to this Cause, and what degree of perfection in each of those attributes may we suppose him to possess?

In discussing this question, Hume is concerned first to emphasize that a fair assessment of the evidence on which we here rest shows that any analogy whatever that is capable of being used as a clue is exceedingly weak. So weak is it, in fact, that if we cannot maintain a complete suspension of judgment (which, where it is possible, would be the most reasonable attitude) we should recognize that any positive conclusion has only a slight probability of being true. The phenomena of the universe are so varied in their properties that selection of any one kind of event as especially similar to the whole and therefore as providing a key to its nature is extremely hazardous. "Can a conclusion, with any propriety, be transferred from parts to the whole? Does not the great disproportion bar all comparison and inference? From observing the growth of a hair, can we learn anything concerning the generation of a man? Would the manner of a leaf's blowing, even though perfectly known, afford us any instruction concerning the vegetation of a tree?"[14]

In the next place, when we examine the total impression that the universe makes upon us, it is not by any means clear that its similarity to a machine is so much closer than other similarities, that the analogy of an intelligent author can be confidently given preference. Taken as a whole, the universe shows analogies with an animal, or a plant, or a colony of organisms, at least as plausibly as with a machine. But if we were to draw our key from those analogies, the First Cause would be conceived as some sort of generative principle, or blind vitality, not as an intelligence.[15] More-over, even though we decide to cast our lot for the mechanical analogy, and appeal to an intelligent author, must we not proceed to view him in turn as an effect and inquire after his cause?[16] In our experience, intelligence is not a self-explanatory thing; it has its own causal conditions through whose operation it arises. This circum-stance surely indicates that, if we hold the universe to be the effect of intelligence, we must likewise hold the intelligence that produced it to be the effect of some more remote cause. And this latter will point still further—we are lost in an infinite regress. But if, seeing the futility of this procedure, we decide that it is necessary to stop somewhere, why not stop before we have taken the first step beyond the experienced effect? Why not simply say that there is some principle of order operative in the material universe, ac-counting for those features in it which resemble a machine, and take no dubious second step, such as identifying that principle with a divine intelligence, at all?[17] Finally, if we blink at all these difficulties, we still must recognize that intelligence, in a being

[14] *Dialogues,* Part II.
[15] *Ibid.,* Parts VI, VII.
[16] *Ibid.,* Part IV.
[17] *Ibid.,* Part IV.

supposed to be the omniscient author of the entire universe, is
so very different in its properties from intelligence as we experience
it that it becomes questionable how far the adopted analogy has
definite meaning. Intelligence in man is

a composition of various faculties, passions, sentiments, ideas; united,
indeed, into one self or person, but still distinct from each other. When it
reasons, the ideas . . . arrange themselves in a certain form or order,
which is not preserved entire for a moment, but immediately gives place
to another arrangement. New opinions, new passions, new affections, new
feelings arise, which continually diversify the mental scene, and produce
in it the greatest variety and most rapid succession imaginable. How
is this compatible with that perfect immutability and simplicity which
all true theists ascribe to the Deity? By the same act, say they, he sees
past, present, and future; his love and his hatred, his mercy and his
justice, are one individual operation. . . . No succession, no change, no
acquisition, no diminution . . . He stands fixed in one simple, perfect
state; nor can you ever say, with any propriety, that this act of his is
different from that other, or that this judgment or idea has been lately
formed, and will give place, by succession, to any different judgment
or idea.

Should we not affirm that "a mind, whose acts and sentiments and
ideas are not distinct and successive; one that is wholly simple
and totally immutable; is a mind which has no thought, no reason,
no will, no sentiment, no love, no hatred; or, in a word, is no mind
at all. It is an abuse of terms to give it that appellation." [18]

The conclusion to this line of reasoning seems to be that while
the evidence indicates the presence of some principle of order in
the world, and while there is some analogy between this principle
and human intelligence so that we cannot entirely reject this clue
to the ultimate explanation of things; yet if we interpret the divine
intelligence so as to give it positive meaning in terms of similarity
to human reason, its plausibility almost evaporates, and the likelihood of its being the true explanation is exceedingly small. And of
course, if we do not give it positive meaning by reference to the
only intelligence with which we are acquainted, namely, our own,
appeal to a divine mind is appeal to a mere word; in this case we
have no genuine explanation at all.[19]

[18] Ibid., Part IV. See also Part III.
[19] Ibid., Parts XII, II, IV.

The First Cause, then, is a being who at most may be somewhat like an intelligence. But what other attributes can we legitimately assign him, and what degree of perfection in any attribute which the evidence justifies ascribing to him at all? Here Hume insists on a principle which flatly denies the Catholic assumption that the cause of various degrees of perfection in any quality must be the superlative perfection of that kind. It is, in fact, more frankly inconsistent with that position than is his predictive conception of the causal relation with the Catholic interpretation of it as productive efficiency. This principle is that when we have no direct experience of a cause, but know it solely by inference from an effect which it has produced,

we must proportion the one to the other, and can never be allowed to ascribe to the cause any qualities but what are exactly sufficient to produce the effect. A body of ten ounces raised in a scale may serve as a proof that the counterbalancing weight exceeds ten ounces, but can never afford a reason that it exceeds a hundred. If the cause assigned for any effect be not sufficient to produce it, we must either reject that cause, or add to it such qualities as will give it a just proportion to the effect. But if we ascribe to it further qualities, or affirm it capable of producing other effects, we can only indulge the license of conjecture, and arbitrarily suppose the existence of qualities and energies, without reason or authority.[20] ·

We must not, in brief, under such circumstances, suppose a cause in any respect greater than the effect, but one exactly equal to it and no more. "Allowing, therefore, the gods to be the authors of the existence or order of the universe; it follows that they possess that precise degree of power, intelligence, and benevolence, which appears in their workmanship; but nothing farther can ever be proved, except we call in the assistance of exaggeration and flattery to supply the defects of argument and reasoning." [21]

It is important to keep in mind that this principle applies only in situations where we can observe an effect but not its cause. It is not Hume's thought that we are limited in this way when we can observe both cause and effect. Then we can attribute to the cause whatever properties we actually find it to possess. When, however,

[20] *Enquiry*, p. 143 f.
[21] *Ibid.*, p. 144.

we cannot observe the cause but only infer its nature from the effect, Hume insists that this maxim must be valid.

What follows when we apply this principle to determine the attributes that may properly be assigned to God, and his degree of perfection in each of them? Well, as to the attribute of power, he must possess this in very high degree, to account for the vastness of the forces which are displayed in his assumed effect. We may not, indeed, ascribe to him infinite power, but his power is clearly very great.[22] As to intelligence, or wisdom, the conclusion above reached applies: if we can properly call God intelligent at all, he must be so in very high degree, but a serious doubt remains as to how far the attribute is allowable or even meaningful. When we come to the moral qualities—justice, benevolence, mercy—the only conclusion supported by the evidence is that the being responsible for the universe is entirely neutral on these matters. The economy which he has instituted is adapted to secure the continued existence of individual animals and their species, but not their positive happiness or well-being. Pain and suffering are widespread among sentient creatures, and their ubiquity is inconsistent with benevolence in the deity, if we suppose him possessed of superior power and wisdom.[23]

Look around this universe. What an immense profusion of beings, animated and organized, sensible and active! You admire this prodigious variety and fecundity. But inspect a little more narrowly these living existences, the only beings worth regarding. How hostile and destructive to each other! How insufficient all of them for their own happiness! How contemptible or odious to the spectator! The whole presents nothing but the idea of a blind Nature, impregnated by a great vivifying principle, and pouring forth from her lap, without discernment or parental care, her maimed and abortive children![24]

To be sure, if we were fully assured by some *a priori* demonstration that the universe is the creation of a being infinite in wisdom and goodness as well as in power, the presence of widespread misery in human and animal experience would not be sufficient ground for rejecting that conclusion. We should be greatly astonished at

22 *Dialogues,* Part V.
23 *Ibid.,* Part X.
24 *Ibid.,* Part XI.

it, and wonder why the actual achievements of such a Creator are
so disappointing in comparison with what we should expect from
him beforehand; the main sources of evil would seem, so far as
we can tell, to be entirely avoidable for a architect supreme in
wisdom and power. But at the same time we should be sensible
of the limitations of our finite judgment in such matters, and recognize that there may be some solution of this apparent contradiction which surpasses our comprehension. However, our situation
is not this. We know of no such *a priori* demonstration. We have
to determine the nature of the cause solely from the effect which
is spread before our observation. And since the effect includes a
vast amount of vice, misery, and disorder, as well as their opposites,
we can only legitimately infer a cause which is proportionate to
the effect in all these respects.[25] Were it not for the high degree
of uniformity and mutual adaptation in the objects composing
the world, we should be tempted to embrace the dualistic hypothesis of an ultimate principle of evil contending with a good power
for control of the universe; but on the whole this is less plausible
than the view that the original cause possesses neither the ethically
approved virtues nor their opposites. It is morally neutral. We find it
true, to be sure, that the ordinary course of experience, while not
adapted to secure human happiness, is in general such as to encourage moral excellence, at least in sagacious men. It is the case
that "virtue is attended with more peace of mind than vice, and
meets with a more favorable reception from the world. . . . According
to the past experience of mankind, friendship is the chief joy of
human life, and moderation the only source of tranquillity and
happiness."[26] However, this circumstance establishes neither morality nor wisdom in the author of nature, for many men do not
learn this lesson; all that is proved is an order of events such as to
suggest the conclusion to those who have the wit to draw it.

His Explanation of Belief in Immortality

So much for Hume's treatment, by his empirical method, of
the problem of God. But the principle of causal explanation just

[25] *Ibid.*, Part XI. *Enquiry*, pp. 146, 149.
[26] *Enquiry*, p. 148.

discussed is of such great historical importance that it deserves further examination; it has, moreover, a vital bearing on his brief consideration of immortality, for which such an examination may prepare us.

Why this difference between Hume's assumptions concerning the relation of a known effect to the cause inferred from it and the assumptions of the Catholic philosophers faced with the same problem? Why is the former so confident that such a cause may not properly be assigned a degree of perfection exceeding the degree displayed in the effect, while the latter are equally confident that supreme perfection may legitimately be attributed to it?

The answer seems to lie in the larger context of interests and attitudes, to which reference has already been made, in which these two modes of reasoning arose. The Catholic thinkers were not primarily concerned that their causal category should supply a basis for prediction and control of the natural events explained by its aid; what they wished was to trace a systematic relation between facts of experience and a Supreme Being in whom man's longing for an infinite good might be satisfied. In this context causality was naturally pictured as essentially "impartation"; whence, it was confidently asked, could a universe containing all grades of perfection, and especially containing a species moved by an urge toward unlimited good, derive its reality save from a being eternally possessing infinite perfection? Hume shared the dominant interests of an age growing in power to anticipate and control physical nature, and finding in the new empirical science, with its emphasis on prediction and verification, an adequate instrument for enhancing and guiding that power. In this context a notion of causality was naturally assumed which implicitly harmonized with these motives—its essence was not impartation, but constancy of observable connection. Governed by such a standpoint, empirical science found it necessary to insist on the validity of Hume's principle of equivalence between any inferred cause and its effect; an unobserved cause cannot be supposed to contain any fundamental properties or any quantity of energy not displayed in the effect. This necessity arises from the following consideration: If, beginning with an observed effect, one attributes to its inferred cause any more qualities or forces than are requisite to produce that effect, he will inevitably predict, from

contemplation of that supposed cause, a different kind of effect than
the one originally experienced.[27] Such prediction will in the nature
of the case be unverifiable. He will expect, in brief, from the operation of his cause, effects which experience will not confirm, because
he has assigned to the cause powers which the original observation
of its effect did not justify. This cannot be held legitimate in an age
whose dominant motive is quest for control of future events by
exact and dependable anticipations about their occurrence.

It is in the hopes of the pious for perfect bliss in a celestial after-
life that Hume finds this fallacy in its most irresponsible form.
Since all our impressions are of happenings in this life, there can
in the nature of the case be no empirical validation of the idea of
future rewards and punishments in another world—no justification
for the optimistic expectation of the faithful for eternity in paradise.
Whence arises this indefensible idea? According to Hume, it is born
of the fallacy just described. From a very imperfect world, viewed
as an effect, people infer a cause endowed with supreme perfection.
Then, turning back from that cause to the effect with which their
thinking began, they say: Surely this sorry world is not the full
product of the infinite wisdom and goodness of such a being;
there must be another, invisible world, in which his perfect nature
is adequately displayed, and where obedient worshipers may share
his incomparable glory. But to reason thus is to correct one mistake
by making another.

What must a philosopher think of those vain reasoners who, instead
of regarding the present scene of things as the sole object of their contemplation, so far reverse the whole course of nature as to render this
life merely a passage to something farther; a porch, which leads to a
greater, and vastly different building; a prologue, which serves only to
introduce the piece, and give it more grace and propriety? Whence,
do you think, can such philosophers derive their idea of the gods? From
their own conceit and imagination surely. For if they derived it from
the present phenomena it would never point to anything farther, but
must be exactly adjusted to them. . . .

Are there any marks of a distributive justice in the world? If you

---

[27] In terms of the Catholic assumptions, no such prediction is permissible.
An absolutely perfect Cause having been established, it is clear that none of its
effects could be absolutely perfect. Otherwise we should have two perfect
beings, hence two gods, and the demonstrable unity and simplicity of the
deity would be violated.

answer in the affirmative, I conclude that, since justice here exerts itself, it is satisfied. If you reply in the negative, I conclude that you have then no reason to ascribe justice, in our sense of it, to the gods. If you hold a medium between affirmation and negation, by saying that the justice of the gods, at present, exerts itself in part, but not in its full extent; I answer that you have no reason to give it any particular extent, but only so far as you see it, *at present*, exert itself.[28]

This summary of Hume's application of his empirical principles to religious issues will indicate that the resulting philosophy of religion is essentially traditionalist in its fundamental conceptions and essentially negative or skeptical in its outcome.[29] Its conceptions are traditional in the sense that prevailing theological definitions of God, miracle, etc., are accepted; no question is raised as to the possibility of revised definitions which might be more adequate to experience and more serviceable to religious thought in an age dominated by the empirical standpoint. There is nothing here comparable to Spinoza's boldness in radically reinterpreting the religious structure so as to harmonize it with scientific assumptions and methods adopted on other grounds. Its outcome is negative in the sense that the important items in the theological creed thus empirically tested are met with the verdict "Not proven," and are either eliminated as unworthy of any sort of belief or shown to possess a very low degree of probability. It should be observed that these convictions are not disproved, either; there is always the possibilty that further empirical evidence may alter our assessment of the case, and in any event human experience is no competent measure of the universe of reality. There may be a host of entities in the cosmos of which, because of their inaccessibility to our perceptual and cognitive faculties, we can have no acquaintance whatever. The point of Hume's arguments is not that we may rightfully deny the existence of what we cannot perceive. It is that by comparing our ideas with relevant facts as they are observed we may

---

[28] *Enquiry*, pp. 149 f.

[29] It should be added that Hume sometimes expressed a point of view suggesting that there were times when he questioned the applicability of his empirical principles to religion, and was inclined to feel that possibly religion rests on a kind of faith which cannot be rationally justified but which none the less has a certain validity. In some of these passages he probably had his tongue in his cheek, but it is not clear that he did so in all. See *Enquiry*, pp. 137 f., 175; and the speeches of Demea in the *Dialogues*.

show the complete unreasonableness of accepting beliefs unjustified
by the perceptual evidence. Many things may exist in which we yet
have no right to believe, because belief in them is incapable of
empirical verification. Hume's challenge to his adversaries, in brief,
is this: Do you believe anything? Produce the empirical evidence.
If you cannot produce adequate evidence you have no business to
believe—although, to be sure, you likewise have no business to deny
that the belief may be true.

Nineteenth-Century Empiricists in Religion

During the latter half of the nineteenth century the outstanding
champions of this point of view regarding religion were J. S. Mill,
Leslie Stephen, T. H. Huxley, and Herbert Spencer. These men
gave it the later development and formulation in terms of which it
is now an influential mode of thought among educated people,
particularly those whose reflective habits have been deeply influenced by the postulates and methods of empirical science. One of
their most important contributions—for which Mill and Huxley
were mainly responsible—was the freeing of the empirical criterion
of truth from its unfortunate earlier dependence on a theory of the
origin of ideas. By them it was stated in terms of the actual procedures of successful inductive science. There the ultimate appeal is
not to the experiences from which our explanatory hypotheses were
derived, but rather to the present or future facts of observation or
experiment which should be found to occur if those hypotheses are
true. Such facts constitute the "evidence" for the truth of the
ideas which lead to our expectation of their occurrence, and
accordingly adequacy of empirical evidence becomes the general
mark of truth in the statements of the empiricist position given
by these men.[30]

In one respect Herbert Spencer hardly belongs in this group.
Though resting upon the foundations provided by empirical science,
he was essentially a constructive metaphysician, confident that he
could prove many things about the realm which transcends human
experience and which others were content to regard simply as
unknown. For him, examination of both science and religion demon-

[30] The reader may refer again here to the illustration on p. 208.

strates the existence of an inscrutable power behind the observable phenomena—the Unknowable, whose inner essence is intrinsically incomprehensible by finite minds, but which is none the less the ultimate source of the forces displayed in nature and in human life. The traditional doctrines about this power he, of course, held to be inadequately evidenced, and incapable of proof.

J. S. Mill wrote a lengthy essay on "Theism," whose purpose, like that of Hume, was to test, in the light of the empirical evidence, the traditional doctrines of religion.[31] His result is very similar to Hume's except on two points. He believes that observed fact, while failing to support the doctrine that the Intelligence probably responsible for the present order of the universe is actuated solely by love for his creatures, nevertheless gives some positive probability to the conclusion that he does desire their good.[32] And since there is some preponderance of evidence in favor of an intelligent and benevolent power as the First Cause of the world, Mill explicitly encourages his readers to allow a hopeful imagination to dwell on this possibility, on the ground that such optimism stimulates our higher feelings and our moral devotion, while it need not blind our estimate of the relevant evidence or the actual degree of probability which the latter yields.[33]

Mill thus swung slightly to the right of Hume; T. H. Huxley moved rather to the left. And in doing so he provided the name under which those who since his day have in general cast their lot with this trend in religious philosophy prefer to be known. Why not, Huxley asked, adopt without qualification the principle characteristic of the empirical scientist when working in his chosen field—the principle that conclusions should be accepted only when supported by adequate empirical evidence and that an entirely uncommitted mind should be maintained elsewhere? Why indulge belief in any proposition when the probability in its favor is so low that there is no possibility of convincing an opponent of its correctness; especially when the issue is such that there seems no likelihood that our limited human faculties will ever light upon decisive evi-

[31] *Three Essays on Religion*, pp. 125–257.
[32] *Ibid.*, pp. 242 f., 190 ff.
[33] *Ibid.*, pp. 244–250.

dence concerning it? Whenever such questions are raised, is not the appropriate answer simply: I do not know?

Huxley coined the term "agnostic"[34] to apply to those who joined him in answering these questions in the affirmative. Such thinkers are not atheists, for they do not presume positively to deny the being of a God; they are not theists, for evidence sufficient to support belief in such a being seems to them lacking. They recognize their ignorance about matters which lie beyond conclusive empirical verification; they strongly doubt whether anyone else, whatever his claims, really knows about them either; and in the case of beliefs concerning supernatural entities, they do not expect that this limitation to man's knowledge will ever be overcome. In matters of religion as traditionally conceived, agnosticism seems to them the only honest and modest position to take. And the adjective "honest" is used advisedly, for Huxley is at pains to insist that the issue raised by agnosticism is more a moral than an intellectual one. "The foundation of morality is to have done, once and for all, with lying; to give up pretending to believe that for which there is no evidence, and repeating unintelligible propositions about things beyond the possibilities of knowledge."[35] When, accordingly, he gives a brief definition of this religious philosophy, both the moral and the intellectual aspects are included.

Agnosticism is not properly described as a "negative" creed, nor indeed as a creed of any kind, except in so far as it expresses absolute faith in the validity of a principle, which is as much ethical as intellectual. This principle may be stated in various ways, but they all amount to this: that it is wrong for a man to say that he is certain of the objective truth of any proposition unless he can produce evidence which logically justifies that certainty. This is what Agnosticism asserts; and, in my opinion, it is all that is essential to Agnosticism. . . . Yet the application of that principle results in the denial of, or the suspension of judgment concerning, a number of propositions respecting which our contemporary ecclesiastical "gnostics" profess entire certainty.[36]

[34] Etymologically, the term means a "not-know-ist." The Greek roots are "a-privative" and the verb "to know."
[35] Huxley, *Essays upon Controversial Questions* (1889), p. 183. This and the following quotation from the same volume are reprinted by courtesy of D. Appleton-Century Company.
[36] *Ibid.*, pp. 350 f. Cf. also pp. 281 f.

And, for Huxley, all propositions about the existence and activity of supernatural beings are included within this number.[37] W. K. Clifford states this principle in more extreme and provocative form as follows: "It is wrong always, everywhere, and for anyone to believe anything upon insufficient evidence."[38] Hume would presumably not have approved such an extreme statement since (as indicated in the footnote on p. 228) he did not unqualifiedly reject the possibility of a different foundation for religious faith than empirical fact but nevertheless valid.

Let us summarize the relation between religion and science from the standpoint of the type of religious philosophy now before us. In terms of the traditionally established conceptions of religion, this relation is conceived to be one of thoroughgoing opposition. Science is built on the method of appeal to observed facts. Religious doctrines are unverifiable by that method, hence they must rest on assumptions quite irreconcilable with those of science. But the empirical procedure appears universally valid to the champions of this philosophy—at least wherever observable facts are at all concerned, and in what significant question, outside of mathematics, are they not concerned? Theology is thus left completely without scientific justification, unless a very low favorable probability, quite insufficient for proof, in the case of certain doctrines, be regarded as justification.

The statement just made is that the "established conceptions" of religion are in opposition to this standpoint. It should be observed that all its prominent representatives occasionally suggest that a conception of religion is possible which would remove this opposition. Spencer's reconciliation has already been noted; likewise, Hume's intimation that religion may possibly rest on a foundation quite other than that of reason and experience. Huxley and J. S. Mill anticipate, in certain passages, the central idea of contemporary humanism, to be discussed in Chapter XI. In Huxley's case these expressions are brief and remain undeveloped;[39] in J. S. Mill

[37] Huxley, it should be noted, denies that agnosticism is a religious philosophy. He is using this phrase, however, in the narrow and positive meaning given it by his theological opponents. *Essays*, p. 285.

[38] In "The Ethics of Belief." (*Lectures and Essays*, Stephen and Pollock ed., Vol. II.)

[39] *Essays upon Some Controverted Questions*, p. 288.

the proposal is elaborated in an essay of some fifty pages.[40] It remained without effective influence, however, until the early twentieth century.

EMPIRICISM AND MORAL PROBLEMS

We may consider briefly the bearing of the point of view now under consideration on moral and social problems.[41] Just as direct observation is the source and criterion of truth, so in the eyes of empiricism our immediate experience of pleasure and pain, happiness and misery, is the origin of our ideas of good and evil, and provides the standard by which to judge them. If such terms are to have definite significance for us they must be traced back to and validated in these direct and indubitable feelings of joy or suffering with which all people are familiar. This means that every attempt on the part of theologians to set up a supposed standard of human good which is derived elsewhere than from such immediate experiences—from tradition, metaphysical theorizing, or supposed supernatural authority—is decisively rejected. Hume challenges those who find such a criterion in the promises of future reward or punishment contained in a sacred book;[42] Mill assails the thinkers who try to discover it in the laws of behavior of nonhuman nature;[43] Huxley insists that it cannot be found in the factors which the theory of evolution shows to be effective in the course of organic history.[44] We guide our way toward such happiness as is available to man, in

[40] The second of his *Three Essays on Religion*, entitled the "Utility of Religion."

[41] The problem of freedom, in any sense which has rendered it a challenging issue to religious minds, loses all force from the standpoint of empirical skepticism, and hence is not discussed in the text. Since causal necessity everywhere is reduced to vivid anticipation of an effect, based on regularity of prior experience, there is no ground for the feeling that human acts are under the control of some fateful and metaphysical necessity. The traditional notions of determinism and of freedom become meaningless. In terms of this viewpoint, the opposite of freedom, if the latter be given an intelligible sense, is simply constraint. Man is free whenever he is not prevented, by physical force or social pressure, from doing what he wishes to do. Freedom is thus an essentially practical problem; so far as it retains theoretical significance it belongs to educational or social philosophy.

[42] *Enquiry*, sec. XI.

[43] In the first of the *Three Essays on Religion*, entitled "Nature."

[44] *Evolution and Ethics* (1894 ed.), especially pp. 79–86.

the present and in the future, by learning through experience what are the conditions under which pleasure is realized and pain suffered. And these lessons are tentative rather than final, for the same reason as applies in the case of other facts of experience. We expect the future to be like the past, similar effects continuing to follow similar causes, and in general orient our actions on that basis, but there is no guarantee that in any given case our expectation will be satisfied, and exact similarity is not even to be hoped for. Certainty, outside of mathematics, is a chimera; we must adjust ourselves to living by a balance of evidence that never amounts to perfect proof.

The bearings of agnosticism on pressing contemporary social problems may be dismissed with a few words. As in the case of the religion of science, no unequivocal conclusions can be drawn here; only a general tendency may be noted. Most of those who are agnostics in their religious philosophy have been strongly influenced by the social standpoint of utilitarianism, whose fundamental contentions are: first, the one above expressed, that human good is to be interpreted in terms of direct experience of pleasure and happiness; and second, that each man's claim to the enjoyment of good is equal to that of any other man. The application of these principles to specific social problems has meant, in general, what is now commonly described as "nineteenth-century liberalism." The utilitarians were vigorous leaders in opposing the more distressing forms of economic exploitation, in supporting the trend toward democracy, and in championing the freedom of the individual to think, speak, and act without regulation by the state except so far as regulation is necessary to protect the same freedom for others. Agnostics in religion today will usually be found to share these social attitudes, but no general conclusion can be drawn as to their position on the political and economic issues which have more recently become the center of debate.

In summarizing, for purposes of comparison, the main assumptions of agnosticism, it will be best to depart slightly from the form previously used. There is really only one fundamental assumption, but it has various implications when considered in relation to the problems of morals and religion.

THE MAJOR DISPUTED ASSUMPTION OF AGNOSTICISM

The ultimate test of the truth of an idea consists in its correspondence with the relevant facts disclosed in sense perception; the ultimate test of goodness or badness consists in human experience of pleasure and pain.

1. Implications Concerning Man's Moral Situation
   a. He is without certainty of the attainment of good or avoidance of ill in the future.
   b. Probability is therefore the guide of life.
2. Implications Concerning Metaphysical Knowledge
   a. Knowledge of ultimates is not verifiable by perceived facts.
   b. Causality means nothing more than constancy of perceived antecedence.
   c. Skepticism is hence the only reasonable attitude in metaphysics; the hypotheses of empirical science alone are capable of becoming verifiable knowledge.
3. Implications Concerning the Supernatural
   a. Supernatural beings or events cannot in the nature of the case be perceived by the senses.
   b. Testimony regarding their supposed effects uniformly lacks adequate evidence.
   c. Neither belief in nor denial of their existence is therefore appropriate for human minds.

SELECTED BIBLIOGRAPHY

Clifford, W. K., "The Ethics of Belief." In *Lectures and Essays* (Stephen and Pollock ed.), Macmillan, 1879, vol. II.
Hume, David, *Dialogues Concerning Natural Religion.*
Hume, David, *Enquiry Concerning Human Understanding.*
Hume, David, *The Natural History of Religion.*
These works of Hume are available in several editions.
Huxley, T. H., *Hume,* Appleton, 1896.
Huxley, T. H., *Science and Christian Tradition,* Appleton, 1894.
Huxley, T. H., *Science and Hebrew Tradition,* Appleton, 1894. Much of the material in these last two volumes is also published in *Essays upon Some Controverted Questions,* Appleton, 1892.
Mill, J. S., *Three Essays on Religion,* Holt, 1874.
Stephen, Leslie, *An Agnostic's Apology,* Smith, Elder, and Co., 1903.

Chapter IX

ETHICAL IDEALISM

THE INTERRELATIONS OF METAPHYSICS, RELIGION, AND MORALS

A COMMON thread runs through all the philosophies of religion thus far discussed. This is the conviction that the core of religion lies in, or at least depends on, certain metaphysical beliefs. God is conceived as the ultimate cause and sustainer of the cosmic order of which we and our doings are a part; correct knowledge about him as so defined is essential to religion and, indeed, is its foundation. The skeptics with whom we were occupied in the preceding chapter share this conviction with other philosophers,[1] and this is why they are skeptics; for them, such knowledge transcends human competence.

We are now to examine a type of religious philosophy, exceedingly influential since it was first formulated, which rejects this conviction. For it, the essence of religion is not metaphysical knowledge, but devotion to moral duty. The threefold relation obtaining between religion, metaphyisics, and morals in previous religious philosophy is in its case radically transformed. Catholicism, Protestant fundamentalism, and Spinozism all agree in treating religion as dependent on metaphysics, and morals as dependent on religion, although they are not agreed in their detailed interpretation of this dependence. For all of them, we can only tell what is right and good for men to do by first understanding the nature of the universe in

[1] Except in their occasional redefinitions of religion which have been noted. See above, p. 232 f.

its bearing upon our welfare. Now agnosticism had made morals autonomous, but no systematic, positive reconstruction of religion had resulted.[2] From the standpoint of ethical idealism this further step is taken, and a different conception of morals renders it possible. Not only are moral principles conceived to be independent of metaphysical knowledge; moral values are the key to the ultimate nature of the universe. Religion is grounded on ethics, and theology is derived from ethical truths. Metaphysical knowledge is either denied, with the agnostics, or is itself radically transformed into a derivative of moral devotion. The gist of the matter, for the previous types of philosophy (excluding agnosticism) is: I understand my universe; I find there God and his absolute laws; hence it is clear what I ought to do. For the present type, it is rather: I see what I ought to do; hence God and the universe in their relation to me become clear.

To take this position is to make a daring assertion of man's moral competence and autonomy. It means claiming the right to reinterpret the nature of God in terms of our moral experience, instead of humbly submitting that experience to the judgment of a God believed to possess moral character and authority independent of our interpretations. It is to say: God must be what man's moral insight demands that he be; if not, he is no God.

When first baldly stated, this seems a very radical transformation of religious philosophy. Yet, if we survey the history of religion with sympathy for this point of view, there is much to suggest that in essence it amounts merely to conscious recognition of a fundamental aspect of religious progress frequently exemplified earlier. When the preprophetic Hebrew picture of Yahweh as a jealous, martial chieftain was replaced in the prophets by the picture of a just and merciful universal ruler—what is this but insistence that later and higher moral ideals have a right to supersede earlier and lower ones in man's conception of the nature of God? When the prophetic picture was itself transformed, under the influence of the exile and of contacts with Persia and Greece, into the idea of a father tenderly caring for the individual and

[2] The agnostics, of course, had to regard the moral life as autonomous, since they rejected both religion and metaphysics as traditionally conceived but did not reject moral theory.

238   TYPES OF RELIGIOUS PHILOSOPHY

seeking his eternal good—what is this but a further insistence on
the same principle? And from the Protestant standpoint, when the
notion that God makes salvation available to man only through the
ministrations of the Catholic hierarchy gave way to the conviction
that he offers salvation directly to the individual, free from intellectual and social control, we have still another illustration, taken
from an age characterized by revolt from the pretensions of human
authority and the corruptions of ecclesiastical domination. According to the religious philosophy now to be studied, man has
many times effectively exerted the right to reinterpret God in the
light of his own growing insight into what is truly great and good,
but before the rise of this philosophy he had not consciously expressed that right as a guiding principle of his creed. This is its
distinctive and significant contribution to religious thought—the
bold affirmation of the doctrine, as a sound foundation for religion,
that man's moral duty is supreme and that theological doctrines
must humbly conform to it.

KANT'S MAJOR PROBLEM

The man who first gave clear enunciation to this view of religion
is the German philosopher Immanuel Kant, who lived from 1724
to 1804, and whose mature philosophy was presented in a series of
epoch-making works published between 1781 and 1790. Kant was
reared in a household which united simple and earnest piety with
stern devotion to moral duty. The effect of this early seasoning of
his mind was that when he later became quite skeptical of traditional
theology he nevertheless retained a firm assurance that there is
something essentially sound both in the religious attitude and in the
main convictions to which it leads, provided only that they are
interpreted aright. It was one of the great tasks of his life to reach
the true interpretation, and it is our first business in this chapter to
see how he carried out this task.

Kant was the intellectual heir of rationalistic metaphysics and
theology, on the one hand, and of empirical science, on the other.
He was most fully acquainted with the former in the guise it had
taken in the philosophy of Leibnitz, as systematized by Christian
Wolff. He was familiar with the latter in the scientific work of

Newton, and before he formulated the fundamentals of his philosophical system he became acquainted with the empirical skepticism of Hume.

If we follow Kant's development, as revealed in his early writings, it becomes clear that the historical opposition between the rationalist and empiricist points of view took deep root in his mind, and gradually became sharpened until he finally saw a clue and invented a method which seemed to promise their reconciliation. For, after having swung several times from one of these standpoints to the other, he became convinced that truth does not all lie on either side in the controversy; the rationalists must be right in certain of their fundamental contentions, and the empiricists in others. His major problem, therefore, as a philosopher, became that of synthesizing these two opposed points of view—not, of course, by piecing them together in the superficial fashion of an eclectic, but by a thorough analysis of all relevant problems under the guidance of a central principle.

It must not be supposed, however, that this was for him a mere technical problem in philosophy. His early training forbade that possibility. Beneath the apparently abstract issue of philosophical method he saw a much larger problem and one of far deeper human concern. He saw a serious and widening cleft between religion and science, in both of which he profoundly believed and whose harmonious adjustment he realized was an inescapable challenge to human thought. His philosophy became the first systematic reconciler of these two great human interests in the distinctively modern sense of that phrase.

It will be worth our while to note why this challenge had become peculiarly provocative in Kant's day, and why it appeared vitally connected with the otherwise technical issue between rationalism and empiricism. Let us recall that prior to the work of Newton the influential trends in science had rested upon a rationalistic rather than an empirical foundation (except in the now antiquated Aristotelian sense of empiricism), and that this foundation had been naturally and easily conceived in a form quite harmonious with the main contentions of the established religious creed. God had created the mathematical order of the universe, some phases of which man as scientist succeeds in rediscovering by the same rational processes of intuitive apprehension and causal deduction that prove the existence of God himself. The medieval unity of religion and science still, in essence, remained, especially for those who dared to follow Spinoza in identifying God with the geometrical structure of the universe. But Newton, hailed as the greatest and most successful scientist of the new era, had combined, in his conception of scientific method, mathematical deduction with empirical verification, and his ultimate emphasis was laid on the latter. This meant that the final test of truth, as the empiricist philosophers, especially Hume, came to see, was no longer intuitive clarity or deductive consistency, but verifiability by sense-perception. Apart from verification through observation, an explanatory idea remains a hypothesis merely; and if it be intrinsically incapable of such confirmation we cannot possibly establish its truth and may be forced to pronounce it quite meaningless. Many men of an empirical temper of mind sensed the threat to religious ideas involved in this transformation of science—the threat which Hume ventured to expose and discuss. Supernatural entities appeared simply incapable of empirical verification, as the latter process was effectively employed in the new science. In brief, rationalism seemed to provide a demonstrative foundation for the truths of religion; empiricism seemed to remove all their support and to issue in thoroughgoing skepticism. It took, to be sure, two generations after the appearance of Newton's major works for these consequences to become sufficiently evident so that philosophers might assess the result; this accounts for the fact that it was the middle of the eighteenth century before men influenced by these historical factors began to see clearly the yawning fissure between science and religion which has troubled so many thinkers since.

Now Kant, as we have seen, believed firmly that there was something profoundly true in religion; he was also deeply impressed by the remarkable achievements of Newtonian science. Here, at last, he thought, was a model of exact and verifiable knowledge about the world. It was knowledge capable of indefinite growth, for its foundations were securely established in universal experience, and its method made sure that every extension of knowledge likewise conforms to our common, direct experience of the facts to which it pertains. Kant did not appreciate in this empirical method all the features that later philosophy of science has found significant, but he did realize quite fully that the objectivity and demonstrability of factual truth in the new science, which virtues he very highly prized, were dependent on its empiricism—its appeal to sense perception as the basic way in which reality is disclosed to our minds. In realizing this he was acknowledging a far sharper conflict between science and religion than European thought had faced since the days of Greek philosophical skepticism. It seemed that if men were to move ahead in the pursuit of verifiable knowledge they must abandon the faiths of religion as entirely ungrounded; if they were to hold firmly to the latter they must turn their backs on the most promising intellectual movement, daily winning new champions, that the Western world has seen. The broad problem of Kant's philosophical career must be understood in terms of this setting; it is the problem of attaining a penetrating understanding both of science and of religion as major expressions of man's rational life, with the task of reconciling them on a basis that could never be shaken. In the midst of his detailed analyses of intricate logical and epistemological matters it is easy to forget this fact, but if one is to comprehend his philosophy it cannot safely be forgotten.

To appreciate the essential features of Kant's influence on subsequent philosophy of religion it is necessary first to summarize the main outlines of his theory of knowledge and his ethical philosophy. His reasoning on these matters provides the main intellectual background for understanding the reinterpretation of religion as dependent on moral principles, which is now a distinctive point of view in Western religious philosophy. In the following exposition of his philosophical foundations we shall, of course, omit everything that is not required to clarify their bearing on the basic issues of religion.

Kant's theory of knowledge was systematically elaborated in his *Critique of Pure Reason,* whose first edition was published in 1781, and whose second appeared in 1787. In dealing with this subject, his synthesis of rationalism and empiricism gives, in general, the palm of victory to the empiricists; the major emphasis of the conclusions established is that human knowledge is limited to the realm of perceptual experience, metaphysics and traditional theology proving totally unable to justify their claim to pose as knowledge. Science, on the Newtonian model, is shown to be adequately grounded and is given the right to proceed on its conquering career, while the skeptics are proved to be essentially correct in their estimate of religion. At first sight Kant's technical formulation of his problem in this book has nothing to do with religion. "How are synthetic judgments *a priori* possible?" is his question. But the issue of religion versus science is deeply involved in this apparently unexciting problem.

Let us see how this is the case.[3] The opposite of "synthetic" is "analytic." Now an analytic judgment (i.e., assertion) is one whose predicate is contained in the meaning of the subject. Consider an example. "Bodies are extended." Since we would hardly define the term "body" without including the circumstance that it occupies space, it is evident that the concept "extended," which constitutes the predicate of this judgment, is contained in the meaning of the concept "body" which forms its subject. A synthetic judgment, on the other hand, is one whose predicate is not contained in the meaning of the subject. "This body is two feet long." Since it is not involved in the meaning of the term "body" that the object to which it refers have any particular length, this judgment is evidently not analytic, but synthetic. There remains for elucidation in Kant's question the phrase "*a priori*." A judgment is *a priori* when it is asserted in advance of experience of the objects about which it is affirmed. The opposite of *a priori* is "*a posteriori*," and a judgment is *a posteriori* when it rests upon observation of the matters concerned. "The next tree that I shall see is an oak" is an *a priori* judgment; "the tree that I have just examined is an oak" is an *a posteriori* judgment.

Now it is evident, according to Kant, that we face no serious difficulty when we ask how analytic judgments are possible, i.e., how we can legitimately and with assurance assert them. Since in their case the predicate of the judgment is already contained in the connotation of the subject, such a judgment consists simply in unfolding part or all of the subject's meaning. We need here no appeal to experience to support us, for if anyone should dispute such a judgment and assert, for example, that some bodies are unextended,

[3] *Critique of Pure Reason* (Kemp Smith trans.), pp. 41 ff.

his predicate would obviously contradict what is implied by his subject. The principle that we must not contradict ourselves is all that we need invoke in justifying the assertion of such judgments. And experience of bodies could not disturb us, for we should by definition refuse to classify as a "body" anything experienced as unextended. Nor, also, is there any serious difficulty in determining how synthetic judgments *a posteriori* are possible. If, having just looked at a tree, I declare it to be an oak, the basis of that judgment and of my assurance in making it is evidently my experience of the tree—the visual perception of those features which identify it as an oak.

But how are synthetic judgments *a priori* possible? How, in advance of experiencing an object, can we assert anything about it that goes beyond what is contained in the meaning of the term by which we refer to it? We should naturally suppose, before examining the matter thoroughly, that such judgments are impossible. There is, however, indubitable evidence, according to Kant, that they actually exist and are confidently used in cognition. Our task is to explain this unexpected and interesting circumstance.

First, all judgments in the science of mathematics are synthetic judgments *a priori*. Take the simple assertion in arithmetic that $7 + 5 = 12$. The subject of this judgment is that part of the equation which stands to the left of the sign of equality. If we analyze the meaning of this subject we find just three concepts—the concept "seven," the concept "five," and the concept "addition" as an operation to be performed. Analysis does not reveal the predicate of the judgment at all; to establish that, we need actually to carry out the addition, and this is a synthesis of $7 + 5$, not an analysis. But might not such arithmetical judgments be *a posteriori*? Do they not rest on experience, which has taught us that whenever we add seven objects and five objects we have twelve objects? No, the most that we could say *a posteriori* is that this has regularly been the case in the past; there would be no guarantee that future additions of seven and five would make twelve. We are quite confident, however, that they *must* do so; we recognize a necessity connecting this subject and this predicate which does not permit any alternative result. The presence of such necessity shows that the judgment is not derived from experience nor subject to its fallibilities, but is *a priori.* Kant adds illustrations from geometry, to establish the same result in that field.

Second, some of the most important judgments in physical science are likewise synthetic judgments *a priori.* Consider, for example, the affirmation, basic to all explanations in the physical sciences, that every event has a cause. Can we derive the predicate of this judgment from analysis of the subject? No, analysis of the concept "event" discloses as its meaning merely "an occurrence in time." To say that it must have a cause is to say something more than is implied in the mere concept of event. And, again, this judgment is evidently *a priori,* not *a posteriori.* If its ground were experience, we could merely say that the events thus far observed have proved to be causally determined; nothing could be affirmed about events in the future. But here, too, there is evidently a necessity for which an *a posteriori* explanation does not account. The entire enterprise of science rests on the assumption that no event happens spontaneously, or by chance—that there must be a cause determining it to occur as it does. And no frustration met under the guidance of that supposition is admitted to be final. Hence the judgment must be *a priori.*

Finally, metaphysical judgments also prove to be synthetic judgments *a priori.* And here the bearing of Kant's inquiry on religion becomes evident. For metaphysics and theology are not separate enterprises for Kant; the metaphysical judgments with which he is vitally concerned are those which give expression to the fundamental tenets of the Christian faith. That the world has an ultimate ground, that the human soul is free and immortal—these are the convictions to which he typically turns when dealing with metaphysical questions. Now no such proposition is analytic. We mean by "world" simply the aggregate of all the external phenomena of our experience; nothing is implied thereby as to whether or not it had a beginning in time and a creative cause. We mean by "soul" the bond of unity in all our internal experiences; but as such it has no reference to any particular temporal duration, nor does it involve either presence or absence of causal determination of those experiences. And the same propositions are clearly *a priori* rather than *a posteriori.* We have no acquaintance with the world as a whole. All that experience has done, or could do, is to present us with a very small portion of the world, over a quite limited period of time. And certainly we have had no experience of its origin, nor of its end. Thus such assertions about the world as metaphysics ventures to make must be one and all *a priori*. A like conclusion emerges with regard to its judgments about the soul. Experience can only tell us that the soul has existed from the time of its birth to the present moment; it gives no possible basis for proof that the soul is destined henceforth to exist forever. The assertion that it is immortal is obviously *a priori*.

Contrary to our expectation, then, synthetic judgments *a priori* would seem to be possible—at least some of them, and in some sense. To be sure, if we only found them in metaphysics (or theology) we might be skeptical on the matter. For in this field disagreement among experts and lack of objective demonstration reign; nothing is permanently settled and there is no systematic progress. This situation might easily suggest that the kind of judgment with which such speculations are concerned is invalid. But the most certain sciences we know—for what knowledge is more certain than mathematics and mathematical physics?—likewise rest on synthetic judgments *a priori*. These sciences can prove their conclusions to anyone capable of understanding the problems to which they afford answers; their foundations are not upset with each new generation, but continued advance is possible on the basis of results already established. We cannot appropriately be skeptical regarding the *a priori* synthetic judgments in them. But we obviously need to understand this strange and challenging caldron of unexpected circumstance.

Kant's famous question—how are synthetic judgments *a priori* possible?—is to be taken in this context. What fundamental factors, he is asking, in the world and in the structure of the mind which seeks to understand it, explain the presence and function of these judgments? And, especially, how are we to account for the fact that the synthetic *a priori* judgments proffered in metaphysics, on which the creed of religion has been supposed to rest, do not seem to possess the same assurance and validity that we find in the judgments of which mathematics and the foundations of physical science are composed? What consequences emerge for the nature and limits of human knowledge? These are the problems to which the *Critique of Pure Reason* seeks a solution.

HIS THEORY OF KNOWLEDGE

Kant is convinced that the rationalists were right in their contention that the cognitive mind is self-active; it cannot properly be regarded as a purely passive recipient, and duplicator through memory, of impressions externally given. Reason has a structure, capable of being disclosed through analysis, and the terms of this structure are hence innate concepts in the sense that they will always be exemplified in any cognitive enterprise on which mind embarks. But, on the other hand, these concepts, of themselves, have no content; they are merely empty forms. Their content is derived entirely from experience. The empiricists were right in insisting that there is no knowledge apart from experience, no cognition of which experience does not supply the necessary body. Their mistake lay in supposing that ideas are nothing but copies of impressions, and that simple impressions are passively received by the mind. There is, to be sure, for Kant, a process wherein the mind merely accepts what is presented to it—namely, sensation, which yields the qualities that we directly apprehend in the appearance of an object—but in all the higher cognitive processes, even perception, mind is active, molding the directly given datum in ways demanded by its own structure. Thus experience, if we mean by it anything more than a blind and unorganized chaos of sensations, is a joint product of external objects, which determine the quality of sensation, and the structure of the mind that is actively occupied in cognizing them.[4]

Kant describes this twofold character of experience by using the traditional categories of matter and form in a novel way. Sensation, controlled by its object, supplies the matter of experience, exhibited to us in the qualitative character of a perceived thing— its color, its sound, its smell, its feel. But there is always a form, supplied by the mind itself. This form is a principle of structure, or order, which disposes the matter of experience in a certain way, gives it a certain organization, imposes upon it a network of regular

[4] *Ibid.*, pp. 21–23, 92 f.

relationships. What we call experience is the sensed matter thus coherently formed; it is not the medley of sensation considered by itself. To experience the sun is not just to bask torpidly in its warmth, with all activity of thought quelled. That is what an animal might do. But human experience is rational, which means that it includes distinctions, relations, patterns of shape and motion, in which objects are perceived and to which their changes conform.[5]

Now it is clear that if we take experience in this fashion, our question—how are synthetic judgments *a priori* possible?—is to be answered primarily by an analysis of the form supplied by the cognitive mind. For the matter of sensation, being produced from the outside, is *a posteriori*, while form, being due to the very structure of the mind, is *a priori*. For that reason, inevitably, form is what we experience *with*, determining the relational pattern of whatever our experience is *about*. Consequently, a synthetic judgment *a priori* is simply an expression of the principle that anything experienced must necessarily conform to one or another of the ways in which the mind is prepared to experience it. What those ways are in detail can, of course, only be disclosed when the mind carefully examines its own essential structure, and Kant proposes to guide us through such an examination.

The analysis which Kant offers holds that the structure of the cognitive mind is complex, involving three distinct faculties, interrelated in certain definite ways. Each of these faculties imposes upon experience its own formal contribution, which is therefore necessarily present in every object as known.

First, there is the faculty of *sensibility*, which organizes experience at the lowest level, that of direct perception. The forms which it contributes are space and time. To perceive anything as a definite object is not merely to receive a horde of sensations—it is to dispose them in a certain order of coexistence and of succession, so that the object gains geometrical character and participates in temporal sequence. It is to fit the object into the infinite patterns of space and time, which are not affairs of sense-quality but a kind of network in virtue of which any perceived quality takes on the property of extension and becomes subservient to principles of measurement. Consider the perception of a blackboard. It is not

[5] *Ibid.*, pp. 65 f.

experienced as a chaotic jumble of blackness, without shape, size, or internal structure. It is a definite object, ordered in space and enduring in time, with definite relations to other objects which surround it. According to Kant, what makes it the latter rather than the former is the faculty of sensibility, imposing on the raw material of sensation its distinctive forms of space and time. The mind does not merely receive that material as sensory quality, impressing no stamp of its own upon it. It transforms it into the content of a spatial object and a temporal event.[6]

Second, there is the faculty of *understanding*. Its function presupposes that of sensibility; that is, it operates not on the raw material of sensation, but on that material as already ordered in space and time. This involves certain important limitations on its functions which will soon be explained. But at present we need simply note that to understand anything is more than to perceive it. It means comprehending it in terms of certain relations which go beyond what is involved in spatio-temporal structure alone. The simplest illustration of the presence and activity of this faculty is found in causal understanding. For two events to be apprehended as causally connected they must already be perceived as standing in the relation of temporal succession. But many pairs of events exhibit succession in time without the earlier being cause of the later. To comprehend two events as in causal relationship thus means adding to the temporal order, provided at the level of direct perception, another structure with a distinctive pattern of its own. This added contribution is the work of the faculty of understanding. Kant finds no fewer than twelve forms provided by this faculty on the basis of the spatio-temporal organization of sensations which its operations presuppose. He calls these "categories," to distinguish them from the two forms of sensibility; causality and existence are historically the most important.[7]

Third, there is the faculty of *reason*, whose function supervenes upon that of understanding as the latter upon that of sensibility. It presupposes that the sensory material upon which it operates is already ordered in space and time and structured in accordance with the twelve categories. Its contribution consists of three "ideas"—

[6] *Ibid.*, pp. 65–67.
[7] *Ibid.*, pp. 93, 104 ff.

those of the world, soul, and God—which provide a further determination not implied by either the forms or the categories. And two of these, at least, are religious ideas. But before we examine the essentials of Kant's doctrine about them it is necessary to note the main conclusions reached with regard to his original problem, as a result of his analysis of sensibility and understanding.

How are synthetic judgments possible *a priori*, and how comes it that those judgments found in mathematics and physical science are objectively valid, permitting confident progress in the sciences which build upon them? Well, if space and time are forms of the mind, necessarily imposed in cognition upon all experienced objects, then those objects clearly must conform to whatever is involved in the essential structure of space and time. Otherwise they could never be perceived as objects. Now, as far as space is concerned, its formal structure is expressed, so Kant maintains, in the axioms of Euclidean geometry. No wonder, then, that we find synthetic judgments *a priori* in the demonstrations of geometry, and that they are cogent to all normal minds! When the mind thinks about any spatial entity in accordance with those axioms it is but retracing, in the shape and figure of a presented object, a pattern of order whose origin lies within itself—in its faculty of sensibility, without whose operation no such presentation could be given at all. That pattern simply expresses the way in which the mind is intrinsically disposed to order an object at the level of perception. Kant tries with less success to show the same kind of intimate connection between the structure of time and the principles of arithmetic, interpreting the latter as ultimately based upon the operation of counting the successive units of a series. The outcome of these discussions is that, on the one hand, we understand how it is that the mathematical sciences consist of synthetic judgments *a priori*, and, on the other hand, we see that common sense and scientific thought are entirely right in trusting these judgments—in making them the foundation of assured knowledge about the world. Deriving from the nature of the mind, they are necessarily valid of all entities which mind can perceive or cognize.

Similarly, if causality and the other categories are forms of the mind at the level of conceptual understanding, we can understand how it is that synthetic judgments *a priori*, expressing the necessary relationships into which these categories place experienced objects and events, are inevitably present in the reasoning of physical science. How else, indeed, should we explain our world than in the way the active nature of our minds prescribes? And it is clear that when science proceeds in its task by the systematic use of the categories—assuming that every event is necessarily connected with some preceding event in the fashion indicated by the causal axiom, and with other events as determined by the remaining categories— it is on the right track and is able to achieve continued progress in widening the bounds of human knowledge. The categories are objectively valid, since all rational minds are so constructed as inevitably to interpret experience in the manner they require. Hence we may have the fullest confidence in the synthetic judgments *a priori* which assert the applicability of the categories to any object of experience. Every event must have a cause, because it is the nature of our minds to explain any event as the effect of some cause.

The astonishing success of mathematics and physical science is thus accounted for, and Kant gives them clear title to proceed in the use of their chosen method without embarrassment by skeptical doubts and without fear that their underlying assumptions will ever be shaken. But how about metaphysics and theology?

In summarizing the part of his argument which has thus far been sketched, Kant enunciates a doctrine which is crucial for the validity of the synthetic judgments *a priori* on which the creed of religion rests. This doctrine is that objective knowledge does not reach beyond the data of possible experience, that is, data capable of being empirically presented.[8] The categories are only applicable to such empirical material, and lead to illusion if the attempt is made to order by their aid objects incapable of being given in sense-perception. What does this doctrine signify, and on what considerations does it rest?

Kant's own way of answering these questions is exceedingly complicated, and involves technical matters that are difficult confidently to interpret. But the steps in his argument that have a vital bearing on religious problems can be detached from their

[8] *Ibid.,* pp. 258 ff.

labyrinthine setting and can be stated fairly simply and straight-forwardly.

We remember, to start with, that the understanding, in all its cognitive activities, is not independent of the faculty of sensibility but presupposes it. Now, in treating of time and space as the forms of sensibility, Kant had noted that although space is a pattern in which we perceive only objects that are external to our minds, time is an order in terms of which we necessarily perceive all that happens within our minds—sequences of feeling, idea, and judgment—as well as changes in external objects. This means that time is an absolutely universal condition of human experience. The most important consequence of this fact is that thinking, as engaged in by us men, is in all its modes subject to the structure and limitations imposed by the nature of time. Whether we think about events of daily experience, or about metaphysical problems concerned with the universe as a whole, our thinking is a temporal process; it takes place *within* time rather than in some realm transcending time. This circumstance involves a fundamental handicap for human thinkers which would not be present for minds (if there are such) that are not limited in this way. It is the handicap of finitude. Although we can intuit time as an infinite whole,[9] no actual mental process in the case of any man extends over the whole of time. It is not merely that we do not live long enough for this to be possible, although that is an important consideration; the crucial point is that any mental event could only be experienced as such when it is recognized as limited to a par-ticular temporal duration and therefore distinguishable from processes which precede, succeed, and overlap it. But this imposes a very important limitation on the function and meaning of all explanatory concepts that we employ in our thinking, as becomes evident when we examine them in detail in the light of this prin-ciple. They are inevitably limited by the structure of temporal process, which we can discover by careful analysis. This means that they can only function after the manner of the categories of the understanding, which are applied under the conditions imposed

[9] *Ibid.*, p. 75. It is doubtful whether Kant finally adhered even to this contention.

by the structure of time, not after the manner of the ideas of reason, which thinkers have supposed to be free from those conditions so that they can apply validly to the entire temporal course of experience taken as a whole. To use language familiar in Kant's day, his vital point is that our human understanding is "discursive." Were we able to survey the entire panorama of existence in one glance, embracing the total stretch of time in a single intuition, our knowledge would, no doubt, not be subject to these limitations. But we are men, not gods. We cannot think our world *sub specie aeternitatis*, but only under the form of time.

The significance of this principle for religious problems can be best brought out by examining its bearing on the explanatory concepts of causality and existence. It had been assumed by traditional metaphysics that these concepts validly apply, not only to objects and events that can be discovered within the spatio-temporal order, but also to the world as a whole and to such a being as God, who stands outside it. God, it had been believed, could be properly said to exist, and to be the cause of that spatio-temporal order considered as an entirety. Kant attempts to show that these beliefs are mistaken, and that human knowledge cannot really include such assertions as these.

So far as concerns the concept of causality, his thought is quite simple. The essence of the distinction between a merely temporal sequence of two events and a causal relation—in which the earlier is cause of the later—is only revealed, and can only be revealed, under the conditions that time provides. It is not, and cannot in the nature of the case, be revealed as applying to the relation between the entire temporal order and something nontemporal. How do we make that distinction, and how do we give it meaning? By learning the difference between merely accidental connections in time, exemplified by the relation between the fall of a limb from a tree and the chirping of a bird which happens to accompany it, and objectively necessary connections, exemplified by the relation between the same fall of that limb and the crushing of the grass as the limb comes to rest on the ground. In the former case there is only temporal sequence between the two events; in the latter case the earlier event is also cause of the later event. Now we do learn this distinction. And it is quite clear that it is a distinction *within* time, for the temporal order is present in both cases; the cause of an effect precedes the effect as well as being its cause. But now suppose we attempt to apply the notion of causality to the world of experience taken as a whole, assuming it to be an effect and inquiring after its cause. In such a situation the meaning of the concept evaporates and its validity is lost. For, owing to the finite limitations of the human mind, we cannot really experience the whole world but only, at best, that portion of it which has been presented in the narrow spatio-temporal field of our personal existence. We do not, therefore, even know whether the existence of the world as a whole can be properly called an *event;* how go further than this, and call it confidently an *effect?* Under these circumstances we are quite unable to distinguish between a causal and a noncausal relation; we cannot realize the distinctive nature of causality here. Were we able to break free from the limitations of finite experience, it might be possible to apprehend a relation between the entire course of events and something nontemporal; but for us this is impossible, since we are human and all our experience is in time. We cannot, of course, positively deny that there are realities to whose nature time as experienced by finite creatures is irrelevant—Kant agrees with agnosticism on this point, too—and we may gain assurance about them through some route other than that of cognitive demonstration. But we cannot *know* them, as we can know that the perceived motion of one body is the effect of motion in another which has regularly preceded it. Our knowledge is limited to the temporal details of finite experience. Causality is an explanatory concept that can only be meaningfully employed as a category of the understanding.

Kant's argument with respect to the concept of existence is less simple, but the central points can be stated without involving ourselves in the more obscure parts of his reasoning.

When we apply this concept to objects capable of being perceived within some spatio-temporal locus, its meaning and validity are apparent. We can distinguish without difficulty between an object that exists, such as a dog, and one that can be imagined but does not exist, such as a centaur. But what can we mean when we say that an object exists which is so inclusive or transcendent that it is incapable of being perceived under such finite conditions? Take again the "world" as a supposed object of knowledge. Clearly we do not mean by it just the aggregate of physical bodies that we have already experienced. It has at least two attributes that that aggregate does not possess; it includes all the bodies that might be experienced but as yet have not been, and it implies that the bodies which make it up are not merely an aggregate but belong to a single orderly system. Is it not obvious that the world, so conceived, is an ideal, rather than something that can be properly said now to exist? It stands for what we hope ultimately to achieve when our knowledge about the various physical objects and events is carried to completion; it expresses our cognitive demand that all of them be capable of explanation as parts of a unitary system. In Kant's technical language, the world is not a "constitutive" category but a "regulative" ideal—that is, it symbolizes the rational interest of the human mind in perfecting its understanding of the medley of external phenomena which confront it; by the aid of such an idea the course of physical inquiry is guided toward the unity of perfect knowledge which is the natural goal of reason. In this capacity the idea is valid. But, thus taken, there is clearly no justification for assertions which imply a claim to knowledge of the world as a whole —assertions about its origin, its ultimate elements, its destiny. These assume that the asserter has gained a completed grasp of the world such as Kant's analysis proves, so he believes, to be impossible for a mind working under the finite conditions and limitations of human thinking.

Similar results are reached in dealing with the idea of the soul. We may properly attribute existence to any particular volition, sensation, or feeling occurring as a temporal bit of our inner life and introspectively observable under the narrow restrictions of time characteristic of human perception. But we cannot properly say that the soul as a whole exists—still less make assertions about the mode of its existence, such as that it is an independent substance, free from causal determination, and indestructible. For these assertions to be justified, our inner life would first need to be lived through to completion, and then we should have to stand aside, surveying it as a single whole and apprehending its essential unity in some larger temporal context. Obviously, none of us is capable of doing this, at least not while we pursue knowledge under the conditions that obtain in this present life. And while those conditions prevail we have no way of telling whether any other kind of life is real, or even possible. The soul, too, is merely a regulative ideal. It expresses our cognitive craving for completed understanding of the phenomena of our inner life as composing a unitary system, and only in this capacity is it a valid idea for knowledge.

If neither the world nor the soul can be known to exist, it is evidently still less possible to affirm any such cognition about God, a supposed original creator, ultimate preserver, and final disposer of both the order of external phenomena and the realm of inner experience. To be sure, there is a regulative ideal operating here too, and if we were to restrict the meaning of the idea of God in human thinking to what is clearly involved in that ideal it would be valid, although we could not say that God exists, for the same reasons that apply in the case of the world and the soul. The external world and the internal soul are somehow both within the same universe. Reason demands that they be capable of explanation in terms of dependence on a single unifying principle. We could mean by God simply that principle. On these terms the deity clearly becomes, however, not an object of human knowledge, but an appealing symbol of the final goal at which it aims. We can, as inquirers, say nothing about him; we can only work hopefully toward that ultimately unified comprehension of our universe that such a principle symbolizes.

But, for religion, God means much more than this. We noted above that by the "world" thinkers mean not only the aggregate of experienced bodies (which they might justifiably claim to know), but the totality of all bodies as bound together in an interacting system (which they cannot plausibly claim to know). In the case of God the religious thinker goes even farther, in the meaning he assumes for the concept, from what our actual experience might justify. Experience might support the claim that in some sense we know there is a sum of all reality (the scholastic *omnitudo realitatis*), including minds as well as bodies. But metaphysics and theology have never been satisfied to mean by God merely this. Indeed, they have not only transcended this concept by making God the unifying principle or "ground" for this totality of existence instead of just the totality itself; they have thought of him as the supremely perfect being, including in his nature every conceivable perfection raised to its superlative degree. And many of them have believed it possible to demonstrate (by the famous ontological argument) that a being so conceived necessarily exists.

Kant must therefore clinch his analysis of this whole problem by showing that the ontological argument is really fallacious. The argument, it will be recalled,[10] attempts to deduce God's existence directly from his absolute perfection, on the ground that a supposedly perfect being without existence would lack an important element in perfection and would thus be self-contradictory. This reasoning, it will be observed, assumes that existence is an attribute that can constitute one of the features of perfection, comparable in this respect to wisdom, justice, love, and the like. The point of Kant's attack lay in his insistence that existence cannot be regarded as a property or attribute whose addition enriches and whose removal impoverishes a concept.[11] Just what is the difference between a hundred silver dollars that are merely conceived and a hundred dollars that really exist? Both have the same number of coins, and the same properties of each coin—roundness, grayish-whiteness, thickness, heaviness, and all the rest. If there were a difference in any of these respects, what we conceive would not be a hundred silver dollars but something else. The difference, then, is nothing that can be stated in terms of properties or attributes; it lies simply in the fact that in the existent hundred dollars there are externally engendered sensations, organized by the mind through the forms and the categories. These sensations, thus ordered in perception, provide real stuff and content for that money. The conceived dollars are alike in every respect but this. Kant holds that this principle applies to all concepts. Accordingly, existence cannot enter into any concept as an implied part of its definition. Define it as and how we please, the question still remains open whether we shall experience anything exemplifying

[10] Cf. above, p. 180.
[11] *Critique of Pure Reason*, pp. 500 ff.

that definition or not. It is impossible to be sure that we will, merely from the definition. We shall never, then, be able to analyze existence out of the concept of supreme or absolute perfection. Any admissible definition of a perfect being remains the same whether we suppose that being to possess real existence or not.[12]

The ontological argument thus falls to the ground. And so far as Kant's main point here appears cogent it illustrates and strengthens his contention that existence, like causality, is merely a category of the understanding, and that all such categories can only be significantly applied under the temporal limitations of finite human experience. They lead to illusion if these limitations are disregarded.

As a result of these analyses, we have, Kant maintains, an explanation of the originally puzzling contrast between the synthetic judgments *a priori* which function in mathematics and natural science and those which function in metaphysics.[13] All such judgments alike are expressions of the essential structure of mind, but the judgments based on the forms and the categories respect the limitations of human thinking and are therefore objectively valid, while the judgments of metaphysicians about the ideas of reason disregard those limitations and are not objectively valid. Thought uses them without error solely if it treats them as regulative guides toward its end of systematic unity in knowledge. Failure to recognize this restriction accounts for the historical circumstance that mathematics and physical science progress from conquest to conquest, each generation building securely upon the achievements of its predecessor and adding its own contribution to them, while metaphysics and theology remain the arena of futile debate, forever occupied with the same problems which they can never settle by any convincing demonstration. It explains why the devotees of these studies do not hesitate to pitch overboard all that their intellectual ancestors have proffered and to erect entirely new founda-

---

[12] In the *Critique of Judgment*, published in 1790, Kant reopens the question whether God may not be used as an objective principle of theoretical explanation. Can we, without God, properly explain the mutual adaptations evident in the organic world? His answer is that a theistic explanation is here highly probable. But he maintains that we cannot give the definite content to the idea of God which is necessary for religion by such considerations; the moral approach alone can provide this.

[13] *Critique of Pure Reason*, pp. 574–593.

tions—these being destined to go overboard in turn. Science may proceed with confidence, but metaphysics is impossible—as knowledge.

The last phrase deserves emphasis, lest we misunderstand the message of the *Critique of Pure Reason*. Like Hume and Huxley, Kant is quite conscious that his analysis has not proved the unreality of God, freedom, or immortality. It has simply shown, if sound, that these matters are beyond the reach of human knowledge.

HIS ETHICAL PHILOSOPHY

In the field of theory of knowledge, then, Kant's reconciliation of rationalism and empiricism gives a decided predominance to the latter; the emphasis is on the limitation of knowledge to data empirically observed. The danger there is that thinkers, moved by confidence in reason, will fall into error through failing to recognize this limitation. In his moral philosophy, to which our attention now turns, a contrary result emerges. The empirical material here has no moral worth; what is significant is a universal rational principle of rightness, of whose validity we can be absolutely certain, although that certainty is practical, not theoretical.

In this field the empirical element consists of the wants and desires which are discoverable by introspective psychology. These naturally move us to action in ways that appear appropriate for securing the ends at which they aim. Such impulses are in themselves neither moral nor immoral; what decides whether our conduct is right or not is the principle by which those desires are controlled. Should we, for example, be guided by the maxim of satisfying as many of these natural interests as possible—should our conduct, in other words, become a pursuit of our own happiness—it would be immoral through and through; we should in this case have surrendered our higher, rational character to become a mere servant of our empirical, sensuous nature, and this is for Kant the very essense of immorality. What this rational character is, and why it is higher than the character expressed in our wants and desires, we shall soon learn. Moreover, in the moral life this surrender is the common danger; hence, although desire is necessary to conduct as sensation is to knowledge, the important matter in discussing problems of conduct is to bring into prominence the rational law which rightfully controls desire.

Man is essentially a rational being, and moral action is at bottom nothing but rational action. But what is it to act rationally? We can find the answer to this question in two ways.

The more direct and rigorous way is to analyze reason, laying bare its intrinsic features and noting what they involve when seen in relation to conduct instead of merely in relation to scientific understanding. Kant finds two such features, namely, universality and necessity. The meaning of these terms is not obscure. In theoretical explanations, for example, reason demands unlimited generalization, i.e., the discovery of a law that is verifiably exemplified in all events of the same kind. Here is exhibited its character of universality. It also demands the exclusion of the possibility that the relation established might sometime fail to obtain. Here is necessity. Indeed, these two features are united in the conception of "law." A law is a principle which is universally exemplified in events of a certain class, and to which they necessarily conform. Consider these features now in their bearing on conduct. To act rationally must be to act in accordance with law. What law? Well, no special law, just the idea of law in general. That is, it is to act in such a way as to respect, in conduct, the principles of universality and necessity. Kant might easily have become lost in a maze of abstract concepts here, but what is concretely before his mind is the fact that men, who are the only rational beings with whom we are directly acquainted, live in social relations with each other. To act in accordance with the dictates of universality and necessity essentially means, then, to be guided in any given situation by the maxim which one would be willing to see become a law for all other men were they in that situation. One must not demand special privileges for himself; it is his business to accept as governing his own conduct the same rule that he would want other people to follow. "Act only on that maxim whereby thou canst at the same time will that it should become a universal law."[14] This abstractly philosophical formulation of the Golden Rule is, then, the principle by which our wants and desires are rightfully tested before being allowed to issue in action. Conduct in harmony with this law and

[14] T. K. Abbott, *Kant's Theory of Ethics*, p. 38.

motivated by respect for it is morally good; conduct inconsistent with it is morally wrong.

The second and less rigorous way by which to find out what it means to act rationally is to observe the moral judgments which we pass upon ourselves and others, laying bare the criteria to which we implicitly appeal when trying to decide what is right to do in any given situation.[15] In such cases we discover the above principle actually operating as a guide to our judgments. Suppose, being tempted to tell a lie or break a promise, we ask ourselves whether and why it would be wrong to do so. We see that it would, and for the reason that we do not want other people to lie or break their promises to us. We do not will it as a universal law that people should tell the truth and keep their promises only when it is convenient or to their interest to do so. If we, then, succumbed to the temptation we should evidently be making an exception, in our own favor, to the maxim which we wish everybody else to follow, and this we see is the very essence of immorality.

The necessity which—so Kant maintains—we may discover in the law of moral obligation, in addition to its universality, appears most clearly when we examine the technical phrase by which he describes it in this connection.[16] He calls it a "categorical imperative." What does this mean? Well, a command which is not categorical is hypothetical—that is, it is one in which we are bidden to perform an action *if* we wish to achieve some end to which it offers the necessary means. All rules of policy or prudence, for example, are hypothetical imperatives; they indicate what we must do if we are to attain happiness or some other good which might naturally be pursued. But it is not necessary for us to pursue any such end, hence no rule of guidance which tells us what must be done to attain it is unqualifiedly necessary. The moral law, however, is a categorical imperative; it commands us without any condition or qualification. It admits no "if." Our ends are subordinate to it as well as our choice of means; or rather, it in itself implies an ultimate end of conduct, namely, respect for rationality and its principle of unexceptional law. Whether in ourselves or in other men, we must not allow rationality to become a means to anything else; it is strictly an end in itself. So far as our individual conduct is con-

15 *Ibid.*, pp. 39 f.
16 *Ibid.*, pp. 30 ff.

cerned, this amounts to subordinating the natural desire for personal happiness to the demands of social duty. So far as our relations with others are concerned, it means avoidance of all temptation to exploit them as instruments to the furtherance of our own purposes; it means treating them with the ultimate respect with which we wish to be treated ourselves. This moral end is necessary because it derives from the nature of reason, which is the supreme and distinctive essence of man.

That the law of duty rightfully claims categorical necessity may be clearly seen, according to Kant, in another way.[17] Suppose that, having surveyed the actual behavior of people in their social relations, we come to the conclusion that this principle of moral obligation is more frequently violated than obeyed, and begin to wonder how a law can be universal and necessary when it is so often implicitly repudiated in experience. We are conscious, however, that, no matter how frequently it is disobeyed in fact, it *ought* to be obeyed always and unconditionally. Its universality and necessity are not such as pertain to an existential fact, after the fashion of a scientific generalization, but such as pertain to a rational command. And in this sense we see that these principles are genuinely present, as absolutely valid in the realm of morals. Even if no man should ever have obeyed the law of duty in a single item of his conduct, we should none the less be clearly aware of his and our categorical obligation to obey it. Like the *a priori* forms of theoretical reason it is in its origin entirely independent of experience, deriving from the rational nature of mind. Unlike them, its validity also stands, entirely independent of sense experience. The nature of its actual content does not at all control or limit the sphere of its relevant application. It is an absolute and unconditional demand. What we can know is restricted by the matter and the temporal structure of finite experience; of what we ought to do we are rationally certain without any such restriction.

RELIGIOUS DOCTRINES AS MORAL POSTULATES

On the foundations supplied by this moral philosophy Kant proceeds to reëstablish the creed of religion which his earlier examination had shown impotent to pose successfully as demonstrative

[17] *Ibid.*, pp. 23 ff.

knowledge. In this novel orientation the significance of religious belief is radically transformed; from being conceived as a kind of metaphysical knowledge—an apprehended insight into the nature of the universe—it becomes a moral faith whose prime virtue is practical, not theoretical.

The vital consideration which, according to Kant, leads us from recognition of our moral obligation to such a reinterpreted theology is that unqualified acceptance of our duty to obey the moral law implies, as we can discover, certain assumptions about the universe and man's place in it. It implies them in the sense that the moral man sees clearly that unless he makes those assumptions he cannot consistently hold to his conviction that the law of duty is a rational command and is categorically binding upon him.[18] We must, in short, if we are to pursue our duty unswervingly, believe the universe to be such that loyalty to the moral law by one who is part of it and dependent on it is always reasonable. Now this belief is not an empty abstraction. Two quite definite factors are included in it. In the first place, we human beings who are summoned to obey the law are creatures of sensuous desire as well as of reason; such desire inevitably influences our conduct, and it does not seem to be necessarily under the control of reason. In the second place, the physical environment around us, to which our conduct needs to be adjusted, is not obviously governed by moral principles. In order to persist in devotion to our duty, then, and to retain our confidence that such devotion is reasonable, we must believe that respect for the moral law can conquer the pull of selfish desire and that the physical world is ultimately subject to moral control. To hold such beliefs would seem to be required from the moral standpoint even though they cannot be demonstrated theoretically.[19] Under this novel garb we face again the main items in the religious creed which had been deprived of cognitive standing in the *Critique of Pure Reason*.

This situation seems, however, to confront us with a serious puzzle. When moral considerations point toward the adoption of beliefs which an examination of the nature of knowledge has de-

---

[18] *Ibid.*, pp. 209 ff.
[19] It will be noticed that one of these beliefs is psychological; the other, metaphysical.

prived of objective demonstrability, what are we to do, and why?[20]
We cannot pretend to know that such beliefs are true, and yet
sincerity and clarity of moral commitment seems to require them.
And surely we cannot contradict ourselves. What is our recourse
in such a dilemma? Kant answers this crucial question by affirming
a doctrine of the "primacy," under these circumstances, of the
practical reason—that is, reason as concerned with matters of conduct—over the theoretical reason, which functions merely as a
faculty of cognition.[21] This means that an apparently metaphysical
conviction which is rationally required by unqualified obedience
to the moral law may be rightly held as well founded even though
it cannot stand as an item of objective knowledge.

In support of this conclusion Kant gives two fundamental reasons. For one thing, the outcome of the critical analysis of pure
reason was agnostic, not atheistic. It did not deny the religious
hypothesis; it simply proved that man is essentially incompetent
to know whether that hypothesis is true or not. The result was
negative, removing certain pretensions to knowledge without denying the object supposed to be known. Whereas, the implications that
follow from acceptance of the moral law, like that law itself, are
positive and unequivocal. Well, surely, we must not abandon a
positive certainty for a question mark. For another thing, theoretical
inquiry, aiming at the attainment of knowledge, is itself a human
activity, a form of conduct. Like other types of human behavior, it
is the expression of a certain interest; comparable, as interest, to the
other characteristic motives which issue in different modes of conduct. Theoretical reason, from this standpoint, is simply one branch
of practical reason; the latter is the all-inclusive expression of the
rational nature of man, of which the quest for knowledge is a
limited part. Now a whole clearly holds primacy over one of its
parts. We cannot, therefore, "require pure practical reason to be
subordinate to the speculative, since all interest is ultimately practical, and even that of speculative reason is conditional, and it is
only in the practical employment of reason that it is complete."[22]

---

[20] No previous Western religious philosophy found itself in such a conflict,
for in none were moral principles autonomous.

[21] Abbott, *Kant's Theory of Ethics*, pp. 216 ff.

[22] *Ibid.*, p. 218.

What, then, is the status of these convictions which are unable to stand as knowledge, but which, as corollaries of devotion to moral duty, hold primacy over demonstrable knowledge? Kant calls them "postulates of practical reason," and he makes it clear that except in one specific respect they must not be regarded as extensions of our theoretical understanding—their validity is that of an assured moral faith. They are not extensions of our cognition, because their acceptance in no way modifies the analysis of knowledge and its limitations given in the *Critique of Pure Reason*. They cannot therefore become the foundation of a scientific metaphysic; systematic deductions cannot be drawn from them and treated as additions to our knowledge. In Kant's own words, "we cannot make any positive use of them in a theoretical point of view."[23] In one single respect, however, they do extend the insight of theoretical reason. We are convinced on rational grounds that the propositions in which these beliefs find expression are true, and that the supersensible entities toward which they point are real. And this assurance the *Critique of Pure Reason* could not give us. Their validity, however, is not that of a demonstrable scientific cognition but that of a faith founded in practical reason. It is a rational faith, because loyalty to the moral law, of which they are corollaries, amply proves itself to be the supreme expression of our rational nature. It is faith, however, not knowledge, because its essential function is not to extend our scientific explanations, but rather to clarify our moral life in its relation to the inclinations of our sensuous nature and to the basic structure of the cosmos in which that life is set. Its articles are ultimate assurances by which we intelligently live, not metaphysical insights by which we break free from the cognitive limitations of finite thought.

What are these postulates of practical reason? They are three: the freedom of the soul from causal determination; its immortality; and the existence of God.

For cognition, as the *Critique of Pure Reason* had taught, no freedom of the will is conceivable. Causality, being a category of the understanding, applies universally and necessarily to every event; only in causal terms can we apprehend and explain it.[24]

---

[23] *Ibid.*, p. 232.
[24] *Critique of Pure Reason*, pp. 469 ff.

Everything that we human beings do, then, when it becomes an object of knowledge, must be regarded as completely determined by a causal chain reaching back to the beginning of our individual career and ultimately to causes entirely outside of and antedating our personal existence. In this way scientific determinism spells religious fatalism; we are made what we are by events which have long since disappeared and are in any case quite beyond control by our moral choices and aspirations. We do what we do, not because we see it is right, but because we are compelled by necessary causes. But when we examine the situation from the point of view of moral obligation we find that freedom is an inevitable postulate of the practical reason.[25] For the law of duty commands us categorically to do the right; and this implies that we must always be able to obey the command, no matter how strong the motives and selfish interests which tempt us to disobey. Whatever we ought, we can. Otherwise it would not be rational to suppose that we confront an unconditional obligation. Therefore, from the standpoint of a moral agent, we must believe that we are free from fatal determination by selfish inclinations, even when an impartial observer trying to understand our conduct would inevitably expect us to succumb to them; we must assume that we are always free to do what the moral law requires, though perchance we have never in our lives done so before. This means the further conviction that over and above our empirical self of impulse and desire, which is all that can be observed by the knowledge-seeking understanding, there is a supersensible moral personality which, as our real self, is ultimately dominant over that lower empirical nature. We cannot know this,[26] but we are morally assured of it, and moral assurance has the primacy over knowledge.

We shall not take the space to describe Kant's attempt to justify by this moral approach faith in personal immortality and in the real existence of God. These parts of his argument have met serious subsequent criticism, even by those who incline to agree with his other major contentions, and would probably not be defended by any contemporary religious philosopher. In fact, Kant

[25] Abbott, *op. cit.*, pp. 187 ff.
[26] Kant sometimes distinguishes freedom from the other postulates by saying that we know it. See Abbott, p. 200.

himself became dissatisfied with them and in his last comments on religion appeared to abandon them entirely.[27] What, however, he intended to replace them by is not entirely clear, unless it be the doctrine that God is disclosed in the categorical imperative itself and the influence which it exerts upon us. The teaching of his closest recent followers on this matter we shall soon examine.

By reconciling in this way religion and science Kant radically transformed theology. From being a kind of metaphysical knowledge it became a morally grounded faith, and a faith whose essential value is to clarify, support, and enrich our moral life. It is not its business to extend our knowledge or to compete with science. For Spinoza, the quest of science is itself the heart of religion; for Hume, it destroys religion's claim to truth; for Kant, science and religion occupy entirely different spheres, and are given distinct functions which are so adjusted that they need never conflict. The realm of possible knowledge belongs to science, and science has complete freedom to explore that realm by its own method. The task of religion is to enlighten our moral devotion and give it cosmic serenity.

When Kant, accordingly, comes to define religion, he does so in terms of this essential dependence in which it stands to moral duty. Religion is "the recognition of all duties as divine commands";[28] not, of course, in the sense that they are duties for us because divinely commanded, but in the sense that clarification of our consciousness of duty leads to the postulation of a holy Supreme Being whose will is revealed in the moral law.

Morality is thus primary and autonomous, religion being secondary and derivative, though yet rationally warranted. Its convictions are rational corollaries of unqualified moral commitment, moving thus in a quite different sphere from that of scientific knowledge and incapable of conflict with it. It is an affair of intelligent conscience or will. "The conception of God is one that belongs originally not to physics but to morals."[29]

Kant did not see clearly that this novel approach to theology, consistently followed, would require some transformation in the

[27] In his *Opus postumum*, edited by E. Adickes in 1920.
[28] Abbott, *op. cit.*, p. 226.
[29] *Ibid.*, p. 238.

meaning of the religious ideas thus validated; in general, he writes as though this procedure established in a new way the same conceptions of God and soul that traditional theology had been impotent to demonstrate. The kind of transformation needed will be seen when we examine Felix Adler's religious philosophy. None the less, Kant did formulate clearly the philosophical foundations of this theological orientation so that others could build with fuller consistency upon them.

In part because of its intrinsic appeal, in part because of Kant's enormous influence on every phase of thought which his writings touched, this ethical approach to religion became an increasingly significant force during the nineteenth century. In the philosophy of Fichte, a younger contemporary and follower of Kant, the moral self is even conceived as an ultimate metaphysical principle, in terms of which the essential structure and go of the universe are explained; and moral faith becomes the avenue by which the individual realizes his membership in the invisible spiritual community which, itself interpreted as a moral will, constitutes supreme reality. Such speculations, of course, go far beyond what Kant would have approved; they turn his practical faith into a new kind of metaphysical cognition. Another younger contemporary, whose conception of religion Kant very deeply affected but whose main contribution lies in another direction, Schleiermacher, will be considered at some length in the following chapter. During the middle decades of the century the influence of Kant's ethical position was exhibited most fully, so far as its bearing on general philosophical problems is concerned, in the system of Hermann Lotze, while a little later both Kant and Lotze became guides to a reconstruction of Protestant theology in the work of Albrecht Ritschl. Largely through such intermediaries as these Kant's ethical idealism entered as a prominent factor the religious philosophies with which we shall soon be occupied, modernism and humanism.

Felix Adler's Religious Philosophy

Of contemporary religious tendencies, the Ethical Culture Movement most fully reveals the influence of Kant's theory of religion. In it a religious society is organized, founded on the common quest of its members for unceasing progress in "knowledge, practice, and love of the right."[30] And the concept "right" is interpreted in essentially Kantian terms—that is, its central postulate is that an inviolable worth is to be recognized in every human being in virtue of his possession of a moral nature. This postulate takes the place, for those united in the Society's fellowship, of a theological creed. Their task is through mutual aid to attain a clearer realization of the meaning of this principle and its implications with respect to specific personal and social problems, to exemplify it more completely in conduct, and to deepen their devotion to the ideal ethical community which the postulate leads them to acknowledge as supreme. With unanimity on such a basic principle for the guidance of conduct, the Society permits, nay, encourages, the greatest diversity in beliefs on other matters, since only thus may the continued clarification of thought be adequately stimulated. And no other belief, in the judgment of its members, is vitally important.[31]

Although there is thus no creed and no source of intellectual authority in the movement, the philosophical principles which have been most influential in guiding the Society's development are those set forth in the writings of Dr. Felix Adler, its founder and for more than half a century its leader. As with Hume in the preceding chapter, we shall allow Dr. Adler to be the spokesman for the solution of the major problems of religious philosophy offered by ethical idealism today, instead of attempting to couch its argument in more general terms.[32]

Taking his stand on Kant's central ethical doctrine that human personality, whether in oneself or in others, must be reverenced and never violated, Dr. Adler endeavors to provide a more adequate and positive statement of that in which ethical personality basically consists than is offered in Kant's concepts of "practical reason" and "consciousness of duty." This is found in the idea that

[30] F. Adler, *The Aim of the Ethical Movement*, p. 2.
[31] It must not be supposed, however, that all members of the Society are ethical idealists, in the sense in which that phrase is here explained. Many are humanists, with a position on morals that is essentially Kantian. See below, pp. 346 ff. and 352 f.
[32] Many details by Dr. Adler's position are, of course, not shared by all contemporary ethical idealists. An attempt is made at the end of the chapter to summarize the doctrines which are characteristic of this theological orientation as such.

each personality is essentially related to other personalities in an ethical community which is implicitly universal—that is, which excludes no one who proves capable of ethical response. And such capacity may be attributed to all human beings; it distinguishes them from inanimate objects and the lower forms of life, which, experience tells us, do not exhibit such responsiveness. Men may hence never be exploited or used as mere instruments. But the relation between personalities in which their ethical community consists is not a merely negative one—that is, characterized simply by unwillingness on the part of each to violate the personality of another. Its more important positive aspect involves mutual furtherance of each other's ends as moral beings. To treat another personality as of absolute worth means to coöperate with him in the quest for all those goods whose pursuit is consistent with recognition of the same absolute worth in other persons whose lives his quest affects.

Dr. Adler takes special pains to insist, however, that this universality of moral obligation does not at all imply a dead uniformity in the detailed character and conduct displayed by ethically earnest persons. Each has his own distinctive capacity and unique contribution to offer to the spiritual life of mankind. With this consideration in mind, we see that to treat another human being as of ultimate value means to bring out, so far as we can, the creative individuality of which he is capable—to foster the growth and expression of that induplicable something by which he may enrich the world. Through such prophetic friendship with others, one's own moral nature enlarges and deepens. Hence an adequate statement of the essential relation in virtue of which the members of the ethical community are bound together must recognize this variegated creativity as well as the more obvious requirements of mutual respect and harmonious interaction. The statement which our author offers of this basic principle of ethical unity is as follows: "The unique difference of each shall be such as to render possible the correlated unique differences of all the rest." If this formula appears rather abstract, the general guiding rule of conduct which it implies as universally valid is quite simple and concrete. It is: Act so as to elicit in others the distinctive excellence characteristic of each of them as fellow members of the ethical whole, and thereby to elicit that excellence more fully in yourself.[33] Like Kant, Dr. Adler maintains that this rule is absolute in the sense of possessing a supersensible and nonempirical warrant, for reasons which will shortly be noted.

But how do we know there is any such excellence to be elicited, either in anyone else or in ourselves? Following Kant, Dr. Adler holds that in the strict meaning of "knowledge" we do not know this. It is a postulate, whose assumption is justified by effects in our moral experience which he believes can only be explained by assuming that there is a real and active energizing in us of a spiritual self. That self is the "I" as a member of the ideal ethical community. There is, he insists, an irreducible difference between a physical event, which can be explained by analysis of the phenomena concerned into their elements and structural relations, and an ethical experience, which derives its entire reality and distinctive nature from its place in a larger whole—namely, the universal ethical community. The method of analysis is fully appropriate to the former, whereas the very essence of the latter would be destroyed by it. A moral act is an act done in virtue of the actor's relation to all other moral beings in the universe. Thus, while the totality of physical nature is incapable of being known, because the analytic method of science is incapable of dealing with it, a moral reality cannot be experienced at all except as related to the whole in which it belongs. Now as moral beings we men are immediately conscious—or are capable of becoming conscious—of such a whole and of our responsibility and worth as members of it. This consciousness has its distinctive effect, meager or great, in our experience. We feel the influence of that whole upon us, and such a feeling can be accounted for only by assuming the reality of the ideal spiritual community which is the object of that consciousness.[34]

The features of Dr. Adler's philosophy which have thus far been considered may be summed up under four propositions: (1) We are conscious of an absolute obligation to treat every moral personality as an end. (2) This consciousness involves the realization of our membership in the ideal community of all moral beings.

[33] F. Adler, An Ethical Philosophy of Life, pp. 73 ff., 116 f., 121, 220 ff. Sometimes the supreme rule is stated more simply still (and more vaguely) in the form: Act so as to elicit the best in others and thereby in thyself (p. 208).
[34] Ibid., Book II, chap. III.

(3) Such realization makes a difference in our character and conduct. (4) That difference proves the reality of the ideal whole whose
pressure is responsible for it.

On these foundations a moral theology is built, and it contains
two major doctrines. First, moral freedom is asserted. This occupies
for Dr. Adler the same essential status and is affirmed on the same
ground as was the case with Kant. Freedom is simply power to
respond to the universal moral whole, and it is present wherever
there is moral experience at all; were it not postulated, the irreducible distinction would be annulled between a physical process,
determined by the structure of its elementary parts, and ethical
awareness. Second, in place of the attempt to find a moral ground
for faith in God and immortality as traditionally conceived, Dr. Adler
simply affirms the reality of an infinite spiritual universe transcending the temporal career of humanity, in which all that is of genuine
worth in each individual is contained and preserved. This doctrine,
he holds, is implied by the nature and absolute value of moral personality as above explained. The spiritual community, whose reality
is attested in our experience and which constitutes the distinctive
environment of moral selfhood, is not restricted to members possessing the particular qualities of men and women, and is certainly
not confined by any spatio-temporal limits. It includes all beings
who are capable of an ethical relation as such. But it is our end as
ethical beings to achieve the full realization of all our potentialities
as members of this community. Now it is clear that this realization
cannot be attained in any finite world. "Only after this truth has
been fully faced and recognized, shall we be in a position to take in
the vast significance of the fact that we are nevertheless under a
certain coercion to persist in our efforts to attain the unattainable,
and in inquiring into the source from which this pressure comes, we
shall be led to infer the influence in us of an infinite nature enshrined
in this finite nature of ours. In other words, to admit the unattain-
ableness of the end in a finite world by a finite being is the very
condition of our acquiring the conviction that there is an infinite
world, and that we, as possessing an infinite nature, are included
in it." In fact, the goal of moral progress may be described, on its
intellectual side, as consisting in the attainment of an unconquerable
assurance and clear vision of the reality of an eternal spiritual

universe to which we belong. The status of such an assurance and vision, however, is not that of cognition, but, as Kant insisted, that of a moral postulate.[35]

An infinite spiritual community thus hovers over the realm of our finite experience, luring it upward to such moral attainment as our capacity permits, and eternally preserving the ethical values achieved.[36] Our empirical individuality is not preserved, however, as the doctrine of personal immortality maintains, and Dr. Adler rejects with equal emphasis the theistic interpretation of ultimate reality. The spiritual community as such takes the place of God.

On the foundation provided by the supreme rule of moral conduct —act so as to elicit in others their distinctive moral excellence, and thereby more fully your own—our author approaches the social problems of contemporary life. These are to be solved, he believes, through the application to them of this absolute maxim, under the guidance of such empirical knowledge as is available about human psychology and sociology. And in the interest of more adequate solutions it is important that this knowledge be continually increased and extended. The proper goal of all social reform, as he conceives it, is very radical and far-reaching; it consists in the transformation of social institutions in such a way that they may become successive phases through which the individual can advance toward the realization of a full ethical personality.[37] At present even the best of these institutions falls far short of exhibiting this character, and the task before us is therefore enormous.

In Dr. Adler's view, the main social groups to which an individual normally belongs should be regarded, from the ethical standpoint, as forming a hierarchical series. First in this series stands the family. Into it each moral individual is born, and it is the institution in whose affectionate enfoldment a truly ethical relation is most readily learned—especially that relation as it can be expressed in the attitude of the mature toward the undeveloped. The best form

[35] *Ibid.*, pp. 130 ff., 150 f., 359 ff. *The Reconstruction of the Spiritual Ideal,* pp. 217 f. The above quotation is reprinted by permission of the publishers, D. Appleton-Century Company.

[36] Faith in the reality of such a spiritual universe is the chief distinguishing feature of ethical idealism, as this chapter uses the phrase, in contrast with the humanism to be discussed below.

[37] F. Adler, *An Ethical Philosophy of Life,* pp. 257 f., 261.

of this relation is more readily exemplified in the behavior of parents toward their children than in any other social situation. From the family an ethical reverence may radiate and gradually penetrate the social institutions which follow it in the series. At the other end stands the church. It is conceived as the attempted embodiment, here and now, of the universal ethical community, "the microcosm of the spiritual macrocosm, or miniature model of the ideal society" which is eternal and infinite. It supplies the normative principle whereby the gradual reconstruction of the institutions that precede it in the series is guided. The three most important institutions which lie between these are the school, the vocational group to which an individual comes to belong, and the state. In an ethically reconstructed society these five institutions would function as a progressive series, through which every person grows toward ethical maturity.[38] Why and how they are related in this order will become apparent as we consider each of them briefly.

The family is peculiarly important, according to Dr. Adler, because the tie of natural affection which lies at its foundation, and which is so warm and selective, provides the most adequate factual support for a truly ethical human relationship. The family is thus uniquely capable of nourishing and disseminating the germ which leavens relationships in the other groups and gradually gives them an ethical organization. In the mutual devotion and companionship which in family life at its best obtain between husband and wife, likewise in the love and guidance which they give the children as the latter grow toward adulthood, the ethical ideal is very largely realized, and the reverential attitude toward personality is encouraged which may gradually mold the other social groups into fuller conformity to the demands of the ideal. A truly moral responsibility of relatively mature and civilized groups toward immature and undeveloped ones everywhere is rooted, so far as its empirical sources are concerned, in the natural affection of a parent for his child. Reverence for the pioneers of ethical attainment in the past, and for leaders in every field of coöperative endeavor in the present, likewise is rooted in the natural gratitude and trust which a child feels toward his parent. And ethical friendship built on mutual respect and interdependence finds its main source in the

[38] *Ibid.*, pp. 241 f., 353.

attachment to each other of husband and wife and of brothers and sisters. But for the family to perform this important moral function, and to perform it more and more successfully, it is essential that the monogamic ideal be accepted. Only when two parents are loyal to each other, and only when their exclusive relation to the children is lifelong, can the spiritual development of parents and children alike be furthered to the highest degree that is possible. Marriage does not exist for the happiness of those who enter it, but for their ethical development, and especially for the development of the children whom they bring into being. From this standpoint, the finest partnership often results from the determined overcoming of incompatibilities which in the case of persons with no controlling ethical purpose would easily lead to divorce. Love when guided by moral reverence never ceases. And since the spiritual training of a new generation is complete at no given age, the finest touches often being added when sons and daughters are grown, the intimate union between the parents should for this reason also continue through life.[39]

In treating problems of education, Dr. Adler is primarily concerned to insist on the responsibility of the school to develop moral personality in its pupils. Its task is never merely to give them information or train them to earn a living in some vocation, as current practice so often assumes. Accordingly, educators should themselves be permeated by the spirit of ethical reverence, education should be conceived as a lifelong process meeting the needs of adults as well as of the young, and systematic moral training must be provided from the lower schools up to the adult classes.[40]

An ethical approach to the vocations involves for Dr. Adler two emphases: Vocational groups should become increasingly conscious of their ethical function in the community as a whole; and the interrelationships of their members need to be so governed as to render the vocation instrumental to their spiritual development. From the former standpoint he classifies the vocations into three main groups: those connected with theoretical and applied science,

[39] *Ibid.*, Book IV, chap. II. *The Reconstruction of the Spiritual Ideal*, pp. 108 ff. In cases of hopeless maladjustment the ethical remedy is separation without remarriage. Cf. *The Reconstruction of the Spiritual Ideal*, p. 118.
[40] *An Ethical Philosophy of Life*, pp. 291 ff.

whose task is to gain knowledge of the finite world and give man mastery over the forces of physical nature; the arts, whose function is to create in finite form semblances of infinite or spiritual reality; and those directly concerned with human relations, whose business is to realize a truly spiritual bond in human intercourse. The industrial problem, considered in this light, becomes one of rendering both employers and laboring groups conscious of their ethical responsibility toward society as a whole and toward each of the other groups to which they are functionally related. From the latter standpoint it is evident that not only must economic relations, as well as all others, be purged of every taint of exploitation, but they must also be transformed into a constructive force toward the eliciting of spiritual possibilities in those whom they bring together. Needless to say, the barest beginnings in this direction are hardly as yet discernible. Progress can hence be made only gradually and through intermediate steps.[41]

"Assuming that the ethical end of life is to be supreme, what kind of industrial reorganization of society will be most in harmony with it? . . .

1. The idea of service is to be preeminent instead of the gain, the wage or salary to be apportioned as the means of sustaining the worker in the best possible performance of the service.
2. The work done by the workers is to be the means of developing them mentally, aesthetically, and volitionally, the educational features therefore to be preeminent.
3. The industrial group is to be transformed into a social suborganism (in the ethical sense a sub-organ of the larger organism of the nation). By this is meant that the employers cease to be employers and become functionaries, while each worker in his place and in his degree likewise becomes a functionary. A common social service group will thus be formed embracing the chiefs and the humbler workers. The chiefs will be the executive and administrative functionaries, and will be safeguarded in the due discharge of their proper functions. The workers will not attempt to wrest from their chiefs as they do at present the directive functions which properly belong to the latter (subject, however, to due control). To each of the lesser functionaries in turn will be assigned a sphere within which a relative independence would be his.

The industry as a whole will be an *organ* of the *corpus sociale,* and this its character will be expressed in its government. The workers, not

[41] *Ibid.,* Book IV, chaps. III, IV.

required to render implicit obedience to rules imposed upon them by masters and superintendents, will have a voice in the legislation of the industry, in framing the policy of the industry, in electing the chiefs, and in this way the development of the will, upon which I lay the greatest stress, will be attained. The will of the worker, at present fettered, will be liberated by the opportunity given it to become enlightened and effectual.[42]

Dr. Adler adds that this plan represents an intermediate stage which might bridge the gap between the present structure of industrial life and the organic constitution of economic relations which is the ethical ideal. It would mark a transitional step in the transformation of what is now, for most people, a mere occupation into a genuine vocation.

The function of the national state, in the eyes of the founder of the Ethical Culture Movement, is to supply the external conditions required for development toward ethical personality of those who are living under the institutions of family, vocation, and the rest. Without protection of life, property, and reputation, without legal maintenance of compulsory education and the monogamic family, such development would be seriously handicapped or impossible. The exercise of force by the state is ethically justified when it is necessary in fulfilling this function. The doctrine thus stated diverges both from the totalitarian conception that individuals and subnational groups exist for the sake of the state, and from the conception of individualistic democracy that the state exists for the sake of its individual members. Each nation is an organism within the total community of mankind, with its own distinctive ethical function. It has no ultimate sovereignty as against the international organization of peoples which the conscience of mankind is struggling to create, nor against the suborganisms of family, vocation, and the like when performing their proper task. On the other hand, it may appropriately foster the distinctive spiritual genius of its people in ways which modern democratic theory, with its excessive emphasis on individual freedom, would not justify.

The corollaries of this conception regarding war and peace are fairly obvious. War is to be avoided wherever possible, but self-

[42] *Ibid.*, pp. 271 ff. Reprinted by permission of the publishers, D. Appleton-Century Company.

defense against aggression may sometimes be necessary. More important, however, is acceptance by each state of the responsibility to aid in the building of a genuine international conscience, leading to a spiritual community of all mankind, from which enduring peace will come as a by-product. Each nation needs to become conscious of its own defects which require supplementation by what other peoples can provide. Such a consciousness would enable the advanced nations to unite for the purpose of developing ethically the backward peoples of the world, so that the richest distinctive contribution to the spiritual growth of mankind can be elicited from them all. Dr. Adler believes that only when the present outrageous economic exploitation of the uncivilized is replaced by the exercise of such a moral responsibility as this will the civilized nations themselves be able to overcome their mutual antagonisms and establish a lasting world peace.[43]

The right constitutional structure of a state he holds to be a kind of organic democracy. It is democracy in the sense that it fully recognizes the indefeasible personality of each of its members, and their right to effective representation in the deliberative and administrative bodies through which the will of the state is expressed. But it is organic rather than individualistic, in the sense that they are represented not geographically, but through the sub-organs, especially vocational, in which their characteristic group interests come to frank and effective expression. Thus the principle of democratic representation is preserved, but it is given, he thinks, genuine rather than illusory embodiment and is adapted to the increasing fulfillment of an ethical function.[44]

The religious society, for Dr. Adler, is the last in this series of social institutions, and its distinctive task is to create and re-create the ideal of the spiritual universe, providing it also with as true an existing model as the spiritual attainment of its members at any time makes possible. As the family nurtures the germ which is capable of expansion in the gradual spiritualizing of the groups which follow it, the religious society fosters the ideal principle and ethical vision which guide the successive transformations in

[43] *Ibid.*, Book IV, chap. VIII. *The Reconstruction of the Spiritual Ideal,* pp. 180 f., 187 f.

[44] Adler, *op. cit.*, Book IV, chap. VII.

the institutions which precede it in the series. Membership in it should be entirely voluntary, and its organization, like that of the state, should be based on the vocational groups represented. Its leaders are ethical teachers rather than a specially privileged clergy. And the bond of unity between its members is mutual furtherance in their common quest for insight into a finer ethical relationship than men have yet glimpsed and for its ever fuller embodiment in conduct.[45]

The Major Disputed Assumptions of Ethical Idealism

1. Assumptions Concerning Man's Moral Situation
   a. He needs certainty by which to live.
   b. He is capable of attaining this certainty in the form of a supreme principle of moral action.
   c. That principle is that inviolable worth attaches to every human personality, who must be treated accordingly.
2. Metaphysical Assumptions
   a. There is no valid metaphysical knowledge.
   b. An infinite spiritual reality may be validly postulated to account for our moral experience.
   c. Acceptance of such a reality involves faith in moral freedom and in the ultimate preservation of all that is of moral worth in every man.
3. Assumptions Concerning Social Duty
   a. Each individual should so act in relation to every other as to elicit his highest excellence as a moral personality.
   b. All social institutions should be so transformed that they become constructive instruments for the realization of this ideal.

Selected Bibliography

Abbott, T. K., *Kant's Theory of Ethics*, London, Longmans, Green, 6th ed., 1923.
Adler, F., *Creed and Deed*, Putnam, 1877.
Adler, F., *An Ethical Philosophy of Life*, Appleton, 1918.

[45] *Ibid.*, Book IV, chap. IX. *The Meaning of an Ethical Society*, pp. 3, 5, 10 f.

Adler, F., *The Reconstruction of the Spiritual Ideal*, Appleton, 1924.
Bridges, H. J., *The Religion of Experience*, Macmillan, 1916.
Coit, Stanton, *The Soul of America*, Macmillan, 1914.
Fichte, J. G., *The Vocation of Man* (Smith trans.), Open Court, 1916.
Hudson, J. W., *The Truths We Live By*, Appleton, 1921.
Kant, Immanuel, *Religion Within the Limits of Reason Alone* (Greene and Hudson trans.), Open Court, 1934.
Martin, A. W., *The World's Great Religions and the Religion of the Future*, Appleton, 1921.
Paulsen, F., *Immanuel Kant; His Life and Doctrine* (Creighton and Lefevre trans.), John C. Nimmo, 1902.
Webb, C. C. J., *Kant's Philosophy of Religion*, Oxford, 1926.

Chapter X

PROTESTANT LIBERALISM

INTRODUCTION

THE RELIGIOUS orientation which appears next in the historical order is the most difficult to expound. Considered from the standpoint of logical coherence, it is not a philosophy but a group of philosophies reflecting no single controlling principle, whether metaphysical, methodological, or ethical. Considered, however, from the standpoint of its historical context and development, it represents a fairly unified tendency in religious thought during the nineteenth and early twentieth centuries. For that reason we shall treat it, in this and the following chapter, on a somewhat different basis from that exemplified in the preceding chapters. Our primary task will be to clarify the features that give it unity as a historical tendency. We shall then note the major lines of divergence that have appeared within it, and something of the variant religious philosophies in which those divergences have found expression.

Our discussion is handicapped to some extent by the fact that there is no generally accepted terminology by which to refer to the distinctions with which we shall need to deal. However, the word "liberalism" will do fairly well when we need to refer to this developing historical orientation as a whole; in contemporary religious discussions this term is often used in such a sense. The most obvious divergences that have emerged within it differ from each other in the degree of conservatism or radicalism which they reveal; we shall call the more conservative forms "modernism" and the more radical ones "humanism." In the case of the latter there is no question about the appropriateness of the word, and the former term will probably be less misleading than any alternative.

Let us begin with a summary description of the historical setting out of which liberalism emerged, and the dominant motives which have guided its development.

The first thing to note is that this religious liberalism gradually and cautiously grew out of the Protestant orthodoxy described in Chapter VI. No great philosopher such as Spinoza, Hume, or Kant, with the bold confidence of an intellectual genius, laid its foundations through a consciously radical departure from the traditional Christian creed and a commitment to some new orientation in religion. There is no point in the history of liberal thought at which a decisive break with the past can be marked. And the more conservative liberals, at least, feel that their religious position is continuous with what has really been central and valuable in the Christian heritage, although in the eyes of their fundamentalist opponents they have abandoned many truths essential to Christianity. This historical continuity and slow growth account for much that would otherwise be philosophically puzzling in their point of view.

That the continuity is with Protestant orthodoxy rather than with Catholicism should be particularly remarked. Of course, the same forces which led to the new development in Protestant circles likewise made themselves felt in the Catholic Church, and during the last decade of the nineteenth century a liberal wing in Catholicism not only became vocal, but attained a position of growing influence. Early in the present century, however, Pope Pius X condemned the movement as inconsistent with convictions vital to the Catholic faith,[1] and within a few years that modernist trend in Catholicism was effectually suppressed. Thus the religious liberalism which is now a significant force in the Western world is an offshoot of Protestantism and must be understood in the light of this background. In some other religious groups which have no authoritative hierarchy, such as the Jews, a similar tendency is evident, but in their case its influence is limited by the small number of adherents.

[1] In the famous encyclical *Pascendi gregis* of 1907.

The second important fact to be noted is that liberalism, like the religious philosophies considered in the last three chapters, has made extensive concessions to the dominant intellectual force of contemporary times, modern science. And this circumstance is the main key to its interpretation. But the nature of the accommodation is different and it is made in a different way. Catholicism and fundamentalism, it will be recalled, assumed their main structure before the emergence of modern science to a position of controlling influence in the Western world, and in general they have maintained the conviction that religious truth is independent of science, authoritative over it, and to be validated by a different method from that which modern science pursues. Spinozism, agnosticism, and ethical idealism, on principle and each in its own way, accepted wholeheartedly what in their eyes was the essence of modern science, and were conscious in doing so that they were forsaking Christian orthodoxy and blazing a novel trail for religious philosophy. Now this is true also of some of the humanist leaders, but most of the thinkers whom we are now considering were not so radical as this. Liberalism, too, comes to terms with the science of the modern Occident, but in its more influential representatives it does so gradually and without the feeling that it has anywhere made a decisive break with the hallowed Christian tradition. This is true even when the supernaturalism foundational to traditional Christianity is explicitly renounced and the conformity of all events in the world to objective, humanly verifiable law is fully accepted.

This circumstance, however, demands further explanation, and the explanation brings to the fore a third important feature essential to the understanding of liberalism. Had the scale of fundamental religious values held by liberals remained that of Catholicism or of Protestant orthodoxy, undergoing no profound transformation, the significant change just observed, no matter how gradually it came about, would almost certainly have been impossible. Liberalism has by easy steps and more or less unconsciously made the transition which Spinoza and Kant achieved consciously and with a single leap. These philosophers said, in effect: The old foundations are no longer intellectually defensible and must therefore be abandoned, but no matter; what is really significant in religion is consistent with science and can be established on a more enduring basis than ever if the full validity of science be recognized. Spinoza found that basis in the nature of scientific knowledge itself, Kant in a realm of moral obligation entirely separate from science; but, for both men, the central values of religion not only were not lost through accepting modern science—they were, rather, brought by it into a clearer and more compelling light. So it has been with liberalism, only less consciously and more slowly. What happened was that during the nineteenth century science vigorously challenged orthodox theology at a number of vital points and in each case forced a choice between two alternatives. One was to reject the scientific conclusion and stand in uncompromising opposition to the assumptions and methods of explanation by which it had been reached (at least wherever religious convictions are involved); the other was to accept it and reinterpret theology in harmony with its implications. Fundamentalists and (with certain qualifications above noted[2]) Catholics adopted the first alternative, convinced that vital religious values would otherwise be lost. But when each of these challenges became insistent and acute there were a number of thinkers who felt that the elements in orthodoxy which these scientific findings threatened were not essential to a true and living religion—that, indeed, the basic values in human life with which religion is primarily concerned, and which it is its business to promote, lie in another realm and are undisturbed by such changes. These were the liberals; for them, theological orthodoxy might be surrendered, in this or that detail of its creed, while what is enduringly significant in their religion remains, and gains new luster by its detachment from those irrelevant trappings.

Such a transformation, and especially such an outcome, are, of course, quite incomprehensible to one of fundamentalist persuasion, and are somewhat puzzling to many others. The process can be more fully explained only by examining in some detail the main foci of conflict during the last century between modern science and Christian traditionalism, and to this examination a considerable part of the present chapter will be devoted. Some introductory clarification will, however, be attained if we recall that Judaeo-Christianity, even in its orthodox form, had emphasized certain virtues which seemed to these liberals clearly violated by an uncompromis-

[2] See above, p. 134 f.

ing hostility to modern science. Ever since the era of the great prophets, sincerity and inward integrity had been praised as essential to true religion; even a certain impartiality and reflective detachment had been encouraged by the sobering lessons of the captivity and the realization that God is the God of all nations alike, not of the Jews alone. These virtues had taken their place among the fundamental religious values of Christianity, and science, whether ancient or modern, is nothing but their systematic expression in the quest for truth about the world, under the guidance of whatever pervasive assumptions have come to characterize it. So when liberals faced a conflict between orthodoxy and science, they felt that they were also facing a conflict within religion itself; if they decided against science, they were violating the demands of certain appealing values basic to their religious heritage, and saying, in effect, that these values are subordinate in importance to those bound up with the traditional doctrines which modern science threatened. It is not surprising that in such a situation many earnest religious minds made the same decision that most thinkers whose interests are predominantly secular have adopted; something vital to their conscience itself would be trampled on if the contrary choice were made. They did not turn to science and forsake religion. Under the challenge of science they adhered to what they felt to be essential in religion at the cost of parting with what was not.

Within the limits of a single chapter it is impossible to treat all the significant forces which have aided in shaping liberalism; the most that can be done is to explain those forces which proved of major consequence, to indicate their connection with the progress of modern science, and to sketch the main forms taken by liberal accommodation to them.

THE POSSIBILITY OF A CONSTRUCTIVE RELIGIOUS EMPIRICISM

The force with which we shall begin may be described as an effort to develop the empiricism of modern thought into a constructive method for interpreting religion and rebuilding theology. And the thinker whose contribution was most decisive in this development was Friedrich Schleiermacher, a younger contemporary of Kant.

In order to appreciate the significance of this application of empiricism to religion it will be well to recall Hume's treatment of theological problems. The outcome of his empiricism, as applied to religious matters, we found to be mainly negative—that is, the foundations of the orthodox creed seemed incapable of producing the empirical evidence necessary if they were to be pronounced adequately grounded. Now, just what was it that made this negative result inevitable? In dealing with nontheological questions, such as the nature of causal necessity, Hume usually supplemented his skeptical conclusion by a constructive analysis; having shown that the prevalent idea about the bond between cause and effect lacked empirical foundation, he looked to see what empirical facts there were which explained the rise of that idea, and then proceeded to a positive reinterpretation of the notion of causal necessity, leading to a new definition of "cause," in the light of those facts. Thus, though causal necessity appeared illegitimate if interpreted as a compulsion between external events, it proved to be entirely valid if conceived as the powerful association of a psychological habit. Why did he not proceed likewise in dealing with religious problems? Well, in a sense he did, but yet in a manner which implies that a generally negative conclusion is none the less to be final. In treating the belief in God, for example, in his brief *Natural History of Religion*, he attempted to portray the factors in human nature which have led historically to the prevalent conception of a Divine Being, but the only one of these factors which did not seem to him rather disreputable was the philosophical demand for an ultimate ground of the experienced universe. Hence Hume felt no temptation to redefine God in terms of what such empirically verifiable processes might reveal, and when the conception of First Cause as interpreted by the theologians proved to lack adequate empirical foundation there seemed no alternative to a thoroughgoing theological skepticism.

In short, to Hume, God was primarily and essentially the solution of a metaphysical problem, not a problem of daily human experience. And the reason why theism had to be rejected—except for a very problematic validity in the case of part of its meaning—lay in its having been defined in such metaphysical terms, together with Hume's failure to consider seriously whether some constructive redefinition, such as he undertook in the case of causal necessity, might be possible.

Now when we examine this situation, considerations appear which indicate the possibility of a more positive empirical method in religion and which are exceedingly important for our understanding of liberalism. One is that, except for philosophers and some theologians, God never has been primarily the solution of a metaphysical puzzle. To most religious people he is essentially the answer to a vital need of daily experience. Such people dimly feel, no doubt, that this involves assigning him a status which philosophers would call metaphysical, since the being through whom this need is met must be related in some way to the rest of the universe. But the divine attributes that would be emphasized when God is viewed in this relation are, from their standpoint, secondary rather than primary. What is primary is his capacity to help them meet the compelling demands of everyday life. Suppose, then, that we should redefine God in terms of this consideration and then ask, as Hume did, whether there is adequate empirical evidence to justify asserting that the being so defined is real. Obviously, the circumstance that God, interpreted as a metaphysical explanation, proved incapable of experiential validation, does not necessarily indicate that theism approached in this way would meet the same fate. Defining God as First Cause, we might as a result of accepting the assumptions of modern empirical science fall into skepticism; defining him as the satisfier of a certain kind of vital need, we might find sufficient empirical evidence for his reality. Whether adequate evidence is available or not depends on our definition of the concept to be tested by it. Now, to be sure, if we are intuitionists or rationalists in our method of seeking truth, it is doubtless incumbent on us to take as final the particular philosophical or theological definition that such a method seems to require. But if we have adopted the tentative, hypothetical method of modern empiricism we seem under no obligation to remain committed to the definition with which our inquiry begins. If the definition with which we start proves incapable of validation we may (and should, unless it seems desirable to abandon the concept entirely) redefine it by the aid of a more careful study of the experiences which have actually given it a living significance to people. Hume drew this conclusion, and was guided by it, in dealing with nonreligious problems; he did not do so in any constructive or systematic way in dealing with religious ones.

Science has clearly assumed the right and the responsibility to proceed in this way. If it had not done so, scientists would become agnostic about the existence of any entity whose previously accepted definition fails to square with the latest empirical evidence. As soon as traditional concepts of space, matter, electricity, energy, etc., prove no longer admissible, they would reject such entities as unknowable, and confine scientific investigation to other things whose established definition still seems to command some verifiable evidence. But since the meanings of all these concepts have undergone radical change in scientific history, this course would obviously mean the death of science rather than its progress. Before many generations had passed, all its fundamental ideas would have become illegitimate and it would be left no problems to attack. The question which we are considering at present might be put in this way: Why should not religion have as much right as science to provide its major concepts empirical reference by redefinition? Why should not theology be reconstructed so as to become systematically responsible to whatever human experiences do in fact underlie men's religious ideas, as the source of their meaning and value?

But, of course, our second definition, or third, might perchance fail to find adequate empirical verification, even though its likelihood of attaining it ought to be greater than that of the first definition— at least if we have intelligently learned the lessons indicated by our failure with the first. What then? Well, if it is legitimate, in acceptance of our responsibility to the relevant empirical facts, to try a second definition when the first fails; is it not legitimate, or even a duty, to keep on redefining the concept in question until we succeed in rendering it adequate to the facts which are supposed to be interpreted by its aid? Or, better still, should we not recognize what is implied in this whole procedure and, in the case of our most basic concepts, at least, pick a definition right away which will render them relatively indispensable and certain? God, for example, may be made a comparatively necessary and solidly established concept by defining him in terms of such an obvious and universal aspect of religious experience that no one who admits the experience can seriously doubt his reality. This is the procedure that modernism, in its clearest and most self-conscious forms, has usually adopted. Professor Wieman, for example, defines God as "that character of events to which man must adjust himself in order to attain the greatest goods and avoid the greatest ills."[3] Now, few people who reflect about human life will question that to attain the greatest goods that are possible man must adjust himself successfully to some feature or features of his environment. In this way God's reality, as long at least as these ideas of environment, adjustment, etc., seem valid to almost everybody, can be placed empirically beyond doubt; the problem that remains is to determine his nature in detail by careful analysis of the experiences to which the definition calls our attention. Thus we can consciously make any concept fully responsible to experience right from the start, by the definition which we provide for it; and only a radically changed experience, or a shift in the fundamental interpretative ideas that seem to us significant, will compel its revision.

But if we entirely accept this essentially tentative character of empirical method, and are ready without reservation to apply it to the definitions as well as the conclusions of theology, a profound revolution is implied in our whole approach to religious problems and in the very foundations of our religious philosophy. It is essential to understand the nature of this revolution. Since on these terms no concept—not even the concept of God—has any absolute rights, all definitions being liable to revision in the light of continuing human experience, God is no longer the central fact in religion or the ultimate principle in theology. His place is taken by man's religious experience. The religious experience of men and women becomes the decisive fact and the final court of appeal by which we test the validity of any theological concept—the concept of God along with others. No such concept, however defined, is any longer absolute. In this revolution the accepted method of theologians since the days of Origen is renounced and its place taken by another. This begins, not with a metaphysical definition of God and proofs of his reality, but with human experience of whatever has religious significance to people. It then proceeds by tentatively analyzing this

---

[3] H. N. Wieman, *The Wrestle of Religion with Truth*, p. 14. Wieman does not call himself a modernist, but this is because the word has a rather narrow meaning for him.

experience to discover the most important factors in it. Theological concepts will be defined in terms of those factors, and theological doctrines will be formulated as hypotheses about significant relations between those factors and other discoverable aspects of human experience. If verified, those hypotheses will assume the status of established laws, though they will always be liable to revision by future experience. The essence of this revolution is well expressed in the title of a book published by Professor D. C. Macintosh in 1917: *Theology as an Empirical Science.*

SCHLEIERMACHER'S THEOLOGICAL METHOD

The historical significance of Schleiermacher's philosophy of religion, to which we now turn, lies in the fact that he was the first to see these considerations with tolerable clarity and to provide a systematic treatment of religion under their guidance. The more general features of his theory are presented in his *Addresses on Religion,* published in 1799, while a detailed reconstruction of theology in the light of this new conception of empirical method is worked out in *The Christian Faith,* which appeared first in 1821.[4] To be sure, like most intellectual pioneers, Schleiermacher did not see all the significant implications of his guiding principle, nor did he, perhaps, adhere with entire consistency to the ones that he saw; but he followed them sufficiently to exemplify the main features of the constructive empirical approach to religion just outlined. As a result of his work, the main features of this approach gradually gained wider influence and acceptance; in the late nineteenth and early twentieth centuries they dominated theological thought in the Protestant world.

Two important points should be in our minds while the major details of Schleiermacher's treatment are discussed. One is that he does not call himself an empiricist, and it is only by surveying his contribution in the light of its larger historical context that we may justly describe it in the terms here used. He regarded his own procedure as a combination of the "descriptive" and "historical" methods; empiricism, as he understood it, he subjects to severe criticisms. His

---

[4] A brief statement of some of his principles of theological method was given in 1811 in a work entitled *A Brief Outline of the Study of Theology.*

terminology in detail naturally reflects this attitude about method; where, for instance, later liberals would ordinarily talk about "religious experience," his preferred phrase is "religious consciousness." But he became the pioneer in the development of what in its broad historical setting may be appropriately called the constructive empirical method in theology.

What he termed the "descriptive" method, and we shall call an empirical one, was derived largely from Kant's procedure in the *Critique of Pure Reason*. But in two important respects he diverges from Kant's ideas in the direction taken by empirical science. Kant had conceived "experience" in such a way that for knowledge to be limited to experience means that it can deal only with phenomena, not with reality. Schleiermacher agrees with this to the extent of holding that a theological interpretation of man's religious consciousness does not give us knowledge of God as he is in himself, but he insists that it does give us real knowledge of God's relation to us.[5] That relation is given in the experience itself and can be truly known. In this significant respect Schleiermacher's position is realistic; theology does not deal with a realm that is merely phenomenal. The other major divergence from Kant consists in Schleiermacher's admission that the conclusions reached by theological analysis and explanation are tentative. They are subject to progressive correction by future experience, and should be explicitly recognized as valid only within a limited historical epoch. When religious experience changes, as it is bound to do, theology will also need to change in order to be true to it. Schleiermacher frankly declares that in these ways religious doctrines are hypothetical and likely to be modified in the light of future experience.[6]

The second point to be kept in mind is that when Schleiermacher develops his theological reconstruction in detail it is specifically Christian experience that he seeks to interpret, not religious experience in general. He loyally places himself within the Christian tradition and restricts his analysis to those features of experience that are historically traceable to the impact of Christ upon the religious life

---

[5] See *The Christian Faith*, sec. 10. Kant himself had suggested in *Religion Within the Limits of Reason Alone* (Green and Hudson trans.), p. 130 f., that God can be known in his relation to man's moral experience, though not, of course, as he is in himself.

[6] *The Christian Faith*, sec. 19.

and feeling of mankind. This means that the range of application of his method is limited by a specific commitment and a conscious devotion to the Christian community. Moreover, in view of his particular heritage, this involves a further limitation, namely, to Protestant experience, since Schleiermacher was distinctively Protestant in his fundamental attitudes and convictions. These restrictions, as will appear in the sequel, have become characteristic of modernism in its most influential forms, though not of humanism.

After these lengthy preliminaries, our summary of Schleiermacher's treatment of religion will not need to be extensive. The essence of religion he holds to be "the feeling of absolute dependence." In every moment of experience we find an element of freedom and an element of constraint; in part we determine ourselves, in part we are determined by what happens around us. But when we penetrate more deeply into our consciousness a region is disclosed in which we have the sense of being unqualifiedly dependent. Even our freedom and self-activity appear not as our own, but as ultimately derived from and sustained by something beyond us. This region is that of religion, and this sense is the heart of religious experience. Schleiermacher assumes it to be universal—that is, capable of discovery by any man who reflects carefully on himself and his feelings. Now the being with whom we are in touch in this consciousness of absolute dependence is God. When Schleiermacher says this it is important to realize exactly what he means, for these same words might be used by a thinker whose method is entirely different. This assertion is not a causal inference nor the conclusion of a piece of empirical reasoning, but a definition; Schleiermacher means that he is defining "God" as the universal, all-controlling reality disclosed in our consciousness of complete dependence. Thus, should there be any reason for doing so, we may dispense with the term "God" and substitute for it any other word which might more suitably refer to this pervasive reality; the function of the term is simply to denote a universal factor revealed in human experience—it has no rights of its own. The experience is the decisive thing and always the court of appeal.[7] In this contention of Schleiermacher, as has been intimated, a thoroughgoing revolution in theology takes place. From being an absolute principle of religious knowledge, God becomes

[7] *The Christian Faith*, secs. 3 and 4. *Addresses on Religion*, II.

for theological method a factor in man's religious consciousness; the meaning of the term is derived from and validated in present human experience.

This does not mean, of course, that God for Schleiermacher is merely a psychological entity. The relation between my feeling and a mountain range whose sublimity I am enjoying is an objective relation, even though it can only be discovered (and truths about its nature verified) in my subjective experience. In the same way God, and our relation to him, are objective in terms of this theological approach, although assertions about him can only be established by looking within, not by looking without. The method is necessarily subjective, but the being we come to know through it is objective.

How shall we proceed to construct the details of our theological system? The answer follows at once from this novel orientation. We embark on a careful descriptive analysis of the religious (more specifically, the Christian) consciousness, i.e., the immediate feeling of absolute dependence, to determine what doctrines truly describe it. Our experience discloses a relation of dependence on something which by definition is God. The basic task of theology is systematic interpretation of this experienced relation.[8] Its doctrines will be conceived and verified as items in such an interpretation. It must entirely subordinate to this the traditional method of deducing its doctrines from the authority of some revelation of God contained in ancient Scripture, or from metaphysical principles set up by speculative theology. It is wholly and responsibly experiential. As a matter of fact, Schleiermacher's actual procedure is not so radically novel as these corollaries would lead us to expect, and it is necessary to watch the use of this method by his later followers to see how drastic a revision of Protestant theology it might encourage. In the main he hospitably embraces the bulk of orthodox doctrines and cautiously reinterprets their meaning in terms of this approach. When he meets items in the creed—such as the dogma of the Trinity —which seem especially difficult to justify on this basis, his inclination is not to reject them, but to find some experiential excuse for their preservation, and at worst to indicate the likelihood of their future revision. But even with this large qualification such procedure spelled a fundamental break with theological tradition and opened

[8] *The Christian Faith*, secs. 15, 16, 18, 30, 50.

the way to a constructive empirical movement in religious philosophy whose full consequences have perhaps not yet become evident.

For our purposes it will be sufficient to illustrate Schleiermacher's method by certain results which he reached, mainly in his treatment of the doctrine of God. One striking result is that, taking the *(1)* Christian religious consciousness rather than some metaphysical theory of God as his foundation, his conclusions about the deity do not form a systematic unit in his theology, but are split into three sections, discussed in widely separated parts of his book. The more specific cause of this outcome is the pervasive influence upon him of the evangelistic tradition in Protestantism, with its emphasis on the experience of sin transformed by that of forgiveness and redemption. Schleiermacher's primary analysis of the Christian consciousness, which provides the scaffold for the details of his system, accepts this tradition; its three basic aspects are consciousness of sin, consciousness of grace, and consciousness of dependence so far as it does not yet involve the felt contrast of sin and grace. Analysis of the latter (which Schleiermacher appropriately treats first) yields omnipotence as the basic attribute of God; from it may be derived such further attributes as eternity, omnipresence, omniscience. Consciousness of sin yields under examination the attributes of holiness, righteousness, and mercy, while experience of gracious redemption discloses the presence of love and wisdom in God. Thus the major themes of traditional theology are preserved, while placed in a radically different setting and tested in a different court.

Another significant result, which was obviously required by his *(2)* empirical principles, is that the meaning of these attributes is determined throughout by their reference to human experience. They do not describe what God is in himself, but simply and solely what he experientially proves himself to be in relation to us. By the attribute of omnipotence, for example, we do not mean to ascribe to God absolute power in any metaphysical sense, but such power as is required to explain our consciousness of dependence. By that of eternity we do not mean to assert that God actually transcends time, but that our religious awareness posits no temporal limit to his activity in relation to us.[9] Indeed, the essential thing in the

[9] *The Christian Faith*, secs. 50, 52, 54.

doctrine of Christ's resurrection is not his historical emergence from the tomb; what the doctrine primarily attests is the Christian experience of Christ as an enduring and present power for redemption in the lives of men.[10]

(3)   A third important outcome is an ambiguity in Schleiermacher's philosophy of religion with respect to the finality of Christianity in relation to the other religions, which has remained unclarified in subsequent modernist thought and which is one factor leading to humanism as a more radical form of liberalism. Schleiermacher voluntarily attached himself to the Christian community and found his supreme values in it. But in what way could he justify such unreserved attachment? Following his method instead of the rationalistic and authoritarian procedure of his predecessors, he could not establish the unique truth of Christianity by appealing to the ancient miracles on which their case in the end rested. Moreover, the tentativeness which is an essential feature of his method forbids claiming absolute truth for any conclusions reached; they must all be regarded as liable to correction, perhaps even radical falsification, when tested by future experience. Does not this imply that finality cannot be asserted of Christianity; must not the possibility be admitted that future experience, in the Western world as well as elsewhere, may find some non-Christian faith superior to Christianity in meeting its religious needs? And even now must it not be acknowledged that the religious possibilities of human feeling are not exhausted in Christian experience; that Western theological history expresses but one interpretation of the sense of absolute dependence among many, while all interpretations are needed fully to describe the religious quest of mankind? Schleiermacher's answer to these questions is ambiguous. At times, especially in his *Addresses*, he appears frankly to agree with these implications. At other times, both in the *Addresses* and in *The Christian Faith*, he attempts to justify on principle his devout adherence to Christianity. This justification takes the general form of affirming that Christianity empirically discloses its superiority to other religions by providing a more adequate understanding and richer development than they of the basic experience which lies at the heart of all religion.[11] But obviously this

[10] *Ibid.*, sec. 99. Schleiermacher did, however, accept the historicity of the resurrection.
[11] See *Addresses*, V.

contention would not seem valid to adherents of other religions. We should not leave Schleiermacher, however, with our attention absorbed in these details. Let us attempt a summarizing statement of the outstanding new thing in his position. Apparently it never occurred to Hume or the other skeptical empiricists that there was such a thing as the religious consciousness in Schleiermacher's sense of this phrase.[12] They defined religious concepts as their rationalist or supernaturalist predecessors had done, in terms of entities which transcend direct experience; finding inadequate evidence for these entities, they concluded that religious faith is absurd and has no legitimate or positive significance. Schleiermacher's great contribution was his insistence that there is something in the present experience of men and women which gives meaning to the concepts of religion, and that by systematic appeal to that experience we can distinguish the valid meanings and doctrinal interpretations from the erroneous ones.

So far as liberalism rests on any basic philosophical principle, that principle consists in this development of empiricism into a positive and constructive method for the interpretation of religion. Its foundation is contemporary religious experience, and its task is to redefine the major ideas of theology in the light of that experience, abandoning whatever lesser elements of the creed seem inconsistent with the new definitions and transforming the others. But the way in which this program has actually worked out, during the century and a half since Schleiermacher's time, has been vitally affected by certain specific achievements which we owe to empirical science in this period. The three most important of these are the theory of organic evolution, the higher criticism of the Bible, and the comparative study of religion. On each of these matters fundamentalism refused to accept the scientific conclusions, holding them to be inconsistent with essential religious truth, but liberals were led by their guiding principles to adopt them and to reconstruct theology in harmony with them. At present the development of psychological science, along Freudian lines, is posing a fourth major issue—whether or not theologians will accept the conception of man which this realistic scientific analysis offers. But unless the principles which have guided the growth of liberalism thus far are renounced, the answer

[12] This statement should be qualified in the case of Mill. See above, p. 232 f.

to this question will undoubtedly be in the affirmative, at least so far as the less conservative liberals are concerned. The three conclusions of empirical science on which liberalism has already, in the main, taken its stand will now be explained and their impact on religious philosophy outlined.

THE THEORY OF EVOLUTION

The theory of evolution became a decisive force in Western thought with the publication of Darwin's *Origin of Species* in 1859. The general idea of evolution as the historical process by which contemporary institutions, customs, and beliefs have come to be what they are and now pass slowly into other forms, presumably more reasonable ones, had become a prominent factor in philosophy during the preceding century and was strikingly displayed in the influential system of Hegel a generation before Darwin's time. The conception of natural selection, as a solution of the problem why organic species are in general adapted to their environment, had been suggested by some of the early Greek philosophers, and since that time had occasionally been championed as an alternative to the dominant view that these adaptations are due to divine purpose. The main significance of Darwin lay in the fact that in his hands the theory of organic evolution in general, and of natural selection in particular, became an empirically verified hypothesis —that is, it was couched in such form as to permit prediction of a great variety of observable facts whose actual presence subsequent investigation confirmed.

The four fundamental ideas in the theory of evolution, as Darwin and his successors in the field of biology developed it, are briefly indicated by the terms "struggle for existence," "survival of the best adapted forms," "heredity," and "variation." In each generation there are produced more organisms than are able to grow to maturity under the environing conditions which they face. Hence they compete with each other for the privilege of continued existence, and the ones most fully adjusted to those conditions survive and produce offspring while the ones less well adapted are likely to perish without descendants. The favorable adaptations of those which survive—whether consisting in the presence of some new organ, or of some advantageous change in an organ already existing—are likely to be preserved, because of the law of heredity that offspring are more closely similar to their parents than to other members of their species. But this similarity never becomes identity; there are always variations between a young organism and its parents, and between it and other offspring of the same parents. Because of this, some among the young of a surviving generation are apt to be still better adapted to their environment than their parents were. Thus variations can accumulate, through generation after generation, until as a result there appears a set of organs quite different from and superior to those present at an earlier period in the process. When the difference has become sufficiently marked, we call the resultant type a distinct biological species, although it has originated by descent from ancestors of another species. The appearance of man, according to Darwin, is to be explained by the operation of these factors.

But the theory of evolution did not merely gain comprehensive empirical verification in the field of biology. It was destined to a broader application. Just as the enormous success of the mechanical analogy in solving the problem of motion in the inorganic world had encouraged attempts to extend it to other fields, and even to conceive the entire universe as a mathematical machine; so the startling achievement of the idea of evolution in reconstructing the tree of life led to its systematic use as an explanatory principle in many areas to which Darwin and his biologist followers had not tried to apply it. Among the inorganic fields, geology and astronomy proved to be most significantly illumined by the conception of evolution; prior to the nineteenth century speculative theories about the development of the earth's crust and the formation of solar systems had been suggested, but during the nineteenth century—in part, even, before Darwin's time, but more rapidly under the stimulus of his success—a vast mass of facts was accumulated which decided between competing theories and indicated more definitely the course of these processes of development. In another direction, comprehensive problems in sociology and psychology were studied under the guidance of the same fruitful idea; the nature of man's major cultural institutions, including religion, and of the human mind itself, was thought to be most clearly explained as the product of a long process of evolution from an ancestry which did not exhibit their most characteristic present features.

In this extension to other fields the theory of evolution naturally lost some of the characteristics which were essential to it when conceived as a solution of specifically biological problems. Those that remained, as apparently validly applicable to all these areas of inquiry, were three. First, the thought that the most comprehensive and illuminating explanation of anything is to be reached by tracing its historical genesis. Second, the conviction that that genesis is not merely a matter of temporal succession, but is also a development. This does not imply progress in any moral sense; it merely implies that a more complex creature often arises out of simpler forms, because it adds to the characteristics displayed in those simpler forms variations of structure and function which, once they appeared, have proved able to maintain themselves. Third, the idea of adaptation, as the principle determining which of the newly appearing variations shall be preserved and which are but temporary. Every such variation emerges in an environment of forces which impinge upon it in diverse ways; only when it is so adjusted to them that a new type of harmonious equilibrium is established, in which they and it together interact, can the new emergent continue to exist or to propagate itself. It is to be remembered, of course, that wherever evolution is present there is also degeneration, since the successful emergence of new forms often spells destruction or gradual deterioration for already existing forms which prove unable quickly to adjust themselves to its presence.

Furthermore, these effects on detailed branches of knowledge do not exhaust the influence of the idea of evolution. So promising did the general conception of evolution seem as a result of these varied conquests that the notion came to be more and more seriously entertained that the universe in its entirety is an evolutionary process, and that its essential character can only be understood in terms appropriate to such a notion. This was an exceedingly radical hypothesis, for it implied a novel basic pattern into which everything that happens in the cosmos is to be fitted, and a novel theory of what a significant causal explanation of anything properly involves.

Prior to this cosmic expansion of the idea of evolution, the

Western world had seen two such comprehensive patterns, with
corresponding theories of the causal relation. One is the pattern
assumed by Plato and Aristotle and more explicitly formulated by
Neo-Platonism in its doctrine of emanation. The essence of this
pattern lies in its tracing all reality back to an ultimate Form or
Being possessed of supreme perfection, various degrees or aspects
of which have been imparted to the different observable entities
of which the universe is composed. This pattern dominated Western
thought in almost all fields down to the rise of modern mechanical science in the seventeenth century, and it is still reflected in
most Western thinking on matters of religion. Viewed from this
standpoint, the vital feature of any instance of causality is the acquisition by the effect of part or all of the perfections exhibited in its
cause; it seems a valid general assumption that the cause of any
effect must be equal if not superior to it in the degree or scope of its
excellence.[13] We have seen the systematic application of this assumption in the Catholic religious philosophy, and the major objection raised against it by Hume—the objection, namely, that this
way of conceiving causes leads us to postulate somewhere in the
universe more perfect effects than those with which our reasoning
began and which can be empirically observed. Hume himself assumes the other basic pattern which Western thought had tried
prior to the day of evolution—a pattern exhibited most clearly in
mechanical science and derived ultimately from the growing demand in early modern times that scientific explanations take such a
form as will permit exact and verifiable predictions. This demand in
turn rests on the desire to control nature, which was almost entirely
foreign to those who shaped Greek and medieval habits of thought,
but which has been a dominant ambition of the modern West.
Clearly, we can hope to control future events only so far as we can
anticipate them with confidence and precision. From this standpoint,
the universe is pictured as a vast machine, whose various motions
succeed each other in accordance with mathematical law. Thus,
given a correct quantitative analysis of any motion as now occurring,
we can predict what exact form it will exhibit at any subsequent
stage. This means that we assume a constancy in the quantity of

[13] The scholastic philosophers formulated this assumption in the technical
phrase: *causa aequat effectu aut formaliter aut eminenter.*

energy displayed at any two successive stages of a mechanical
process; if the later lacked some energy present in the earlier, or
possessed more, we could not, given the earlier, anticipate with
exactitude what the later course of the motion would be like. Now,
the conception of the causal relation appropriate to this pattern of
thought is that it requires a quantitative equivalence between any
cause and its effect. Cause and effect are each specific motions, and
express the same amount of energy. To be sure, when this theory of
causal explanation was applied, as by Hume, to matters in which
exact quantitative analysis is at present beyond us, the requirement
of precise mathematical equivalence is not insisted on, but the more
general demand is maintained that any cause inferred from its
effect be so conceived as to permit the clearest possible prediction of
whatever effects are empirically verifiable. The revolution in theology involved in this doctrine of causal connection has been noted;
Kant was convinced of its inevitability, as well as Hume.

A cosmic extension of the idea of evolution leads naturally to a
third metaphysical pattern and theory of causality. The essence of
this pattern consists in picturing the universe as a vast historical
process, in which more complex entities are continually being generated out of simpler antecedents, maintaining themselves whenever
surrounding conditions permit. All the empirical knowledge at
present accepted in the various sciences fits with tolerable harmony
into such a cosmic scheme. The most influential form of this theory
at present is called "emergent evolution." From its standpoint the
broadest and most distinctive types of variation which have proved
capable of preservation and propagation are spoken of as emergent
levels; the three outstanding levels are inorganic matter, life, and
conscious mind.[14] The first of these apparently existed for aeons
before the second appeared, and the second for many millions of
years before the third, which seems to be present only in man. But
even the most complex forms of mental life trace ultimately back
genetically to the simplest types of inorganic substance. How is
causal explanation naturally conceived in this metaphysical context?
Obviously, as at bottom a genetic relation. The effect is generated
out of the cause and may be—in fact, normally is—more complex

[14] See the works of such recent philosophers as Lloyd Morgan and
S. Alexander.

than the cause. Here, again, the demand for successful prediction
is present, and in this respect the present theory agrees with the
mechanical conception of causality. But it is distinct from it in its
insistence that in wide areas of empirical fact—perhaps universally
—the later stage of a process is not merely equivalent to the earlier,
but exhibits new properties some of which may be preserved and
repeated thereafter. The causal relation must, then, be so construed
as to allow for this circumstance. The variations, in their first
appearance, are from this point of view left unexplained, since it is
impossible to anticipate their character in detail; all that can be
predicted is that novelties of some sort will occur. But such a general
prediction must in terms of this approach be embodied in the notion
of causality which it implicitly involves; the cause—whether it be a
single event or a group of determining conditions—may be simpler
than its effect because the latter, in arising out of the former, is likely
to reveal properties and ways of behaving that are absent in the
cause. It will be noticed that in one major respect this assumption
about causality is exactly the opposite of the ancient and medieval
conception; for the one, a cause does not need to exhibit all the
qualities displayed in its effect, while for the other the ultimate cause
must contain more and higher perfections than are revealed in any
effect.

What, now, were the main consequences of the theory of evolution for religious thought?

The most important specific consequence was that a naturalistic
view of man's origin and nature was implied. Prior to the successful establishment of Darwinism the account of the creation of
man given in the first book of the Bible—and of the creation of
other living species as well—had been almost universally taken as
the literal scientific truth.[15] Most of the available facts accumulated
earlier than the nineteenth century appeared to indicate that biological species are quite distinct from each other and that the
essential characteristics of each species are preserved from parent
to child. Thus the theory of special creation was not only explicitly
taught by the Bible, but seemed harmonious with the available
biological data. The new scientific doctrine, however, taught that
man is first cousin of the anthropoid apes, and that he is descended

[15] That is, since the victory of Christianity.

with them from a common ancestry through a process of natural evolution. This conception, to those who accepted it, not only deprived man of his distinctive dignity as a special creation of God in the latter's image, and placed his origin and development under natural law; but also removed one of the prime evidences for the reality of a supernatural Creator possessing the intellectual and moral qualities characteristic of man. As long as man was viewed as the object of a special creative act and the highest product of divine power it seemed necessary to attribute to his Author all the distinctive perfections which man at his best exhibits, but when his appearance became intelligible as the outcome of purely natural forces, operating according to biological law in the simpler creatures that constitute his ancestry, a wise and good Creator no longer appeared needed to explain the facts. Indeed, the course of natural selection as pictured by the evolutionary theorists seemed quite irreconcilable with human ideals of intelligence and love; the various species prey mercilessly upon one another, each intent solely upon its own survival and well-being, while vastly more individuals are constantly being produced than can possibly, in view of environing conditions, grow to maturity. A nature "red with tooth and claw" confronted pious contemplation instead of a nature shot through with beneficent purpose.

To some thinkers, especially among Catholic theologians, a compromise appeared possible. It was quite in line with their Aristotelian premises to surrender man's body and his physical functions to the claims of natural evolution, but must we not insist on the special creation of that which most obviously distinguishes him from his animal forbears—his mind and soul? Here an evolutionary variation appears which strikingly sets off its possessor from other living creatures, being of distinctive value and dignity; how is its original appearance to be accounted for? The answer of the champions of evolution was to apply in detail the evolutionary theory to problems of comparative psychology, showing that prominent characteristics of the human mind can themselves be interpreted as the outcome of a gradual process of selection and adaptation. Even before 1859, Herbert Spencer had published his *Principles of Psychology,* in which man's mental faculties were explained as evolutionary products, and it was not difficult for his successors to render the explanation still more persuasive. Human thinking, for example, came to be portrayed as a biological function making more advantageously for survival than the "trial and error" behavior of the lower animals, but as genetically related to it; the essential differences between the two were accounted for not by the special creation of intelligence as a novel faculty, but by the appearance of specific variations which gradually telescoped the process of trial and error, enabled the consequences of this or that act to be anticipated, and hence permitted adjustment to environmental changes with more confidence and less danger. Thus man's soul as well as his body seemed capable of explanation in terms of natural selection. This was a very radical challenge to Christian theology.

The most important general consequence for religious thought arising from the dominance of evolutionary ideas lay in the fact that it provided a purely natural explanation of the adaptation of organs to the ends which they serve—an adaptation which previously had provided the main argument for a divine purpose as controlling the economy of nature. These many and varied adjustments, in creatures without intelligence, seemed to point toward a wise providence guiding the formation of the organs involved and insuring that they function as effective means toward their appropriate ends. The analogy of intelligent contrivance, exhibited in the human invention of machines for the realization of certain desired ends, presented itself as the only adequate analogy in terms of which such striking and often minutely detailed adjustments could be accounted for. We have seen that even pre-Darwinian skeptics, such as Hume, found some degree of cogency in this argument. From the evolutionary point of view, however, no supernatural intelligence is needed to explain the facts. All that has to be assumed is that nature continually produces more creatures than can survive and have offspring under their environing conditions, and that each new generation exhibits variations as compared with its parents—usually minute differences but sometimes more prominent ones ("mutations," to use the technical term). If these assumptions are sound it will necessarily follow, without any superintending providence, that in general the creatures now in existence will have such a detailed structure as secures their preservation and well-being in the surroundings which they face. Those less happily adjusted have simply been eliminated in the struggle for survival. And the answer of the evolutionists to the main objection of the Catholic theologians[16] is that sometimes mutations appear in the form of rather complex organs capable all at once of performing a quite novel function, which may be exceedingly advantageous to the creatures in whose behavior it is exercised. The occurrence of such striking variations has been experimentally verified both under natural and under artificial conditions. Thus the first appearance of a wing enabling its possessor to fly would seem to be explicable without departing from the naturalistic assumptions of the evolutionary theory, especially when we consider such a familiar intermediate form as that of the "flying" squirrels.

Now Protestant fundamentalism found it impossible to reconcile this evolutionary view of man with Christian doctrines which seemed to it essential. The basic irreconcilability lay in the fact that a literal interpretation of the Bible—which for the fundamentalists constitutes the way to religious truth—could hardly fail to find the doctrine of the special creation of man taught in it. Acceptance of the theory of evolution seemed, therefore, to involve abandonment of the hallowed Protestant conviction that the Bible in all its parts is an infallible revelation of divine truth. Moreover, the hoary traditional conceptions of man's religious need and of his destiny were undermined by the evolutionary view of man. Those conceptions demanded the penetration of man's natural life here below by a supernatural order on which it depends for whatever real good is ever attained. Man has a soul whose destiny lies in that supernatural realm; apart from divine grace he is impotent to secure forgiveness for the guilt which condemns him to an eternity in hell; and when that grace comes it performs a miraculous transformation through which he becomes an heir of heavenly bliss. Both the profoundest need of man and the nature of his salvation could only be described in essentially supernatural terms. Whereas, from the standpoint of the theory of evolution, man's entire make-up and history, as well as his origin, appeared capable of explanation as part of a purely natural order governed by genetic laws verifiable everywhere in the biological field.

16 See above, p. 109.

Those who in the face of this situation became liberals, however, found it possible to reconcile religion with the theory of evolution. Few of the more conservative among them—the modernists—accepted all the implications that may be drawn from an unqualified expansion of the evolutionary viewpoint into a comprehensive cosmology, as the more radical liberals were likely to do, but even they did accommodate their Christian beliefs to the Darwinian explanation of the origin of man and of the course of human history. Since this involved some profound readjustments, it is important to note the main factors which made them possible.

First, and foremost, these modernists, like other liberals, were thinkers who had become persuaded that modern scientific methods of investigation and explanation are essentially valid. The two major assumptions of the newer science—that the world is an intelligible order and that the ultimate test of truth is detailed empirical verification—seemed to them sound. They knew that the major concern of the scientists who were engaged in building up the theory of evolution was not hostility to religion, but loyalty to empirical truth, and they felt that theology was doomed if it set itself in irreconcilable opposition to their results or methods. Religion itself demands loyalty to truth, hence it must adjust itself to truth wherever discovered and also to the most efficient ways of establishing truth. Otherwise, intelligent and honest men would have to abandon it.

A second, and perhaps equally important, consideration lay in the fact that as modernists sought to clarify the readjustments that would be demanded by acceptance of the theory of evolution, it appeared to them that the facts and values that are really central in religious experience remain untouched by it and that what must be surrendered never was religiously essential at all. Here the constructive empirical approach to religion championed by Schleiermacher proved an indispensable aid. From this standpoint no traditional Christian doctrine, however clearly taught in the Bible, is absolutely vital to contemporary religion; it is an intellectual interpretation of past religious experience, using the scientific assumptions and categories then available, but it is not final for us. What is certain for us is something that no scientific fact or truth can destroy, namely, our own religious experience—the circumstance directly verified in our inner lives that through ideas and ideals that have come down through our Christian heritage we have found great spiritual goods that men sorely need, such as peace, hope, guidance in perplexity, strength to overcome temptation. The realization of these values in many individual lives is a fact, and the only fact that is quite fundamental; for modernists, theology is but an attempted explanation of it and may at any time need revision. Now, there is no irreconcilability between this fact and the theory of evolution. Whatever may have been man's origin, by whatever process he has come to occupy his present position in the biological world, it remains that he is here, with whatever capacities and experiences now characterize him, including his capacity to aspire toward spiritual ideals and to achieve significant progress in their realization. If man is genetically akin to the lower animals, and is the product of natural evolution, then evolution must be recognized as a process issuing in the emergence of just such a creature as he proves to be, and may properly be viewed in the light of its most interesting product. All that is necessary to theology is full acceptance of the facts of contemporary religious experience and the value that they signify for those in whose lives they appear. Everything else is secondary, and may properly be reinterpreted or even abandoned if it conflicts with other verifiable facts, such as those which appear to demand the theory of evolution for their explanation.

Besides these two basic factors, at least three minor ones played a significant part in the theological reconstruction that was directly due to the idea of evolution.

One was the presence of philosophical systems which, on the one hand, championed a generally evolutionary interpretation of human history and, on the other, defended the truth of an essentially religious view of the world—indeed, a view not only religious, but in many respects specifically Christian. Such philosophies began to appear as a part of the so-called "romantic movement" late in the eighteenth century, and were exceedingly influential throughout the century that followed; outstanding among them was the philosophy of Hegel, which for many decades reigned supreme in German thought, then became the dominant intellectual force in

England, and finally acquired a similar position in America.[17]
Another factor was the circumstance, evident in the details of these
philosophical systems, that the reconstruction demanded was not
as radical as it might conceivably have been. Evolution seemed not
to be flatly inconsistent with belief in God; at least it was still possible to suppose that the long natural process culminating in man has
been guided by a divine purpose even though science as such finds
no need of postulating any providential control, and that a still
greater end than has thus far been realized is destined to be
achieved in the future if men devotedly coöperate with God in
promoting it. Moreover, an exalted place for Jesus of Nazareth in the
religious history of mankind could be claimed without contravening
evolutionary ideas; in fact, many modernists adopted the position
that he was the supreme creation of the evolutionary process in
human form, and reinterpreted the doctrines about him in the light
of this conception. A third factor, which must not be neglected, lay
in the fact that an evolutionary interpretation of religious history
opened a way of relief from distressing difficulties that morally sensitive souls had always felt in the orthodox view. Since the latter
held that the entire Bible is a revelation of the one true and eternal
God, it was compelled to accept everything in it as expressing the
divine Will. Thus the Psalms which breathe vengeance on Israel's
enemies, the vivid threats of eternal torture in hell-fire, the passages
in which the Hebrews are commanded to massacre their captives—
men, women, and children—must be regarded as disclosures of
God's character equally with the passages in which he is portrayed
as the spirit of suffering and redeeming love.[18] Thinkers who felt
the moral appeal of the latter conception and who found the essence
of true religion in it had ever found it difficult, if not impossible, to
reconcile two such different pictures of the divine. For them, the
theory of evolution brought a sense of profound relief. The Biblical
story of Judaism, and even of Christianity, could be regarded as an
evolutionary growth—a process of development from cruder and
less adequate ideas of God to higher and more ethical ones. Thus

[17] Hegel's conception of development is, of course, markedly different from
that of the Darwinian theory; it is for him a rational process, following a systematic logical pattern.

[18] Ps. 35, 69. Matt. 13: 38–43; 25: 41–46. Judg. 20, 21.

the picture of God as a merciless judge and ruthless punisher appeared, so it seemed, as an early stage in the gradual advance of
man's religious conceptions which finds a culmination in the passages
in John and Paul which emphasize self-giving love as the
essence of God's relation to man. Indeed, even fundamentalism had
been forced to mitigate this conflict of ideas by a semi-evolutionary
theory. According to it, there have been two dispensations in God's
dealing with mankind, that of the Old Testament and that of the
New, in the earlier of which his full beneficence was not as yet
overtly displayed.

THE HIGHER CRITICISM OF THE BIBLE

As a result of these factors, an increasing number of Christian
thinkers since Darwin's books appeared have accepted evolution as
a true theory and have revised their theological ideas in conformity
with it. But it is evident that the factor last mentioned involves an
unorthodox theory of the Bible and of its inspiration. The Bible
itself becomes viewed as a product of natural evolution—a collection
of books displaying man's progressive understanding of God as he
grows in moral and religious insight, rather than a supernatural
disclosure of absolute truth. This alone was an exceedingly radical
idea, and had there not been other forces working simultaneously
toward the same result it is doubtful whether it would have been
seriously entertained by more than a few especially bold thinkers.
But there were such coöperating forces, which we must now
examine. The most decisive influence that led directly to this novel
view of the Bible is generally referred to in contemporary discussions as the "higher criticism," which again is a development
rejected by fundamentalists but in general accepted and even welcomed in the liberal camp, including the modernists.

The "lower," or textual, criticism of the Bible has always been
recognized as legitimate by responsible scholars, even those of
decidedly fundamentalist persuasion. The aim of such criticism is
simply to determine, as accurately as may be, the original text of
the Biblical writings. The oldest manuscripts on which our present
Bibles are based were copied many centuries after the original text
was written and are separated from it by many intervening copies

and versions. Now according to the theory of divine inspiration,
as generally maintained, only the words set down by the original
writers were supernaturally revealed; those who later transcribed
and translated them were subject to ordinary human fallibilities.
And since the oldest texts now available show a large number of
variant readings, some of which concern passages theologically
important, it would be exceedingly difficult to make the contrary
position plausible. The "higher" criticism, however, is the attempt
to determine the historical meaning and truth of what the text says,
and to do so by the same methods that scientific investigation has
found successful in dealing with secular writings. This quickly
leads to results inconsistent with the traditional view of the divine
inspiration of the Scriptures, hence fundamentalists have not recognized it as legitimate. From their standpoint, the meaning of Sacred
Writ must be interpreted in ways harmonious with the doctrine that
an omniscient deity is the author of every statement in it.

There are serious difficulties in this position, which will soon be
illustrated. If we ask why they did not constitute a disturbing
challenge to Christian scholars prior to modern times, the answer is
twofold. Throughout a large part of the pre-Reformation period
allegorical interpretations of Scripture were encouraged. The real
intent of many passages, it was supposed, can hardly be found in
their literal meaning but must lie in some hidden spiritual truth
which they symbolize. Obviously, to the user of this method no
difficulties in the text would be insuperable. And when allegory fell
out of fashion, ecclesiastical authority, basing itself on established
tradition, solved the problem. It decided between alternative interpretations of puzzling passages by an organ of truth at least as
ultimate as that of the Bible itself. But Protestants had rejected
Catholic tradition as being frequently mistaken, and had rebelled
against Church authority. Moreover, they had opened the Bible
freely to the study of laymen, insisting that every man's conscience
and judgment are competent to find God's saving truth in it. This
meant that allegorical meanings, while not denied, were rendered
subordinate to the plain, literal truth of its statements. Only such
truth was straightforward and unambiguous, capable of confident
interpretation in the same sense by different readers.

When, in this historical setting, Protestant scholars plunged into the systematic study of the Bible to discover its exact meaning, they gradually became conscious of perplexities that placed them in a serious dilemma as long as they felt obligated to be loyal to the traditional theory of divine inspiration. They found numerous contradictions in the Bible, where it seemed impossible for both of two statements to be true. Many of these consist of discrepant accounts of the same event. For instance, in the story of Noah's flood the patriarch is first told to preserve in the ark one pair of every species without distinction of clean or unclean; then he is bidden to save seven couples of the clean beasts.[19] Jacob's change of name is located at two different places, first at Peniel, second at Bethel,[20] and two discrepant accounts are given of the origin of the name Bethel.[21] Deuteronomy insists upon the restriction of legitimate sacrifices to the Temple at Jerusalem, whereas in the biography of Elijah God is represented as dramatically recognizing a sacrifice on an altar at Mount Carmel, far from Jerusalem. Use of such altars is clearly approved in other passages in the historical books.[22] Some of the discrepancies are particularly interesting, because of the fact that they turn upon obvious presuppositions of the text rather than upon direct statements. In the later books of the Old Testament and in the New Testament Moses is regarded as the author of Deuteronomy; yet in Deuteronomy 34 not only are Moses' death and burial described but the description ends with the statement: "And no one knows the place of his burial *to this day*."[23] The last phrase of this quotation clearly implies that it was written by someone living at a later date. Another type of case appears in the topographical references in the books attributed to Moses. In Deuteronomy 1: 1, for example, it is stated that Moses' words were spoken "beyond the Jordan in the wilderness," which implies that the writer was on the Canaan side of the river, which Moses never reached.

Moreover, at least one pair of passages in the Bible indicates that the traditional theory of divine inspiration, with its claim of infallibility for the content of the revelation, is not intended by

[19] Gen. 6: 19; 7: 2.
[20] Gen. 32: 27–30; 35: 10, 15.
[21] Gen. 28: 10–22; 35: 9–15.
[22] I Sam. 7: 6, 9–11, 17; 9: 12–14, 25; 10: 3, 5, 12.
[23] Deut. 34: 6.

Scripture itself. In Ezekiel 26 the prophet proclaims as a divine revelation the message that the city of Tyre is to meet destruction at the hands of Nebuchadrezzar, king of Babylon, and he portrays in graphic language the complete desolation into which she is to be plunged. After a hard assault, however, Nebuchadrezzar failed to capture Tyre, and subsequently led his army down the coast toward Egypt. Accordingly, in Ezekiel 29 the prophet announces another revelation, in which God promises the conquest of Egypt to Nebuchadrezzar as a recompense for his defeat by the Tyrians.[24] There is no hint in the later of these passages that he now doubts the authenticity of the earlier revelation because the prophecy it contained failed to be verified as and when he expected. Apparently, what is essential to a divine revelation, in his mind, is not its factual infallibility, but the truth of the moral lessons it embodies. Of these he was always confident. In this pair of chapters the Bible itself seems clearly to teach that "divine revelation" must be understood in a sense which will allow its content to be historically fallible, liable to correction in the light of further experience.

These inconsistencies challenge explanation. But any attempt to explain them, while adhering to the orthodox view of supernatural revelation, plunges us into an almost intolerable dilemma. The only wholly frank and candid answer would seem to be to say that God's ways are inscrutable, and that what therefore seem contradictions to our finite minds are not contradictions to an omniscient mind. But this is a perilous answer; it implies that God's use of thought and language rests on entirely different principles from ours. Man's mind and God's mind have no common measure. In that case we will not know how to interpret with assurance any part of the Bible, since even the passages that seem simple and clear may on that supposition really mean something quite different from what we naturally assume. Scripture, then, becomes useless as a guide to our salvation. Nor, of course, can the problem be solved by returning to the authority of tradition and the Church, without sacrificing everything for which Protestantism has historically stood.

When the methods of the higher criticism were applied to the problem posed by these inconsistencies they reached as definite and as illuminating results as had been attained through their applica-

[24] Vss. 17–20.

tion to other ancient writings. The essence of these methods lay in their refusal to assume that the documents examined disclose an infallible, timeless truth, and in their effort to discover the meaning of the statements contained in them by clarifying the specific historical situations which their authors were attempting to meet. In the endeavor to recover these situations by appeal to internal evidence and also to what we know in other ways about the period concerned, the basic questions asked, whether about the Bible or any other writing, are: What is the date at which this book was written? What was the author's purpose in writing it? What distinctive features of language and of style are exhibited? Who is the author, the one assumed by tradition or someone else? What earlier materials, if any, did he use? How reliable were those materials—that is, when and by whom were they written? How competent is his testimony, and how trustworthy, in the light of these various considerations, is the writing which we owe to him? Such questions were asked about the Biblical books by a few philosophers as early as the seventeenth century; during the last half of the eighteenth century some Protestant scholars probed more systematically for answers to them; and by the middle of the nineteenth century sufficiently comprehensive theories had been suggested so that detailed research, aimed at their testing and correction, was stimulated and in many theological centers effectively prosecuted. The results of these investigations are exceedingly challenging to champions of the orthodox view of revelation, for while, as is usually the case with any scientific inquiry, there are many questions on which critical opinion is still in doubt or divided, almost complete agreement obtains on certain broad solutions of some of the fundamental problems. And if these solutions are adopted the nature and significance of the Bible becomes an essentially different thing from what it has been to those who view it solely through precritical eyes.

In order to elucidate these differences it will be well to describe briefly an especially provocative illustration of the critical method as applied to the Bible. The first main part of the collection of books known among Christians as the New Testament consists of the four Gospels, which constitute our main source of knowledge about the life and teachings of Jesus. Each of these Gospels offers a separate account of the Master, and naturally there are interesting similarities and differences between the four stories. Prior to the appearance of the higher criticism Christian scholars did not think of these similarities and differences as constituting a problem to be investigated in the way that would be taken for granted in the case of four secular biographies. Each of the Gospels was believed to be infallibly true in its every statement, since each was a revelation to man from an eternal and omniscient mind. From this standpoint, the central problem consisted in working out what is known as a "harmony" of the Gospels—that is, a single biography of the Nazarene teacher which would include the material from all four books without duplicating accounts of the same event. Difficulties in this enterprise arose at two points. For one thing, descriptions which obviously refer to the same occurrence are often discrepant in some particulars. The method in such cases, of course, was to add the discrepant features to each other wherever they are not flatly inconsistent; if consistency proved simply impossible, to assume that the contradictions arose from errors by copyists of the early manuscripts. Variations regarding these features sometimes appear even in our extant manuscripts. For another thing, the historical sequence of events is not always the same. This is a special difficulty when John is compared with the other Gospels, but even they do not entirely agree with each other in this respect. Here was a more serious puzzle for the orthodox conception of revelation. In general, it could only be met by a confession of human ignorance as to how a reconciliation might be made, or by concessions which really compromise the infallibility claimed for all the four accounts. Sometimes it was not easy to decide whether two stories referred to the same event or not; in such cases the only safe procedure for the orthodox scholar was to assume that they did not, and to treat them accordingly as descriptions of two different happenings.

The higher critic, however, finds evidence in the Gospels which leads him to another solution of these difficulties. In the first place, the account given in the Gospel of John varies so markedly from that of the other Gospels, and is so obviously colored by certain metaphysical tendencies prominent in Hellenistic philosophy—

notably those reflected in Philo's work—that he sets it aside as in the main of little historical reliability. Whatever may be the case with much of the detailed material now included in it, the book itself, according to him, is a late product, written not earlier than the second Christian century, and designed to meet philosophies then spreading among Gentile Christians which held that the divine Logos through whom men are saved is not to be identified with the man Jesus and never appeared in a tangible human form. A good case may, indeed, be made for the correctness of this Gospel's account on a few matters where it varies from the other three— especially on the temporal relation between the crucifixion and the feast of Passover—but it is difficult to be confident of its historicity in the case of most other variations. Hence, biographies of Jesus written from the higher critical point of view depend primarily on the material from Matthew, Mark, and Luke, and follow a chronological sequence developed from their account.

But these three Gospels (known as the "synoptic" Gospels) themselves exhibit very striking similarities and differences, which suggest a very definite theory for explaining the main facts. Mark, the shortest of the three, is included almost entire in Matthew, and half of it is included in Luke. By the word "included" two things are meant. First, not only are the same events described in essentially the same way and order, but there are also extensive coincidences in the language used, such as would hardly be explicable if there were not a common source of the three accounts. Second, when the slight alterations, additions, and condensations in this common material are examined in detail, practically all of them are readily explained if it be assumed that Mark existed first and was used by Matthew and Luke, while the contrary assumption leads to insoluble difficulties. It is thus concluded that Mark was the first Gospel to exist in substantially its present form. When, further, the non-Marcan portions of Matthew and Luke are compared, exactly the same situation appears again. Not quite half of this part of Matthew and slightly less than a third of this part of Luke reveal such identities in language as to indicate a second common source besides Mark, and a source already existing in Greek as well as the original Aramaic. This source consists entirely of sayings and discourses of Jesus, and since nothing is known about its author it is referred to in scholarly discussions as Q.[25] When Mark and Q are set aside, there remains somewhat less than a third of Matthew which appears to be derived from sources unique to the first Gospel, while almost exactly half of Luke was drawn from materials used only by him.

Now when, on the basis of these results, we raise the question when and why these Gospels were written, the answer given by the higher critic, derived mainly from internal evidence, runs about as follows: Mark was written not far from A.D. 65, probably at Rome. Its selection from available narratives about Jesus and sayings by him, and its characteristic emphases, were determined mainly by the problems confronting the Roman church at that time. Q was written sometime between A.D. 45 and 65, probably in Antioch, and reflects the need felt by Gentile Christians in Asia Minor for teachings of Jesus which would provide authoritative guidance in dealing with the perplexities characteristic of their life at that time. Matthew was written at Jerusalem sometime in the seventies. Its typical emphases are those that would be expected of a Jewish Christian moved by vigorous hostility to the Pharisees and anxious about problems of ecclesiastical organization and authority. Luke was written last of the three, probably in Caesarea sometime between A.D. 80 and 95. Its selection of details and emphasis are what we should expect from a humanitarian, home-loving Gentile Christian of that period who was conscious of the main problems affecting the Gentile Christian communities.

The higher critic observes that both Matthew and Luke, in their corrections of Mark, not only improve his style but also remove implications which seem to detract from Jesus' power and insight or which reflect upon the loyalty and good sense of the disciples. He naturally concludes that other corrections of the same sort were probably already made in the original documents of Mark and Q, so that the actual life and teaching of Jesus can only be

---

[25] The first letter of *Quelle*, the German word meaning "source." Since Luke follows his sources more closely than Matthew, the content of Q can be most simply and confidently stated in terms of the passages which contain it in Luke. E. B. Redlich, in a recent *Introduction to the Synoptic Gospels*, assigns to Q as a minimum the following material from Luke (with, of course, the parallel passages in Matthew): 3: 7–9, 16–17; 4: 3–12; 6: 20–49; 7: 6–8, 18–28, 31–35; 9: 57–62; 10: 2–16, 21–24; 11: 9–52; 12: 1–12, 22–59; 13: 18–35; 14: 11, 26–27, 34–35; 16: 13, 16–18; 17: 1–6, 20–37.

doubtfully reconstructed from the materials now available. At any rate, the full authenticity of any of these materials cannot justifiably be assumed; human fallibility is evident in all of them. Especially in the case of passages bearing upon issues which are known through other evidence to have been hotly debated by Christians during the period when the Gospels were being written, the critic points out that it is exceedingly difficult to tell how far they are colored by strong convictions on the matters then under discussion, and how far they accurately report Jesus' own mind or action. We have no quite certain historical truth, even about him.

Why such an outcome is unacceptable from the fundamentalist standpoint (and, with some reservations, to Catholicism) is evident enough; one can hardly adopt it and at the same time hold the traditional view of the Gospels as constituting an infallible divine revelation to man. With the liberals, including those whom we are calling modernists, however, the case was, in general, otherwise. Their disposition to admit the validity of the methods and assured results of modern science inevitably led them to feel that opposition to the application of scientific method to the understanding of the Bible would be inconsistent and futile. And those who had already been influenced by Schleiermacher's ideas, or had fully accepted the evolutionary conception of history and were thinking about the development of religion in terms harmonious with it, were quick to see that the story of the Bible offered by the higher critic is precisely what would be expected if these conceptions are valid. The Bible from this point of view is essentially a record of man's past religious experience, reflecting at each stage the fallibilities and limitations of his outlook as well as his dominant loyalties, ideals, and hopes. Its agreements and disagreements, both major and minor, are just what we should anticipate in a collection of books of this kind. In principle, the Bible is not different from religious literature written at the present time as an expression of deep-seated need and pious feeling. This means, of course, that the concepts of inspiration and revelation must be radically reinterpreted, so that we may mean by them man's halting and gradual discovery of divine truth rather than a supposed absolute disclosure from God's omniscience. Finally, here, as in the issue directly raised by the theory of evolution, it seemed to liberals—especially, to modernists—that genuinely religious values were enhanced, not destroyed, by accepting the critical view. Doubts and uncertainties engendered by the contradictions of Scripture no longer paralyzed earnest thought or confused moral insight. Modern Christians felt themselves one in a new and more intimate way with the Biblical authors in the never-ending quest for a fuller understanding of God and a more intimate appreciation of the mind of Christ. After all concessions to the higher critic had been made, the fundamental things still remained—that men and women today have religious experiences with the characteristic values which they bring, and that, so far as Christians are concerned, these experiences are primarily aided, renewed, and guided by the records of Jesus' life and teaching contained in the Gospels. As long as these truths abide and are experientially verified, the liberal is sure that nothing really vital to his religion has been lost, and these evidently do not depend on any special doctrine of Biblical inspiration.

It is important to observe, however, that this new view of the Bible meant at least as radical a transformation of the fundamentalist theory of religious authority as the latter had meant in its contrast with the Catholic doctrine. Catholicism, it will be recalled, insisted upon the recognition of three distinct levels in the hierarchy of religious authority. Divine truth was originally revealed to the prophets and apostles; it is interpreted by the pope and the bishops of the Church; and as so interpreted is submissively accepted by other Christians. Orthodox Protestantism had fully agreed as regards the first of these levels but had taught that the distinction between the other two is mistaken—they should entirely coalesce. Every Christian has the right and the duty to interpret the Bible for himself, his conscience and reason being guided by the Holy Spirit. Now the modernist conception of the Bible and of divine inspiration obviously carries the implication that the distinction between the first level and the others is really unwarranted. When the authors of the Bible wrote their message they were in essence in a situation no different from that of any earnest contemporary thinker who is moved to interpret life for the benefit of whoever may find guidance in his writings. "Slowly the Bible of the race is writ," and every pious mind may add his contribution to it.[26] New, il-

[26] James Russell Lowell, *Bibliolatres*.

luminating truth is open to anyone's discovery. All three levels in the structure of religious authority thus, from this standpoint, merge in one. So far as the Bible, as now composed, continues to hold a distinctive place, this is merely due to its proven power over long centuries to enliven and guide the higher aspirations of men, not to any unique intrinsic prerogative.

THE SCIENTIFIC STUDY OF COMPARATIVE RELIGION

We may be relatively brief in dealing with the third major issue on which liberals made extensive concessions to science while traditionalists did not—the issue precipitated by the scientific study of comparative religion. It will not only provide a further illustration of the points brought out in the above discussion of evolutionary theory and the higher criticism, but will also serve as a more explicit introduction to the differences between modernism and humanism.

During the greater part of Christian history prior to the nineteenth century, Western religious thinkers had little interest in understanding and explaining the non-Christian religions of whose existence they were aware. The problem was to convert people from them to the true saving faith and to guard Christian communities from their pernicious influence. From time to time, however, sporadic attempts were made to account for the origin and spread of these religions; such attempts became more common in the seventeenth and eighteenth centuries, as the reports of explorers and traders made Europeans more vividly conscious of the variety of religious practices in the Americas and the Orient. The explanations offered were, however, far from scientific. With practically no exceptions, they were not only *a priori*, but dogmatic; the available facts were fitted into a scheme which was determined by acceptance of the Christian or some other specific viewpoint as alone true, by comparison with which all other religious claims were pronounced false and vicious. Under these circumstances, as might be expected, descriptions and analyses of available facts showed little approach to impartiality. They were thickly colored by horror at the degraded ideas of the deity found among savages, or by commiseration with the wretched plight of people wandering in the darkness of religious error.

The explanations offered by thinkers who dealt with the history of religion in this manner are illustrations of what may appropriately be called the "degeneration" theory of religion. Of this theory there appeared, in the centuries just mentioned, two main forms. One was held by orthodox Catholics and Protestants who felt bound by their view of the Bible to interpret religious facts in conformity with its historical statements. From this standpoint, it seemed evident that the original religion of mankind—that practiced in the Garden of Eden by Adam and Eve—was a pure and true monotheism, uncontaminated by any form of error. But Adam and Eve sinned, and their descendants fell deeper and deeper into moral degradation. As a result of this collapse of man's original virtue he lost his high ethical conception of God and began to entertain a cruder polytheism. He believed in a host of demonic powers which he thought might be persuaded to satisfy his selfish wishes through magic and sacrificial gifts. This tendency of religion to degenerate continued to display itself throughout human history except for those areas influenced by the work of the Hebrew prophets and of Christ. These teachers were specially sent by God in his mercy for mankind to combat this otherwise fatal trend toward idolatry and corruption. Thus Christianity is essentially a re-establishment, through God's gracious and loving aid, of the early religion of Eden, when Adam and Eve lived in an intimate filial relation with God; the other religions exemplify the various barbarisms and pernicious crudities into which that pure faith has degenerated among peoples to whom God did not send accredited messengers.

The other form of the degeneration theory is that held by many of the deists and those whom they influenced. They believed in a religion "of nature," which prevailed originally among mankind, and which involved a simple and rational set of beliefs about God, moral obligation, and human destiny. This natural religion had, however, become corrupted, largely as a result of the machinations of clever priests who saw in man's susceptibility to superstition an opportunity to expand their authority and power. They taught that they were the special agents through whom the divine governance of men was to be exercised, and that access to God and influence over him could only be secured by special techniques in which they alone were competent. From this standpoint Judaism and Christianity, as well as the other religions, illustrate this historic tendency toward corruption; all alike need to be purified from superstition and reduced to the rational religion of nature which had obtained in the beginning. Some of those who adopted this theory made a single (and not always sincere) concession to Christianity in affirming that the essence of Christ's teaching lies in the fact that it proclaimed, with new and more compelling sanctions, just this original religion of nature.

Neither of these forms of degeneration theory could, of course, maintain itself unchallenged in an age permeated more and more by the attitude of modern science. During the eighteenth and nineteenth centuries facts relevant to the historical and comparative study of religion were accumulated with increasing rapidity, facts which could only with considerable violence be fitted into the degeneration scheme. Doubts about the Garden of Eden story and the supposed primitive Golden Age of mankind, together with the increasing influence of an evolutionary point of view in the study of human history, bereft the assumptions underlying the degeneration theory of their traditional supports and opposed them by other assumptions at least equally plausible. Of still greater importance than these changes, however, was the growing realization that a truly scientific study of comparative religion involves above all else the application, in gathering, describing, and interpreting facts, of the same scrupulous impartiality that is a fundamental aspect of the scientific approach to other subjects.

This meant that religions could not properly be classified initially as true or false, and then described in the incurably prejudiced context that such a classification betokens, but that they must be studied in the light of objective features of similarity and difference —features capable of being verified by any honest and competent observer, no matter of what religion he might personally be an adherent. The scientific necessity of such impartiality may be readily seen if we consider the situation in which some other science— astronomy, for example—would be caught if investigators began their work by classifying all theories in that field as true or false and then prosecuted their further research under the rigid guidance of such a classification. The varied material of religious history demanded, then, examination on the unprejudiced initial assumption that whatever religious creed, if any, might be true, all faiths alike are natural expressions of human need and are to be analyzed and compared on the basis thus indicated. All are anthropological phenomena, exhibiting in diverse environments and in variegated ways certain common human tendencies and concerns. All are forms of man's religious experience. In Schleiermacher's language, each develops some natural but more or less distinctive relation to the divine, in which man may feel himself to stand, and it takes all of them together to disclose exhaustively and satisfy entirely the religious nature of man. None could be assumed in advance to enjoy any unique privilege.

Now words need not be wasted to show that the scientific study of comparative religion in this manner cannot be wholly acceptable to the Catholic or to the fundamentalist. And even modernists, as the more conservative liberals, accept it with a certain qualification, arising from their loyal attachment to the specific religious values for which Christianity stands and their conviction that these values are superior to any embodied in the non-Christian religions. Humanists found no difficulty at all here, since in their case, as we shall soon see, such attachment is renounced on principle. But modernists share with them the scientific assumption that human history is the arena of natural law, and they are willing to pursue the study of religion with the impartial scientist as far as they can without imperiling the values which, if lost, would seem to take with them everything worth while in religion.

The most prominent outcome of this concession to scientific impartiality is the subordination or abandonment by modernists of many beliefs which Christianity shares with other religions and which seem peculiarly difficult to maintain in a scientific age, with a corresponding concentration on the moral insights and social ideals that they find especially emphasized in the Christian faith. Belief in ancient miracles (especially miracles connected with the birth and death of a great religious leader), supernaturally authenticated scriptures, expectation of a glorious second coming with a divine judgment upon all men, the idea that sacraments have miraculous efficacy, confidence in the supernatural power of prayer—all these things are characteristic of many civilized religions. Modernists note that they express everywhere the same psychological needs and appeal to the same kind of dubious historical evidence. The more one studies them in an impartial manner, with scrupulous regard to all the relevant considerations, the less does it seem plausible to maintain that the special boasts of any particular religion on such matters are well founded. The claims of all religions to supernatural authentication in these ways can hardly be true, and yet the objective evidence for all claims is of the same kind. Therefore it would seem that all must be rejected, as expressions of just such an unscientific attitude toward nature and uncritical belief in testimony as the theory of evolution would lead us to expect in the early religous history of mankind. The higher criticism of the Bible likewise points in the same direction; passages which by its criteria appear on other grounds to be of dubious dependability include a number of those which the comparative study of religion leads the modernist to reject as incredible. As a result of all these considerations, the disposition of modernist thinkers is openly or tacitly to surrender belief in the traditional Christian creed so far as it contains these supernaturalist claims, and to revise and reinterpret their theological structure accordingly.

On the other hand, the comparative study of religion itself, pursued in an entirely scientific spirit, clarifies the distinctive differences between the religions as well as their common features. Among these differences are the ethical ideals and social programs characteristic of each religion. Humanists wish to maintain an attitude of full responsiveness to all these envisioned values, unqualified by commitment to any single religion that has come down from the past. Modernists believe it possible to combine a quite impartial analysis and description of these differences with personal loyalty to the ideals that are especially emphasized in Christianity and uniquely expressed in the life of its founder. Thus while the traditional supernaturalist conception of Christianity seems to them, in general, no longer valid, a view which thinks of its essence as a distinctive way of life and a high type of moral idealism can, they believe, be maintained in full harmony with the assumptions, methods, and results of science.[27]

[27] The main problems which arise from this belief will be examined in connection with the more detailed contrast between modernism and humanism which follows.

Selected Bibliography

Abbott, Lyman, *Theology of an Evolutionist*, Houghton Mifflin, 1897.

McGiffert, A. C., *The Rise of Modern Religious Ideas*, Macmillan, 1915.

Mackintosh, H. R., *Types of Modern Theology* (chaps. I–VI), Scribner, 1937.

Randall, J. H., and Randall, J. H., Jr., *Religion and the Modern World*, Stokes, 1929.

Schleiermacher, F. D. E., *The Christian Faith* (Mackintosh and Stewart ed.), T. and T. Clark, 1928.

Schleiermacher, F. D. E., *On Religion: Speeches to Its Cultured Despisers* (Oman trans.), Kegan Paul, 1893.

Redlich, E. B., *The Student's Introduction to the Synoptic Gospels*, Longmans, Green, 1936.

White, A. D., *A History of the Warfare of Science and Theology*, Appleton, 1896, 2 vols.

Chapter XI

MODERNISM VERSUS HUMANISM

INTRODUCTION

THE FURTHER clarification of religious liberalism which is needed for our purposes will be best secured if we now develop in some detail the contrast between modernism and humanism which thus far has been presented only in general terms. And a typical defense of liberalism, first in its more conservative and then in its more radical form, can be most effectively summarized in terms of such a contrast.

For a hundred years and more the liberalism which has been discussed existed as an influential force only in the conservative or modernist form, except for such partial anticipations of humanism as appeared in the thought of J. S. Mill or that of his contemporary Auguste Comte. But early in the twentieth century this radical liberalism assumed a more definite shape and became quite articulate.[1] Its leaders were drawn in part from Unitarian ministers and theologians, who already represented the most liberal wing of Protestantism, in part from pragmatic or realistic philosophers who became convinced that if religion is to have any significant and valid meaning today it can only be in the form which finds systematic statement in the humanist position.

An analysis of this contrast should begin by returning to the basic idea and method of religious liberalism, described at the opening of the preceding chapter. That idea and method are expressed by

[1] Notably in "The Humanist Manifesto," published in 1933. (See *The New Humanist*, Vol. VI, No. 3.)

the phrase "religious experience." Now, just what is the essence of religious experience? How shall we identify it, and distinguish it clearly from those phases of human experience that are not specifically religious? It is necessary to do this in order to have the basic material to which our constructive empirical method can be applied —analysis of the major factors that can be discovered, definition of religious concepts in terms of them, formulation and verification of particular doctrines, etc.

Well, most liberals who came after Schleiermacher have not followed him in finding the essence of religious experience in man's feeling of absolute dependence. This seems to them a somewhat narrow and passive psychological foundation, characteristic, to be sure, of certain types of experience that may properly be called religious but not essential to all. They tend to find the heart of religious experience in a broader, and at least equally universal, kind of human need or concern, together with the active quest for its satisfaction. Men have, of course, many and various specific needs —the need for food, for shelter, for companionship, for active achievement, and the like. None of these particular needs appears to be distinctively religious; even the need for participation in a symbolic ritual is capable of being satisfied in other than ecclesiastical ways, as the secret fraternities and orders well know. The essence of religion is therefore, they think, not to be found in the attempt to satisfy any of these specific cravings. And it is dubious whether there is such a thing as a religious instinct; psychologists increasingly fail to discover it. But over and above these various special needs, all men, or at least most men, feel a more general and comprehensive need, the need of integrating the scattered and more or less conflicting parts of themselves—their impulses, emotions, sentiments, interests, ideas—into a coherent and effective unity. Man has a natural demand, not only for this or that object as the goal of this or that inner drive, but also for an organized personality in himself, mobilized in its entirety in face of the totality of his environing universe. There must be a wholeness within realized in full response to the vast wholeness without. Now this integration of personality, so it is contended, is the vital good that religious faith in the past has brought to men; only it has been interpreted in terms appropriate to traditional theology rather than in those suited to an empirical psychology. The sense of sin is a description, in such terms, of what is essentially a consciousness of failure to win such a unified self because of disturbing factors within; experience of redeeming grace is realization that the integration longed for has been gained through the aid of some external power. So with the other concepts fundamental to orthodoxy. What religion has always really meant for men is such an inner transformation and such a guiding plan of life as bring unity of character and wholeness of vision to individuals distraught, discouraged, lost in apparently hopeless conflicts, incapable of poise, serenity, or self-control. Those who find such emancipation find salvation, in any tenable interpretation of what salvation concretely means to an individual in the living present.

A self thus integrated and mobilized reveals two general aspects, an active and a passive. On the active side it is characterized by devotion to some appealing cause, person, or ideal, guided by a vision of an overarching and commanding good. In devoted service to this, all one's energies are organized and wrought into effective and dependable instruments. In giving himself thus to this supreme good one finds himself for the first time as a real personality, in which all his partial selves are united and harmonized by a single dominant purpose. On the passive side it is characterized by a sense of release from inner discord and a feeling of serenity, of power, of sincerity and purity of aim, of confidence and courage, and of harmonious relation with the deep-seated forces in the surrounding universe. The attainment of such an integrated self is for any man or woman a great good, one which spells not only moral gain but also an increase in mental alertness and physical vigor.

THE MODERNIST PERSPECTIVE

But at this point the crucial difference between modernism and humanism comes to the fore. The modernist interprets this experience of integration in terms of his commitment to a distinctively Christian faith. As he develops that interpretation, what is uppermost in his mind is the fact that Christianity, at its best, has provided a way that is still essentially valid for realizing such integration. Christian people through the ages, he is sure, have found experi-

entially that the most effective way for them to attain this goal is
through acceptance of the ideals for which Christianity distinctively
stands and personal loyalty to the spirit exemplified in its founder.
He wishes to preserve continuity between his own religious experience and that of the Christian past.

Hence a problem inevitably arises, on which modernism and
humanism diverge. If our appeal is in the end to the verifiable facts
of human experience rather than to any traditional dogma, must we
not admit that the great religious good may come to men quite
apart from Christianity? And if so, can we claim any absoluteness,
or even unique value, for this religion as compared with others?
The answer of modernists to the first of these questions is, in general,
yes. In non-Christian countries people will naturally find the key to
the kind of self-integration they crave and suppose to be possible
in non-Christian ways. Indeed, even in Christian lands many may
so misunderstand the true essence of Christianity or be so repelled
by its traditionalist, superstitious, and socially irresponsible adherents that they will discover the needed inner unity and vigor
through commitment to causes that at present seem secular rather
than religious. But these circumstances merely indicate the partial
failure of Christianity in the past. Were the real significance of
Christ's gospel known and fully appreciated, such individuals might
well find in it, they believe, a vitally important contribution with
which their quest for religious truth could hardly dispense. And at
this point the typical modernist answer to the second question
becomes easily understood.

Perhaps no absoluteness can be claimed for Christianity, in any
sense which would conflict with the tentativeness of empirical
method or would appear to dogmatize about men's religious experience in the future. But when we compare the great religions which
today compete for the loyalty of civilized peoples, and survey their
history, modernists believe that sufficient justification can be found
for attributing a relative superiority to the values for which the
Christian religion distinctively stands, and for expecting that the
longer earnest men and women everywhere face the deeper problems of life the more they will come to feel this superiority. The main
emphasis in this argument is likely to be one derived from the social
idealism of the modernist viewpoint. It seems to most modernists

that the non-Christian countries have made no significant social
progress under the stimulus derived from their religions. Their major
customs and social institutions, with the evils as well as the virtues
that are characteristic of them, have for millenniums remained without substantial improvement. War and social injustice are regarded
as inevitable, like the weather. Whereas, in Christian lands there
has at least been some progress toward the moralizing of the basic
human relations, and a persistent demand that social wrongs shall
not be permanently tolerated. Slavery has been well-nigh abolished,
women emancipated, industrial exploitation aggressively attacked,
and a new conscience against the horrors of war aroused. Doubtless
Christianity is not the sole cause of this difference, but there is surely
some significant correlation, they are sure, between its demand that
the spirit of Christ be expressed in all man's social relations and
these outstanding historical facts. While, then, the supernaturalism
of traditional Christianity must be surrendered or subordinated in
an age of science, the ethical ideal of loving service to one's fellows,
incomparably exhibited in the life and teaching of Jesus as well as
in his sacrificial death, is shown by historical as well as critical
analysis to be superior to any alternative, and to contain greater
promise of ultimate victory. It meets a profounder and more universal human need; it challenges fuller realization, both in every
individual's inner life and in the social institutions by which he is
enfolded, today as much as ever before. Recognition of these circumstances validates, they believe, an attitude of personal loyalty
to the historic Jesus, and justifies attachment to the Church which
he founded.

A corresponding attitude will, of course, be natural, from the
modernist standpoint, toward the Bible. Rejection of its infallibility
and of the miracles reported in it does not at all, modernists think,
affect the fact that it is the record of some of man's greatest religious
insights and the source of our knowledge of the Master's life and
sayings. It is now indispensable for religious inspiration, illumination, and guidance. It is still a unique revelation of God to man, not
in the sense of a supernatural truth mysteriously dictated to its
writers, but in the sense of a vivid portrayal of supremely valid
ideals such that by its aid our souls find power for effective living in
a way that no other literature quite equals.

How about the meaning and validity of the concept of God? Many modernist thinkers revert to the assumptions of ancient metaphysics at this point, merely applying those assumptions to the present religious experience of people instead of to the wider range of facts with which the Catholic argument began. These assumptions can be employed either in the form of a causal or in that of a teleological explanation. If it is the former, the reasoning will proceed in this way: The religious experience of people is an indisputable fact—that is, their experience of self-unification through devotion to some vision of goodness or beauty, bringing inner peace and power for nobler living. Now this fact must have an adequate cause in the vast cosmos of which man's life is a part, and this cause by definition is God.[2] If it is the latter, it will start with the thought that the religious life of man is a life of temporal effort and struggle toward the attainment of an ideal end. That end is progressively, though slowly and haltingly, realized in the spiritual achievement of individuals and the moral transformation of society. Such progress indicates the effective guidance of human life by a goal of supreme perfection, toward which as a result of that control it tends. God is that ideal of human excellence, constantly molding the course of history into greater conformity to his nature. He is the consummation of the moral and religious evolution of the human race, now active in leading it onward—the "far off, divine event toward which the whole creation moves."[3]

It will be observed that both these arguments imply acceptance of the ancient and Catholic conception of causality—that goodness in an effect indicates at least equal goodness in the active power to which it is ultimately due. And most modernists who use them believe also that they justify conceiving God as a person. That is, personality in the effect indicates significant kinship, at least, to personality in the cause, even though, because of the latter's infinity and transcendence, the concept thus applied must be acknowledged a halting symbol rather than an exhaustive and precise description.

But some modernist theologians distrust these assumptions, recognizing that they are alien to the methodology of empirical science, and perhaps therefore out of place in an analysis of religious experi-

[2] H. E. Fosdick, *As I See Religion*, Harper & Brothers, p. 26 f.
[3] Tennyson, *In Memoriam*, final stanza.

ence intended as a basis for the empirical verification of religious doctrines. They tend to define God by using categories derived from the modern theory of evolution in place of the categories of ancient metaphysics. Such reasoning will take something like the following form:

Religious experience does not occur in a vacuum; like any experience, it involves an environment. Every significant human achievement of value, including distinctively religious value, is a process in which one is actively related to, and dependent on, the world around him. Alone, man can accomplish nothing; he cannot even become himself. When he attains anything that seems to him good he has in so doing adjusted himself to some factor in environing nature to which he had formerly not been so successfully attuned. He has become accommodated to some real and important feature of his universe. Now, has not the term "God" always meant to religious people essentially that power in the world to which we gain right adjustment when achieving the greatest goods of which human nature is capable, especially the good of harmonious unification and effective invigoration of personality? May we not thus define God by applying the idea of evolutionary adaptation to our analysis of religious experience? Such a definition will not, of itself, of course, indicate the divine attributes—these remain to be determined by formulating hypotheses under the guidance of this definition and then testing them by further examination of our experience—but it indicates the most fundamental fact, from man's standpoint, about God, and shows the direction that detailed inquiry in theology will appropriately take. Thus, as long as empirical method finds it natural to use these evolutionary categories, the reality of God can be made relatively certain by defining him in this way, and no assumptions uncongenial to empirical science will be involved.

What position does modernism take on the immortality of the soul?

Well, arguments similar to those by which God is established fail here; the human soul can hardly be made immortal as God can be made real, by definition. The fact that we now experience ourselves as existing does not establish our existence in the future, either causally or teleologically or as an implication of successful evolutionary adjustment. But if God has been identified as a factor in the universe that in some sense is working toward the full achievement of personality in us, then belief in immortality seems naturally to follow as a well-grounded faith, if not as a coercive proof. Whatever progress toward personal integration we experience appears to show that the cosmic power which supports the values that are revealed at their best in a fully unified human personality is more deep-seated in the structure of reality than the powers contending against these values. In the end the universe is on the side of personality and the worth that it distinctively embodies. But if this be a more justifiable faith than its pessimistic contrary, it seems equally permissible to believe in the immortality of such personality. Its possibilities of spiritual growth are never exhausted in three score years and ten; the apparent purpose of the cosmos would seem to fail at a crucial point if the main enterprise that we find fostered in it—the building of rich and noble personality—is in all individuals cut off by death. The same factor that accounts for its presence and for whatever achievement is already attained may be trusted to preserve it for a still greater achievement in the invisible beyond. Most modernists have renounced the orthodox ideas of hell and eternal punishment as inconsistent with the truth that God is love, and the traditional pictures of heaven they also regard as merely symbolic. But that there is an opportunity beyond death for selfhood to continue its quest for a finer good seems to them a valid hope and faith. The universe is on the side of the highest values; the highest values are enshrined, but only partially realized, in the integration of human personality in our present lives; therefore we may conclude that their fuller realization takes place in the continued existence of such personality in another realm beyond the grave.

A few modernists regard the hope of full personal immortality as somewhat too daring; even they, however, usually hold that the values attained in human selfhood are preserved in some form and are not destroyed by death.

Buttressed by these encouraging convictions, the modernist looks forward hopefully to continued religious progress in the evolving life of humanity, and energetically participates in the tasks which it lays upon his shoulders. He is an eager champion of modern science and wishes to see it accomplish still greater wonders in the future than it has in the past, both in disclosing the law-abiding structure of nature and in applying the knowledge so gained to the practical amelioration of human life. The only matters on which a conflict might arise between science and his religious faith are the historic uniqueness of Jesus and the ultimacy of Christian values in comparison with others. He shares the scientist's distrust of the miraculous and therefore disbelieves in a providence conceived as superintending the details of nature's happenings. The divine purpose is gradually realized in the world through orderly progress in which man coöperates by meeting its necessary conditions. Prayer in the form of petition for special benefits the modernist usually rejects, as both futile in a world controlled by causal law and in most cases immoral; men should not treat God as a cosmic errand-boy to serve their whims, but should themselves accept the responsibility to transform the world under divine guidance into a place in which Christian ideals reign. Prayer, however, as an opening of the inner life to the fuller play of spiritual influences from beyond one's present horizon is not only legitimate, but a tested means to nobler living; the uplift that comes is then no miracle, but the appropriate effect of meeting a necessary condition of moral growth. Especially does the modernist labor anxiously to bring about an end to the internecine warfare between Christian sects. A unity of Christendom, or at least as wide-reaching a unity as proves possible, on a modernist foundation, is his aim. This aim has already been partially realized, and the momentum of the drive toward unity among Protestant denominations is rapidly gaining. From the modernist standpoint, the differences which separate the sects are not fundamental; they concern items of metaphysical or historical dogma which are irrelevant to genuine Christian values. The important thing is not rigid adherence to ancient creeds, which need restatement today in any case. The one really vital matter is coöperation among those who believe in the ideas symbolized in Jesus of Nazareth, toward the end of more fully exemplifying those ideas in personal conduct and in the great social institutions which pervasively influence modern life.

BASIC HUMANIST CONVICTIONS

To the humanist, much of this reasoning represents a failure to carry through the principles of empirical method consistently, and to recognize all that is involved in identifying religious experience as the experience of realizing fuller personal integration.

If we are in earnest, he holds, in our commitment to empirical method with appeal to present psychological facts, and if we really mean that the essence of religion is to be found in the integration of personality around devotion to a supreme ideal, then in strict logic it is permissible to convert this definition and affirm that whatever is empirically discovered to perform this function for men and women is religious.[4] Wherever, through any means, people find aid in achieving and perfecting this experience they find religion. And the appropriate further step of empirical method is not to attempt an immediate demonstration that such an experience is to be won best by traditional Christian loyalties, but rather to engage in an impartial study of contemporary human life and see how various people who have made significant progress in this direction have achieved their success. But as soon as such an impartial examination is embarked upon it becomes quite clear to the humanist eye that neither the claim of modernism for a clear distinction between Christianity and other religions, nor for a significant distinction between the religious as traditionally conceived and the secular, can be made good. People find a satisfying unification of personality in all the manifold ways in which they find it; each of those ways should, then, be included within the scope of religion. It will be helpful to elaborate briefly each of these two criticisms.

Humanists will admit, of course, that in the Western world, with its distinctive historical background, its long-fostered attitudes and habits, large numbers of needy men and women will continue to find inner peace, joy, and moral guidance through devoted adherence to Christ and voluntary loyalty to his teaching as they understand it. But in non-Christian countries, for exactly the same reasons, most people will secure the same result through commitment to the best that their own religions render available, and in fact often continue to do so even after the Christian message has been proclaimed to them. Who, being faithful to empirical method, can venture to claim that their experience is not genuine, and not the best solution to their anxious and living need? Moreover, in

---

[4] J. Dewey, *A Common Faith*, pp. 13–17.

Christian countries, too, a generation has arisen which finds so many intellectual and moral perplexities in the supernaturalism traditionally associated with Christian faith that the latter is obviously a source of perplexity and embarrassment rather than of support and illumination. Men are turning to all sorts of new cults and unorthodox enthusiasms in the endeavor to find what they lack; it is evident that they will either miss the supreme religious good entirely or attain it in non-Christian ways. But experience shows that they often do attain it, and by our impartial empirical approach is not the path they follow, whatever that may be, properly called religion?

Here it becomes evident also, from the humanist standpoint, that the familiar segregation of life into religious and secular concerns is just as untenable as the claim of final religious value for one particular religion as against others. Any devotion to an appealing good in the form of an artistic vision, the advancement of scientific truth, an enticing social cause, a personal friendship, a family trust—whatever specific form it may take—through which an individual finds himself, attaining serenity and unity of purpose, is *ipso facto* religious, and its value as such is clearly established, so far as he is concerned. But such commitment may assume so many varied guises, and may embrace so much of what is ordinarily thought of as nonreligious behavior, that we cannot draw any clear line between the religious, on the other hand, and the secular, on the other. Religion, conceived in terms of this approach, embraces the whole of life, at least the life of any person who lives it under the control of an organizing ideal; nothing can be excluded from it except discord and evil. True religion, for any man or woman, is just wholehearted absorption in whatever envisioned greatness empirically brings integrity of selfhood and promises to be a constant, dependable source of continued growth toward the goal of perfect harmony, within and without. For humanists, before us lie all the significant values that promise joy in human living, Christian and non-Christian, religious in the customary sense and also secular; the door should be open to the richest achievement of which man's powers prove capable, without any restriction to the ways which past religious loyalties have emphasized. Religion is man's eager, unshackled quest for whatever goodness and fineness life makes possible.

Indeed, the humanist goes further than this, and offers positive criticisms, which appear to him justified by the empirical method, of the modernist attempt to identify loyalty to the life and teachings of Jesus with pursuit of the moral and social values which call for fuller realization today. It seems to him clear that Jesus did not embody all the values that are religiously significant today, and that the attempt to find them in him is historically unwarranted.

That Jesus was a man of remarkable human sympathy and of self-sacrificing heroism is clear. Also, that in his teaching the best moral insights and social attitudes preached by his predecessors, which still today challenge more widespread and effective realization, were detached from much that is irrelevant in their previous context, is clear. And doubtless he radiated an indefinable personal quality, capable of arousing not only devoted attachment, but also wondering awe, such as few of the great men of history have possessed. But candid examination of the Gospel stories discloses another side to the picture, which in view of the moral and intellectual problems of contemporary life demands, in humanist eyes, honest recognition.

Jesus had no appreciation of the value of intelligence as the most dependable human faculty for analyzing the perplexities into which men fall and for providing wise guidance in dealing with them. Simple and childlike trust in the Heavenly Father and humble obedience to his will was the sum and substance of life's wisdom to him. His theory of the world, which to his mind justified this confident faith, is squarely opposed to the scientific naturalism that a frank assessment of experience increasingly compels modern men to accept. Far from thinking of nature as an objective, law-abiding order, to which man must patiently learn how to adjust himself while assuming responsibility intelligently to transform those parts of it that are amenable to human control, he believed it to be directly subject in all its details to the purposive care of a personal being. Every hair of our head is numbered; no sparrow falls without his supervision. Repent of your sins, have faith in God, and love your neighbor as yourself, is his counsel.

This basic attitude precluded, of course, any obligation on man's part to interfere in political and economic matters. Since God will at his chosen time and in his chosen way supernaturally take charge of human affairs and establish his kingdom, these things may entirely be left aside as no responsible concern of religion. Social institutions are accepted as they stand. Man cannot, to be sure, serve both God and mammon, but he can and should serve both God and Caesar. As for economic relations, there is much in Jesus' parables which suggests that he took for granted and without criticism the economic structure prevalent in his day, with its assumption of an absolute right on the part of employers to make such profits as they are able and to treat their workmen according to whatever whim may seize them. Those who work but an hour in the evening may be rightfully paid the same wage as those who have toiled through the long heat of the day, if the employer so will. In fact, God's relations with men are at times compared with those of a haughty and capricious employer with his workmen; he is master of body and soul, and may properly do with them, in time and eternity, whatever it may please him to do. He is subject to no standard of right beyond his own arbitrary will.[5] Though appreciating the tender affections that family life makes possible, Jesus insisted that loyalty to him requires his followers to be ready to abandon these for his and the Gospel's sake. Ordinary prudence in the form of intelligent forethought of future needs is a moral vice, since it implies lack of full confidence in the Heavenly Father's providence. His position on all these matters was doubtless profoundly affected by his expectation of an early establishment of the divine kingdom, bringing an entirely new order of earthly affairs; in such a situation material cares and social responsibilities (except so far as concerns the basic attitudes necessary for admission to the kingdom) were naturally almost negligible. Can we really approve, also, the humanist asks, the surge of self-exaltation that occasionally found expression through Jesus' lips—the claim to a unique familiarity with God, control of the powers of nature, and unlimited judicial authority over mankind?[6] This mood is easily understandable in view of the Messianic expectations in the light of which Jesus interpreted his career. But does not the deepest ethical insight of modern times feel it to be inconsistent with the modesty of true friendliness, the humility appropriate to awareness

[5] Mark 12: 14–17. Matt. 20: 1–16. Of course, Jesus believed that God is kindly disposed toward those who turn to him in sincere repentance.
[6] Luke 10: 17–24.

of one's many limitations, and the genial readiness, demanded of moral leadership in a democratic age, to learn from the deeper experiences of others while sharing with them the significance of one's own?

Surely, the humanist contends, we cannot, in the light of all these circumstances which are quite obviously displayed in Jesus' teaching and conduct, honestly regard him as embodying the highest moral and social ideal which challenges realization today, or as a person whom we should seek to imitate in all respects. But to insist on the vital importance of an attitude of personal loyalty to him, and at the same time to encourage a careful study of his biography in the mood of such enthusiastic attachment, as modernists usually do, cannot fail to confuse and weaken rather than to clarify and strengthen many of the social attitudes and responsibilities that most evidently need courageous development and guidance today.

We must, then, discriminate, humanism maintains, even in our appreciation of Jesus and the moral ideals that Christianity intimately associates with him. Our attitude must be one of intelligent selection rather than a fervent attachment which in the nature of the case is at least partially blind to deficiencies challenging supplementation or correction. We must view him as we do the other great religious teachers of the past, recognizing that all alike have given a contribution of enduring value to the religious growth of mankind, with which we cannot afford to dispense, and that none is properly to be accepted wholesale. Otherwise we shall lie in constant peril of intellectual stultification and moral bewilderment. Our most fundamental religious attachment cannot be to any historic source of present ethical values, but to those values themselves—all values which seem to promise enduring satisfaction to the struggling and aspiring life of humanity. Love, continually growing in wisdom and in empirical responsibility, proves itself by the test of experience to be unqualifiedly good; but this cannot truthfully be said, humanists hold, of any historical religious heritage.

From the humanist standpoint, therefore, modernism is in this respect but a diluted and less consistent fundamentalism. It admits the legitimacy of applying scientific method to many phases of religious experience which fundamentalists protect from its dangerous assaults, but it has its own fundamentals which are not

exposed to the full light of impartial examination. When it comes
to the personality of Jesus and the moral ideals which in Christian
thought are bound up with him, the appropriate attitude, modernism
feels, is not one of full scientific impartiality, but one of devout
allegiance. Humanism, however, demands a thoroughgoing adherence to science, on these as on all other matters, in the interest of
intellectual clarity and moral honesty. If we are to be loyal disciples of Jesus as a moral leader, then it insists that we should
unflinchingly follow what careful historical study shows to have
been his example and the principles of his teaching, without rejecting or correcting any of them; if we are not willing to do this,
then we should frankly recognize the selective method that we are in
fact adopting and pursue it consciously and courageously. In the
long run it will not do to identify commitment to our own highest
contemporary ideals with loyalty to the historical Jesus who only at
certain points championed or exemplified those ideals.

But does not humanism have its own still more attenuated list of
fundamentals? If not, how can it stand for anything whatever that
is positive and significant, as every religious faith must in some sense
do; if so, does it not thereby run afoul of the same criticism?
Does not allegiance to this or that human value imply that, so far
as it is concerned, the impartiality and tentativeness of scientific
method have been displaced by enthusiastic devotion?[7] The reply of
the humanist to this query is that he adheres to an objective empirical method throughout, but that the consequence described does
not in fact follow. The attitude taken is one of complete and unreserved welcome to any promising values that may come upon our
horizon from any quarter, non-Christian or secular as well as traditionally religious; so far as he attaches himself to any absolute value
it is just the value of an open soul itself, ready for unending growth
through future experience and for unprejudiced comparison of newly
envisaged goods with those which have been previously assumed to
be highest. But he finds as a matter of actual experience that certain
broad types of human value do prove capable of maintaining themselves under this challenging test, of steadily gaining in clear and
compelling cogency as a result of every attempted criticism. They
change, to be sure, in the detailed mode of their application to con-

---

[7] This criticism will be stated more fully below. See p. 361 ff.

crete cases, but they remain the same in essential meaning. The main goods that he finds to be thus entirely harmonious with an impartial and open mind are the pursuit of truth, the creation of beauty, the realization of love and friendship, and the delight of sharing with others whatever goods are capable of being coöperatively sought and mutually enjoyed. These things, then, occupy a distinctive place in his ultimate ideal, but they remain there, he insists, not as objects of pious attachment but as values that in fact prove dependably fertile in the course of growing experience. His only object of absolute allegiance is human good as such.

The true bond of religion is, therefore, from the humanist's standpoint, neither a metaphysical dogma nor a form of historical loyalty, but commitment to those appealing human values that universal experience, so far as it gains in clarity and insight, attests as good. Only on these terms, he believes, can we hope to see realized some day a genuinely catholic religion of all mankind, drawn from every historic creed, and united by principles which increasing wisdom will ever support.

Of these differences between modernism and humanism, the one which cuts deepest is the humanist's unqualified acceptance of a naturalistic conception of the universe; it is because of this that he tends to abandon the term "God" instead of redefining it in harmony with his basic convictions, as modernist theologians do. Modernists reject the supernaturalism of traditional orthodoxy, to the extent of giving up belief in miracles and detailed manifestations of divine providence, but most of them are convinced that there is a personal being[8] guiding the course of nature and of history as a whole toward wise and good ends. With few exceptions, humanists do not believe that any such conviction is warranted. They hold that the universe is an impersonal order throughout, taking no account of ends that are desirable from the human standpoint; so far as man attains any enduring good he does so by intelligently controlling those natural processes which he can learn how to master and by wisely adjusting his expectations and emotions to the overwhelming forces that are beyond his sway. How do humanist philosophers defend this belief?

The more general arguments for this unqualified naturalism were

[8] Or at least a being who is best understood through the concept of personality.

noted in the chapter on Spinoza. But with three centuries of scientific progress intervening, contemporary thinkers naturally supplement such arguments by considerations that could hardly have been given much weight in Spinoza's day.

Among these considerations a prominent place is accorded those derived from the enormous and undisputed success of science. In a brief period of history it has progressed in the most astounding manner, both toward a detailed understanding of how things happen in the world, and in the application of this knowledge toward a larger human control of nature through practical invention and scientific industry. Now this unquestioned success would seem to be clear testimony, so humanists contend, to the soundness of the basic assumptions characteristic of the scientific movement which has achieved it. And what are those assumptions? Well, prior to the rise of modern science men for long centuries had sought to understand nature by the method of deduction from rationally intuited principles and by supposing that apparently teleological processes were the key to its essential structure. They had pictured it as an organic system aiming at the attainment of a supreme good, and had construed its detailed doings by deduction from the idea of such a purposive hierarchy. But this procedure gave rise to interminable controversies and fostered serious errors. By contrast, modern science is historically distinctive in that it has quite abandoned the teleological idea that the concepts "good" and "perfection" supply fundamental clues for the interpretation of nature, and has insisted that deduction is an inadequate tool without empirical verification. The replacement of teleology by the assumption that the world is a nonpurposive order implies that man must regard himself as a part of nature rather than as in any comforting sense a special favorite, except to the degree that he succeeds in making his good a natural end by learning how to manipulate what happens around him toward its attainment. To be sure, in the biological sciences teleology is still of some value in guiding the quest for verifiable laws, but to those familiar with Darwinism this does not mean that nature purposively takes account of biological ends; it is merely a consequence of the demonstrated truth that in the long run organs and functions are not likely to survive unless they successfully serve the purposes of the creature in whom they appear. The replacement of confidence in deduction by the demand for verification of hypotheses through observation implies the same naturalistic principle—the scientist may not assume that facts will always accommodate themselves even to his most rationally guided expectations; he must submit his anticipations to the humble exercise of sense perception, in which nature is allowed to present its own story. Both these fundamental and distinctive features of modern science, then, confirm the basic conviction that the pervasive pattern of the world is not affected by human hopes, preferences, or ideals of good, but is a neutral structure to which man must submit, except as concerns the limited area which he may reasonably aim to control. Elsewhere, his weal and woe are irrelevant to what exists in the universe, and a dependably good life can be won only by accepting this fact and adjusting our emotions to it.[9]

But science not only attests this truth by her successful principles of method. Many of her detailed conclusions, especially in the biological and psychological sciences, point toward and clarify the same result. So, at any rate, humanist thinkers contend.

Just as the Copernican astronomy ended the pretensions of the celestial bodies to a divine status, showing that heaven and earth are alike the scene of corruption and belong to the same realm of predictable physical law, so post-Darwinian biology and psychology, rightly understood, have ended man's pretensions to any special prerogative in the cosmic scheme, except as through the exercise of his intelligence he secures and maintains it. The new biology not only makes him a part of the tree of life, genetically related to the lowest forms of the animal kingdom and capable of survival only as he continues to adjust himself successfully to environing conditions; when its principles are used as a basic clue to the understanding of the world as a whole it also becomes evident that the entire realm of life arises out of and is dependent on a physico-chemical order whose vicissitudes it must share. Since we know of no other part of the universe in which the specific conditions obtain which seem necessary for its existence here, it appears likely that life is a local and episodic phenomenon in the cosmos at large. Sooner or later some crucial change is sure to take place in the forces on which life as we know it depends—the destruction of our

[9] W. Lippmann, *A Preface to Morals*, chap. VII.

solar system, for instance, in case living creatures prove capable
of surviving less radical catastrophes—and then man with all the
values which he prizes will disappear, presumably forever. At least
there is no empirical evidence that any goods which human existence
has made possible could be preserved through such a calamity and
make any significant difference to the world's subsequent state.
Nature in her massive fertility may, to be sure—perhaps now does—
produce elsewhere in the universe intelligent beings of a sort, but
we have no spiritual contact with them; our achievements and
values will, as far as we can see, remain permanently alien to their
concerns and will perish when we perish.[10]

The new psychologies extend the evolutionary scheme to include
the life of the soul as well as that of the body, and thus bring an
end to the influential mind-body dualism which in the past has
encouraged many religious thinkers to feel that even though man's
physical being be surrendered to the order of nature his spiritual
essence is a quite different affair, rightfully claiming a superior
origin and a more hopeful destiny. Nature is perennially fruitful in
all manner of ways, some of which issue in organic products fortunate enough to be more successfully adapted to survival than the
forms out of which they emerged. What we call "mind," with its interesting and distinctive properties, is one of these emergent
products, just as life itself is a historical emergent from physicochemical structures. It is preserved merely because it gives to its
possessors powers of adjustment to environing conditions which
prove in practice superior to the best faculties of competing organisms. Archaeology and anthropology show, moreover, that these
powers originally appeared in weak and obscure forms; they have
gradually developed to the state exhibited in the geniuses of civilized life through the operation of the same evolutionary laws that
account for their first emergence. Physiological psychology and
many abnormal mental phenomena indicate the pervasive and detailed dependence of mind upon its varied organic conditions, notably those of the nervous system. The Freudian psychologies still
more thoroughly upset the complacent rationalism and moral optimism unconsciously present in the traditional methods of psychological analysis and classification. They show that empirically

[10] G. Santayana, *Reason in Religion*, pp. 259 f.

the dominant force in human nature is not man's faculty of intelligence, shared, as he fondly supposes, with divinity, but a horde of subconscious drives, passionate impulses, and cantankerous emotions, only fitfully illuminated and weakly guided by gleams of reason. In fact, reason itself, under Freudian investigation, proves to be no separate faculty, uncontaminated by the less seemly energies of mind while authoritatively supervening to control them in the light of clear knowledge. Clarity of insight and impartial truth are at best ideals toward which *homo sapiens* may haltingly approximate; in actual practice his most objective thinking is permeated by irrational complexes and distorted by blind urges which constantly lead him astray. Reason is at best largely rationalization, and the operations of what we call "understanding," especially in matters metaphysical and religious, are mainly wishful thinking.[11] When man's mind is examined in the light of these considerations, humanist thinkers find it easy to see why the comforting theologies and egotistic idealisms of the past have been so widely believed in spite of their conflict with the most obvious facts of experience. They have been accepted and cherished not because they are true, but precisely because they are false; the real world in its cold and implacable unconcern for human interests is too intolerable for men to face, and therefore they have overlaid it in fancy with the warm projection of their hopes and aspirations. The universe of religious belief is the universe as they passionately wish it to be, superimposed upon the world of harsh fact which is then industriously harmonized with it as far as possible.[12] From this standpoint, the argument for the reality of God or a spiritual order from the universal agreement of mankind loses all its force; in fact, we must rather presume that any widespread human belief whose main tendency is to console people in adversity and encourage them in weakness is not true but false.

The humanist, then, accepts the thoroughgoing naturalism implied by all these considerations, reconciling himself to being part of a purely impersonal order of events in which none of his concerns whatever has any special privilege. This means that from his viewpoint prayer in the sense of petition is no longer relevant, the nearest justifiable approach to it being meditative self-examination and sin-

[11] E. A. Burtt, *Right Thinking*, chaps. III, IV.
[12] J. W. Krutch, *The Modern Temper*, chap. I.

cere opening of the depths of one's nature to all the forces which
uplift and sweeten. It means that worship in the traditional sense of
self-surrender to a supernatural power becomes transformed into
reverence for the social good and a manly assertion of the dignity
of human life in its rich potentialities of beauty and greatness. It
means that the comforting faith in some cosmic guarantee of human
values is replaced by a resolute readiness to face the tragedies and
crises of life in terms of our knowledge of their naturalness and
probability, finding in the sense of friendly comradeship with our
fellows a more than satisfying compensation for loss of the cozy but
illusory feeling that underneath are the everlasting arms of a divine
protector. Sentimental hopes and all forms of wishful thinking are
to be discouraged, while a more virile attitude of intelligent aspiration is progressively fostered by education and rooted in social
custom. And the new psychologies, social as well as individual, far
from being taken as a threat to man's moral and spiritual interests,
are to be seized as the source of suggestive opportunities for dealing
(more intelligently than religious therapy has done in the past) with
the challenging social perplexities and personal entanglements that
threaten disaster to modern life. Verified knowledge is always power
toward wise ends, in psychology as in physics. Knowing more clearly
and realistically what human nature is like, in ourselves and in
others, we can render our aspiration toward enduring good more
intelligent and effective than it has been when confused by sentimental faith and prudish veiling of the dark wildnesses of our
character. We can follow the path of social and mental hygiene with
the reasonable hope that increased understanding gives, even though
that same understanding completely blast, as it doubtless will, all
simple solutions and easygoing panaceas of the terrific problems of
human life.[13]

Because of this radically naturalistic orientation it seems best, to
most humanists, to abandon the term "God" instead of harmonizing
it with their beliefs by drastic reinterpretation. The vast majority
of religious people in the West, they are sure, mean by this word a
supernatural being who created physical nature and providentially
disposes all that happens in it toward good ends; this is the meaning
hallowed by the orthodox creeds and theological systems. In view

[13] "A Humanist Manifesto" (*The New Humanist*, Vol. VI, No. 3), p. 2 f.

of this fact, is it not deceitful and dishonest to continue to use the word in religious discussions which such people will hear and read, if we intend by it something quite contradictory to this comforting doctrine—if what we really stand for is a conviction which flatly denies all that this belief implies for them? We have frankly rejected theism; shall we retain "God"? Shall we not thereby encourage a serious intellectual and moral confusion—an intellectual confusion between two diametrically opposed convictions about the universe, and a moral confusion between two conflicting ways of life? Shall we not inevitably seem to encourage people to live by trust in the beneficence of a superhuman person enthroned behind nature, when what our real principles require is that they be challenged to face unflinchingly the fact that there is nothing in nonhuman nature that cares for their concerns and to make the thoroughgoing adjustment and accept the moral responsibility that this consciousness brings?

Let us then offer the world a religion without a God. Not all humanists go to this extreme—John Dewey being the outstanding exception[14]—but most of them draw precisely this conclusion.

But can we then justify calling what we believe and practice a "religion"? If we make as clean a sweep as this of the furniture with which in the past men have been familiar in the home of their religious imagination, what is left that could properly pass under the name of religion? Except for the religion of science, all the philosophies with which we have previously been occupied would say, nothing. What remains is a social aspiration; religion has quite disappeared. But from the humanist standpoint, what is left is properly thought of as religion because it meets the same needs that religion at its best has always met; even though it meets them by uniting men in devotion to the dependable supports of human joy here on earth rather than by turning their eyes to a supposed transcendent providence. To humanists it seems clear that men who have believed in supernatural powers have not believed in them for their own sake, but for the human values of comfort, hope, and assurance that have been vividly associated with such belief. The goods in human experience brought by religion have always been the central matter; beliefs in unseen helpers have been important

[14] See *A Common Faith,* p. 50 ff.

because it has been widely thought that realization of the supreme blessings of life depend on them. Humanist insistence on this point is supported by careful studies of religious history. It is contended that Western theologians have fallen into the habit of interpreting religion far too narrowly, because of the historical emphases of the particular religions with which they are most familiar. When we study sympathetically primitive and Oriental religions we discover, so humanism maintains, that what is common to religion every-where is no solacing metaphysical faith, but simply a resolute quest for the greatest goods life seems to promise, by the aid of whatever techniques are available.[15] Belief in supernatural beings is often present, of course, but it takes the most varied forms, some of which, e.g., fetishism and orgiastic totemistic sacrifices, horrify the sensitive Western theologian even more than a complete absence of supernaturalism would do. And some religions, at least, have been quite naturalistic in the humanist sense; this is true of the primitive Buddhism taught by Gautama and of Confucianism as many Chinese understand it. In all these cults, however, there is a systematic attempt to attain a fundamental adjustment for man in face of the insistent challenge that life presents, and the values of peace, poise, and confidence that such adjustment brings. This endeavor humanism also retains.

So religion, from the point of view of this radical liberalism, does not involve any metaphysical creed; at its center lie the major ethical values and valid social principles which challenge realization. Intelligent and devoted commitment to these is true religion.

Moreover, the humanist is sure that careful study of the history of religion demonstrates a relevant truth here that more orthodox Western theologies find it hard to recognize. Such study, he believes, clearly indicates that all religions, whether their adherents are aware of it or not, have been relative, in their fundamental ideas, to dominant human needs and values. Such values are the central and controlling feature in all religions. The divine beings of primitive belief are just the natural powers of sky, sun, earth, rain, certain animal species, streams, the sea, on which men depend for the physical sustenance that at that stage of human evolution is their most insistent need and major preoccupation. As nations develop,

[15] A. E. Haydon, *Man's Search for the Good Life,* especially chap. III.

the need for a broad political unity expresses itself in religion by the elevation of some ancestral leader to a ruling position among their divinities, or by attributing to some specially emphasized natural power the human qualities of an idealized chieftain. Hebrew religion at the period of the Palestinian conquest exemplifies this situation; Yahweh is essentially a storm god embellished with the attributes of a martial hero. As group conflicts become increasingly important, in the course of the internal specialization of national life into many classes with distinct interests, and as external intrusion of nations on each other through military aggression and imperialistic exploitation threatens to be constant, the social ideal of a peaceful unity of all mankind becomes insistent. As it gains clarity, the attitudes which are necessary to realize and preserve such unity—equity, mercy, kindliness, love—are brought increasingly into prominence. These new demands are gradually expressed in an altered conception of the high divinities of peoples; the idea that there is only one God of all the world arises, and that his major attributes are not those of sternness and power but those of wisdom, justice, and love. The period of the prophets exhibits this stage in the case of Hebrew religion. And since these new moral and social ideals take somewhat different form in different nations, the fundamental character of the revised religion varies accordingly. In China, where the emphasis is on social order and stability, the supreme divinity is an impersonal principle of order in the universe, and the practical aspect of religion consists mainly in concentrated attention on the rules necessary to maintain dependable cöoperation in the natural and basic human relationships of sovereign and subject, parent and child, husband and wife, and the like. In Europe, where the emphasis was on love, knowledge, and effective leadership, God is conceived in more personal form; he embodies these qualities in their highest perfection, and human aspiration is encouraged by dramatic symbol and moral teaching to focus upon them as expressing its ideal end. Indeed, humanists see in the history of Christianity itself the clearest evidence of the same principle. During the time when the obvious and paramount need in western Europe was for authority, discipline, and unified organization, the claims of the Catholic Church, which met these needs, were almost everywhere recognized as valid, and the religious life of men fell into a corresponding pattern. When the demand for freedom, initiative, and responsibility for the individual became vigorous, it expressed itself not only in altered political and economic structures, but in a new form of Christianity—that in which the characteristic emphases of Protestantism are central. Thus man's major religious ideas, humanists hold, are everywhere shaped by the dominant needs and values of the people holding them. God, far from being the creator of man, is always himself created by man; any conception of him is a result of the play of man's idealizing imagination over the quest for the appealing goods that life renders possible. "The dim and shadowy outline of the superhuman deity fades slowly away from before us; and as the mist of his presence floats aside, we perceive with greater and greater clearness the shape of a yet grander and nobler figure—of him who made all gods and shall unmake them. From the dim dawn of history, and from the inmost depth of every soul, the face of our father Man looks out upon us with the fire of eternal youth in his eyes, and says, 'Before Jehovah was, I am.' "[16] But nonhumanist religions, while always exemplifying this truth as much as others, are blind to it, insisting that the essence of religion—at least in their own case—lies in something quite other than the quest for human values. The humanist plea is that we should all recognize frankly that this determinative position of man and his needs in religion is universal and inevitable. We can reverence only what we sincerely feel to be good, and our ideals of what is good historically change with our basic concerns. Let us consciously make our religion the expression of what we believe to be man's highest needs and ideal values, with full realization of all that this involves for our theological ideas, instead of doing so unconsciously under the mistaken notion that religion is really something else.

When we seriously consider the matter in this light, humanism contends, it becomes evident that nothing more than this is essential to religion. For the high goods that man's experience is capable of realizing are not dependent on metaphysical considerations for their goodness. Whatever conclusion we may reach about the world beyond man—whether naturalistic or supernaturalistic, materialistic or idealistic—it still holds true that some things in human experience are beneficent, others harmful; some are better, while

[16] W. K. Clifford, "The Ethics of Religion" (*Lectures and Essays*, Vol. II).

others are worse; and wise discrimination is therefore the basic key to enduring happiness. The great problem is so to order our conduct as to realize the best that is possible for man. And this is the problem of religion, rightly understood, for the great common faith of religion has always been that nothing but the best—salvation, in theological terms—is good enough for man.

LIBERALISM AND CONTEMPORARY SOCIAL PROBLEMS

It remains to sketch the position of liberalism on the insistent social problems of contemporary times. Here, as elsewhere, there is considerable variety of ideas, and all that can be done is to portray what appears to be the dominant trend, first for modernists, and then for the more radical humanist position. In the case of both, the guiding idea is twofold: on the one hand a frank facing of the fact that the modern world is struggling to meet new, complex, and very puzzling issues, and on the other an eager determination to provide the leadership necessary if those issues are to be solved in such a manner as will express and promote the highest ideals that men can glimpse. The task of religion, as influential modernists see it, is not to save individuals from a hopeless world destined to supernatural destruction, but to permeate the network of our daily social relations with the justice and love which the spirit of Christ demands, for only in a Christian world can persons be fully Christian. The humanist emphasis would be that this task involves the establishment of such conditions as will render participation in these ideal goods genuinely and securely open to all men. This means a radical reform and redirection of most of the social institutions under which people now live, so that they will respect rather than flout the ideal of a free and universal society in which people voluntarily and intelligently coöperate for the common good. But the practical program of humanism in carrying out this task and in meeting the insistent social issues of contemporary life is closely akin to that of modernist leaders, being merely somewhat bolder at certain points. We may begin with the problems affecting family life.

So far as these are concerned, modernists incline to hold that no simple and dogmatic solution, based on traditional standards of authority and sexual purity, can today be adequate. They are as concerned as Catholic and fundamentalist theologians to insist that family relations be so ordered as to further the highest spiritual development of those who enter them, and not to be merely instrumental to present individual happiness. But it seems to many that this does not imply a rigid adherence to the rules taught in the Bible or established in tradition. New possibilities, opportunities, and responsibilities in married life have been opened up by the changes of which we are reminded by such phrases as "the emancipation of women" and "the discovery of dependable methods of birth control." Moreover, modern psychology has laid bare serious emotional tensions that lack of happy adjustment between husband and wife may frequently bring. With the best will in the world, many individuals cannot overcome these disturbing effects. Where that is the case, continuance in a hopeless marriage is apt to mean not merely the negation of happiness, but also the undermining of conditions necessary (in the case of the children as well as the married partners) for the successful integration of personality and the inward peace, courage, and health that always accompany such integration. Hence, although modernists deplore the rapid increase of divorce in all Western countries today, they are apt to admit that frequently such separation, with opportunity for remarriage, is the only appropriate solution for maladjustment in this or that particular case, and this in the interest of religious values themselves. At least, an absolute prohibition of divorce, or permission of it merely on grounds of some specific sin, such an infidelity, seems to them an entirely antiquated and empirically indefensible method of meeting the difficulty.

For similar considerations, a freer attitude toward birth control is evidenced by most members of this group. Like all religious teachers who are familiar with the major distractions to the spiritual life, they wish men and women to subordinate the quest for sensual satisfaction—so apt, as it is, to disintegrate a personality—to the higher values of loving companionship as devoted partners and parents. But two considerations make them hesitate to endorse the uncompromising opposition to birth control manifested by the Catholic Church, and lead many of them to a qualified approval of its use. For one, they recognize realistically the appalling moral difficulties as well as physical dangers, especially in the case of poor families, that unwelcomed pregnancy brings, and it seems to them clear that in many cases the only way to relief for the overworked wife and mother is through the intelligent practice of contraception. For another, experience of marital intimacy supports, they think, the principle that the sexual relation, expressing in its unique way a happy oneness in mutual giving and receiving, may contribute to the higher values of love and friendly harmony between husband and wife instead of usurping their place, and is thus not inconsistent with the quest for spiritual goods even when quite detached from its reproductive function. But if this is the case, then scientific birth control should be regarded as a means to be used toward religiously valuable ends, not as a sheer evil to be uncompromisingly denounced. And the way to test and direct its uses is to appeal to man's present experience of its morally significant consequences, not to dogmatic authority derived from the past.

These changes of attitude do not merely, of course, reflect a readiness to relax orthodox prohibitions. They imply a positive responsibility and a constructive principle, namely, that ways must be found, under the new conditions of modern life, to realize to the full the spiritual possibilities of the family relationship. And both the greater equalitarianism between husband and wife enforced by contemporary social conditions, and the more understanding companionship between parents and children which modern educational ideals encourage, provide, modernists think, an opportunity hitherto impossible for a deeply satisfying coöperation in all the interests and activities of the home. It is the business of religion to seize this opportunity and make the most of it, not to pass it by in blind adherence to ancient standards of obedience and holiness whose validity contemporary religious experience does not confirm.

Humanist thinkers accept these ideas also, and some of them adopt a more extreme position which modernism would not approve. The more radical among them incline toward the solution of regarding sex as an essentially harmless pleasure which should be regulated only by personal taste and preference, and should be taken into account by public law only when children appear, who clearly have the right to adequate parental care.[17] Thus the so-called "companionate" or experimental marriage, as long as the

[17] C. E. M. Joad, Thrasymachus, pp. 54 f.

stork keeps his distance, would be a perfectly proper way of meeting the difficulty set by the economic unpreparedness of most young men and women for a family.[18] Those less venturesome feel that this solution does not adequately meet a real ethical problem that has been emphasized by all great religious teachers of the past. They are sure that sex is only a true good when controlled and interpenetrated by the love which naturally wishes to express itself in the joys of lifelong companionship and the mutual acceptance of parental responsibility. The serious problem is how to realize effectively this principle under the difficult and rapidly changing conditions of the modern world.[19]

As for the political issue between democracy and dictatorship, liberals are practically unanimous in their vigorous support of democratic ideals and methods. But their support is not simply grounded in the historical considerations which mainly account for the similar stand on the part of fundamentalists. They have been profoundly influenced by Kant; liberty and tolerance of others' rights are in their eyes necessarily demanded by respect for the personality of every man and woman, based on the recognition that each individual is a unique center of joy and sorrow, an irreducible focus of moral and spiritual possibilities. Every person must be treated as though he counts for something in the world, and can decide better on the basis of his own experience than any self-imposed authority can decide for him where his highest good lies and the main ways in which it is to be pursued. This implies a fundamental equalitarianism in their social theory. In face of the rising bevy of dictatorships abroad, with the violent revolutions and counterrevolutions which they bring, accompanied by ruthless suppression of civil and religious rights, liberals pin their faith on democracy as essentially the method of peaceful evolution in political affairs, providing for new governors with changed policies whenever the majority of citizens so demand, and preserving for the individual such freedom of self-expression as is consistent with stability and social justice. Thus viewed, democracy presents itself as the way of friendly and coöperative progress toward ends which will take account of the interests and needs of all members of the

18 See B. B. Lindsey and W. Evans, *The Companionate Marriage.*
19 W. Lippmann, *A Preface to Morals,* chap. XIV.

political community. Viewed in this light it symbolizes and embodies, so liberals hold, a valid religious ideal as well as a living political principle. Fascism they deeply distrust, since it threatens, in its apparent aims as well as its ruthless dictatorial means, the personal and social goods which seem to them important; communism they likewise vigorously oppose so far as the same dictatorial methods are used. In its ultimate ideal communism is, however, essentially right; to reorganize our social life on the basis of the Marxian principle "from each according to his ability, to each according to his need," would but express in economic relations the valid ideal of subordinating selfish gain to the love and service of others.

There is little difference between modernists and humanists on these political issues. If humanists have made a distinctive contribution here it is in clarifying more fully what is involved in the democratic ideals of freedom and equality of opportunity for all men. In discussing these ideals they have emphasized a principle which they believe answers the main objection of those who criticize such equalitarianism on the ground that it will not work. Whenever the ordinary man is given greater rights and larger powers—so the criticism runs—he shows that he knows neither how to use them wisely nor how to preserve them. Equalize income, for instance, today, and tomorrow the larger share of it will already be gravitating toward the hands of those with more than the average share of foresight and cleverness. Hence, the conclusion is drawn, we might as well accept a world in which freedom varies with power to secure and exercise it. But from the humanist standpoint this criticism entirely misses the point. It misses it because freedom has been conceived in a merely negative fashion, as consisting in nothing but removal of previous handicaps and oppressions. Of course, men and women who for ages have been ground beneath the heel of privileged social groups will not at once, when the heel is taken away, show alertness and discriminating wisdom in the use of their new opportunities. They will make all manner of mistakes and easily become the prey of novel forms of exploitation. But this simply means that genuine moral and social freedom is a positive thing, not mere emancipation from restraint. Men must gradually learn how to be intelligently free, through education and respon-

sible practice; the great task of a democratic community is to add
to the negative removal of oppression those positive instruments and
encouragements through which alone the common man can attain
effective liberty, dignity, and self-respect. Failure to realize this truth
and accept this responsibility is the major weakness of the social
institutions which are called democratic in the contemporary world.

What about the position of typical liberals with regard to the
economic tensions of the modern world? In such matters, the characteristic position of these thinkers involves frank recognition of the
serious social evils which are entailed by the prevalent form of organization in industry, and a resolute insistence on the attainment of
such a solution as will end these evils and make the economic relations under which men live consistent with valid human ideals. They
are disposed to admit that capitalism has in the past brought many
benefits to mankind, notably in stimulating the invention of labor-
saving machines and encouraging the large-scale production at low
prices of all sorts of goods required to meet human needs. In days of
rapid expansion of industry its values perhaps far outweighed the
ills which it brought. None the less, in their judgment it has always
been an essentially unethical method of harnessing man's industrial
life, since it makes the activities necessary to satisfy economic wants
depend on the pursuit of personal profit by business leaders; whereas
in a truly humane scheme of economic relations the gain-seeking
motive would be entirely subordinate to that of service to the community. And at the present time, they hold, the evils of capitalism,
especially its systematic exploitation of both wage earners and consumers, together with the danger of war which its uncontrolled
operation brings, have become so intolerable that a drastic reorganization of our economic structure is imperatively demanded. Human
rights—the right of all men to a secure share in the benefits that
industrial progress has rendered available—are superior to property
rights on the part of the wealthy few.

In the case of not a few liberals this demand leads to a forthright
championship of socialism—the ownership by the people as a whole,
operating through their various governmental agencies, of the means
of production and distribution. Some hesitate to go this far, but
agree on the desirability of strict public regulation of industrial
activities, to the end of protecting the interests of the consumer and

assuring steady employment at fair wages to the workers. Most of those who are not doctrinaire socialists see large promise in the consumers' coöperative movement. This enterprise offers a peaceful method whereby groups of consumers may organize to provide for their own economic wants and gradually displace capitalistic agencies by successful competition. Unlike state socialism, it does not add enormously to the responsibilities and temptations of politicians. Most modernists, also, are sympathetic champions of the right of labor to organize for collective bargaining in its own chosen way, since under present conditions only by such group pressure can the terrific disadvantage of the worker in making contracts with his employer be reduced to a minimum, and public opinion be forced to recognize labor's just demands and to support their protection by law.

Again, there is little difference between modernists and humanists with respect to the principles and practical programs to be followed in these matters. Humanists have, perhaps, supported organized labor somewhat more unqualifiedly than most modernists do, and have given a typically humanist answer to a frequently voiced criticism of the labor movement. That this movement often seems on the surface to be a divisive thing, promoting class warfare, is due mainly to the circumstance that our habits of thought have in general been set by the unjust economic order in which we now live, so that we think of employers as in some sense having rights over against those of the total community of which they are a part. But according to humanism there are no such rights. All rights attach to individuals as members of a larger whole and as responsible to contribute to its genuine good. All men and women therefore have ultimate rights and also social responsibilities as workers; none have any rights as masters of workers in the interest of profit for themselves. This does not, it need hardly be said, mean approval of all policies of labor leaders, nor does it mean blinking the difficult problem of the successful administration of industry in a socialized commonwealth.

The ideal goal of industrial evolution, for liberalism, then, is in general such an organization of business relations as will render each participant a loyal servant of the needs of his fellows and will guarantee to those dependent on him economic security and a just share in the well-being of the community to which they belong. Only thus can the economic life of mankind become a foundation on which the spiritual goods of love, kindness, wisdom, and creative achievement are steadily enriched without being constantly corrupted and contradicted by festering social injustice.

The leaders of liberalism, in both its conservative and radical wings, are more unanimous in their vigorous opposition to war and their earnest attempt to promote the cause of world peace than in their commitment to any other single social program. To their minds, war is today what slavery was a century ago—the outstanding social evil and the supreme moral challenge. Except, perhaps, when waged strictly in self-defense, it accomplishes no genuinely valuable social end, while its staggering losses and hideous horrors for civilians as well as for those in the armed forces, under use of the new scientific engines of destruction, now threaten the destruction of all the gains of civilized progress. Democracy itself could hardly stand the strain of another world war. Here is a tremendous responsibility for the intelligence and social conscience of mankind, which liberals resolutely face. They seek to promote international understanding by all available means, to arouse in local communities all the wisdom and earnestness that can be brought to bear on the problem of war, and to rally unceasingly the forces which can bring pressure on governments to adopt and extend policies making for peace. They believe in reduction of armaments to the minimum required for self-defense, and they aid in the exposure of activities on the part of armament manufacturers which foster distrust and discord between nations. Not many adopt a position of absolute pacifism, involving a pledge not to bear arms for one's government under any circumstances; a determined aggressor must be checked, by force if necessary. What is perhaps more significant than any of these matters, they seek to clarify the underlying causes of war, especially those existing in the form of economic ambitions and rivalries, and to attain a thoroughgoing solution of the larger problems which these causes pose.

THE MAJOR DISPUTED ASSUMPTIONS OF LIBERALISM

1. Man needs not only the satisfaction of particular wants, but also the attainment of a harmonious, integrated personality.

2. Present human experience is the criterion of truth and the standard of value.
3. Experience of growth toward a unified personality reveals each individual as interacting with environmental forces, social and cosmic.
4. Those forces operate in a law-abiding order.
5. Religion has the responsibility for transforming human life, individual and social, so that it will express true values as fully as possible, guided by verifiable knowledge of that order.

ASSUMPTIONS ON WHICH MODERNISM AND HUMANISM DISAGREE

Modernism
1. The kind of religious experience which most fully fosters the value of integrated personality is that which traces historically to the life and teachings of Jesus.
2. The forces of good are more deep-seated in reality than the forces which oppose it, hence faith in continued progress toward the realization of such values here and hereafter is legitimate.
3. God many be properly defined as the cosmic factor, disclosed in religious experience, on which human growth in the realization of these values most depends.
4. All religious concepts, such as revelation, inspiration, grace, salvation, must be redefined in the light of present experience, interpreted in accordance with these assumptions.
5. To transform individual and social life so that it expresses true values means to bring it into closer conformity to the spirit of Jesus.

Humanism
1. Moral and religious values are relative to man's changing experience. Christian conceptions of them are not final.
2. The sharable social values, however, such as those of scientific truth, artistic creation, loving friendship, and devotion to democratic causes, maintain their excellence in the face of all doubt and criticism.
3. Intelligent devotion to these values does not require any cosmic guarantee of their ultimate victory or eternal preservation. Such devotion is the essence of religion.

4. The universe, in fact, takes no account of human good or ill except so far as man learns to control parts of it toward the realization of his chosen ends.
5. The joy of comradeship in the quest for sharable social values is a more than adequate compensation for faith in a superhuman helper.

Selected Bibliography

Ames, E. S., *Religion*, Holt, 1929.
Auer, J. A. C. F., *Humanism States Its Case*, Beacon Press, 1933.
Dewey, J., *A Common Faith*, Yale University Press, 1934.
Fosdick, H. E., *As I See Religion*, Harper, 1932.
Haydon, A. E., *Man's Search for the Good Life*, Harper, 1937.
Horton, W. M., *A Psychological Approach to Theology*, Harper, 1931.
Mathews, S., *The Faith of Modernism*, Macmillan, 1924.
Potter, C. F., *Humanism, A New Religion*, Simon and Schuster, 1930.
Santayana, G., *Reason in Religion*, Scribner, 1905.
Sellars, R. W., *Religion Coming of Age*, Macmillan, 1928.
Ward, H. F., *The New Social Order: Principles and Program*, Macmillan, 1919.
Wieman, H. N., *The Wrestle of Religion with Truth*, Macmillan, 1929.

Chapter XII

THE NEW SUPERNATURALISM

DURING the decade of the 1920's an observer of the religious scene in the Western world might easily have persuaded himself that the forces which found expression in modernism and humanism were winning a complete victory, in non-Catholic circles at least. The outcome of the first World War seemed to be a triumph of individualistic liberalism and democratic socialism over the powers that had been opposing these principles; faith in the ability of man to progress under the guidance of such ideals seemed fully justified. And the liberal movement in religion was precisely the movement which was prepared to reinterpret theology in terms of such a faith. The day of religious convictions quite irreconcilable with these confident hopes appeared to be over.

Now, as one surveys the scene from the vantage point of the mid-twentieth century, these conclusions are seen to have been radically erroneous. Since then there have come the rise of the Nazi power under Hitler, the second World War with its release of revolutionary tendencies throughout the world, the expansion of communism to a dominant position in eastern Europe and Asia, and the rapid weakening of democratic influence and conviction over a large part of the Western world under the pressure of these forces. Individuals and groups that twenty-five years ago were facing the future with unclouded democratic optimism are now shrinking from it with anxiety and apprehension.

It could hardly fail to be the case that under the stress of these circumstances the religious picture would also undergo a profound alteration; and indeed new forces in religious philosophy have become increasingly vigorous that a generation ago would have seemed to have little promise of widespread success. As is inevitable in such a situation, when we look back at the period of liberal dominance with these forces in view, it is evident that significant factors leading to the emergence of these new trends were operative then, though obscured by the pervasive strength of the liberal confidence in man and the persuasiveness of its appeal to human experience as providing our criterion of truth and of value.

An Altered Perspective in Religious Philosophy

So radical has become the alteration due to these circumstances that emphases which reflect it are appearing even in recent interpretations of the philosophies with which we have above been occupied. Such reinterpretations have not as yet been strong enough to modify those philosophies profoundly. But their presence testifies to the vigor of the new forces that are affecting men's thinking in the troublous times into which the world has now plunged. It will clarify our understanding of the new trend in religious thought that is most influential in our day if we begin by noting how some champions of these earlier philosophies are reconceiving their position in this situation.

The leading Catholic philosophers today are referred to as neo-Thomists rather than as Thomists, and the prefix has more than a merely temporal significance. Their basic doctrines are still those defended seven hundred years ago by Thomas Aquinas, but they are accommodating themselves to contemporary forces in a number of important ways. Two of these may be mentioned. On the one hand the encompassing framework of Aristotelian metaphysics, without which their philosophy would lose its distinctive character, is being stretched more than ever before to allow an adequate place for the modern scientific discoveries and theories that are not irreconcilable with essential Catholic doctrine. This is evident in Catholic natural philosophy and social philosophy alike. On the other hand (and here the emphasis with which we are now concerned is more directly obvious) it is increasingly recognized that contemporary men are approaching the problems of religion, not so much through a concern for ultimate explanations of their universe as through a concern for successful practical and emotional adjustment to life under the harrassing conditions of modern times. Some neo-Thomist thinkers are restating the Catholic viewpoint in terms which they hope will make it relevant and convincing to those whose religious perplexities are determined by this approach.[1] The metaphysical foundations are subordinated to guidance in dealing with these perplexities.

Agnosticism has been sufficiently outflanked by the liberal willingness to reinterpret traditional concepts and doctrines in the light of present human needs so that it is no longer the disturbing force that it was fifty to a hundred years ago. The idea of God as First Cause in the orthodox sense now contends against respectable definitions which seem to have more verifiable meaning in terms of human experience, and therefore are not so readily disposed of by the agnostic argument. Among the sophisticated young intellectuals today scepticism has taken a novel turn which is quite understandable in the light of the humanist position and the new emphases in present-day philosophy. During the century from Hume to Huxley the main preoccupation of religious thinkers was with the facts uncovered by science and the problem of reconciling them with religious faith. This situation was met by Immanuel Kant with the contention that the heart of religion lies in certain commanding values, not in any facts that could be upset by scientific discovery. And when the liberals attempted to verify religious truths by an appeal to experience, the experience they increasingly had in mind was an experience of satisfying personal values, not of mere facts considered apart from the integrating value that individuals might realize in them. But are there any values which can successfully claim objective validity in filling the role that these thinkers assign them? It is natural that keen minds should raise this question, especially in an age when the stable social patterns of the past are slipping away, and that some should come out with a negative answer. In their case we should find ourselves in the presence of a new and very devastating skepticism—a skepticism about basic human values instead of about the reality of supposed metaphysical facts.

[1] See for example Monsignor Fulton J. Sheen's *Philosophy of Religion,* published in 1948, in which the traditional metaphysical arguments are postponed to the latter part of the book.

The central contentions of this skepticism are two—either of them being capable of emphasis apart from the other, but both being frequently combined. One is asserted by a number of influential philosophers who have been impressed by recently developing forces in social thought, such as the cultural relativity of human values as revealed in anthropology, the Marxian doctrine that these values reflect class economic interests, and the obvious ease with which socially accepted preferences can be exploited to serve the interest of self-seeking groups through clever propaganda. From such considerations they draw the disturbing generalization that assertions claiming validity for this or that value are really nothing but expressions of the asserter's emotions. He is trying to induce other people to like what he likes or approve what he approves, but if their attitude is different from his the claim has no standing; no objective demonstration, either logical or factual, is possible in these matters, and when people disagree there is nothing more to be said except in the way of nonrational persuasion.[2]

The other contention draws its strength from the widespread conviction that valid explanations of anything must be couched in terms of the precisely measurable physical conditions which underlie or accompany it. This belief is the main support of physiological and behavioristic psychologies. Now when our experiences of value are first reduced to subjective emotions, and then these emotions are explained in terms of their physical correlates, the sense of value with which we began seems to have been destroyed, and replaced by something to which no one could attribute any appealing value. Let us see what happens when this method of reductive explanation is applied by Mr. Joseph Wood Krutch to the values which have been regarded as spiritually most significant, both by orthodox theology and by champions of the liberal movement.

Love and true understanding have been the values most consistently emphasized in this connection, but Mr. Krutch maintains that the attempt to order life on the supposition that these are valid ultimate ends is self-defeating, especially if the two be pursued together. For true knowledge about love (or any other exalted value)

---

[2] This position has been championed by a number of influential contemporary philosophers, such as Bertrand Russell, A. J. Ayer, Rudolf Carnap, C. E. Stevenson.

tends in the nature of the case to destroy the worth of that emotion; under the scrutiny of objective, dispassionate analysis it forfeits all dignity, not to say grandeur, and becomes a trivial or even ridiculous thing. This is partly because the attitude of calm detachment, essential to clear knowledge of anything, is incompatible with the attitude of enthusiastic attachment, which is necessary to the conviction that any object has real value. Thus true knowledge is irreconcilable with a feeling of the worth-whileness of anything, even of true knowledge itself. It is partly because accurate knowledge of human emotions, especially, perhaps, the emotion of love, must be stated in terms of the physiological conditions present whenever love is expressed. The lover must be described as suffering from a "fixation"; and when he holds his sweetheart's hand the two must be portrayed as "quietly sweating, palm to palm."[3] Now, since these terms of objective analysis have no appealing emotional associations, the reduction of love to such categories, which is necessary to exact knowledge about it, destroys its exalted value and emotional grandeur. It is debunked—transformed into a quite silly performance. In brief, to make a religion out of love one must believe with all his heart that this emotion is great and good, but true knowledge of love deprives it of all greatness and goodness. The same effect of knowledge has been, indeed, exhibited universally. Modern science destroyed the supernaturalism of earlier times by showing just what in the cosmos man's life depends upon; when dispassionately and objectively revealed, that hitherto mysterious entity lost its divinity and became a natural order of causes and conditions. According to Mr. Krutch, the liberal is blind to the fact that accurate knowledge of man himself—especially of his desires and emotions—must inevitably have the same outcome. Man loses the nobility and dignity ascribed to him by religious feeling when thus understood and is no longer even a fit subject for tragedy. At worst, his behavior is monstrously farcical; at best, it is pathetic.[4]

How about art? The new skeptic points out that this aspect of culture is just as incapable as scientific knowledge or love to serve as a dominant value for religion. The most obvious feature of art is its uncompromising individualism. The artist takes it for granted that

[3] Quoted by Krutch from Aldous Huxley.
[4] *The Modern Temper*, chaps. III, IV, V.

he has a right to express whatever seems to him to be significant, and the critic of his result no longer assumes the privilege of judging the artist's preferences but only his degree of success in achieving what he set out to achieve. Let his ends be what they will; only his means may be legitimately criticized. But, if we accept this artistic individualism and regard its characteristic values as entirely legitimate, we will tend to destroy the foundations of social morality. Since any human end is in that case beyond criticism, there will no longer exist any bad men or women, only relatively successful or stupid ones. St. Francis and Benvenuto Cellini are equally great artists in the career which they pursued, only their adopted style is different. Neither should be criticized for his style, and both may be equally admired for their success in expressing it.[5]

Philosophy itself is an art in the broad sense of the term, namely, the sense in which art includes anything created by man, that inevitably therefore reflects some type of order congenial to the human mind. Every philosophy does this, for even if the urge realistically to accept facts as they are overcomes the pull of wishful thinking, the structure which is "found" in Nature is still the structure determined by human logic. A long-influential philosophy is simply one which succeeds both in expressing, in its chosen order, some fundamental need of man, and also in attaining a large measure of harmony with the external world. Now, past philosophies radically fail us today, and perhaps the greatest human need is for a new and truly great philosophy in this sense. If to concentrate religion on the values of art means to make it the determined quest for such a philosophy, Mr. Krutch would interpose no basic objection. But he is still severely skeptical of its chances for success. In view of the disintegrating effect, above explained, of scientific knowledge upon enthusiasm for any human values, such a philosophy would have to insist upon an absolute separation between the serious concerns of human life and the entire realm of scientific truth, allowing neither to affect the other. This, however, hardly seems possible in any way which could appeal to a substantial number of contemporary thinkers. We have committed ourselves to science for better or for worse, and any propositions which appear to be entirely separated from scientific truth seem to us no more than fictions—often pleas-

[5] *Ibid.*, chap. VI.

ing, no doubt, but still fictions and therefore incapable of supporting a philosophy seriously claiming relevance to the real world. It is theoretically possible that human beings might arise who would not be troubled by such a sundering of knowledge and value from each other, but they would be so different from ourselves that their emotions and enthusiasms could hardly be regarded as a genuine solution of our difficulties.[6]

The only plausible way out of the dilemma, for Mr. Krutch, would seem to be the (otherwise) imminent destruction of civilization as we know it and its replacement by a more animal-like existence pursued by more naïve people who have not yet progressed far enough to be caught in our perplexities. But presumably they will in time repeat our mistake and meet the same fate. "Ours is a lost cause and there is no place for us in the natural universe, but we are not, for all that, sorry to be human. We should rather die as men than live as animals."[7]

The outcome of this line of reasoning seems to be that an irresolvable contradiction lurks in the position which humanism holds in common with more traditional religious philosophies. According to that position, when an individual commits himself to such values as love and honest understanding of his world, experience supports the commitment and guides him toward an integration of these values in a supreme end to which he may be consistently devoted. If Mr. Krutch is right, a skeptical doubt paralyzes such a commitment; it appears that we must choose between true understanding and these other appealing values—it is impossible to have both. The attempt to find meaning and validity for religion in the form of earnest commitment to enduring values is thus undermined.

The main effort today of thinkers who may in general be classed with the modernist wing among the liberals is to find some way of saving the major concepts of Christian theology from the subjectivism which seems to haunt the appeal to human experience as the ultimate criterion of truth in these matters. Thus they hope to meet successfully the skepticism just described. Scientific method, it would appear, leads to objective results when it is applied to experience of

[6] *Ibid.*, chap. VII, secs. III, IV. *Experience and Art,* chap. VII, secs. III, IV.

[7] *The Modern Temper,* p. 249.

external facts, but when a similar procedure is applied to our inner experience of goods and bads it uncovers only subjectively variable preferences which cannot honestly claim objective validity. Can we avoid this unfortunate outcome while still applying a responsibly experiential method to the field of religion?

A number of influential thinkers are answering this question in the affirmative. We may consider briefly two illustrations. One is a group whose position goes by the name of "naturalistic theism." It distinctively emphasizes the realistic assumption of modernist theology—that the experiences which are significant for religion and give meaning to the concept of God are experiences of a reality in man's environment, not merely of some psychological process in himself. It hopes then by experimental action in relation to the environment to verify objective truths which, as such, will satisfy man's need for rational understanding and for dependable guidance in pursuing the goal of adequate adjustment to his world.

The intellectual foundations of this position lie in the thought of such recent philosophers as Whitehead, Bergson, Dewey, and Samuel Alexander. Amidst their differences on other matters, these thinkers all agree in emphasizing creative process as basic in the universe; it is exhibited not only in man's quest for distinctively human values, but also on a broad scale in the natural evolution outside of man. Now the evolutionary process, taken as a whole, cannot become an object of religious sentiment, for it brings much into existence that is evil and inharmonious, lacking for that reason capacity for stable endurance. But there are certain fundamental aspects of this temporal advance, or factors within it, which by virtue of their intrinsic nature make for the realization and preservation of order, value, and harmony. These, too, operate not only in human striving but in the animate and inanimate cosmos at large. Such phases of the natural creative process can, according to the naturalistic theists, be identified and known in this their distinctive character, and they are of supreme religious significance. They constitute that aspect of the universe which attracts religious feeling, giving it clarified guidance and stable support. In fact, from this standpoint, these elements in the cosmos, in their interactive wholeness, represent what religious thought has always in essence meant by the term "God." Thus the theory becomes a "naturalistic theism." It is theistic rather than pantheistic, because God is not identified with the entire universe, but only with those features within it which promote order, love, and wholeness. It is naturalistic rather than supernaturalistic, because the God thus conceived is no transcendent being lying mysteriously beyond the realm of facts which human science can explain, but is a part of the total natural structure of things, capable of being known as such by man—clearly apprehended, that is, in his distinctive role in the cosmic scheme.

The most prominent exponents of this point of view in circles mainly concerned with religious and theological issues are F. R. Tennant in England and H. N. Wieman in the United States.[8] For Wieman, God is that complex of interactions in society and in nature at large on which we depend, and to whose essential structure we must conform if the maximum possible value is to be realized in human experience. What this essential structure is in detail we cannot demonstrate in advance, but can only experimentally discover under the guidance of this general definition. It is evident, however, that the maximum value which its reality renders possible must be some system of experienceable enjoyments in which each enhances and supports all the others and leads thereby to new and richer enjoyment.[9]

The influence of the novel perspective of our day upon Wieman's thought is revealed in the fact that while in his earlier books the factors which give meaning to God (as above defined) seemed to be located mainly in the world of metaphysics, in his *Source of Human Good*[10] they are identified with processes operating in the interaction of man with his fellows. These processes, when responded to, save men from fear, anxiety, and despair by luring them away from their present longing for security and protection to adventurous participation in the forces that are always creating the maximum good that is possible under given conditions.

---

[8] See the former's *Philosophical Theology;* the latter's *Religious Experience and Scientific Method, The Wrestle of Religion with Truth, The Source of Human Good,* and his essay in D. C. Macintosh, *Religious Realism.* Tennant is more conservative than Wieman; in his case the main historical influence is the philosophy and psychology of James Ward.

[9] *Is There a God?,* p. 13; *The Wrestle of Religion with Truth,* pp. 14 ff., 21 ff.; *The Issues of Life,* pp. 221 f.; D. C. Macintosh, *Religious Realism,* p. 162.

[10] Published in 1946.

An illustration of a somewhat different sort appears in the work of Professor Charles Hartshorne. His theological method is on the whole more conservative than that of most modernists; instead of assuming that the traditional concept of God is to be replaced by one derived directly from contemporary religious experience, he asks: In what specific ways is it necessary to revise that concept when it is subjected to the most searching logical and experiential criticism? The distinctive result which he reaches by this procedure is insistence on a clear distinction between the traditional attributes that can be asserted of God absolutely and those which must be asserted relatively—i.e., in such a way as to allow for a process of temporal change in God's nature. According to the orthodox Christian theology, both Catholic and Protestant, whatever attributes can be assigned to God are expressive of his changeless essence and can therefore be assigned without qualification. They characterize the divine nature absolutely. Hartshorne believes that this position leads to irreconcilable contradictions. These can be resolved, however, if the above distinction is drawn. Consider, for example, the attribution of love to God. If we mean by this word what our highest human ideal of love would imply—and if we do not, what dependable meaning could it have?—careful examination will show that it involves an absoluteness in certain respects and a relativity in others. God as love would be absolute or unchanging, in that his kindly concern for each of his creatures would be unfailing under all circumstances; but he would be relative or changing, in that it would make a difference to him whether his creatures respond to his love or not. In the case of those who do, new values enter his experience which do not appear in the case of those who do not. The only alternative to this conclusion would be to regard God as completely impassive, indifferent, and self-sufficient, but none of these adjectives is consistent with the attribute of love.[11]

The outcome of Hartshorne's work is thus a revision of the traditional metaphysical theology so that it will conform to an accurate analysis of the attributes which embody our ideal of personal goodness.

As might be expected, a new form of humanism also seems to be emerging. It offers a restatement of the humanist position such that

[11] C. Hartshorne, *The Divine Relativity,* pp. 16 f., 25 ff., 35 f., 41–59.

—so its proponents believe—the factors in the contemporary scene which are leading many others to an antihumanist doctrine can be adequately met without abandoning the central convictions of humanism. Again, we may illustrate by two modes of thought which obviously belong under this general description.

One presents itself as a branch of the "existentialist" movement, which in most of its other representatives leads in a direction quite opposed to humanism. The outstanding champion of this branch is the philosophical novelist and dramatist Jean Paul Sartre. The motives expressed in his way of thinking are largely determined by the general religious disillusionment which has affected so many young intellectuals today, and also by the specifically devastating experiences which were the lot of Frenchmen during the Second World War. These experiences induced skepticism about all the values that they had believed in before, and a conviction that they must rebuild from the ground up. Their guiding attitude might be expressed as follows: "God ought to exist but he doesn't; we therefore have to face, on our own, the meaninglessness of life and give it such meaning as we can by our resolute action." The key principles which Sartre emphasizes in this connection are those of freedom and responsibility. Since there is no God who created man according to some preconceived plan and thus determined what his essence must be, there is no inevitable fate to which man is predestined; he is free to shape his own nature, to make of himself whatever he can and will. And when he accepts the responsibility for self-determination in this way, he cannot avoid the awareness that he is responsible for others also. He is his brother's keeper.

The way in which these two principles are interconnected, for Sartre, is indicated when he says, "To choose to be this or that is to affirm at the same time the value of what we choose, because we can never choose evil. We always choose the good, and nothing can be good for us without being good for all."[12] That is, to make oneself, through action, one kind of person rather than another is to assert the value of what one has thus chosen, and to assert it as valuable for oneself is to assert it as valuable for all.

The fact that choice involves commitment to a certain value would seem to require no special defense; how does Sartre justify the

[12] *Existentialism*, trans. by B. Frechtman, p. 20.

further contention that whenever one is choosing he is choosing for others as well as for himself, and is thus accepting responsibility for them? The answer seems to be that, in being conscious of ourselves, we are in the nature of the case conscious of others too, and of their equal right to whatever value we seek for ourselves. In this form Sartre makes his own the Kantian interpretation of the Golden Rule. Whenever we choose we cannot escape (except by a kind of double-dealing) the thought: "What if everyone acted that way?" Every act is inevitably exemplary; in it one is not only making himself into whatever he becomes, he is also creating a certain image of what he thinks man universally ought to be. His act confers a universal, and not merely personal, value on whatever is achieved through it. Thus, only through dishonesty can man evade the responsibility of acting in such a way that humanity in general might guide itself by his actions.[13]

Even though God does not exist, then, and there is no eternal pattern of value for us to copy, man has the capacity and responsibility of freely creating a human community by his own choice and action. Only this theory, Sartre believes, gives man real dignity, and a status transcending that of a mere object.

The other mode of reinterpreting humanism takes specific advantage of the lessons which are rapidly accumulating in the field of psychotherapy, and thus endeavors to deal with the deep emotional problems which traditional theologies handled in terms of the concepts of sin, guilt, grace, and forgiveness. From this viewpoint, such problems are very real and perhaps universal, as Christian theology has claimed, but an adequate solution can be achieved on a humanist foundation; the orthodox religious psychologies are too narrow in their assumptions and encourage an unfortunate dependence in the sick souls for whom they provide a cure. All the wealth of psychoanalytic literature now available is relevant to this reinterpretation, but a conscious application of it to the development of a new religious humanism is found in the work of Eric Fromm, especially in his *Man For Himself* and *Psychoanalysis and Religion.*

According to Fromm, people in general adopt one or another unfortunate "orientation" in their attempt to adjust themselves to the demands of life. There is the "receptive" orientation, in which

[13] *Ibid.*, pp. 20, 24.

a person feels that all good comes to him from the outside and that the only thing he can do is passively to receive it. If he is religious, he expects everything to come to him from God and nothing from his own activity. Another is the "exploitative" orientation, dominated by the feeling that good things can only be won by wringing them from his environment through force or cunning. A third is the "hoarding" orientation, in which a person has no faith that anything new can be got from the outside world; his security is based upon hoarding whatever he has and giving as little as possible to his fellows. He withdraws from free interaction with others, as threatening to take from him something that he is eager to possess. A fourth, especially characteristic of American life today, is the "marketing" orientation, in which one feels himself to have only the value he can command in the strenuous competition for success; he is what he can sell himself for on the personality market. Contrasted with these orientations, which lead to inner conflicts because they do not make for real health or happiness of soul, is the "productive" orientation, in which a man has become conscious of his powers and is making himself into a healthy and happy person through their free, rational, and responsible expression.

But will not such an orientation mean disregard for the welfare of others? Does it not betoken an essential selfishness? Just the contrary, according to Fromm. Selfishness and self-love, for him, are not only far from identical; the former arises just because one has become incapable of the latter. Love in its true sense is not a passive state, in which one's desperate yearning is satisfied by the one for whom he yearns; it is an active concern for his beloved. It is characterized by care, and by a responsibility to express that care in appropriate ways; it is guided by knowledge of the one loved and by a "respect" for him in the etymological sense of the word—an ability to see him as he is in his individual uniqueness. Now anyone capable of loving another in this way will also love himself in the same way, for he too is a human being with all the qualities and powers of an object of love. Love is not a fixed quantity which must be taken away from one object if it is turned toward another.

From this it follows that my own self, in principle, must be as much an object of my love as other person's. The affirmation of one's own life, happiness, growth, freedom, is rooted in one's own capacity to love, i.e., in care, respect, responsibility, and knowledge. If an individual is able to love productively, he loves himself too; if he can love only others, he cannot love at all.[14] One who loves only others thereby shows that his love is not a productive quest for life and happiness but a demand that others give him the goods that he is unable to achieve for himself; and this is the essence of selfishness.

True love, in terms of this analysis, is thus an expression of strength, freedom, and happiness; it is the only genuine form of self-realization. Love that is associated with a sense of duty and of sacrifice, and is thus contrasted with concern for oneself, is not really love but some diseased substitute for it.

FORCES EXPRESSED IN THE NEW SUPERNATURALISM

These emphases in Fromm's humanism run directly counter, however, to the most influential new movement in religious philosophy whose appeal is spreading more and more widely in the Western world, especially among Protestant circles. There is no generally accepted phrase by which to characterize it, but its central feature is helpfully disclosed if we call it the "new supernaturalism," and that term will therefore be used in the subsequent discussion.

We may best understand the main forces which are finding expression in this religious viewpoint if we approach them first historically and then psychologically. On the historical side the basic factor is the increasingly obvious failure of the optimistic liberal hopes which pervaded the Western world with such seeming justification at the close of the first World War. Bereft of these hopes, man in the mid-twentieth century is haunted by a deepening sense of insecurity and disillusionment, which constantly feeds the emotions of fear, anxiety, distrust, and despair. Behind this change lies the inability of his leaders to take wise advantage of the situation created by the victory of democratic liberalism in 1918, and to consolidate the conditions under which such liberalism could continue to be the decisive force shaping the cultures of the world. The victors were too short-sighted, and too grasping after immediate self-advantage, to be able to reconstruct Europe in such a way that the rise of Mussolini and Hitler to power might be forestalled, and to follow

[14] *Man for Himself,* p. 130. See also *Psychoanalysis and Religion,* chap. IV.

such policies with Russian communism as would encourage it to become a responsible participant in the peaceful reordering of the international scene. As a result, the second World War became inevitable, with its vaster destruction and its more complete collapse of the restraints which previously, so far as civilians at least are concerned, had mitigated the violence and the horror of war. At the close of this holocaust there was only a year or two of hopeful recovery, to compare with the decade of optimistic expectancy that followed the first war. Russian communism profited by its greatly strengthened position and the misery of common people in Europe and Asia, to promote the international communist revolution by a novel strategy of insidious infiltration and appealing propaganda— a strategy so clever that the rest of the world has not yet learned[15] how to cope with it effectively. America, tyro in international politics and ambiguous in her own controlling evaluations, was suddenly thrust into the position of leadership among the forces making for liberal democracy in the world, but has found it exceedingly difficult to devise any successful counterstrategy in the struggle with communistic totalitarianism. The other nations, striving against fearful odds to recover from the ravages of the last war, seem unable to give enough concerted force to the United Nations Organization so that the two gigantic powers might be compelled to subordinate their fear and distrust of each other to policies serving the world's peace and security. In the meantime the development of super-atomic bombs and the threat of an even more catastrophic hydrogen bomb, together with scattered military episodes in various parts of the world, increase the danger of a third world war and make the anticipation of it an unimaginably horrible nightmare. Men everywhere, but especially in the Western world, feel themselves swept toward tragedy by forces entirely beyond their control.

One particular aspect of this historical change deserves emphatic mention, since its effect upon the new theological current is very profound. In the era of democratic optimism leaders in all branches of Western culture were not only dominated by a general faith in man's ability to progress on his own resources toward the Kingdom of God on earth; they were also moved by the unqualified conviction that his faculty of reason is a dependable guide in this progress. The

15 This was written in 1950.

intelligence of men, they were sure, while finite, is essentially competent to discover truth on any subject to which it applies itself, and the ongoing march of science, natural and social, seemed to give continued corroboration to this assurance. There were, to be sure, even before the rise of Hitler and the challenge of communist strategy, forces which were weakening this confidence in the objectivity and power of reason. There was the insistence of orthodox Protestantism that man's ways of thinking are inevitably corrupted by sin as long as he remains unredeemed by divine grace. There was the increasing influence of the doctrines of Nietszche, Freud, and Marx, contending that human reasoning is inevitably, to some degree, a rationalization of controlling biases—unconscious if not conscious, biases of the economic class to which the reasoner belongs if not biases determined by his individual compulsions. But as long as the world seemed progressing toward democratic-liberal goals, these factors accomplished little beyond stimulating a parlor skepticism and justifying a rebellion against moral convention among the intellectual elite. As it became caught in the maelstrom leading toward the second war and the increasing fear of a third, this skeptical relativism acquired a more vivid relevance and seriously undermined man's rational self-confidence in two ways.

On the one hand, there was the more and more obvious fact that not enough people possessed the wise understanding of themselves and their fellows that is essential to anticipating possible catastrophes and adopting the policies needed to safeguard the world against them. Here was a clear historical demonstration of the failure of reason to function successfully in the way liberal optimism had assumed that it always could, and a failure under circumstances providing a crucial test of its pretensions. On the other hand, it became obvious that Hitlerite propaganda and communist strategy achieved the large measure of success that they did by applying to their own ends this skeptical relativism. They learned how to exploit very skillfully the rationalizing hypocrisies of liberal statesmen and defenders of "free enterprise"; they acquired astonishing facility at profiting by the fact that the quest for truth among men everywhere is subtly mixed with, and profoundly affected by, their desires for security, for comfort, for competitive standing, and for a sense of belonging to their group. Under the stress of these disturbing experiences, it is not surprising that confidence in reason among Western thinkers has for a couple of decades or more been steadily undermined, and that the undermining in many cases has amounted to a complete collapse. Feeling unable to save himself from impending catastrophe, and no longer trusting reason as a guide to the true and the good, Western man is easily led to hope that a supernatural source of truth and goodness may break in to save him from himself; he turns thus in various forms to the cult of unreason.

In this situation theology has adopted an essentially psychological approach to religious problems in a different sense of "psychological" than was exemplified in the procedure of liberalism. The adjective generally used to describe this approach is "existential." Since, as we have noted above, one branch of existentialism draws corollaries from the meaning of this word quite different from the conclusions drawn by the thinkers we are now to deal with, it is important to understand what it essentially signifies in current discussions. Liberalism, we recall, appealed to man's experience of achieving integration as providing material for reinterpreting and verifying religious doctrines; the thinkers who employ the word today appeal rather to the widespread sense of disintegration, to enforce a different psychological emphasis and to validate a different set of doctrines. In this tragic situation it seems to them clear that man by his very nature cannot avoid a profound concern for himself, and that everything he does is done under the stress of this inevitable concern. He is confronted by nothing less than the alternatives of living or dying; his thinking in general and his philosophizing in particular cannot but reflect this poignant fact and whatever way he takes of meeting it. In these matters of morals and religion there is no such thing as dispassionate reflection, determined merely by the nature of the object one confronts, and if there were it should be distrusted as essentially inadequate. Thinking here is "existential" in the sense that it does not deal with essences abstracted from their living embodiments; it deals with the world of a thinker who exists as a concrete individual and is profoundly concerned about the weal and woe of his existence. This psychological orientation, in its contemporary form, was exemplified first in Sören Kierkegaard, who in the middle of the nineteenth century wrote a number of works, now becoming widely influential, in which this concept of "existential" was basic.

Moreover, the existential thinkers whom we are soon to expound are confident that the traditional Christian ideas of sin, grace, faith, and forgiveness find valid meaning in this experience. When man is concerned about himself, in a way which is not the expression of incurable despair but involves hope for the future, he is concerned about himself as a sinner before the bar of divine judgment. In less orthodox language, he is conscious that his plight is due not simply to evil forces impinging on him from the outside, but to forces that lie within himself and for which he is responsible. And the sin with which he must primarily come to terms is "original" sin—that is, a deep-lying obstruction within that sunders him from his true good and separates him from peace with God and with himself. From this standpoint, no solution of the problem of life is possible without removing this obstruction. Now man is impotent to remove it himself, for as long as it is there all his faculties, including reason itself, are its tools and cannot be employed to dislodge it. Only through God's redeeming grace can the sinful self be shattered, and replaced by a spiritual self in which reason can dependably fill the very modest role which truly belongs to it.

In the judgment of these thinkers, recent history has fully confirmed these emphases and has given a new relevance to this theory of human nature and experience. Whatever one may fondly believe about his own thinking and that of the group to which he belongs, it is only necessary to look at the thinking of others to see that it is largely motivated by self-interest in some form, and that the proud belief that it is not so motivated is a major cause of the blind fanaticisms, unconscious imperialisms, and furious injustices that have brought the world to the brink of disaster. Unless we become conscious that such motivations are operating in our own case, too, so that we may become imbued with modesty about our own fragmentary truths and achieve a forgiving tolerance toward the fragmentary truths of others, the round of fanatical violence breeding equally fanatical violence remains hopelessly unbroken; with the steady invention by science of more and more lethal weapons, that way lies total destruction—at least of Western civilization, perhaps of the human race.

This new supernaturalism takes varied forms, not all of which are of wide influence. Indeed, our unavoidable dependence on vague and ambiguous words in discussing basic religious issues becomes unfortunately evident here; some people regard themselves as supernaturalists today simply because they prefer a rather cramped definition of "nature." If "nature" includes only the physicochemical world, and the processes which can be exactly verified by scientific method, it is fairly clear that our most important problems trench upon a realm of "supernature," which thus gains significance because what we really care about has by definition been excluded from "nature." When men who thus narrowly limit the realm of the natural come to interpret those experiences in which we directly feel the impact of a power beyond ourselves, supporting our higher aspirations but apparently not localized in any specific physical or social object, an explanation in terms of the supernatural seems clearly required. Such experiences, construed in terms of these assumed definitions, attest the presence and activity of a being belonging to something other than the "natural" order of events.

THE DIALECTICAL THEOLOGY

We shall not take the space to deal with supernaturalisms generated merely by this circumstance; let us turn to the most vigorous and challenging form of this contemporary trend. In European theological thought it appears in the so-called "dialectical theology" whose best known leader is Karl Barth and whose outstanding philosophical interpreter is Emil Brunner.

Barth defends an uncompromising transcendentalism, more extreme than that of Neo-Platonism or Augustine. God is Supreme Sovereign of the world, who speaks to man in his Word (the Bible) but who is entirely separated from and discontinuous with human thought and experience. We can respond to the Word, and our lives thereby become changed, but we cannot by human thought explain God. All the attempts to do so in the various theologies of the past are, in his view, inadequate, and even presumptuous in their assumption that the Infinite God can be known by man; the best attempts to describe him today will inevitably betray their futility by the logical contradictions and paradoxes which in the nature of the case they will reveal. When God comes to man he breaks in upon the course of temporal experience from another realm, that of eternal being, which is entirely inconstruable in experiential terms. This irruption transforms the subsequent course of history, but it has no historical causes and human philosophy is impotent in its presence.

What is the task of theology under these presuppositions? It clearly cannot be a very ambitious one. Barth states it in language which is traditionally Protestant: theology is the "service of the Word of God"; that is, its task is to clarify by means of human thought and speech the revelation which God has given in the Bible. But in two fundamental respects—not to speak of minor ones—Barth's meaning differs from that of Protestant orthodoxy when it uses such phrases. For one thing, Barth entirely rejects natural theology as a supplement to the direct appeal of divine revelation. This rejection is, of course, required by his unqualified denial of competence to human reason. Hence theology includes no rational or historical argument aiming to establish the claim of the Bible to be a revelation from God. In fact, unless and until God speaks in its pages to some particular human soul, and is responded to by that soul, it is no revelation, strictly speaking, but only the possibility of one. Thus, as soon as the Bible is mentioned in theology at all, it appears as the authoritative Word of God, obediently accepted as such, whose message is to be humbly and reverently elucidated in terms of modes of speech adapted to present human need. For another thing, the same unbridgeable gulf between the transcendent reality of God and the essential incapacity of human thought about God introduces an important element of humble skepticism or reverent relativism into Barth's theology. Kantian agnosticism and modernistic tentativeness leave their mark on his system at this point. Theology, being a human product, can claim no finality for its doctrines. It has erred in the past, and is always liable to err. Its task is never finished. The standard to which it always appeals in its interpretative work is, of course, none other than the living, compelling Word of God itself; and since the latter stands in mysterious discontinuity with all human reflections about it, it may at any moment require the responsive theologian to revise any previous interpretation that has been proposed. It is on this ground that the dialectical theologians accept the validity of the higher criticism, and are ready to solve any historical problem that may arise about the Bible in whatever way the canons of impartial historical scholarship may dictate. The outcome of theological effort is thus always tentative and always incomplete; it must recognize its limitations and not in any sense attempt to think of itself as a branch of science. God cannot be made an object of human knowledge. For these reasons, the method of theology can be neither that of systematic demonstration nor that of experiential description. It is, in a brief phrase, that of obedient, responsive interpretation.

The central reality in the Bible, without which it could not disclose itself as the Word of God, is, according to Barth, Christ. There is no cogent argument for his divinity; indeed, there were those who came into his direct presence without awareness that the Infinite God was in him. But those to whom he speaks a divine message need no other evidence. In his redeeming grace they have found God, and that is enough to show them where in history and in literature the Word of God is uniquely disclosed.

Barth developed his theology mainly in terms of a concern to clarify what a pastor should preach to troubled souls in his pews. Brunner, whose lifetime career has been that of a theological professor, aimed to present the dialetical theology in such a way that it might answer the questions of intellectuals who are concerned to achieve a philosophical orientation about the world and who have been strongly influenced by the assumptions of liberalism. Christian theology cannot, he is sure, afford to pass them by. In the work which comes to grips most closely with the fundamental issues here, his *Revelation and Reason,* he insists that the Christian thinker has both a general and a specific task to fill in relation to the problems of such persons.

The general task is to remove misunderstandings that these intellectuals may be under, as to what a true interpretation of the Divine Word really implies, especially in its relation to the knowledge progressively built up in the secular sciences. Christian theologians in the past and the present have often fallen into serious errors in this field, justifying distrust and opposition on the part of honest seekers after truth. It is the duty of the Christian philosopher to correct these errors and to show that there is and can be no conflict between faith and reason when each is rightly understood.

The specific task is, if possible, to convict of sin those intellectuals who have succumbed to the liberal confidence in reason—challenging them by the forthright contention that what they take to be intellectual honesty is actually a fundamental dishonesty.[16] What they call intellectual honesty is really a clear display of the sin of arrogance and self-will. They are willfully demanding "the right to define the whole range of truth from the standpoint of man." But it cannot be defined from the standpoint of man. Man is not self-sufficient—neither his reason nor any other faculty in him. Their own lingering doubts and scruples, the conflict between various theories of truth and reality—these reflect the sense of guilt, the bad conscience which expresses itself in this illusion of the "autonomous" human reason. Only when they contritely repent of this proud arrogance, and let God speak to them from beyond their human criteria of truth, will a true intellectual honesty be attained. This honesty will be grounded in humble obedience to God who is the transcendent source of all truth, and in whom alone the ultimate criterion thus lies.

Hence, far from reason displacing faith by its own pretensions to unqualified validity, faith includes reason, and makes a place within its total perspective for all that a sound rational understanding of the world, by whatever method, establishes. A Christian philosophy will apply this principle in detail to the various problems which interest philosophers. It will show, for example, that although there is no distinctively Christian logic or mathematics, the farther we go in the direction of questions involving serious personal decision, the greater the difference that will appear in our answers according as they express the Christian faith or not.[17]

NIEBUHR'S THEORY OF HUMAN NATURE

Reinhold Niebuhr has become the outstanding spokesman in America for a religious philosophy akin in its theological fundamentals to that of the dialectical theologians abroad, and his viewpoint is becoming increasingly influential among Protestant circles elsewhere. He began his career as a Protestant modernist, but an early

---

[16] *Revelation and Reason,* p. 213 ff.
[17] *Ibid.,* p. 383 ff.

acquaintance with labor problems led him to adopt a soberly realistic attitude toward the quest for justice in economic and political affairs. He became convinced that the shallow optimism among religious liberals, expressed in the belief that man was steadily progressing toward the wise solution of these inequities, revealed a proud and irresponsible complacency that could only be corrected by a new acceptance of the Augustinian-Calvinist doctrine of original sin, and of man's need for salvation from beyond himself through the forgiving grace of God. After developing this conviction through a number of "tracts for the times," appearing between 1928 and 1940,[18] he systematically elaborated the substance of his philosophy in his Gifford Lectures on *The Nature and Destiny of Man*, published in 1941 and 1943. His thought has been considerably influenced, among others, by Paul Tillich, now his colleague on the faculty of Union Theological Seminary, who by a somewhat different route had also been led to a position which combined a democratic socialism in politics with a return to orthodox Protestant emphases in theology.

Niebuhr tells us in the preface to his Gifford Lectures that this "study is based upon the conviction that there are resources in the Christian faith for an understanding of human nature which have been lost in modern culture." What this means is that modern Western culture has mistakenly committed itself, with complacent confidence, to psychologies and philosophies based on the optimistic belief that man can be understood in his own terms and is able to work out his destiny on his own resources, whereas the orthodox Protestant faith, rightly understood, can correct this tragic error by a truer conception of man. It replaces this man-centered orientation by the conviction that human nature can only be adequately understood through its relation to God, before whose judgment man is a sinful creature and whose redeeming love alone can save him from sin and despair. This theory of human nature, he recognizes, cannot be logically or empirically demonstrated to those not prepared to accept it, for any demonstration inevitably rests upon some set of

---

[18] Along with some more substantial writings, e.g., *An Interpretation of Christian Ethics*, 1936. He published in 1932 *Moral Man and Immoral Society*, which represents the stage of sober and somewhat pessimistic realism referred to above.

basic presuppositions; and the narrow and optimistic presuppositions about man characteristic of modern thinking must be abandoned, or at least seriously questioned, before those who have blithely adopted them will be willing to consider different presuppositions which reject this shallow optimism. But he hopes that the experience of our generation has been sufficiently disillusioning to shake many thinkers out of that optimism and give them a readiness to examine the Protestant alternative on its merits. He is confident, of course, that when that alternative, as he interprets it, is accorded a chastened and humble acceptance, it will prove adequate to take account of all the truths about man that other theories have glimpsed, as well as the very vital truths to which they have been complacently blind.

According to Niebuhr's fundamental analysis, man can only be fully understood in terms of two dimensions of his nature and their essential relationships.[19] In virtue of one—the "horizontal" dimension—he is a part of nature and involved in all her processes. This side of man's being not only includes his body, which is obviously subject to nature's vicissitudes; it also includes much of what we would regard as belonging to his mind. His desire, emotion, will, and purpose bind him to the natural changes going on within and without; even his reason, so far as it operates under the influence of these forces in him, is a part of nature rather than enjoying a status above nature. But in virtue of the other—the "vertical" dimension—he is related to God as the transcendent source of his being. The side of him that is disclosed in this relationship is that which religion has traditionally referred to as "spirit," whose essence is the capacity for free self-transcendence. Man is able at any time, Niebuhr holds, to become aware of himself—not merely of this or that particular act or feeling, not merely of any limited segments of his nature—but of his total self as it now is. This capacity gives him a locus of freedom from causal involvement in nature and reveals potentialities which can only be satisfied by a relation of obedient harmony with God, who is the supernatural and perfect embodiment of all spiritual excellence. Man's plight and privilege, which differentiate him from other creatures, is to be torn between God and nature, and the

[19] R. Niebuhr, *The Nature and Destiny of Man*, Vol. I, chaps. 1, 6.

universal problem which he has to deal with arises precisely from this circumstance.

For, existing in these two dimensions of being which involve such different potentialities, man is conscious of inevitable tension and intolerable anxiety.[20] By virtue of factors each of which is essential to his nature, he is pulled in different directions. On the one hand, he knows that as a part of nature he is a finite and dependent creature, subject to all the contingencies to which other creatures have to submit. On the other hand, he is conscious that his capacity of self-transcendence opens infinite possibilities before him; he is never limited merely to the forms of achievement and the degree of free self-realization that he has won to date. He desperately needs a way of relief from the anxiety aroused by this intolerable dilemma, and the way universally chosen by men is the way of sin—more specifically, the sin of pride which is the root of all sin. That is, instead of humbly recognizing that the true center of his being is in God, which is a step always theoretically possible, he attempts to resolve the tension by proudly claiming independence and sufficiency for himself, despite his obvious finitude and weakness. This proud self-assertion is the essence of sin. Although it is the strategy universally employed, man is not fatally compelled to it by causal necessity and is hence responsible for adopting it. He could at any time have chosen God instead of himself; in fact, he has only been able to pursue this strategy by a certain voluntary blinding of himself to what he really knows—namely, that he is not the self-sufficient determiner of his own destiny. He refuses to look honestly at this fact which so stubbornly affronts his self-esteem, preferring to dwell in admiring confidence on his significant historical accomplishments, in the boastful pretense that they are all of his own achieving.

Such pride, according to Niebuhr, appears in four main forms, each of which may express the self-assertion either of an individual or a group. There is pride of power. The self, anxiously feeling itself insecure in its finitude, refuses to admit its insecurity or to accept a really dependable security through humble trust in God; it grasps for more power over things and over other persons, in the desperate belief that it can thus make itself secure. Thus arise the manifold

[20] *Ibid.*, chaps. 7, 9.

and terrible injustices that darken man's social life. There is pride of intellect. Man, anxiously aware of the uncertainty of his knowledge, is unwilling to admit his finite handicaps and the measure of ignorance which must inevitably haunt him; he affirms his own relative and limited truth to be the final and absolute truth, willfully obscuring the conditioned character of his knowedge and the taint of self-interest which always in some degree distorts it. There is pride of virtue. This is the Pharisaic pride of self-righteousness, of which the good man who is conscious of his goodness is guilty. Refusing to recognize the element of imperfection in every moral achievement and the consequent need of a humble realization of continuing sinfulness, he affirms the unqualified rectitude of his own quite relative standards of goodness and haughtily condemns as vicious all who fail to square with his moral demands or who reject his criteria. This form of pride is responsible for the most appalling cruelties in history, since men who are sure that they know what is absolutely right are likely to persecute without restraint or mercy those who refuse to accept their moral authority. Finally, there is spiritual pride, which arises when the self-righteousness just described claims divine sanction and support for its relative standards of virtue. This is evident in the pretensions of the Catholic Church, which identifies itself with the Kingdom of God on earth and holds its pope to be the vicar of Christ when guiding the faithful in matters theological or moral. The same vice can appear, however, among Protestants too, in the blithe conviction that their acceptance of a truer interpretation of the gospel than that of Catholicism, and their more complete humbling of man's pride before God, guarantee them a superior virtue. Nor is this form of pride exhibited only in avowedly religious people. One confronts in essence the same phenomenon wherever a higher than human warrant is claimed for man's attempt to establish moral control over his fellows, as in the communist appeal to the Dialectic of History to justify the dictatorship of the proletariat and give ethical sanction to its ruthless pursuit of world domination.

In these illustrations we have kept in mind the fact that pride can be collective as well as individual—that is, be asserted in behalf of groups as well as by any particular individual. And collective pride can be both more plausible and tempting, and also more grievous in its effects, than individual pride. It is more plausible and tempting because when exercised in the name of a group it can more easily seem justified than when it is asserted by an individual for himself; the group does achieve a certain universality and impartiality in relation to its members which none of them as an individual would dare to claim. Thus a group, in its relation to other groups and their members, is in a position to be far more cruel and ruthless in its will to domination than any individual could possibly be.

The tragic outcome of these various forms of proud self-assertion is the multiplication of injustice and misery throughout the world. And because of this inevitable effect, the insecurity of those who are guilty of pride is increased rather than lessened; the more desperately man grasps after power, certainty, and prestige, the more insecure he is rendered by whatever measure of success his blind will apparently achieves. He arouses increasing distrust, hostility, and eagerness for vengeance among those whom he suppresses and maltreats; sooner or later they combine effectively against him and topple him into defeat and ruin. The futility of solving the problem of anxiety in this way Niebuhr believes is clearly evident to any honest view of history and of current affairs.

What hope is there for man in this ominous plight? Only by abandoning the effort to resolve his tension through trust in his own power and wisdom, and by turning toward God in humble faith that the divine can and will do for him what he is unable to do for himself.[21] This means a repentant awareness of his sin, especially the basic sin of pride and all that it has brought in its train; this shatters his self-esteem and self-confidence, making him willing to shift his center of reference from himself to God. It means a recognition that he is standing before God as a transcendent Judge, who condemns his willfulness and dishonesty, leaving him no resource for salvation except in dependence on the divine mercy. But, to man's wondrous good fortune, God has already revealed himself in the form of a merciful Savior as well as in that of Lawgiver and Judge. The train of events recorded in the Bible, culminating in the death of Christ on the cross, constitute a unique disclosure of God to man —a disclosure of his forgiving love. In virtue of this love, as revealed in the suffering Christ, he takes man's sin and sorrow into himself,

21 *Ibid.*, chap. 5, especially pp. 129 ff., 140 ff.

inducing thus the contrition and willingness on man's part to give himself to God which could not otherwise have been aroused. Through the transforming experience thus initiated man's old sinful self is crucified with Christ, and is replaced by a new self whose center is no longer itself but God. This new self is justified by faith and can thenceforth live in serenity and creativity, growing toward a more perfect exemplification of the divine law of love. It is already saved "in principle." It must, however, never allow itself to assume that sin is no longer present and that moral perfection has been actually achieved. This would be to succumb to the temptation of pride on a new level; it would mean a reassertion, on that level, of sinful self-sufficiency. No matter what his achievement to date, man always remains subject to finitude and to the corrupting taint of self-interest; he always remains dependent on God's grace and forgiveness. Constant recognition of this fact, and constant readiness to confront contritely any new form of self-centeredness that might appear, are the best safeguard against sinfulness on some new level, and are the only attitude that can render possible steady growth in grace and truth.[22]

His Interpretation of History

Thus far we have been summarizing Niebuhr's religious psychology as it bears mainly upon the problems of an individual, lost in anxious tension and in search of salvation—the theory developed in the first volume of his Gifford Lectures. In the second volume, while the perplexities of the individual are not forgotten, the main emphasis shifts to a philosophy of history. Niebuhr is confident that non-Christian interpretations of history suffer from one or another fatal weakness, being based again on an inadequate understanding of man; only the Christian view, as he understands it, gives a perspective comprehensive enough for a true insight into the meaning of history.

In the first place, this view attributes a real significance to the historical process, as contrasted with the classical Greek belief that this process, being an affair of change and time, is intrinsically meaningless and that only in the eternal is true meaning to be found.

[22] *Ibid.*, chap. 9, especially p. 260 ff.

From such a standpoint, the problem of life and destiny is to escape
from time and history into the timeless. In the second place,
Niebuhr's view challenges the optimistic assumption, permeating
modern thought from the Renaissance onward, that the significance
of history can be realized in the historical process itself, by man's
progressive achievement of the values open to him under the guidance of his own reason. Man is incompetent to give meaning to history in this way; only through the revelation, within history, of the
grace of God who stands beyond history can the meaning of human
evolution be understood and realized. For, in the last analysis, the
source of this meaning is the sacrificial love of God for man, uniquely
revealed in the death of Christ, and introducing thus a creativity
into history that man would not have been able to achieve on his
own. But this sacrificial love inevitably stands in a paradoxical relation to the historical process, the paradox being incapable of a fully
consistent explication in terms of rational logic.[28]

Why is this so? Well, on the one hand, such love fulfills human
history, as marking the ideal which the historical process is seeking
to approximate more and more perfectly. All men should ideally love
God and each other as God loves them; in the light of this ideal the
evolution of history is from the childlike innocence of the first Adam
to the loving perfection of the second Adam, namely Christ. On the
other hand, it negates human history, since in the nature of the case
no complete embodiment of such love in history is possible; and
any assumption that it has been achieved is a sinful presumption—
shown in the light of the divine ideal to be self-centeredness, not
true love. Indeed, the negation is deeper and more perplexing even
than this statement indicates. It is often the duty of a Christian
citizen to struggle for the highest relative justice that is possible
under any given historical circumstances, and this may mean asserting his power against others in ways which he knows fall short
of the demands of true love. Hence, in the nature of the case, a
certain tragic contradiction is never removed from history; the ideal
is historically possible in the sense that no limits can be set to the
realization of brotherhood on the surface of our planet, but it is not
possible in the sense of ever being fully actualized within history,
or being able always to dictate our conduct. The ultimate realization

[28] *Nature and Destiny*, Vol. II, chaps. 1, 3.

and validation of sacrificial love lies beyond history, in the eternal nature of God.

The most important chapters of Niebuhr's subsequent discussion apply this paradox to man's effort to achieve, first his intellectual, and then his political, goals through the processes of history.[24] In terms of the former quest the paradox takes the form: Man has and has not the truth; in terms of the latter it becomes: Man can and cannot achieve justice.

Man has and has not the truth. He has it in the sense that every scientific discovery and every philosophical insight embodies a partial apprehension of truth; and there is no limit to the possibility of its further attainment by the honest application of valid methods of thought. In the case of the more comprehensive philosophical and theological systems, what renders them partial at any given time is not merely the narrow range of any man's experience but also the taint of self-interest expressed in their implicit postulates; but again there is no limit to the possibility of becoming aware of this egoistic taint, with the assumptions which reflect it, and therefore of attaining a less limited approximation to the truth. The tragedy of Catholic theology for Niebuhr is its intolerance on principle—the proud insistence that its set of assumptions and the doctrines built upon them possess divine warrant. The tragedy of orthodox Protestant theology, whose deeper understanding of sin should have guarded it against the error, is the intolerance arising from its conviction that the fully correct interpretation of the Bible has in its doctrines been once for all expressed. Both these theologies have forgotten that man also has not the truth—that is, they are blind to the fact that he does not have it in final and absolute form. Indeed, the only ground of assurance that we can grow from a more partial to a less partial truth is our willingness to refuse to claim truth as a certain and final possession; whoever makes that claim is simply freezing himself in his present errors and effectively blocking the way to their correction.

Now the secular movement stemming from the Renaissance came to see clearly that human perspectives are finite and varied; hence it was able to practice the virtue of tolerance toward divergent claims to truth, assured that in the sifting process of continued inquiry and

[24] *Ibid.*, chaps. 8, 9.

discussion truth would finally prevail over falsehood. In this lies its outstanding contribution toward an adequate solution of the problems arising from man's inveterate eagerness proudly to claim finality for his partial truths. But this movement fell into a grievous error of its own, in its confidence that the victory of truth can be achieved within history and without benefit of the factors derived from the working of divine grace in man. Since intelligent persons cannot help seeing that final truth never is really attained in history, there is a threefold danger in this secular optimism that Niebuhr believes can only be effectively guarded against by the Christian view.

There is first the danger of indifference and irresponsibility on vital issues of truth and falsehood, which attitudes are always easy when there seems to be no way, on our present intellectual resources, of adjudicating competing claims. If, in the second place, this irresponsible paralysis becomes total skepticism—expressing a despair of ever being able to discern truth from falsehood—the whole intellectual enterprise is threatened with the abyss of meaninglessness; when we have lost our criterion, and have no way of finding one, the very search for truth becomes hopeless. But since man cannot pursue his daily life in such blind skepticism, the third danger is the one most likely to appear at this juncture—the danger exemplified by the dogmatic pretensions of Nazi and communist ideologies, and by the persuasive appeal that they exercise over lost and bewildered minds. Men cannot get along without believing something to be true. Hence "new fanaticisms are the much more probable consequence of the modern position than complete skepticism. In these fanaticisms an ultimate position and a final truth are implicitly or explicitly insinuated into what was provisionally regarded as a realm of partial and fragmentary truths. Thus new religions emerge in an ostensibly irreligious culture."[25] But one who has accepted understandingly the Christian view will be protected from these dangers. He cannot be indifferent to truth because his thinking will be existential—that is, moved by a real concern to understand himself aright, so that his soul may win life in place of death. He cannot fall into total skepticism because, while he knows that he himself cannot attain final truth, he trusts God who is the

[25] *Ibid.*, p. 239.

source of all truth. And he will not be the prey of new fanaticisms because he will know that no human claim to have achieved the absolute, even when made on behalf of ostensibly universal values, can be more than a deceitful pretense.

Likewise, in the political realm, man can and cannot achieve justice. He can achieve it in the sense that there is no limit to the possibility of the fuller realization of brotherhood in men's social relations; the justice actually attained can always be corrected in the direction of the perfect mutual love which constitutes its ideal norm. From this standpoint brotherhood is the fulfillment of justice. But it is also its negation. Man cannot achieve justice, in the sense that, no matter how far he progresses toward the approximation of brotherhood, there is still a gap between what the ideal requires and what has been actually attained. And nothing is more flatly negated by true brotherhood than the pretense that some present conception of it, or some institution set up for implementing it, really embodies the ideal symbolized by the word.

This fact—that the ideal negates as well as fulfills every actual achievement of justice—can be seen, Niebuhr insists, both when we examine the laws which are believed to express the nature of justice at any given time and place, and when we survey the political structures and organizations which administer those laws. In each case we find a compromise between what ought to be if the true norm of justice were fully realized, and what actually is. The laws of justice are on the one hand instruments by which an ever larger measure of mutuality and community among men is progressively attained, under guidance of the ideal of impartiality and equality. On the other hand, they are positive contradictions of that ideal; the form they take is always limited by a realistic recognition of the powerful play of self-interest among those whose conduct they are to regulate, and even the most equitable form that could be taken would be inevitably tainted by man's incapacity to attain a universal perspective. Niebuhr illustrates this aspect of the paradox by the problem of establishing a just law of unemployment insurance.[26] Any law actually passed will be a compromise between the community's sense of moral obligation to the unemployed and the unwillingness on the part of those whose employment is reasonably

[26] *Ibid.,* p. 249 f.

secure to foot the bill that a really adequate mode of insurance would cost. The law will also reflect the inability of even the most impartial human imagination to envision just what true justice would require in this matter. As for the structures of justice, exemplified chiefly in the organs of government, they too are always a compromise between what a rational ideal of an organization administering justice would prescribe and the actual equilibria of group pressures in the community at any given time. So far as the compromise makes concessions to the latter it constitutes a negation of justice. Because some concessions to the latter are unavoidable, there are always two major possibilities of evil in the way government functions. If it is too strong, wielding an excessive degree of centralized power, it is likely to degenerate into tyranny, denying the freedom due to individuals and minority groups; if it is too weak, the balance of power between contending interests in the community, being insufficiently controlled by a more impartial force, may break out into anarchy. Democracy, Niebuhr holds, has made two vital contributions to the theory and practice of politics. It rejects the traditional aristocratic idea that those who occupy some privileged status in society should as such wield the power of government, in favor of the idea that government should be in the hands of persons directly responsible to the governed; and it gives constitutional standing to the right of resistance to unjust government, as, for example, in the principle that a minority has rights even against the prejudices of the majority.

The true attitude toward government, he thinks, was in essence formulated by the later Calvinist thinkers. They insisted that the criterion for a legitimate government is not merely its capacity to maintain order and peace but its ability to govern justly, and they realized also that if justice is to be more and more fully approximated the acts of government must be subject to free democratic criticism, which makes possible continued responsiveness to new prophetic insights into the meaning of justice. On the practical side, the duty of the conscientious Christian citizen is to find the right balance between the task of achieving a more perfect brotherhood in the functioning of the historical institutions under which he lives, and the task of achieving the best relative form of justice among the alternatives actually available. The latter task involves the readiness to employ force against those who would plunge us into greater injustice than we now suffer from, both within our own society and in the form of hostile foreign governments. Hence Niebuhr believes that pacifism is fundamentally irresponsible; in the utopian belief that love can be actually realized here and now, it would under threat submit to tyrannical power, and thus place men in a position where the struggle for freedom and brotherhood would be under even greater handicaps than it is at present.

Niebuhr concludes his philosophy of history and destiny with the following summary: "Thus wisdom about our destiny is dependent upon a humble recognition of the limits of our knowledge and our power. Our most reliable understanding is the fruit of 'grace,' in which faith completes our ignorance without pretending to possess its certainties as knowledge; and in which contrition mitigates our pride without destroying our hope."[27]

NEO-SUPERNATURALISM AND SOCIAL PROBLEMS

We can be relatively brief in treating the bearing of the new supernaturalist position on contemporary social problems. On these matters only certain basic principles, and a few major corollaries, are held in common by all the thinkers with whom we have been occupied; elsewhere, there is considerable divergence of interpretation. And so far as Niebuhr is concerned, what is most vital in his position has been already brought out in expounding his conception of the ideals of love and justice, and of the ambiguous relation between them.

The central principle, of course—and here lies the radical difference between this position and that of liberalism—is that the standard and norm of what is good for man lies not in him, not in anything that can be discovered in his experience, but in God. Just as God, being the transcendent source of truth, condemns as well as fulfills all human criteria of truth, correcting them by a norm to which man by himself cannot attain, so God as the transcendent source of good condemns as well as fulfills all human ideals of individual perfection and of social relations. We must find our real good in him, and be guided in its pursuit by his revelation to us in

[27] *Ibid.*, p. 321.

the Bible, especially in the unique disclosure of his love for man in the sacrificial death of Christ. The essential difference between this doctrine and that of Protestant fundamentalism lies in the fact that, while for fundamentalism the Bible provides an exhaustive set of answers to all moral and social questions, the new supernaturalists are ready to supplement its teaching by lessons derived from an empirical study of history and anthropology.[28] They are confident that these lessons fully confirm the basic truths disclosed in the Word of God, and in detailed interpretation of those truths they are glad to profit by whatever an honest and realistic assessment of human behavior may teach. The Bible, by itself, does not explicitly instruct us what to do in the varied situations we confront, but gives us only a general command; in obeying that command in each choice or action we need all the understanding that is available, from whatever quarter. Here, as in such matters as the higher criticism, the humble tentativeness and flexibility of the new supernaturalism make possible a continuing adjustment to scientific discoveries that the more rigid fundamentalism has found difficult.

But we begin to meet divergences among the leaders of this group even when we examine their interpretation of this central principle. Brunner interprets it in language that reminds us throughout of the Augustinian-Calvinist tradition, and when he applies it to detailed problems he reveals a fairly consistent adherence to traditional Protestant principles. It is in the Will of God that man's real good lies, and he begins to attain it only when he abandons his proud demand to determine what is good for himself by satisfying his sinful desires, and submits obediently to the divine command. The essence of that command, so far as its ethical implications are concerned, is to love God through loving and serving our neighbor. What does this mean, in terms of our attitude toward the main social institutions through which much of our activity will inevitably be expressed? It means accepting those institutions, especially the family and the economic structure of our culture, as part of the divine order of creation; we discover the neighbor whom we are to love and serve primarily by fulfilling, in the spirit of Christian responsibility, the duties of the "calling" in which we find ourselves

[28] Karl Barth, in much of his writing, seems to revert to the fundamentalist position on this matter.

placed. It does not mean, however, passively accepting the evils that may appear in the present functioning of those institutions. God is redeemer of the social order as well as its creator, and the task of redemption may require revolt against its present forms and replacement of them by something new.[29]

Niebuhr's interpretation is somewhat different on both these points. He would hesitate to say unqualifiedly that man's good is determined for him by a transcendent Will; this sounds too much like sheer, fateful imposition from the outside. Despite God's transcendence there is continuity between man and the divine; we rightly think of God as embodying in perfection the excellences that human experience at its best enables us to glimpse. Hence the revelation to man of divine love is not an arbitrary command to obey, but a clarified disclosure of what man obscurely knows to be good but would never be able by himself to discover in its absolute form. And when Niebuhr deals with the challenging social problems of our day his thought is continually haunted by the sense of an unavoidable conflict between love and justice as well as by the positive harmony between them. Justice is always being transformed under the guidance of the ideal of love, but in concrete social decisions we may be forced to violate the requirements of love in order to achieve the best relative justice that is possible. This conviction was expressed in extreme (and somewhat pessimistic) form in his *Moral Man and Immoral Society*, but in essence it has remained with him throughout his subsequent thinking. A realistic assessment of the way in which progress takes place in the economic and political spheres, he is sure, shows that absolute pacifism (as taught, for example, in the Sermon on the Mount) is not only futile but actually stands in the way of realizing the relative justice that under the circumstances at hand would be superior to available alternatives.

When we come to these basic issues of politics and economics we find that in general the leaders of the new supernaturalism tend toward a democratic socialism as the wise solution of contemporary problems in this area. The socialistic emphasis gives meaning to the second phrase of the slogan in which at one time Niebuhr expressed

---

[29] *The Divine Imperative*, trans. by D. Wyon, pp. 56 ff., 83 ff., 205 f, 214 f; *Christianity and Civilization, passim.*

the gist of his position: "Theologically to the right; politically, to the left." The readiness with which socialism can be allied with dictatorial totalitarianism, however, as shown in the fascist and communist social structures, has qualified their extreme socialistic enthusiasm of two decades ago, and led to an emphasis on socialistic methods through which democracy can be more confidently preserved.

With respect to the essential validity of political democracy, then, there is complete unanimity among these thinkers, and here they are at one also with the other philosophies which have been influential in Western religious thought except (in part) Catholicism. In its insistence on expressing, through its political forms, each individual's right to freedom and his duty to respect the freedom of others, democracy is the political implementation of a true normative understanding of human nature. Man does realize in this way, so far as political action goes, what God is calling him to be. As for the need of socializing democracy, all these thinkers agree in criticizing the extreme individualism of the democratic conceptions that have prevailed in the past—the individualism that has strongly influenced both fundamentalism and liberalism. Such conceptions have failed adequately to realize that the Christian ideal is not the isolated freedom of the mystic, but a "community of free personalities."[30] However, disagreement appears again in their interpretation of what this emphasis implies for political and economic reconstruction. Niebuhr, for example, is confident that the ideal of equality provides an ultimately valid norm by which to guide this reconstruction. Every major step of social reform in the past, he believes, has involved the correction of some inequality of opportunity or privilege; the question to ask about any inequalities that still remain is whether they can be justified before the bar of a true Christian understanding of man, and the answer usually is that they cannot. Brunner, on the other hand, profoundly distrusts the ideal of equality when systematically employed in this way. All men are equal in the sight of God, to be sure—he never questions this basic Christian truth—but no society of people who are not saints could operate successfully without rewarding special functions with special priv-

[30] E. Brunner, *Christianity and Civilization*, II, p. 134.

ileges. Indeed, he even maintains that true fellowship is impossible without inequality, though here it is inequality of endowment rather than inequality of privilege that he has in mind.[31]

It is evident that much remains to be done in clarifying the social implications of the new supernaturalist position, and perhaps full unanimity is not to be expected even when this process has gone much farther.

The Major Disputed Assumptions of the New Supernaturalism

1. Assumptions Concerning Man's Moral Situation
    a. Man is lost in sin, which prevents his attainment of truth and goodness, and obscures his understanding of them.
    b. By himself he is totally impotent to gain release from sin.
2. Metaphysical and Historical Assumptions
    a. There is a God who transcends the realm of man's temporal experience and biased reason, but who may break into it to save those who respond in faith.
    b. This is the God whose Word is revealed in the Bible, and especially in the self-giving love of Christ on the cross.
    c. God also speaks to man in the created wonders of nature, but until redeemed from sin man cannot interpret them aright.
3. Assumptions Concerning Religious Knowledge and Authority
    a. Every Christian is free to interpret the Divine Word as it acquires meaning for him in each perplexing situation.
    b. There is no authoritative or final interpretation of the Bible; an honest and obedient responsiveness to its message will show itself in a humble tentativeness about all conclusions reached.
    c. The task of theology is to place man's redeemed reason at the service of the Word, clarifying its bearing on present perplexities.
4. Ethical Assumptions
    a. The sacrificial love of God is the ultimate norm of what is good for man.
    b. Man's duty is to serve God through loving service of his fellows in community.

[31] *Ibid.*, p. 67, *The Divine Imperative, loc. cit.*, p. 213; Niebuhr, *The Nature and Destiny of Man*, Vol. II, p. 254 f.

BIBLIOGRAPHY

Aubrey, E. E., *Present Theological Tendencies*, Harper, 1936.

Barth, K., *The Doctrine of the Word of God*, T. and T. Clark, 1936.

Barth, K., *The Word of God and the Word of Man* (Horton trans.), The Pilgrim Press, 1928.

Brunner, Emil, *Christianity and Civilization*, Nisbet and Company, 1948 and 1949, 2 vols.

Brunner, Emil, *Revelation and Reason* (Wyon trans.), The Westminster Press, 1946.

Brunner, Emil, *The Divine Imperative* (Wyon trans.), Lutterworth Press, 1937.

Davies, D. L., *Reinhold Niebuhr, Prophet from America*, MacWhelan, 1948.

Horton, W. M., *Contemporary Continental Theology*, Harper, 1938.

Niebuhr, Reinhold, *Christianity and Power Politics*, Scribner, 1940.

Niebuhr, Reinhold, *The Nature and Destiny of Man*, Scribner, 1941, 1943, 2 vols.

Niebuhr, Reinhold, *Moral Man and Immoral Society*, Scribner, 1932.

PART III

Basic Issues in Religious Philosophy

Chapter XIII

THE SCOPE AND CERTAINTY OF RELIGIOUS KNOWLEDGE

THUS far we have made no attempt to engage in a critical discussion of the major questions on which the types of religious philosophy examined adopt contrary positions, or even to indicate in any systematic way what these questions are. Some of them have, of course, occasionally been emphasized, and to some extent clarified, when the later philosophies were expounded in their relations with the earlier. Moreover, at the end of each chapter a brief formulation has been offered of the main disputed assumptions of the type of philosophy there discussed, so couched as to facilitate critical comparisons. In a concluding survey of the field, which is now appropriate, we may well embark on such comparisons directly and come to grips with some of the challenging issues which separate these philosophies. In this discussion, as in the preceding pages, impartiality will still be the central note. The purpose will be not to convert the reader to the assumptions that seem to the author sound, but to contribute to a clear apprehension of the crucial foci of conflict. Complete impartiality is doubtless beyond anyone's attainment, but a vigorous effort will be made to approximate it, and the reader is urged to detect and discount any lurking biases that may appear in these concluding chapters. The most important thing is for each one who pursues these pages to attain a position from which he may more confidently advance toward his own satisfactory solution of the fundamental problems of religious thought. Five major problems of this kind will be chosen. They are more or less interconnected, and any selected starting point is to a large degree arbitrary.

401

One of the most important of these issues will be brought vividly before our attention if we return to the Catholic philosophy and place ourselves at the point where, according to its argument, natural reason is compelled to recognize its essential limitations and to look expectantly for supplementation by a divine revelation. It has been proved, if the earlier reasoning is as sound as Catholic thinkers believe, that God exists as a personal being, that the human soul in its spiritual essence is immortal, and that the ultimate destiny toward which its nature points is supernatural, since that destiny depends on conditions which man by his own power is unable to provide, and requires knowledge which man's natural reason (heretofore its adequate guide) is impotent to attain. Hence—so the conclusion is drawn—his reason needs help in the form of a supernatural revelation, and since goodness and love have been shown to be attributes of God we may be confident that such a revelation is available. All that is needed further, by the use of natural intelligence, is a clear basis for choice between the various claimants to this role.

Now the crucial consideration which requires this important conclusion is the recognition that human intelligence, unaided by special help from God, is limited. Its knowledge is finite, not infinite. And this limitation is of two sorts, which it is essential to distinguish. On the one hand, since every man begins his individual career without any knowledge, and gradually acquires what understanding of his world he succeeds in gaining through a temporal process of learning, it is evident that at any given time he must be ignorant of many things which wider experience might bring within his cognizance. But since no man lives long enough to make his experience quite complete, and since even within his lifetime he does not command all the facilities which aid one's acquisition of knowledge, this limitation is never entirely overcome. No one does know all that he might know in virtue of his intrinsic capacity to know. This consequence of man's finitude, involving recognition of his temporal and instrumental handicaps, is admitted by every serious philosophy. According to the Catholic thinkers, however, man's mind lies under a further and more important limitation also. It is finite not merely through lack of time and opportunity to exercise its powers to the best advantage, but also in the nature of those powers themselves. Since its first objects of knowledge are material things perceived through the senses, from which it gradually abstracts the universal essence, its knowledge, during our present life, is never entirely freed from matter nor from sensuous imagery. And even in the next life, apart from special illumination by God, man's apprehensions are such as would be appropriate to a dependent creature and hence far inferior to the understanding possessed by the Infinite Source of all reality and truth. Thus human knowledge is essentially and not merely contingently limited. Its powers of understanding are affected by a congenital weakness. Now this kind of finitude is not admitted by most other philosophies; hence its assertion precipitates an important issue in religious philosophy.

To the Catholic mind this distinction is important, because if it be valid there is at hand a plausible answer to the plea that would naturally be made if only the first of these two sorts of finitude were recognized. In that case the objection of many thinkers to the Catholic argument would take this form: To be sure, the knowledge that each of us now possesses as to the nature of our true good and how to attain it is incomplete and may be partially mistaken; but no knowledge is intrinsically beyond man's attainment; hence we should increase our understanding of these important matters by all means within our power, rather than look for supernatural knowledge by which to make good our defects. If, however, human intelligence is inherently defective, this answer does not seem sufficient. Should there be the possibility of remedying that inevitable ignorance by a revelation from Infinite Wisdom, it appears plausible that in such a direction lies our salvation.

A major problem challenges consideration, then, at this point, and in their answers to it all the other religious philosophies which have been examined diverge in one fundamental fashion or another from the Catholic position. The problem is this: If human intelligence is essentially deficient, not simply through lack of time and appropriate facilities, how can we be confident that the preceding course of reasoning, by which the existence of a personal God who cares for man has been established, is sound? Or, to put the same question in reverse order, if we were entirely competent to reach that result and may justly regard it as certain, why may we not go ahead in continued exercise of the same power of reason, and answer all the other questions which are important for our well-being? We need more knowledge, no doubt, but is there any ground for questioning our ability to attain whatever knowledge is attainable, since we have already confidently reached such ultimate and basic truths as these? Do you hold that we are incapable of attaining more, because of a fundamental incompetence in our intelligence? Then is there not a paralyzing doubt thrown on the validity of the results already reached? If the chance is infinitely small that our own reason would hit upon the right method of attaining its supreme good, is not the chance also infinitely small that it was right in the course of argument by which it proved the existence of a God able and willing to supplement our weakness by a supernatural revelation? In short, assuming that the human mind is intrinsically competent, then, given time and appropriate experience, it can presumably solve all problems that can be solved and needs no revelation from a superhuman mind; but if it is not intrinsically competent, then is it not likely to be mistaken in drawing the conclusion that supernatural aid is available? In reaching that conclusion it was making use of particular sense perceptions, which are admittedly infected by error, and axioms of causal explanation, which in view of the essential finitude of the mind that adopts them may, it would seem, also be quite fallible.

Now, the answer of the Catholic philosophers to this objection is, at bottom, that, although the mind's starting point in sense perceptions is intrinsically defective, the metaphysical axioms by which we reason our way from them to the Ultimate Cause and determine the latter's essential attributes are not so—they are absolutely true and can be clearly apprehended as such. Recognition of the mind's essential weakness is not intended to impugn their certainty, but merely to affect the scope of the results which man is able to establish by them and the manner in which those results are rendered intelligible to his mind. Thus we may, beyond peradventure of doubt, establish God's reality and his possession of such personal attributes as intelligence, will, goodness—and this is sufficient for the remaining contentions vital to their position.

With this plea in mind, the above problem can be expressed in more specific form. Suppose we grant for the sake of argument that these causal axioms are entirely sound[1] and that we may confidently

[1] Whether they are so will be considered below. See pp. 425–429.

affirm that a God infinite in goodness exists. But can we with equal confidence affirm that God's goodness must be of such a sort as to lead him to provide a special revelation for man's guidance? This does not clearly follow from the mere idea that he is infinitely perfect. Take a situation which is analogous in certain respects. The domestic animals are dependent on man, and look up to him as a superior and more perfect being. But his perfection does not necessarily involve performing those acts which are required to satisfy their needs; he uses them rather as means for the fuller attainment of his own ends, and feels entirely justified in so doing. May not the relation between God and man be similar—man existing, as some of the confessions have explained, solely for God's glory?

Moreover, even if we reject this analogy as mistaken, and suppose with the Catholic philosophers that God's goodness does include loving regard for man's good, still is it quite clear that this regard must take the form of providing supernatural guidance in furthering his salvation? Is it not possible that God might consider the development of self-reliance as the greatest good for man, and therefore purposely leave him to his own resources in discovering what is good and how to attain it? In short, when we hold that God's goodness means supplying supernatural aid to man are we not thereby implicitly assuming that we can not only know that he is good, but also know what that goodness would lead him to do in his detailed relations with his creatures? But is not this to make ourselves equal with God in knowledge of the good, and if we can tell with such confidence what particular modes of conduct must be characteristic of Infinite Goodness, will we not just as confidently be able to tell, by the same reasoning, what particular modes of conduct are appropriate for attaining such goodness as is suited to finite creatures? In this case there would be no need of supernatural revelation; seeing what God ought to do to take care of our salvation, we can see with equal clearness what we ought to do to take care of it ourselves. On the other hand, if we hold consistently to the assertion that man's intelligence is so defective that he cannot pilot his own way to ultimate good, then should we not draw the conclusion that he certainly cannot tell what God's infinite goodness is like— whether, for instance, it would make provision of special help in

man's quest for salvation, or not? In brief, in the light of these considerations, must we not face the alternative?—If man's reason is competent to tell that God's goodness implies the provision of a supernatural revelation, it needs no such revelation, being able to decide
equally well what man's own attainment of good requires; if it is
incompetent to point the way to human salvation, it is still more
incompetent to conclude with assurance anything about infinite
providence—the latter may be entirely incomparable with our finite
ideas of good and may disappoint all the expectations which they
would lead us to entertain.

Of course, the Catholic philosopher believes, while engaged in
this reasoning, that a divine revelation to man is an actual fact,
present in the Christian Scriptures, and hence an argument that
would render it *a priori* reasonable readily appears cogent. But,
according to the nonsupernaturalist viewpoint, acceptance of any
supposed revelation as an actual fact depends upon the prior conviction that there is in the universe a God able and willing to supply
it. For, if we did not believe this, could we not always readily conclude that the supposed revelation is to be accounted for on the
assumption of liberalism, namely, that it is a product of the same
moral enthusiasm and other psychological factors that we invoke
to explain any contemporary religious writing? In that case the
alleged miracles of Scripture will be treated as we treat reports of
miraculous events in other primitive literature, and thus no clear
evidences of a supernatural status for the revelation will remain.
There must still be faced as a historical fact, of course, the remarkable growth of the Christian Church, but since other successful
religious movements also started with small and unpromising beginnings, it does not seem evident that the particular success of
Christianity would appear strictly miraculous except to one already
favorably inclined toward its supernatural claims. Indeed, there are
thinkers who have regarded the arguments for a personal God as
convincing, but who do not accept the claim of any special scripture
or historical movement to embody a revelation from him, and hence,
rejecting all positive religions as being alike mistaken, have con-
tented themselves with natural theology alone. For them, God is
good, but his goodness is primarily displayed in the beneficent
order of nature which is directly present to the observation of all

men everywhere, not in any written book known only to a limited geographical area and thus raising perplexities which, they think, a rational mind finds difficult to solve.

The basic challenge which other religious philosophies pose for Catholic thinkers to face is therefore this: Can you, in the presence of these difficulties, render clearly intelligible and fully persuasive your contention that human reason is initially competent and is able on some ultimate matters to attain certain knowledge, while being in other matters quite fallible and essentially incompetent, on its own resources, to proceed further? Is it, perhaps, the case that the reason which is expected to operate in this way is from the very beginning a *humble* reason, so that when it finds itself under fundamental limitations it is disposed to adopt a trusting faith instead of turning to skepticism?

Obviously, there are two major alternatives to this position with respect to the competence of human intelligence. One is to deny its capacity to attain saving knowledge entirely. This is, in general, the doctrine of Protestant orthodoxy and of the new supernaturalism. The other is to affirm its intrinsic competence to deal, by its own resources, with any problem which may be significantly set before it, and thus to reject the notion that its achievements either need or should expect supplementation by a supernatural revelation. This is, in general, the doctrine of the other four religious philosophies. They differ greatly among themselves in the way in which they interpret this competence of man's mind, especially with regard to the degree of certainty which it may attain, but all alike hold the notion entirely chimerical that such weakness as man exhibits can be remedied by the gift of supernatural knowledge.[2]

In fact, they are sure that trusting acceptance of such knowledge means, actually, adopting the beliefs of certain other men instead of our own—the prophets, that is, and the authoritative ecclesiastical spokesmen. Because, for Catholic and orthodox Protestant theory, God does not disclose his truth to us directly, but only through them. But if it is proper to trust their intuitions of truth, why not ours? Such is the basic plea of those who oppose the supernaturalist position on this matter. Doubtless, they will admit, the ancient

[2] The position of modernism on this matter is, to be sure, somewhat ambiguous. Cf. above, pp. 288 f., 294 f., 326 ff.

prophets and the church leaders were men of unusual spiritual sensitiveness and sagacity, and the new ideas which have come to the world through them are very important. However, recognition of this fact does not imply that as a general principle we should take their intuition or reason as a criterion of truth in place of our own. Wherever ours disagrees with theirs we should, of course, take special pains to be sure that we are not making a mistake in following our own insight, but when the latter is clear how can we do other than follow it? Indeed, in view of the fact that there are many ancient seers who teach partially irreconcilable doctrines, and many competing religious interpreters, can one who is vividly conscious of this disagreement take as his ultimate criterion of truth the judgment of any of them?

Let us leave aside for the time being the fundamentalists and new supernaturalists, assuming with the other viewpoints that man's natural reason is at least partially competent and that its competence includes the power to establish, by inference from facts of experience, conclusions regarding the nature of the universe and other truths important for religion. How certain is the knowledge which it is capable of establishing? Here arises a closely related problem on which religious philosophies sharply differ. Is that knowledge absolute, so that we may be serenely confident that the conclusions reached are beyond the possibility of reasonable doubt, or is it fallible—liable to mistakes which future experience may require us to correct? On this issue Catholicism, Spinozism, and ethical idealism take the former view, while the agnostics and liberals adopt the latter. And the members of each opposing camp assign, in general, the same reason for their stand on this issue, however much they differ on other matters. Those who defend certainty in religious knowledge are confident that the possibility of salvation—of man's attaining his ultimate good—is dependent upon it, while those who reject certainty find no adequate evidence that it is attainable, and hence insist that we must accommodate our beliefs and attitudes to its absence.

Holders of the former of these two viewpoints are convinced that there is such a thing as an ultimate reality in or behind the universe, possessing a certain positive and constant character. For the Catholic this ultimate reality is a personal God, for the follower of Spinoza it is the mathematical structure of the universe, for the ethical idealist it is a moral order; but for all alike it has a definite nature which is eternally and indubitably there. Now, if there be such an entity at the heart of things, successful adjustment to it must clearly be involved in man's attainment of his highest good, whatever else such attainment may require. In case it is God, our lives must conform to his plan; should it be an order of necessary law, we must accept with peace and resignation our humble place in it; if it is a community of moral beings, we must make its rule of conduct unqualifiedly our own. Our basic religious attitudes must be built around the central core of harmonious adaptation to the ultimate nature of reality. But this, these thinkers believe, is impossible unless we can know with certainty what that nature is. Should such certainty be unattainable, then man's supreme good will likewise be unattainable. For in that event we shall either quite fail to gain the needed adjustment or, if we appear to gain it, the achievement will be merely accidental; there can be no assurance in our minds that the decisive step necessary for salvation has been taken. And without such assurance something essential to an adequate adaptation is lacking; our convictions will be wavering and changeable rather than settled, and no core of stable faith will have been formed about which a mature, disciplined personality may develop.

There is a positive, changeless nature in the universe; man's highest good involves squaring himself in conviction and character with it; and this is impossible without assured knowledge of what that nature is[3]—these are the crucial assumptions of the champions of absolute certainty in theology.

From the latter viewpoint, an honest survey of human experience indicates that no such absolute knowledge really is attainable, and that the inward assurance of certainty is illusory. Its defenders note, in the first place, that people who feel entirely certain are often confident of things which are mutually contradictory and cannot all be true. They observe, in the second place, that the convic-

---

[3] For the ethical idealists, of course, it is an assured rational faith rather than knowledge, strictly speaking. But this is because, following Kant, they restrict the term "knowledge" to the conclusions of natural science. That it is certain, they hold as much as the others.

tions of such persons sometimes change in spite of themselves; from being quite certain that there is a personal God they become persuaded, under the stress of some new experience, that there cannot be a God; or, from a settled assurance that authority is out of place in religion, they become sure that the Catholic hierarchy is the rightful interpreter of religious truth. These circumstances prove, in the eyes of the thinkers now under consideration, that the subjective sense of certainty is not trustworthy and is no adequate criterion of truth; it merely indicates that for one reason or another the conviction now dominant has succeeded in displacing other alternatives. But different beliefs may have their innings later, and one of them may be true rather than the one now so confidently held. In the third place, these philosophers are persuaded that the very nature of human knowledge is such as to render certainty impossible, so far at least as questions of empirical fact are concerned. Our knowledge is always restricted by the range of our experience to date, and by the means and methods of observation that we have used. There is never any guarantee that future experience will merely repeat the past; in fact the likelihood, judged by our previous experiential growth, is that it will bring many changes, some of which will lead to a revision of our erstwhile theological creed. In their view, we should fully recognize and accept the inevitability of these features of human experience, and take even our firmest convictions as tentative rather than final. It is ridiculous to claim absolute insight when our experience and conduct frequently belie it. Hence, they urge, let us frankly acknowledge this state of affairs, revise our ideas of man's supreme good in the light of it, hold our knowledge as always ready for correction by changing experience, and develop the religious character and attitude appropriate to such a situation. This attitude will be fundamentally one of welcoming growth and new insight, on matters of central importance as well as on others. There will be no absolute certainty, not even the certainty of continued development, since while we have no warrant that any previous conviction will be preserved, there is likewise no proof that it will not be. Expectation of novelty rests merely on an empirical generalization from the past, not on any *a priori* truth.

With the agnostics, this emphasis on the merely probable and tentative character of knowledge leads to an essentially negative position; the metaphysical or supernatural entities postulated by the other camp, being no longer objects of certain knowledge, become irrelevant to man's quest for the good. Either there is no ultimate reality or man cannot surely apprehend it; hence he is thrown on his own finite resources to work out such measure of happiness as he may. Liberals attempt a more positive and constructive religious philosophy on this foundation—one in which truth is always relative to growing experience. And some in the humanist group, faced by the thoroughgoing skepticism to which this relativism leads thinkers like Krutch, endeavor by rational analysis to justify pausing short of such a paralyzing doubt. Although no truth or value be absolute, experience shows, they hold, that certain types of good are capable of self-maintenance and self-enhancement in the presence of the most penetrating criticism, and that devotion to them makes possible the stability of character and the emotional confidence requisite for a happily integrated personality.

Even the new supernaturalists, it will be recalled, accept in large measure the doctrine that religious knowledge is tentative rather than certain. They are sure that a transcendent God exists, and that his revelation to man is disclosed in the Bible and especially in the recorded death of Christ, but in all other matters our judgments may at any time prove to be mistaken. In their case, however, this position is grounded at least as much in a deep religious humility as in this realistic recognition of historical shifts in theological opinion.

Which of these positions is right? Can man live his religious life by relative truths, or must he have an absolute? And if the latter, what absolute must he have? How, further, are we to decide between these alternatives? In our attempt to answer these questions, some historical clarification of the problem might help.

The major achievement of Greek thought was the discovery of mathematics, in its distinctive character as demonstrative knowledge. From axioms and definitions—real definitions, in the sense that they were confidently believed to apply to objects and relations in the physical world—thinkers of Hellas found it possible to prove with clear rational cogency a wide range of theorems which also seemed valid of the real world. Now, the human mind naturally seeks such demonstrative cogency wherever it can be attained, and its definitive attainment in one field of experience at once established an ideal for scientific knowledge everywhere. Scientific method came to be conceived as essentially identical with the mathematical method, involving two major steps—the intuitive apprehension of axiomatic truths or first principles that are valid of nature, and the deduction of further and more specific truths from them. Mathematics became the model which all science was expected to imitate; indeed, only where this model could be exemplified did knowledge in the strict sense of the word seem to be present. We have seen in earlier chapters how theology inevitably turned to this model when it sought to provide a systematic treatment of its themes, and how Aristotle, although insisting on an empirical origin and genesis of scientific knowledge, was yet so completely under the spell of the mathematical ideal that he regarded these empirical processes as merely preliminary to science, the latter consisting, properly speaking, of the demonstrative system of truth later erected on such foundations. In early modern thought mathematics was again invoked to provide a universal method of knowledge in the interest of scientific certainty, which seemed to Descartes and his followers to have somehow been lost through failure to follow faithfully the mathematical pattern. This time the emphasis was not simply on the intuitive clarity and deductive consistency of mathematical thought, but also on the exact measurability and impartial necessity of the distinctive kind of order which it believes to obtain in the world.

Then came the empiricism of modern natural science. Behind it lay the aggressive this-worldliness of the leaders of modern Europe, with their daring ambition to master the realm of physical nature. They were interested in anticipating and controlling future events of perceptual experience far more than in squaring themselves with ultimate reality. But when men's reflection about the world began to be swayed in any widespread fashion by this interest it gradually became evident that the mathematical method, by itself, was impotent to anticipate the detail of perceptual fact. No matter how clear our intuitive apprehensions may be, no matter how rigorous our deductive demonstrations—the objects which later perception will have to recognize may fail to correspond to the expectations which those apprehensions and demonstrations justify. The most certain explanation of past facts, in short, may prove inadequate to future facts. Moreover, the Spinozistic interpretation of the essence of mathematical order encouraged its own transcendence in this direction. If Nature is a necessary structure, operating with no reference to human good or ill, it follows that she is under no obligation to conform, in detail at any rate, to man's ideas about her, and hence she may at any moment present him with perceptions which disappoint his most confident expectations. Once this lesson is clearly learned, and men still prefer the adventurous attempt to anticipate future fact to the secure contemplation of the systematic order realized in our explanations of past fact, a profound transformation in their fundamental intellectual attitudes takes place. Demonstrative certainty is no longer of the essence of scientific knowledge; it becomes subordinate to a different basic ideal—the ideal of adequacy to future experience. Since, looking at our world from this standpoint, we know that we are going to recognize perceptions yet to come as facts, to be taken fully into account even though they differ from what our present knowledge leads us to expect; and since experience continues to present us plenty of new facts of this sort— we find it necessary to regard even our most certain knowledge as hypothetical instead of final. Its function now is not so much to systematize previous reflection as to guide anticipations of future perception. Hence its method becomes regulated by canons which experience shows to be serviceable to this end, but yet there is no guarantee whatever that in any particular case this function will be successfully performed. The modern empiricist thus abandons the demand for certainty in scientific knowledge, and is satisfied instead with the prospect of its progressive correction through continued inquiry and novel discovery.

One of the important results of this transformed orientation is the general recognition of a fundamental difference between pure mathematics and the sciences of empirical fact. Previously, as was natural in view of the historical circumstances just surveyed, no such cleavage seemed to obtain. Mathematically certain knowledge about physical nature was believed to be possible. Radical empiricists have attempted, of course, to render plausible the other extreme position which is theoretically tenable—that mathematics itself is really empirical and its theorems as hypothetical as those of natural science. It would appear today that this attempt has failed. Dominant trends at present hold that all science which purports to deal with perceptual fact is tentative and subject to correction by future experience, but that mathematics, when abstracted from its application to such facts, exhibits another kind of knowledge and remains essentially what the Greek thinkers took it to be. So far as its own internal structure is concerned, it is a science of demonstrative cogency; its theorems follow necessarily from the definitions and postulates without dependence on anything external. Absolute certainty is to be sure, not possible even here; we sometimes make mistakes in a mathematical calculation and that indicates a bare possibility that all of us have been mistaken every time we have added 2 + 2. But still there remains an important difference between such blunders as mathematicians occasionally commit and the errors into which we may fall regarding empirical facts. When the former are corrected by concentrated attention, universal agreement among mathematical experts usually reigns thereafter. But the latter seem to be constantly at the mercy of a contingent factor, so that no single correction, however carefully and conscientiously made, carries any warrant that correction will not be needed again. The general outcome thus seems to be that mathematical knowledge is certain in a legitimate sense, but that knowledge of empirical fact is never so.

It is worth noting that the tentativeness of empirical knowledge, now widely granted, has come to be increasingly supported by a consideration of another order than those thus far emphasized. It has been observed by many thinkers that the claim of absolute certainty is intimately bound up with the dogmatic attitude; when one is sure that he knows the truth he is also sure that all who disagree with him are wandering in error, and whenever he deigns to argue with them this assurance is apt to be rather obvious. Recognition of the tentativeness of knowledge, on the other hand, is essentially associated with modesty and with readiness to admit that there may be truth in the point of view of others where they hold different opinions from our own. If we are open to correction by future experience, there is always the possibility that some other person may already have learned the lesson that subsequent facts are destined to teach us; the process of amendment may be hastened if we accept his aid. Openness to the correction of our previous ideas by future perceptions, as a controlling attitude, thus involves openness to their rectification by the experiences and interpretations of others. This means not merely a thoroughgoing modesty and tolerance in our social behavior, but a more positive friendly-mindedness—a pervasive feeling that our own experience and belief can be greatly enriched by a sympathetic understanding of the beliefs of others, and that where we differ from them we can rarely be entirely right and they entirely wrong. Now, such modesty and generosity seem to be in harmony with the moral ideals which have long been gaining emphasis in Western thought, and this ethical tendency operates strongly to support the rejection of claims to certainty in favor of the tentativeness which is its natural corollary in our attitude toward knowledge.

Where do metaphysical, theological, and ethical convictions belong, with reference to these two kinds of scientific knowledge? Do they belong with mathematics or with empirical truth? So far as metaphysics and theology are concerned, the trend, except for Catholic circles and the more conservative Protestants, has been in the direction of refusing them the certainty of mathematical truth. This trend has been gradual, of course, and vigorously opposed by those who feel that certainty in knowledge is essential to religion, but its influence has on the whole been increasing.[4] These two subjects seem to be dealing with matters of fact, while pure mathematics is concerned only with relations between concepts—concepts of number, of figure, of order, and the like. Certainty is attainable, according to those who follow this trend, only in these conceptual relations; mathematics at once becomes contingent if applied to anything beyond the realm of concepts. If, then, we mean by God, immortality, and moral freedom anything more than conceptual possibilities, the challenge we must face is how to make convincing the claim that truths about them are capable of the certainty which other factual truth seems to lack. Are not our clearest ideas on these matters subject to the correction of future experience as much as our ideas about any other actually

---

[4] Kant's discussion of the ontological argument marks the historical turning point here.

existent affair? Or is this entire empirical trend of thought a radical mistake, at least if it be taken to apply to religious convictions? May we appropriately, so far as they are concerned, refuse to admit that future experience can ever belie them any more than clearly apprehended mathematical truths, and, perhaps, refuse even to recognize as a fact any experience which threatens to cast doubt upon them?

So far as ethical insight is concerned, a problem arises which modern thought appears to find peculiarly difficult. It is by facing the difficulties and taking a stand on them that ethical idealists and humanists attempt to reach an adequate answer to the major issue now under discussion. Certain kinds, at least, of moral truth seem on examination to be essentially different from both mathematical theorems and empirical knowledge. When we say that something *ought to be,* we do not appear to be asserting either that its presence is empirically verifiable or that there is any mathematical necessity about its existence or nature. It seems thus to belong to a third class of propositions, quite distinctive in comparison with the other two types. But such propositions must either be certain or not certain. Suppose, now, we are led to believe, as is the case with ethical idealism and humanism, that religion is essentially an affair of moral value, not of metaphysical demonstration. Shall we hold that the propositions which express our insight into ultimate values are certain, or tentative? The former of these two philosophies gives one answer, the latter the other.

For ethical idealism, the ultimate law of moral obligation is rationally certain, and whatever implications about the universe acceptance of it clearly involves are also rationally certain. Such implications do not, to be sure, constitute metaphysical knowledge, since their function is practical rather than theoretical, but they none the less permit the same degree of assured conviction that Catholic philosophers and Spinoza have claimed for their metaphysical assertions. Humanism accepts the same principle of moral obligation, although in the form of a social ideal rather than as a rule of duty, but for it that principle is tentative rather than *a priori* certain. However, it contends that this ideal is one of the forms of human value which prove able to maintain themselves in the face of novel experience and thus provide a relatively stable focus around which religious devotion can be built. It hopes thereby to combine the complete openness to new experience that is characteristic of the empirical attitude with the continuity of character and purpose that appear essential to any serious life. Occupying this position, it faces a challenge on both sides. The criticism of the ethical idealist is: Can you really build either morals or religion on the shifting sand which is all that the tentative method of empiricism provides? Must you not have some more deeply grounded assurance —some rock of certain refuge in times of emergency—on which to establish your religious faith? The challenge of the Krutchean skeptic is: Can you really make good your contention that some forms of value are capable of maintaining themselves in the presence of novel experience, at least if you imply by this that their value is thereby really confirmed as against alternative forms? The more you come to understand impartially these values to which you are enthusiastically committed, the more dubious you will be about their value, for impartial understanding is intrinsically irreconcilable with enthusiastic attachment. And is it not experientially evident that almost any broad aim maintains itself in the way you describe, once a man has passionately abandoned himself to its pursuit? The quest for power grows by the experiences to which it leads, especially if it be guided by cleverness and shrewd insight into the character of others, just as readily as the quest for friendship or for scientific truth. And yet power and friendship are antithetical as dominant values. Can you, adopting an empirical relativism, justify your assumption that certain values rather than others are verifiable as a stable center of religious devotion?

It may be observed incidentally that this problem of certainty has a bearing on the position taken by the various types of religious philosophy with reference to the structure of religious authority. According to Catholicism not all persons are capable of certainty on the same matters, at least when we pass beyond the questions which can be answered by natural theology. The prophets and apostles had a justified assurance that certain messages which they spoke came to them as the direct inspiration of God, and that they were not mistaken in discriminating between these and other convictions which carry no such infallible warrant. Since the canon of the Bible was closed, however, such inspirations no longer come, and everyone else who feels similarly sure that he is the medium of a new supernatural disclosure is bound to be mistaken. Further, in virtue of his place in the apostolic succession, the pope may be legitimately certain that when he defines the doctrine of the Church on matters of faith or morals his pronouncements are infallibly true. Should anyone not in the position of papal authority feel such certainty, however, he is inevitably in error. On these matters other people may appropriately have assurance only that the true revelation did in fact come through the authors of the Bible and that the true interpretation is determined by right of apostolic succession. Protestant fundamentalists and new supernaturalists agree with the Catholic thinkers so far as the special certainty of the prophets and apostles is concerned, and the delusion from which anyone else would be suffering who should assume himself capable of it. But they deny that the pope may justly be more certain than any other Christian regarding the interpretation of religious truth. The Holy Spirit guides all alike in their earnest endeavor to determine the meaning of the Bible; no one has any special privilege in the sense that his assured conviction becomes the criterion of truth for others as well as for himself. The other four philosophies, especially since the results of the higher criticism have become available, make the same denial regarding the special claim of the prophets. For them, there is no adequate evidence that ancient religious leaders stood in any different relation to Omniscience than that of prophets of contemporary times. The past is to be, and can be, understood by analogy with the present, and cannot properly be regarded as providing entirely distinctive insights into religious truth, capable of becoming an authoritative criterion for present experience and reflection. In short, the men of the past were really no more certain on these matters than we are. Here, of course, the challenge is: Which of these three alternative doctrines can be made convincing in face of the arguments of its opponents? And what decides our answer? Does it depend on the degree of confidence that we have in our individual intelligence as compared with our reverence for the religious tradition we inherit?

Chapter XIV

THE ESSENTIAL STRUCTURE OF THE UNIVERSE

A SECOND major issue connects directly with the themes which have just been discussed. Among the matters on which we attempt to reach an understanding judgment—whether absolutely certain or fallible—is the general structure of the universe in which we live. No question is more fundamental for religious philosophy than the question what sort of affair this structure is.

With regard to this problem the most challenging divergence appears between the Catholics, fundamentalists, new supernaturalists, and most modernists, on the one hand, and humanists together with followers of Spinoza, on the other. The former hold that the main pattern of the universe is teleological, expressing a purposive plan; while the latter maintain that it is a realm of neutral and impartial law, capable ideally of statement in mathematical form. Since this difference involves momentous consequences for one's philosophy of religion, it will be well to clarify it rather fully, probing the underlying assumptions of the alternative answers.

The basic conviction of the one party is that in the last analysis what happens in the universe happens because of its tendency to avoid some evil and realize some good. We experience ourselves as essentially controlled in our behavior by desire or purpose; we do what we do because it seems to promise the attainment of ends that we envisage as good. Even our unconscious conduct is teleologically oriented, in the sense that it is adapted to secure certain ends, of advantage to ourselves or our families, rather than others. We observe that the behavior of our fellow men is similarly motivated and we have constantly to take account of that fact in our relations with them. Moreover, the entire organic world appears to operate on the same principle; growth toward maturity presents itself in all its significant details as a striving for the attainment of ends which promote the continuance and well-being of the species, and express the selective and adaptive potencies of the striving creature. As for the inorganic world, while it does not seem so clearly pervaded by teleology in its internal economy, it obviously does provide a vast system of means which contribute toward the realization of organic ends. Especially is its stability and order adapted to the support of all rhythmic organic processes and to knowledge of its events, on man's part, in terms of dependable law. All of nature below man in some sense then exists for the service of his ends, while he similarly exists for the sake of whatever ends present themselves to him as ultimately good. And even these brief considerations call our attention to a hierarchical order in the teleology of nature. Creatures lower than man in the scale of existence—that is, lacking his distinctive capacities—pursue or express the kind of perfection to which their powers are suited, and every such form of perfection is limited in the definite ways implied by the specific nature of those powers. But man's unique capacity is intelligence, and intelligence is intrinsically able to apprehend not only this or that limited good, but also universal good—good in its essential and absolute nature. This indicates that man occupies a privileged position in the universe. His good is the final good of the entire teleological system, including while also transcending the ends toward which all other creatures strive. Can we, now, adequately interpret all these facts unless we suppose that a teleological structure is basic to the universe, goodness or perfection being a real cause of what happens in it? Must we not hold that Absolute Good or God is the ultimate cause of all events, that man's distinctive good is the same as that of the universe at large, and that therefore, despite his present limitations, he is destined for an infinite perfection in which those limitations are transcended? So reasons the defender of the teleological theory. To be sure, he admits, there is no guarantee that in any individual case that high end will be reached, but the nature of the universe is such as to set it before man as his appropriate goal, in comparison with which all the joys of his present existence are partial and incomplete.

To the other point of view, in its extreme form, all this argument seems a systematic rationalization of human wishes. For it, the mere fact that we and other living creatures desire objects and pursue ends proves nothing more than that we are naturally moved to seek them. It does not prove that those objects and ends are good, still less does it indicate that the essential structure of the cosmos is purposive. These objects and ends, when attained, frequently are disappointing, and this shows, in the first place, that they are not ɪeally good, but only mistakenly seem to be so. Also, our desires for them are often entirely futile, which indicates, in the second place, that exact and dependable knowledge about ourselves and our world cannot be expressed in teleological terms at all. The reason for this conclusion is that accurate knowledge of events, from the point of view of modern science, is knowledge of them in their constant relations with other events, events which occur with them in unexceptional regularity. But many contingencies so often prevent a desire or instinctive tendency from attaining its object that the relation between these two events is in fact far from constant. Given a craving, its end may be realized or it may not. Likewise, given a satisfying attainment, there is no guarantee that a specific longing was actively instrumental in bringing it about—it may have been hit upon accidentally. These considerations strongly suggest that clear knowledge must be expressed in other than teleological categories and assumptions. Such appear to be available both in the mechanical and in the evolutionary pictures of the world. Although these differ greatly from each other in detail, they agree in conceiving the universe as an order of neutral causal relationships, in which events happen, not with any reference to their goodness or badness or to whether or not they happen to be desired, but simply because other events which determine them have occurred. By tracing the connections of things from this standpoint we can secure, so it is insisted, an understanding of nature which eliminates chance and contingency wherever possible and reduces them to a minimum elsewhere. Thus our knowledge is less likely to be falsified, and predictions based on it are less likely to be disappointed by the outcome. A man desires, for example, to wed the lady of his choice; but, unless many other circumstances are favorable, the fact that he has the desire is no dependable indication that it will be satisfied. A man drops from a tenth-story window; he will surely fall to whatever solid substance is underneath, whether as a would-be suicide he wants this result or as a victim of sudden violence he experiences it with terror. If, then, we seek to understand what happens in the universe in terms of constant laws of interconnection, must we not take the latter situation as basic and typical rather than the former? Must we not assume that Nature is without any controlling end—that she is not a purposive or moral order, but an order of impersonal fate?

Moreover, when we look at the whole cosmos in the light of this theory, does it not prove possible to fit organic tendencies and human desires into this system of neutral causes and effects along with everything else? We long for a certain apparent good, but, having attained it, find ourselves disappointed. Why, then, did we long for it? Not, surely, because of its goodness, since we now discover that it is not good. Must we not say: We longed for it because there were determinate causes, having nothing whatever to do with the goodness or badness of the object, which were working upon and in us to produce that longing? And, if so, must we not offer the same explanation in the case of those desires which do lead to genuine satisfaction? They, too, must be regarded as produced, not by the quite contingent circumstance that their issue is happy, but by the presence of conditions which engender them. From this standpoint, while it is reasonable, in view of man's essentially appetitive nature, to seek by our practical activity situations which promise the most stable and enduring happiness, we must not suppose that their goodness has anything to do with their factual occurrence or their causal relations. Goodness is entirely dependent on and relative to organic experience of satisfaction or frustration; it is not a cause of anything that happens and is therefore not a principle in terms of which we can properly understand the structure of events in which we exist. The universe is an impersonal order to which, if we are wise, we will accommodate ourselves, in emotion and in idea; it is not a purposive plan in whose essential goodness we may place a joyous trust.

Between these extremes there lie, of course, an indefinite number of intermediate positions. The more influential of these, historically, are attempts to combine the basic ideas of the extreme doctrines in various ways. During the seventeenth and eighteenth centuries the most widespread attempt of this kind consisted in supposing that the order of physical nature is a determinate mechanical structure with no internal teleology, but that as a whole it is the creation of a purposive deity characterized in the main as the Catholic philosophers had portrayed him. Thus teleology is held to be ultimate in the universe, while a large area within the world is believed to be nonteleological in its detailed behavior. The position of the ethical idealists, from Kant's day to the present, may be regarded as a major variant of this attempt. For them the world of physical nature is believed to be entirely mechanical, but it is also merely phenomenal; ultimate reality is a moral order whose essential structure is established by the law of duty and its constant attraction upon all those in the phenomenal realm who are capable of moral response. God's place is taken by an infinite spiritual reality, nontheistically conceived. During the nineteenth century and the early twentieth a view held by many was that the biological realm, including the course of human history, may be properly understood in teleological terms, but that the physicochemical, and especially the astronomical, order, on which all organic life in the end depends, is blind mechanism. In this case, due to that ultimate dependence, the reign of impersonal law is final in the universe, teleology constituting only a significant factor in a subordinate field which exists at the mercy of nonteleological forces. It seems evident from these instances that it is impossible to combine the two principles of interpretation in such a way that one will not be definitely subordinate to the other. Apparently, any consistent cosmological picture (leaving out the possibility of some third alternative) must choose between them as ultimate principles; either the basic structure of the universe is teleological or it is causal in an impersonal sense, but it can hardly be both.

Which of these alternatives shall we hold to be warranted, and how shall we justify our decision? The challenge to those who champion an ultimate teleology is: Can you, in view of the frequent experience of frustration and the importance of dependable knowledge of events, render convincing your insistence on the validity of a purposive interpretation of the universe? The challenge to their opponents is: Can you, in view of the fact that each living creature is constantly seeking what seems to him good,

and therefore naturally looks upon his universe as a complex of ends
and of means available for their attempted realization, make convincing your elimination or subordination of such teleological categories? And an *argumentum ad hominem* may be here introduced.
"After all, does not the explanation of your adoption of this impersonal naturalism lie in the fact that you desire as an end the confident
predictability and accurate knowledge to which that impersonal
order will provide the necessary means? But this is not to subordinate
teleology, it is to provide an unusually striking illustration of it."
Thus in the eyes of the teleologists, the opposing view of the universe
is left incomplete; their antagonists proclaim explicitly the structure
of the world as they systematically envision it, while forgetting and
leaving implicit the ultimate end for the sake of which that view
is adopted. To the antiteleologists themselves, of course, this picture
of the world seems to be no means to an end, however significant
the achievements which its recognition encourages; it presents itself
simply as a generalization from undeniable facts of experience.

How can we tell which of these alternatives one ought to adopt?
There is a temptation to answer this question, at least initially,
in some such fashion as this: Consult your most pervasive and
insistent experiences of the way in which things happen in the
world, and accept the general cosmological picture which is most
clearly harmonious with them. If they point toward a teleological
structure of events as fundamental, adopt the appropriate metaphysical view; if they point toward a neutral and impersonal order
as fundamental, adopt the radical naturalism which that conception involves. And perhaps in the end one can find no clearer and
more adequate guide to his decision than this.

But an important question arises at this juncture which demands
serious consideration. Perhaps the facts, as such, are not coercive
either way. If they were, it would be strange that sincere and intelligent inquirers should, in their presence, reach such widely different interpretations, fraught with such momentous consequences for
religious philosophy. It may be that, whether we are conscious
of it or not, the deciding factor in our cosmology is not the experienced facts, but our underlying assumptions regarding the
proper way of rendering them intelligible—our deep-seated convictions as to what constitutes an adequate explanation of any factual

occurrence. Perhaps the same events, viewed in the light of one such conviction, will support a certain metaphysical picture, while, viewed in terms of another assumption, they will appear to justify a different conclusion.

It has been noted in the preceding chapters that, so far as fundamental problems of religious philosophy are concerned, the Western world has witnessed the dominance of three very different assumptions of this kind. Ancient and medieval thinkers, almost without important exception—and in religious matters, at least, many moderns have agreed—were convinced that no set of facts is adequately explained save in terms of an ultimate cause which has imparted to them whatever degree of goodness or perfection they exhibit. To such thinkers, this was a direct and practically unquestioned corollary of the general principle that nothing can arise from nothing; if that is a sound maxim, they reasoned, surely it follows that a higher excellence cannot arise from a lower. Now this implies that the goodness in things is a real and effective cause of their existence and nature, and thus the teleological method is validated; it implies also that the ultimate source of all things must be a Being possessed of supreme perfection, various aspects or degrees of whose excellence are imparted to the finite entities which make up the world of nature. Should this assumption be denied, it would seem to such thinkers that certain definite and obvious features of the facts that we are trying to explain simply remain unaccounted for, and to leave them thus is clearly to be illogical. A second conviction, dominant historically during the period when the successes of mathematical mechanics encouraged a generalized picture of the universe after its model, agrees with the first in holding that nothing can arise from nothing, but insists that just as any cause must be adequate to its effect, so the full effect must be empirically equal to its cause. For the same reason that we are compelled to ascribe to the cause whatever attributes and powers are requisite to account for the properties of its effect, it is our business to hold that no feature of the cause fails to gain complete expression in its effect. There must, in other words, be an essential equivalence between the two, so far at least as concerns their basic and measurable characteristics. Otherwise we would naturally predict, from our description of the cause, a different and in certain respects greater effect than experience could ever verify. When, now, we apply this assumption about the nature of an adequate explanation to the cosmological problems posed by religion, a very different theory of the universe is reached from that required by the assumption above considered. We cannot suppose the ultimate cause—taking it for granted that such exists, which is questionable on empirical grounds—to be supremely perfect, for then the world of experience which constitutes its effect would be supremely perfect, and this it obviously is not. We can only ascribe to such a cause precisely those qualities and that exact degree of each which we see adequately displayed in the effect, and no more. Thus, given a quite imperfect effect, we may only legitimately postulate an equally imperfect cause. And, since such a cause will not correspond to the established theological conception of a God supreme in wisdom and goodness, we will on these foundations inevitably be led either to agnosticism about the reality of God or to a radical redefinition of God, transforming him into a human ideal without metaphysical potency or into a moral principle justifiable to faith but not to knowledge. A third major assumption, encouraged by the theory of evolution and increasingly influential since Darwin's day, agrees with the second in rejecting the idea of a supremely perfect cause, but disagrees with both the first and the second in entertaining a very daring notion—that in a real sense something can and does arise out of nothing. A total effect may be more complex than its causal conditions, and may display qualities and modes of behavior which those conditions entirely lack. Behind this historically radical idea lies, of course, the belief that scientific evidence adequately proves the actual emergence of living things and creatures possessing minds out of an inorganic world quite void of either life or consciousness. Since such is in fact the case, evolutionists reason, our theories of the causal relation and of what is needed for a sufficient explanation of any set of facts must be accommodated to it, and this means that we should not insist that the total cause must even be equal to the effect in all its properties and modes of action; a part of the effect simply comes unpredictably and irrationally (if you like) into being. From the other two points of view such a theory of explanation is absurdly illogical. Defenders of the first viewpoint say: If the historical facts out of which such effects have been generated fail to show all the properties of the effects, that simply means that one needs to look elsewhere for the complete cause—in realities incapable of empirical observation, if need be. Defenders of the second viewpoint usually say: These affairs that you call life and mind are not real in the sense in which the physicochemical processes underlying them are so: they are simply highly complex forms of inorganic change, and for clear knowledge must be regarded as reducible to such. For both first and second viewpoints, time is not creative; it is a subordinate rather than an ultimate aspect of the universe.

The metaphysical pictures which issue from these three diverse assumptions are very different. The first leads to a conception of the cosmos as essentially a process of emanation of various kinds and degrees of imperfect being from an all-perfect source. The second encourages the notion of the universe as a series of transformations in time, preserving always the same quantity of material and energy, with the same fundamental properties. The third requires a picture of reality as an evolutionary development, in which new, more complex levels of existence from time to time appear, maintaining themselves whenever environing conditions permit. Now, it may be that the same experienced facts can fit with tolerable harmony into any one of these pictures, according to the explanatory assumptions that we implicitly or explicitly take to be warranted. At least this would seem extremely likely if we note the further circumstance, doubtless inevitable, that people always tend to select and emphasize those facts which are especially suited to the principles of explanation which they have espoused, and to neglect or minimize the more refractory ones.

How, then, can we tell which assumptions regarding adequate causal explanation are sound? This seems to be the crucial problem challenging us. There is, to be sure, a possibility that should not be forgotten. It may be that even though the facts which directly confront a thinker appear reconcilable with any of these three assumptions, there is a certain long-run pressure of factual experience which encourages one of them and discourages the others, so that in this sense factual considerations still remain the final court of appeal. But long-run facts will hardly be sufficient to tell us clearly, here and now, which cosmology, of the several available, we ought to champion.

If we ask the question, Why have there been these broad historical changes in men's underlying convictions regarding the way
in which facts may properly be explained? it appears that a very
suggestive answer can be given, although it remains doubtful how
far that answer helps us decide which of these convictions to adopt.
Suppose we consider in the light of this question the dominant
character of the successive periods in which these assumptions have
severally prevailed, and the pervasive interests and attitudes which
that character expresses. The fundamental attitude of most Greek
thinkers was aesthetic and contemplative. They had no zeal either
to harness physical nature or to reform the world, but they prized
the virtues of unity and harmony; they delighted to contemplate the
diversity of changing events as flowing from an ultimate changeless
principle which was the source of whatever order and significance the
events disclosed. In late ancient and medieval times a certain otherworldly interest became joined with this aesthetic attitude; the
present realm of social and natural fact seemed hopeless in its radical
imperfection—a thing to be escaped from into mystic union with
the perfect substance which transcends the present unpromising but
happily quite transient scene. Under these circumstances, since the
facts of experience which attracted general attention seemed capable
of interpretation as part of a teleological scheme expressing such an
aesthetic and mystic interest, it was the most natural thing in the
world to assume the validity of that scheme and the soundness
of the principles of explanation which it implied. Modern Europe,
when it began to gain emancipation from the cultural forces by
which it had been educated, revealed in its typical thinkers a quite
different dominant urge—a practical ambition to control Nature
and render her subservient to man's ends. This involved assuming
as an axiom that she was capable of control—that is, that future
events can be exactly predicted by analytic examination of present
events which are destined to lead to them through chains of causal
connection. This assumption itself implied, in turn, as explained
in Chapter VIII, the theory of essential equivalence between any
cause and its effect. In this context the appropriate conviction regarding adequacy of explanation is that whatever features of an
effect we are concerned to render intelligible require a cause which
has precisely the same degree of the same fundamental properties as

they exhibit. Similarly, the appropriate metaphysical picture is in the broad sense mechanical, representing the universe as an order of determinate sequences in which nothing of the past is lost and nothing significantly new is ever gained. Finally, the enormous successes of modern science, together with the world-wide expansion of European political and economic power, culminated in the nineteenth century in a pervasive optimism and confidence in progress among typical Westerners. It seemed ever so much better to be a vegetable than a stone, a rational man than a vegetable, and (although this aspect of the doctrine might sometimes be left unexpressed) a sensible European than a superstitious Oriental. And did not biological science clearly indicate that organic life, emerging from its inorganic matrix in very rudimentary forms at some remote period in the past, had gradually struggled its way upward through the various species of creatures to its present culmination in the highest types of humanity now spreading an enlightened culture over the world? Thus the cosmos seemed to be steadily moving toward a richer and wiser level of attainment, or at least—for the scientific-minded wished to avoid partiality—toward more complex products exhibiting a greater variety of qualities and modes of behavior. Now the natural expression, in metaphysical reflection, of this optimistic faith in a wiser and greater future, was the assumption that effects transcend their causes in the number of properties and powers of action which they reveal, and that the universe as a whole is an evolutionary process, ever pregnant with unpredictable but promising novelty which appears whenever given half a chance.

Thus the major metaphysical ideas that have obtained in the history of thought in the West would seem to be correlated with the dominant spirit of each age—that is, with the pervasive attitudes and insistent concerns shared by its intellectual leaders. If our present problem, then, be restated in the light of this circumstance it would seem to involve the prior question: Which of these controlling attitudes is on the whole the soundest one, and why? Or should we, perhaps—for there are many signs that the epoch of confident optimism has reached its end—endeavor to anticipate the dominant mood of the coming age and forecast the metaphysics which it will find congenial?

It has been indicated in the preceding pages that our view of man and his destiny depends in the main on our answer to this problem about the essential structure of the universe. If we accept an ultimate teleology we shall readily accept also a privileged place for man in the cosmic scheme since, generally speaking, his distinctive faculties appear more capable than those of any other species of using the rest of the natural world as means toward his chosen ends. Inasmuch, also, as the supreme good which he can conceive is in some sense universal and infinite, the teleological view readily encourages the conviction that the world is so constituted that this perfect and all-inclusive good is intrinsically attainable by man. This aspect of the problem may be briefly elaborated. To be sure, it is theoretically possible to hold a cosmic teleology which is quite impartial with respect to man's place in nature as compared with that of other living creatures, but no influential religious philosophy in the West has championed such a doctrine, inasmuch as the same considerations which support a teleological metaphysic in general likewise point toward a hierarchy of functions and ends in which man's role stands very high. The conception of the universe as an impersonal order, on the other hand, in which things happen not because of the appealing ends which they realize, but by the pressure of their natural causes, involves a radically different theory of man and of his cosmic prospects. He has, of course, all the properties which he has, and his experiences are what they are, but from this standpoint he appears at best but a minor part of Nature, accommodated in all that he does to her all-encompassing order, and in no sense a creditor to whom she owes special obligations. At the present time this doctrine usually takes the characteristic form provided by the theory of evolution—man is one product of a vast temporal process, his ideals of goodness and his heritage of reason being just as fully the outcome of simpler natural antecedents as his erect posture and his remarkably flexible hand. His destiny, individual and collective, is whatever it historically proves to be, but in any event there is no metaphysical warrant for belief in survival beyond the grave, and no encouragement for the idea that the life of the human race is more than a transient episode in the drama of universal existence. This does not, perhaps, detract from man's dignity, but it suggests the appropriateness of a very deep humility. Need it take aught from the strength, courage, tenderness, and hope with which one faces the challenge of life?—here is the important question.

So far as immortality is concerned, in lack of a more extensive consideration of the distinctive problems posed, two brief remarks may be made. One is that metaphysical naturalism does not necessarily mean denial of immortality, provided we believe in the competence of human intelligence to attain absolute and unchanging truth. Let Spinoza be our witness here. If we assume, as many thinkers have, that knowledge involves in some sense the identification of the mind with what it knows, must not that in us be eternal which is capable of allying itself with what is eternal? The other is that influential forces in modern thought encourage the suspicion that the best forms of religious devotion, like high patriotism, are sufficiently selfless not to require the assurance of personal compensation. Perhaps the greatest good which religious experience renders available is its own reward, entirely sufficient without the assurance of everlasting life. On the other hand, there is much in the testimony of great spirits to suggest that, while their deepest experiences spurn any *demand* for immortality, they at the same time strengthen the sense of its *reality*.

Chapter XV

RELIGION, METAPHYSICS, HISTORY, AND
SOCIAL ETHICS

WE MAY now attack a third major issue of religious thought. It
is a matter which affects the problem of ecclesiastical organization
as well as questions of theological principle. There are really two
distinct questions here, but when one has been sufficiently clarified,
the other will not detain us long. Let us begin with a problem concerning the relative importance in religion of metaphysics and
of social ethics. On it, ethical idealism and humanism stand together against the other philosophies expounded. Which is really
central in religion—the true foundation of theology and the sound
basis of church unity—an ultimate metaphysical belief or a common
social ideal? Does the heart of religion lie in some theory as to
the nature of the universe, which must be held by all church members if they are to have a sense of significant community with each
other, or are metaphysical convictions subordinate to agreement
on a fundamental ethical principle or general goal of social progress?
Throughout the whole history of Western religious thought,
prior to the appearance of ethical culture and humanist groups,
it had been taken for granted by all influential thinkers that the
former of these assumptions is correct. Religion, they were sure, is
different from morals, and in some sense supplies its needed foundation. A conviction of oneness with the forces that are deep-seated
in the universe, about which propositions can be clearly known and
formulated in a creed, was in their judgment essential to religion,
and agreement on that creed is what binds the members of a
religious community together. Such members may differ widely
in their detailed understanding of what social duties religious faith

prescribes, but these differences are not of major consequence provided a common metaphysical faith and common ideals of personal conduct are present.

Ethical idealists and humanists challenge this assumption. They are profoundly convinced that under the conditions posed by modern thought it is inevitable that any group of men and women, all of whom alike hold high social ideals, will differ markedly in their metaphysical notions, and that some will be quite agnostic with regard to theories of ultimate reality. Yet such people need to be united in coöperative devotion to the social ends to which they are all committed, and the community of purpose thus attainable is perhaps more important than their separation on the matters about which they disagree. Now these two types of philosophy are confident that the unity thus established is a religious as well as a moral unity, for devotion to ethical value rather than acceptance of a metaphysical creed is for them the heart of religion. The effective bond of unity in religion, they therefore think, must be found in a common social purpose, and beliefs about the universe can be allowed to take a quite subordinate place.

Moreover, when they view the previous history of religion from this standpoint they are persuaded that their opponents have been mistaken in supposing that cosmological belief ever is as central and important as pre-Kantian theologies have claimed. What has always really been primary, they think, in the doctrine of God, is not his status in the cosmos, but his embodiment of moral character and his ability to bring a valuable enrichment of experience to those who have faith in him. Thus, if these features can be preserved in religion, they think that the metaphysical attributes can be subordinated or even denied without loss. And they feel that the real bond of unity in the Christian Church has not been the conviction that God controls the universe, but that he is like Jesus of Nazareth in possessing a loving character, which all Christians are expected to emulate in their relations with others. Especially they are sure that in contemporary times, influenced, as such times so profoundly are, by the empirical assumptions of modern natural science, religious organizations will increasingly lose the support of socially-minded thinkers if they continue to insist that common convictions about the nature of the universe be held by all their members. The vital thing, in their eyes, is agreement on the foundations of social ethics and on the broad features of the social program which express their bearing on present-day problems in industry, politics, and international affairs. A far more effective church, they are convinced, can be formed out of people who agree in this way on socialism or pacifism, while differing in their cosmology, than out of persons who hold the same metaphysical creed but strongly diverge on these pressing social issues.

Which of these divergent alternatives should we espouse? And on what principles can we decide? Is our decision determined mainly by the conclusions we reach on the question whether metaphysical knowledge is attainable or not? Or is it a matter of our fundamental intuitions as to what is most vital in our religious experience, and our forecast of what elements will prove to be central in the future religious life of the world? And if so, how tell which intuitions are in the right? If we judge the question merely by the evidence of history, it is fairly evident that those who pin their faith in metaphysics have the better of the argument; the long story of religion, in the West and also in India, seems to support their contention, and efforts to build a strong church on devotion to a common social purpose alone have so far been meager and of not unquestioned success. But can we confidently assume that this will continue to be the case?

The most effective defense of the position that the essence of religion is found in devotion to a common social ideal, rather than in a shared metaphysical theory, probably consists in the contention that the moral factor in religion has progressively gained emphasis and clarity throughout the whole history of theological thought, but that, in the Western world, it is only under the distinctive and novel influences of modern times that this factor has been able, in the minds of any considerable number of people, definitely and explicitly to subordinate all other elements to itself. But if the forces which have issued in this result are enduring and not transient, the change it has brought about in the religious attitudes of many people will also presumably be enduring and may be expected gradually to become more widespread. Ethical idealists and humanists are confident that this is the case, since in their eyes the moral emphasis in religion and the distinctive assumptions of modern science—which are the two main influences here involved—are but the expression of the deepest needs and the most insistent experiences of which humanity, when it becomes mature, is capable. For them, insistence on a metaphysical theory as an affair of primary importance is an indication of religious childhood; when men and women are grown up they are bound to put away childish things, or at least to subordinate them to a different outlook.

The most effective defense of the more traditional position probably consists in an elaboration of its insistence that the structure of the universe must be taken seriously. If action in pursuit of a high ideal is to be wise and successful it must be guided by true understanding of the total pattern of events within which that action proceeds. Has our understanding in the past been mistaken? Then let us correct it in whatever way our clearest insight into the nature of reality requires. To be sure, in an age which needs a radical revision of this sort it is likely that past metaphysical creeds will lose much of their uniting force. But in the long run earnest men can be effectively united only by a common understanding of the truth about themselves and about the vast whole of which they are dependent parts. Spinoza believed this, as Aquinas and Calvin did.

It is now time to turn very briefly to the other question mentioned at the beginning of the present chapter. This is the question whether loyalty to some particular historical personage or tradition is essential to religion, or whether it may be dispensed with in favor of some general philosophical orientation. The former alternative is held by Catholicism, fundamentalism, modernism, and the new supernaturalism, while the religion of science joins with ethical idealism and most humanists in defense of the latter.

Here it is important that the precise difference between the two viewpoints be carefully observed. The latter position does not deny a very significant place in religion for its great personalities; nor does it deny the pertinence of high admiration for their heroic character and profound gratitude for the new insight, moral power, and courageous hope that have become the possession of mankind through them. And, it agrees, we may often properly be guided by their influence in the intimate details of daily life; the best way frequently to clinch a difficult moral decision is to ask ourselves how such a revered personality would be likely to meet the situation confronting us. But this position does not approve zealous devotion to any founder of religion when that feeling strikes so deep as to suspend, as far as he and the ecclesiastical tradition which stems from him are concerned, our critical faculties, with the result that attachment to him becomes superior, in our experience and reflection, to open-minded respect for impartial truth. From this viewpoint, such devotion is bad on several accounts. It means that we become less than fair in our appreciation and understanding of other outstanding religious personalities and what they have contributed to the religious life of mankind. We should not, so it is contended, place ourselves in a position where we cannot use to the full the aid of all these geniuses. It means that we become blind to real defects in the personality of our chosen leader, measured against the spiritual needs of contemporary life, and that we fall into historical confusion through identifying his example and teaching with what our own chosen ideals prescribe. It means that the central object of our religious concern is some event in past history, rather than the important truths verifiable in the present and the human needs insistently challenging earnest attention in the immediate future. It means that we easily become the prey of exploitation on the part of those who are consciously or unconsciously ready to use our uncritical loyalty to ancient seers for the sake of increasing their power and furthering their ends in the present. Hence, in the judgment of those who emphasize these matters, such fervent discipleship should never be allowed to supersede our complete openness to truth and our recognition of novel aspects of human value as they appear on the horizon.

Those who hold the other alternative are convinced that this is to confuse the religious with the philosophical attitude. Philosophy, no doubt, must make objective truth always its primary consideration; this feature it has in common with science. Both seek universal principles which, as universal, are necessarily abstract, lacking the vivid concreteness of individual exemplifications of their distinctive quality. And perhaps a few philosophers, it will be allowed, can be sufficiently satisfied by these abstractions so that in their religious life no strong demand for a more warm and personal attachment arises. But surely, maintain the defenders of this view, such is not the case, and never will be the case, with the mass of men who feel the pull of religious emotion. They need an individual human symbol and exemplification of that to which they are religiously attached; without it devotion fades away, to be replaced, if at all, by a cool recognition of truth and a matter-of-fact attack on life's problems. In the judgment of these thinkers, genuine religious feeling can live, in the vast majority of human hearts, only under the guise of commitment to a person. Contemplation, for example, of what happened on the Cross of Calvary can be of religious significance only if it leads to an awe-struck reverence, gratitude, and devotion centered upon the noble personality who suffered there, not if it merely encourages the recognition of general principles or high social ideals. Religious men need an individual Savior, not a partially successful illustration of some universal standard of value. Religion is no formula, representing a merely abstract entity; it is enthusiastic response to the appeal of a great personality.

Which of these alternatives shall we accept? Are people essentially different on this matter, some being capable of a satisfying religious experience in the presence of a general philosophical principle or ideal, while others need the warmth which adoring attachment to a person provides? The crucial theoretical problem is perhaps this: Is universal truth the ultimate consideration in religion as in other fields, or may it be subordinated to the more vivid values capable of embodiment in some particular historical individual?

Chapter XVI

MAN AS SINNER

IN VIEW of the vigorous influence today of the new supernaturalism, it is important to consider seriously a fourth issue on which it, along with Protestant fundamentalism, takes a distinctive position against the other religious philosophies that we have examined. According to this position, man's first step toward health and wholeness must be the humbling recognition that he is a sinner in the eyes of God. This is a prerequisite, these thinkers are sure, to any genuine further progress, because without it whatever man does and thinks (especially about himself) will be corrupted by his sin; instead of moving in the right direction he will inevitably be lost in self-deception, and the poison of pride will continue to infect his entire self. To other philosophies, this is a completely unjustified pessimism about human nature; it implies a kind of impotence and perversity in man—also a passivity in his relation to God—that a sound religious perspective cannot accept. Indeed, from the standpoint of some of them—the religion of science, agnosticism, humanism—the very concept of sin is an unfortunate and misleading one; a serious attempt to understand the depths of human nature would do well to discard it and analyze the relevant facts in other terms.

Is man a sinner? And if he is, how shall we most adequately and realistically understand this sobering fact about him? What should we do, after honestly recognizing it, to meet successfully the problem that its presence poses? In other words, are the two philosophies that insist on this deep-seated corruption of man essentially right, in their diagnosis of the facts and in the curative treatment which they prescribe?

A correct answer to the problem of diagnosis would seem to lead naturally to a correct answer to the problem of cure; so we may confine this brief discussion to an analysis of the former—of the theoretical questions concerning the understanding of human nature that are involved. And there would seem to be two basic issues on which our attention will need to be focused. One is the primary issue as to whether—in theological language—man is a sinner or not. In William James' rather pithy way of expressing it, do all men need to be "twice-born," the second birth being necessary in virtue of the deeply perverting effect of sin, or are some able to grow naturally toward spiritual perfection without any convulsive awareness of being lost, and thus without experiencing any such second birth?[1] But then there is a second issue which must be considered, irrespective of our answer to the first. Assuming that some people, at least, do need to experience this shattering consciousness of sin, how shall we most clearly understand what happens when it takes place? Are the fundamentalists and new supernaturalists right in so analyzing it that all the creative activity which appears in it is assigned to God, and man accorded only a helpless and passive role? Or, as Fromm's reinterpretation of humanism affirms, should it be understood in a way which allows man effective participation in this creative renewal of himself?

In order to clarify these issues at all adequately we shall need to remind ourselves of certain very broad and general facts about religion, and this will require some reference to religions which grow out of a different background from that of Christianity.

When we examine the various civilized religions of the world, and compare what they have in common with contrasting features of primitive religion, we find that they all agree in insisting that man as he stands is incapable of true happiness, but needs to be remade before he can realize such happiness or even understand what it is. Primitive religion, by and large, is unconscious of any such need. It assumes that man's natural desires form the core of his true self; these desires press legitimately for satisfaction, and religion provides one important set of techniques by which their satisfaction can be assured. While a different note is not entirely absent, in general the divinities of primitive religion are conceived

[1] *Varieties of Religious Experience*, Lecture IV.

as powers which man can either coerce or persuade to satisfy his
natural desires for continued life and well-being. Civilized religions
discard this assumption in favor of a more penetrating analysis
of human nature. According to them, these desires which make up
the substance of the natural man are not unqualifiedly good.
As long as they are present they (or at least some of them) ob-
struct the way to man's fulfillment of his most wonderful potentialities, in virtue of which he can realize with his fellows and with
the universe a deep harmony which primitive religion is unable
to glimpse. In order to attain this harmony our natural urges
and yearnings must be radically disciplined, not just satisfied;
we need to be transformed into personalities in which they fill a
quite different role from that which they fill in their undisciplined
form. In short, our very inmost selves need to be, and can be, reshaped into something other than they naturally are, and only
when thus reshaped can they enter into the true happiness of
which man is distinctively capable. And so all these religions provide a psychological analysis which teaches this lesson; all, likewise, provide a method by which this radical transformation is to
be guided toward its goal.

But only those civilized religions which believe in a definitely
personal, transcendent God find themselves led to analyze this
situation in terms of the concept of sin. In their case such a concept
is almost inevitable. God, thus understood, embodies among other
things the absolute standard of rightness, to which he wishes us
men to conform; the attempt to satisfy our cravings is constantly
violating that standard, and constantly paining his fatherly concern for our true welfare. Our undisciplined nature, in short, is
rebelliously sinning against him, and we need redemption from
this sin in order to become heirs of the blessedness that is open
to us. Just as inevitable, however, is the absence of any such concept in nontheistic religions, but that does not mean that these
religions have not dealt seriously and profoundly with the same
human problem. It only means that their analysis of it, and their
practical solution for it, proceed in a different framework and
employ different categories.

It will be worth while to develop this statement briefly, by
reference to two of the nontheistic religions, Confucianism and

early Buddhism. Each of these religions is deeply concerned with the problem arising from man's undisciplined desires and offers a fundamental remedy; neither of them employs any concept similar to that of sin. But they differ from each other on the point that is central to our present discussion. In general, Confucianism assumes that the "once-born" man is the typical case; hence it provides an analysis and cure which aim to bring about a progressive transformation of our desires, so that they will be in full harmony with the highest possibilities of our social life and of our relation to the universe at large. Buddhism, on the contrary, assumes that our natural desires are radically wrong at their very core. They must be ultimately eliminated, and replaced by a character so different from the character dominated by these desires that it appears to be the complete Nirvana[2] of the natural man. In Pauline language, our old self must die and give way to a new self whose existence and life are radically discontinuous with what the old self exemplified. Hence the method employed—the famous "eight-fold path"—is so devised that it will lead step by step to an honest awareness of the extent to which cravings still infect our character, to a more and more radical rejection of them, and thus to a final state in which they will have faded completely away. But in both Confucianism and Buddhism this curative process is one in which the individual to be cured takes the initiative and exercises the responsible effort that is needed; he is not conceived to be passively dependent for his salvation on a transcendent divine power.

It is evident from this brief summary that these two religions agree with Western supernaturalism in holding that there is something radically wrong with the natural state of man, and that this wrong must be corrected before he can enter into a dependably happy and creative relation to himself, to his fellows, and to the universe. But in dealing with this problem they do not employ any concept analogous to the concept of sin; nor do they believe that this necessary reshaping of human nature is, or should be, carried out in dependence on any supernatural power. Moreover, along with these similarities and differences, they exhibit in their own way the provocative contrast between the "once-born"

[2] That is, "annihilation" or "nothingness."

and the "twice-born" doctrines about how the reshaping is to be achieved. Buddhism agrees with the typically Protestant insistence that there must be a wholesale purging of the poison of evil in man, while Confucianism believes in the less drastic method of gradually perfecting what is already good and thus reducing the evil.

When, in the light of these comparisons, we return to the challenging issues about sin in Western thought, two clarifying conclusions are strongly suggested. One is that the blithe evolutionary optimism about man which has been especially characteristic of Western liberalism during the last century may be blind to some important and sobering facts. It may well be that there is a wrongness in the human heart which cannot be adequately dealt with merely on the assumption that all that is needed is continued progress from the good that has already been achieved to the better that lies ahead. It may be—as the new supernaturalists insist—that this exuberant confidence in progress is itself one of the factors seriously hampering the deeper cure that is needed, encouraging a complacency which as long as it is present obstructs any more radical transformation of man by making it seem unnecessary. It may be true—as they insist—that even our faculty of reason is caught in this wrongness, along with everything else in our nature. The discovery, by various recent trends in psychology, that much of what we call reasoning is really a rationalizing of our hidden desires, and that perhaps no reasoning is wholly free from this taint, is very significant evidence. If that is the case, doubtless whatever complacency we have about ourselves will be able, in various subtle ways, to use reason to protect and justify itself against the threat of any disturbing awareness of our wrongness within. It may well be that the true perfecting of character cannot take place without an honest confronting of all these possibilities—a full recognition that they are present in oneself as much as in other people—and without a more radical way of dealing with them than the optimistic belief that man is naturally evolving in the right direction permits. The other suggested conclusion, however, is that all this can take place without necessarily employing the theistic concept of sin. And when we view the problem in terms of this broad perspective, it may appear that while that concept helpfully emphasizes some features of the situation that needs to be faced, it obscures others, and perhaps encourages certain attitudes that are detrimental to the remedy that would alone be really adequate. Let us develop this thought by summarizing the arguments that opposing thinkers employ in criticizing each other's position here.

Why do those who believe that man is a sinner, and needs consciously to recognize that he is, deeply distrust those who believe otherwise? Fundamentally, because it seems clear to them that this refusal to recognize one's sinfulness betokens a complacent self-righteousness that is the most serious sin of all. It is the most serious sin because wherever it is present it prevents any humbling awareness of whatever taint of self-interest still infects one's character, and prevents thus any real progress toward the complete abandonment of self, in love, that is the spiritual ideal. It is for this reason that, from their point of view, the basic human sin is pride—not sensuality, not injustice or cruelty, not even loveless-ness. Because, where there is no pride, these other sins can be removed, through humble recognition of their presence, and sincere repentance; but where pride has not been given up, all other sins are able to hide and protect themselves under its cloak, thus continuing to poison one's character because they are not honestly recognized and confronted. And it seems to these thinkers clear, from observation both of man's individual rationalizing and his collective hypocrisies, that this proud complacency is readily able to use reason as a willing tool in its self-justification. What individual has not, to some degree, sincerely mistaken the prosecution of his own subtle advantage for service of his fellows? What nation has not justified its quest for dominance over others by confusing that dominance with the true welfare of the world? And any such analysis is naturally expressed by Western theologians in terms of the concept of sin. They take for granted the theistic foundations of Western religion and have not been seriously concerned to find out how such problems have been dealt with elsewhere in the world; hence they identify without question this radical wrongness in human nature, revealed primarily in pride, with sin against God.

Why do those who reject this analysis distrust the theology of sin? For two reasons. In the first place, it seems clear to them that there are many "once-born" souls who naturally grow toward spiritual perfection (and who would include among its virtues a modest readiness for self-criticism) and that wherever this happens it is the most fortunate way to achieve religious progress. These souls had, perhaps, a happy environment in their childhood, which encouraged the early formation of sound moral habits and an attitude of loving concern for others; in their case no shattering consciousness of a radical wrongness within seems ever to be needed. Their religious life is a steady advance toward a richer realization of the inward peace of self-giving, and a fuller expression of responsible wisdom in their social conduct. Thinkers who are impressed by these once-born souls are inclined to take them as religiously typical, and to feel that what is most needed is to bring about the social conditions in which more of the younger generation can exemplify this form of spiritual growth. In any case, they are sure that the theology of sin is untrue to this kind of religious experience, and hence cannot properly claim (as it usually does claim) to be a universally valid analysis. In the second place, it seems to them that the notion of sin is haunted by certain unfortunate implications which lead to spiritually dubious consequences, even in the case of the twice-born souls who apparently need to come to terms with some deep-lying wrongness in themselves. It does not encourage, for example, they think, clear discrimination between a constructive and a partially destructive use of the awareness of wrongdoing. It does, to be sure, avoid the completely destructive feeling of despair, because God is conceived not merely as Judge but also as Savior. But when one's sense of guilt is interpreted as sin against God, the whole picture of God in the Old Testament as well as the New inevitably affects his feeling and attitude. The constructive turning away from self-centeredness toward what is truly good is thus confused with fears of punishment, with a tendency to prostrate oneself before majesty and power, with a childish acquiescence in the authority of "father"; even a morbid preoccupation with one's trivial mistakes as well as one's major delinquencies may be fostered. Moreover, they are sure that even in its best forms it encourages a paralyzing sense of impotence on man's part—a lack of manly self-reliance—and an utter dependence on the supernatural, which imply a wrong ideal of spiritual perfection.

But at this juncture we broach the second of the two issues to be discussed, and it will be best to sink an elaboration of the thought just expressed in a consideration of this issue, to which the problem of sin as such is secondary.

Taking it for granted that there is such an experience as the "second birth," and that many persons need to undergo it in their quest for spiritual perfection, on what basic assumptions should it be analyzed and interpreted? It would seem that an adequate interpretation must have two characteristics: it must be in terms that are fair to the relevant facts, and it must be in terms that reflect a sound conception of the kind of transformation that needs to be accomplished. Does the fundamentalist and new supernaturalist analysis meet these two requirements? And if not, how should it be corrected?

The outstanding feature of that analysis, as we noted above, is that it assigns all initiative and redeeming action in this process to God, leaving for man only a helpless and passive role. All that happens, from beginning to end, is the effect of divine grace; salvation, when it comes, is due entirely to God. The main reason for this interpretation is that any real process of self-criticism and self-transformation does involve a "moment" of ceasing to struggle, of consciously rejecting what one now is, of waiting for new forces to be released; and if this phase of the experience is emphasized as the crucial one in the entire process such an interpretation becomes very plausible. When one discovers (as those who undergo the second birth do discover) that even his sincerest effort to do right reflects the distorting power of the wrongness within, when he realizes that even the clearest exercise of his reason inevitably involves a taint of rationalizing, he feels his whole present self to be impotent; he can do nothing but abandon it, in waiting and emptiness, and whatever forces then come in which make for spiritual renewal (and they do come in if he is in earnest) seem to enter from the outside—from a power not himself that is creating in him a new personality, more akin to what his ideal of perfection demands. And if those who interpret this experience have also assumed without question the theistic concept of a transcendent God, the orthodox Protestant analysis becomes unavoidable.

What have the critics of this analysis to say here? Mainly, two things. The first concerns the very difficult problems about God that are thrust upon us if we make this interpretation. We seem forced to accept the doctrine of predestination, in its most extreme and rigorous form. For it seems obvious that some people go through this transformation and thus, being released from domination by sin, become heirs of eternal bliss; while some do not, and are therefore condemned to whatever destiny awaits the unrepentant and unregenerate. Now if all is due to God, the difference between these two situations must be explained as the consequence of an arbitrary and inscrutable decision of the Divine Will. But how can this inevitable conclusion be reconciled with the doctrine that God is supremely good, and that his goodness is distinctively exhibited in his love for all men—his desire that all alike be saved? And how can one feel reverence toward such a God? If, on the other hand, what happens in this process of personality-remaking is due in large part to man—to his active participation—then this serious theological difficulty becomes avoidable. In that case we can explain the difference between these two situations as due to different degrees of active response on man's part to the challenge of critical self-awareness and self-judgment; God does not need to be saddled with the responsibility of having eternally predestined some men to hell.

The second thing that the critics can say concerns the spiritual ideal reflected in the interpretation. Are not self-respect, and a certain kind of self-confidence, valid spiritual virtues? Are they not necesary to the fulfillment of personal and social responsibility? Does not a mature spiritual character show a fundamental autonomy in judgment and action, no longer dependent, as a child is, on a father's will as to what he should be and do? Does not the fundamentalist and new supernaturalist interpretation reflect, then, a child's acceptance of helplessness, a child's demand for the kind of security that complete dependence on a father's decisions for him provides? This is very easy in an era of social upheaval when individuals feel discouraged and impotent, but is it morally good? Should not man think of himself rather as responsible for his own destiny, and creatively participate in its determination? If such is the case, then the process of radical self-renewal should be analyzed, if possible, in terms which harmonize with this spiritual ideal. And it would seem that in a matter of this kind such an analysis is always possible, without violating any of the relevant facts. What has to be done first, of course, is to bring out all the factors that can be verified as playing a significant part in this process. But the question, which of those factors should be interpreted as belonging to the action of God, and which to the coöperating action of man, would appear to be undecided in advance and certainly not determined merely by the discoverable facts. Any decision on that question is a part of our way of reading those facts and fitting them coherently into our theology. So, at least, the critics of the traditional interpretation can plausibly insist. Indeed, their extreme contention would be that the very conception of God which theology is employing here is a product of man's idealizing imagination, as it clarifies the more appealing features that his own nature has disclosed.

Which solution, then, of these serious issues is the right one? They have always been of prime importance, and ever since the day of Augustine no Western religious thinker of first rank has been able to neglect them. But in our day their challenge has acquired a new and insistent poignance. How can we meet that challenge with true understanding?

Chapter XVII

METHOD IN RELIGIOUS PHILOSOPHY—THE ROLE OF FAITH

How CAN we reach confident answers to such questions as the ones which have just been critically analyzed? In view of the circumstance that keen and honest thinkers have been led to such different conclusions about them, we face a fifth major problem in the fact of their mutual opposition. This is the problem of method in dealing with the challenging issues of religious philosophy. When men who are eager for truth reach irreconcilable answers to important questions, it seems clear that not all of them can be following the method which is appropriate in such matters. What is the right method, and why is it right?

By and large, as was noted earlier,[1] four main methods of pursuing theological questions can be distinguished in Western thought. They may be called, respectively, the authoritarian, the intuitive, the rationalistic, and the empirical methods. Most influential religious philosophies combine two or more of them in some distinctive way.

A method is authoritarian if it locates its standard of truth in some sacred writing handed down from the past, or in the pronouncements of some ecclesiastical institution. Protestant fundamentalism illustrates an ultimate appeal to authoritarian method in the first of these two forms; Catholicism, in the second. But Catholicism, unlike fundamentalism, holds that the validity of this authoritarian appeal can be justified by a prior argument grounded in experience and reason. Hence the initial method which it employs is in part empirical (in the Aristotelian sense), in

[1] See above, p. 133.

448

part rationalistic. Authoritarianism is sufficient as a method of last resort to those who are convinced that the authority to which they appeal possesses a higher than human sanction. This is the case when the Bible is believed to be, or to contain, a unique revelation from God. To those who are not so convinced, the question at once becomes pertinent: what method was used by that supposed authority? And the answer seems to be: one or more of the other three methods mentioned.

Let us consider them. The intuitive method is exhibited in clearest and most extreme form in the thinkers known as "mystics." Who is a mystic?

The mystic is an individual in whom religious experience takes the form of an unusually vivid integration, one of whose major aspects is a sense of having gained direct insight into the nature of ultimate reality and of man's relation to it. Sometimes he finds it hopeless to attempt a statement of this insight in ordinary language. Usually, however, he feels that such a statement is due his less fortunate fellows, and then a serious difficulty arises. The reality with which he has been in touch often appears quite unverifiable by ordinary human experience, and his description of it may even seem self-contradictory, or at least highly paradoxical. These features do not trouble the mystic because of his complete confidence in the trustworthiness of the illumination that has come to him; if reason and daily experience fail to approve his discoveries, so much the worse for reason and experience—their inadequacy is thereby clearly indicated. But paradox and lack of harmony with facts of ordinary life do trouble those who are not mystics. They find it very difficult to believe that these so-called "insights" are genuinely such, or can properly be trusted, since the greater part of life is lived under different guides. Now, while not many persons exemplify the extremes to which mysticism may go in its outstanding representatives, most religious people do have experiences which give them a sense of exaltation above the humdrum level of ordinary existence and which possess a certain cognitive quality, at least to the extent of strongly suggesting or supporting doctrines which otherwise might seem inadequately buttressed. Memory of these experiences then suffuses daily life with a certain assurance which encourages distrust of reason and of sense perception wherever they run counter to the ideas which such experiences had seemed to confirm, even though in secular matters these processes are still regarded as sufficient.

③ The rationalist in religious philosophy profoundly distrusts mysticism because of its esoteric character, and especially because its descriptions of reality sometimes seem to violate the axioms which reason regards as basic to all clear understanding. His absolute principle is that truth can never be self-contradictory, and therefore wherever he meets paradox or apparent inconsistency he is sure that truth has been missed. His most certain principles are the ones he finds exemplified in careful analytic reflection on all problems which reason is concerned to attack, secular as well as religious. He insists, then, that the ultimate intuitions of religious philosophy must be such that from them systematic demonstrations can be made, the resulting doctrines being logically bound together in a coherent order. He may distrust mere sense perception as much as the mystic does (although modern rationalists are less likely to do so than those of an earlier period), but unless the canons which seem to be prescribed by the nature of reason are fully respected his assent will not be won.

④ The empiricist is suspicious of both mystic illumination and reason unless they are explicitly rendered obedient to facts disclosed in sense perception. He rejects the insights of the former as entirely illusory unless they are frankly treated as tentative hypotheses capable of verification by experienced facts that are available to all normal people. He accepts the rational axiom that thought must not contradict itself, but holds that all demonstrations of reason, outside of the purely mathematical sciences, are inconclusive apart from such verification. Nothing else seems to him quite so dependable or clear as a fact of direct observation, and only when an idea can be shown fully to square with observed fact is he confident of its truth.

These four methods are capable of being combined in various ways, especially the first and second, and the third and fourth. In fact, few religious philosophies fail to give a significant role to at least two of them. The normal way in which the authoritarian and intuitive methods are combined is evident throughout religious history. Ancient seers or prophets gained some important intuitive insight into the meaning of life, which then, as handed down through tradition, became an authoritative revelation of the divine to their followers in later generations. The normal way in which the rationalistic and empirical methods are combined is exhibited most clearly in the history of science. The outcome of this history is that rationalists nowadays accept the responsibility to take facts of sense perception as their starting point in the acquisition of knowledge about the world, and as providing much, if not all, of its detailed content. Empiricists, on their side, do not attempt to get along without reason, since a perception remains nothing but a perception until it is related in some orderly way to other perceptions; such relating is not itself accomplished by the senses but is the work of reason, and is guided by principles that can never be fully verified by perceptual experience. Also, to a degree, the second and third methods may be combined; this happens whenever a rationalist accepts some illuminating intuition as a dependable basis for systematic demonstration of detailed doctrine, or the followers of a prophetic mystic accept some responsibility to render his insights logically coherent. Can the first and third methods be combined? Yes, but apparently, in the West, only in the ways exemplified in Catholicism and orthodox Protestantism.[2] In Catholicism natural reason is believed able to demonstrate, by its own canons as applied to certain historical data, that the Church has divine authority to interpret saving doctrine to men. Such authority then is accepted, in part on rational grounds. For Protestantism, in all but its liberal forms, the authority of the Divine Word must be accepted at the very beginning; reason then fulfills the humble role of giving a systematic exposition of that revelation. Indeed, many modernists reveal an element of authoritarianism in their attitude toward the Bible, although it is not explicitly recognized as a part of their theological method.

But the second and fourth of these methods can be combined only if we are willing to adopt a radical dualism in our cosmology —that is, if we draw a sharp line between transcendent reality, whose nature is revealed by intuitive illumination, and the world of ordinary experience, to be understood by the method of empiricism. Such a combination has occasionally been defended by

2 And in a few sects of less extensive influence, such as the Mormons.

important thinkers, and in a less definite form is implied by the practice of many religious people, but as a philosophical standpoint it has never been widely influential. Philosophers and theologians usually insist on a unity of method in dealing with factual reality even though they may be dualists or pluralists in other respects.

The most challenging issues today in connection with the problem of method are those which concern the degree of validity that may properly be assigned to the authoritarian and intuitive methods as over against the way of reason and experience. The new supernaturalism has in its own fashion given respectability to authoritarianism again, after the long dominance in Protestant theology of a liberal empiricism. And intuition in some form has always had its champions in this field. But our age is the age of modern science—which means that a strongly empirical emphasis dominates its thinking and that respect for the principle of rational consistency is taken for granted. In such an age a persistently vital question is this: Is this empirical and rational method, properly conceived and applied, adequate in dealing with religious questions; or does it need to be corrected by some source of authority, or supplemented by some sort of mystical insight? Is it a sound demand that all truth about factual reality must be verifiable in the experience of the ordinary person, or is some religious truth gained only by direct intuition of supersensible reality, mediated through authoritative tradition to those who are dependent on the intuitions of others? On this issue agnosticism, humanism, and the more radical modernists take the former position, while Catholicism, fundamentalism, and the new supernaturalism adopt the latter.

From the standpoint of champions of the former view, the latter method is untrustworthy, chiefly on two accounts. They see that intuitive insights, except for certain very broad features, vary greatly, and reflect the central ideas of the historical faith in which the one who accepts those insights has been brought up. These considerations seem to them both to impugn the method as such and to show that it is not as independent of other factors as the believer in intuition assumes. They see also that it is readily capable of social exploitation. When some individuals claim to have discovered truths important for human welfare which the mass of mankind are unable to check by common experience, it is easy for the former, or for persons who assume to stand as their interpreters, to exercise power in spiritual, if not also in material, affairs over those who look to them for leadership and guidance. In this way the easy and frequent alliance of intuitionism and authoritarianism seems to them a social danger as well as intellectually unjustified. The empirical method, on the other hand, is prized because it is essentially democratic. A fact of sense perception is common property among all normal persons, and therefore a method which appeals to such facts as its final criterion of truth is a method which all can apply in the same way, reaching the same results by its use.

Those who believe that there is validity in the intuitive method distrust empiricism because it seems to them palpably inadequate, especially in religious matters. They see that even facts of external perception are not always as objective as empiricists are apt to assume; these data are capable of being related in different ways and interpreted by different principles of explanation, and thus often seem to support diverse conclusions. They believe, moreover, that when religious experience is concerned some of the most important facts are events of inner experience, disclosed only by introspection of one's inward attitude or state. But such facts are very ambiguous, elusive, and fluctuating; it seems almost impossible to establish any definite doctrine clearly by their aid alone, or to refute irreconcilable doctrines that appear supported by the introspection of others. Moreover, these thinkers ask, is not the experience of the prophetic mystic still an experience even though not commonly shared, and must not an adequate empirical method take it fully into account? In short, they contend that empiricism must be broadened if it is to become adequate to the most significant religious facts, and that when thus revised it loses the very features which most appeal to those who champion it. Suppose we grant the main empiricist contentions; there still remains before our eyes the baffling problem of discriminating the facts that are really relevant to religious problems, of analyzing them clearly, and of determining how they should be interpreted. This is the basic challenge to the em-

piricist view. The challenge to their opponents, of course, is to
render the methods of intuition and authority convincing in face
of the circumstance that even less than empiricism do they seem
to lead to any single impartial conclusion on the matters with which
all these methods are attempting to deal.

What, after all, *is* intuition? The empiricist is apt to assume that
it is always a mysterious and esoteric affair, characterized simply
by its difference from the methods which he has come to trust.
Is this so? Is there a kind of intuitive insight whose distinctive
nature is to draw together, in a unity of meaning, facts which
for the empirical method remain disconnected or inharmonious?
There is much in the history of mysticism to suggest an affirmative
answer. But if so, how shall we distinguish such valid insights
from the intuitions which seem to be merely products of wishful
thinking? What can serve as a criterion here?

So we return to the crucial issue. In the light of all these considerations, which standpoint ought we to adopt? Empiricism has
many obvious and appealing virtues, but it seems of questionable
applicability to the crucial questions of religious philosophy. Intuitive insight seems naturally and spontaneously applicable to
them, but it lacks the methodological advantages which modern
thought has increasingly come to regard as essential. And there
are always those who claim authority in religion; is the claim
ever justified?

It is in connection with the problem of method that the difficulty
which many religious thinkers feel concerning the relation between
faith and knowledge should be considered. Conclusions established by the way of rational analysis of perceptual experience
are ordinarily recognized by thinkers who are not mystics as being
properly called "knowledge." True mystics, by contrast, usually
insist on applying this term to the insights gained in the mystic
experience, and refuse to admit, as other than illusory, truths
reached by any less exalted method. Since, however, they are
decidedly in the minority, general usage has accepted the former
implied definition of knowledge, and has recognized the established sciences and philosophy as its most prominent exemplifications. The term which is then commonly applied to modes of
assurance reached by routes other than reason and ordinary ex-

perience is "faith." It may be faith in one's own superempirical insight, or in another's insight as handed down by tradition or interpreted by some authority. Our present major issue may accordingly be stated in this form: Is the way of knowledge adequate in religious matters, or does it need to be supplemented by the way of faith?

Except for the agnostics, the Spinozists, and some humanists, all influential movements in religious philosophy have allowed a significant place for faith as a supplement to knowledge, but their interpretation of this concept and especially of its relation to knowledge varies greatly. To the Catholic, faith is necessary because knowledge, in the form of natural theology, cannot include all truth essential for salvation; the essence of faith is acceptance of needed supersensible truths, and such acceptance is involved in sincere commitment to God and submission to the authority of his Church. To the fundamentalist, it is required for the same reason, but it consists rather in trust in the divine revelation given through the Bible—a trust held warranted by the latter's moral appeal and its miraculous evidences. In ethical idealism, the nature and significance of faith become quite transformed. Faith is needed because knowledge is only competent in the phenomenal realm, being impotent in metaphysics; it is just as rational, however, as knowledge, since it results from the exercise of reason on the moral obligations of man and their implications regarding the nature of ultimate reality. These apprehensions are just as certain as knowledge—perhaps more so—but they are of quite another order. Liberals, of course, differ considerably among themselves on this matter. Some modernists think of faith as a quasi-mystical addition to rational understanding, arising from the circumstance that the explanations of their religious experience offered by science (represented here by the psychologist) appear less than just in their eyes both to the high value and to the cosmic implications of that experience. Faith is thus an extra-scientific warrant for the validity of the explanation they hold to be sound. In the case of many, faith is used primarily in a narrower sense; it means devoted commitment to Christ and his way of life, and is necessary because the superiority of the religious and moral values bound up with him can never, they will admit, be scientifically demonstrated. With humanism, a further transformation appears. Those among its champions who use the word mean by it essentially the eager adherence on man's part to whatever social good seems to be supreme, but it is empirically grounded and hence not rational in the sense in which it is so for ethical idealism. It is required because such commitment, while not sharply sundered from scientific knowledge, in a vital sense precedes and outreaches it. Pursuit of science itself implies that one regards the kind of knowledge it discovers as worth pursuing and hence as a significant human good, but its value cannot be established by the method of science. To the new supernaturalists, faith is the trustful and obedient response to God on the part of the repentant soul, a response which involves full acceptance of the Biblical revelation, and which chastens reason so that it places itself submissively at service in interpreting the divine Word.

Here is rather impressive testimony to the human need of some mode of assurance transcending what can be won by the ordinary empirical and rational processes of knowledge. If these philosophies are right, man must in some sense live by faith and not merely by knowledge. But just what is faith? Is it, in its essence, a kind of higher knowledge—an insight into metaphysical reality? So many have believed. Is it acceptance of some revelation which supplements our knowledge? So many have also taught. Or is the immediate confidence which it brings of another sort than that which attends the acquisition of knowledge? Is faith, perhaps, rather our voluntary commitment to a great leader? Is it devotion to an ultimate moral principle or value which is not, properly speaking, an object of knowledge even though our acceptance of it provides the foundation for whatever wisdom in living we attain? Many have accepted one of these conceptions of faith. Faith brings assurance, but assurance of what? And how are we to construe the relation between faith and knowledge as derived by the ordinary means of perception and reason—the sense and way in which the former supplements the latter? Is it just an addition, or is the relation more complex and intricate? Possibly knowledge itself rests upon faith, a doctrine taught by thinkers as different in other respects as Augustine and John Dewey;

perhaps faith rests upon knowledge, a position held in different ways by Spinoza and the early empiricists. Where lies the truth in such baffling matters? Apparently we need some adequate answer to these questions of method in order to deal more satisfactorily with the issues earlier raised. What should our answer be?

Or—for there is a more radical possibility—should religious philosophy abandon the assumption that its task is to establish *truth* on these difficult matters, and accept the more modest and humble role of contributing to progressive but never-ending *clarification* of them? The present volume, in the interest of maximum impartiality, has explicitly restricted itself to this latter function— is that all, perhaps, that theology and religious philosophy can ever really accomplish? Should we reconcile ourselves to its limitations and give our energies to the development of its possibilities?

The five major issues which Part III has endeavored to clarify do not by any means exhaust the important conflicts involved in the ultimate assumptions of the competing religious philosophies that have occupied our attention. More than these chapters would be needed to consider all of them. But these five are peculiarly focal and basic. If one reaches a tolerably clear and confident answer to them he will find that his solution of most of the other problems in religious thought has been reached by implication. Clarification of these, therefore, has seemed especially needed. It is important in each case to see the central point at issue in relation to its background, and something of what is involved in each of the major alternative answers.

By way of summary of Part III, these crucial issues may be succinctly stated. Is man competent to attain all needed religious truth for himself, or does he require and can he gain supplementation by a supernatural revelation? And is he capable of certainty in his religious insights, or of empirical tentativeness only? Is the fundamental structure of the universe a teleological or an impersonal order? Which is of central importance in religion—a metaphysical faith, a historical attachment, or devotion to a moral principle or social ideal? Is man in his natural state radically sinful? And by what method are questions like these to be answered? In what sense, if any, does man need to live by faith?

In the introductory chapter some suggestions were made as to where, in such fields as the history and psychology of religion, contemporary students might hope to make significant contributions to our deeper understanding. In the philosophy of religion the greatest and most insistent need is the further critical examination of these fundamental problems. Doubtless, most readers of the present discussion will be primarily concerned to reach their own more confident answers to them. A place of honor, however, awaits those who can and will contribute to such progressive criticism, and thus aid in the reflective guidance of all subsequent thinkers who are eager to come to terms with the realities on which man's happiness and destiny depend.

SELECTED BIBLIOGRAPHY TO PART III

Alexander, H. B., *God and Man's Destiny*, Oxford University Press, 1936.
Bennett, C. A., *The Dilemma of Religious Knowledge*, Yale University Press, 1931.
Bennett, J. C., *Christian Ethics and Social Policy*, Scribner, 1946.
Bennett, J. C., *Christianity and Communism*, Association Press, 1948.
Bergson, H., *The Two Sources of Morality and Religion*, Holt, 1935.
Brightman, E. S., *Philosophy of Religion*, Prentice-Hall, 1940.
Brightman, E. S., *The Problem of God*, Abingdon, 1930.
Burns, C. D., *The Horizon of Experience*, Norton, 1934.
Durant, W., *On the Meaning of Life*, R. R. Smith, 1932.
Ferré, N., *Faith and Reason*, Harper, 1946.
Fromm, E., *Man for Himself*, Rinehart, 1947.
Fromm, E., *Psychoanalysis and Religion*, Yale University Press, 1950.
Hartshorne, C., *The Divine Relativity*, Yale University Press, 1948.
Haydon, A. E., *Man's Search for the Good Life*, Harper, 1937.
Haydon, A. E., *The Quest of the Ages*, Harper, 1929.
Hocking, W. E., *The Meaning of God in Human Experience*, Yale University Press, 1912.
Hocking, W. E., *Thoughts on Death and Life*, Harper, 1937.
James, W., *The Varieties of Religious Experience*, Longmans, Green, 1902.
James, W., *The Will to Believe*, Longmans, Green, 1897.
Jones, R. M., *Pathways to the Reality of God*, Macmillan, 1931.
Krutch, J. W., *The Modern Temper*, Harcourt, Brace, 1929.
Laird, J., *On Human Freedom*, Allen and Urwin, 1947.
Lamont, C., *The Illusion of Immortality*, Philosophical Library, rev. ed., 1950.
Lippmann, W., *A Preface to Morals*, Macmillan, 1929.

Lyman, E. W., *The Meaning and Truth of Religion*, Scribner, 1933.

Martin, J. A., Jr., *Empirical Philosophies of Religion*, Columbia University Press, 1945.

Montague, M. P., *Twenty Minutes of Reality*, Dutton, 1917.

Montague, W. P., *Belief Unbound*, Yale University Press, 1930.

Newton, J. F., *My Idea of God*, Little, Brown, 1927.

Nicholson, J. A., *Philosophy of Religion*, Ronald Press, 1950.

O'Brien, J. A., *Truths Men Live By*, Macmillan, 1946.

Otto, M. C., *The Human Enterprise*, Crofts, 1940.

Otto, R., *The Idea of the Holy*, Oxford University Press, 1926.

Overstreet, H. A., *The Mature Mind*, Norton, 1949.

Santayana, G., *Reason in Religion*, Scribner, 1905.

Sartre, J. P., *Existentialism*, Philosophical Library, 1947.

Schweitzer, A., *The Philosophy of Civilization*, Macmillan, 1950.

Talbot, N. S., *The Riddle of Life*, Longmans, Green, 1929.

Taylor, A. E., *Does God Exist?* Macmillan, 1947.

Tillich, P., *The Religious Situation*, Holt, 1932.

Trueblood, D. E., *Foundations for Reconstruction*, Harper, 1946.

Trueblood, D. E., *The Logic of Belief*, Harper, 1942.

Tsanoff, R. A., *The Moral Ideals of Our Civilization*, Dutton, 1942.

Tsanoff, R. A., *The Nature of Evil*, Macmillan, 1931.

Tsanoff, R. A., *The Problem of Immortality*, Macmillan, 1924.

INDEX

(The main treatment of the more important topics or thinkers
is indicated by italics.)

121 f., 127 f.; for fundamentalism, 153 f., 159; for Spinoza, 190 f.; for Hume, 217, 224 ff.; for Mill, 230; for Kant, 255 ff., 265 f.; for Schleiermacher, 291 ff.; for modernism, 329 ff., 357; as treated by humanism, 339 ff; for naturalistic theism, 366 f.; for the new supernaturalism, 377 f., 382 f., 385, 387 f., 392, 396
Golden Rule, the, 148, 259, 370
Good, idea of the, in Plato, 47 f., 53 f., 69
Grace, doctrine of, in Augustine, 74, 78 ff., 84 f.; in Schleiermacher, 293; in fundamentalism, 153 ff.; in the new supernaturalism, 385, 392
Greek Catholicism, 74, 96 f.
Gregory the Great, Pope, 88

Haeckel, E., 192 f.
Hartshorne, C., 368
Hebrew religion, development of, 16–40
Hegel, G. W. F., 296, 306 f.
Higher criticism of the Bible, 17, 295, 308–318, 322, 378 f., 393
Hinduism, 7, 73
History of religion, 5 f., 318 ff., 346 ff.
Holy Spirit, the, 34, 74 f., 149, 155, 157, 418
Hosea, 21, 27
Hugo of St. Victor, 92 f., 95
Humanism, religious, 232, 268, 280 f., 324, 332–358, 359, 365, 368 f., 370 ff., 411, 416 f., 419, 432 f., 435, 438 f., 446 f., 452, 455 f.
Hume, David, 176, 207–229, 239 f., 258, 266, 281, 285 f., 295, 299 f., 303
Huxley, T. H., 229 ff., 258
Hypothesis, role of, in modern science, 204 f.; applied to theology, 288 f.

Immortality, doctrine of, 10, 30, 36–40; in Plato, 51 ff.; in Aristotle, 62; in Augustine, 79, 81, 87; in

Catholicism, 95, 119–123; in fundamentalism, 154, 160; in Spinoza, 191 f.; as treated by Hume, 227 ff.; in Kant, 244, 254 f., 264 f.; in Adler, 271 f.; in modernism, 330 ff.; critical discussion, 431
Impartiality in the study of religion, 4 f., 10, 13 f., 457
Incarnation, doctrine of, 40, 328
Induction, canons of, 203, 229
Inspiration of the Bible, 419 f.; for orthodox theory, 308 ff.; for modernism, 328
Integration of personality, religious significance of, 325 f., 332 ff., 357
Intellectual love of God, in Spinoza, 191
Intelligence, nature of, 119 ff., 140, 343, 362 f., 373 ff., 379 ff., 384, 388 f.; competence of, critical discussion, 401–408
Intuition, method of, 133 f., 448 ff.
Inwardness, emphasis on, in the prophets, 22, 25 ff.; in Jesus, 32 f.
Isaiah, 21, 22 f.

Jacob, 310
James, William, 439
Jeremiah, 21, 24, 26 f.
Jesus of Nazareth, 28, 31–34, 36 ff., 40, 65 f., 74 f., 129 ff., 157, 160, 163, 290 f., 294, 307, 313 ff., 319 f., 328, 332, 335 ff., 359, 379, 385, 387, 392 f., 396, 433, 437, 455
John, Gospel of, 31, 38 ff., 65, 308
Joshua, 17 f.
Justification by faith, doctrine of, 155 f., 160 f., 385 f., 396

Kant, Immanuel, 85, 169, 180, 238–267, 268 ff., 281 f., 284, 290, 300, 352, 423
Kepler, J., 177, 204 f.
Kierkegaard, Sören, 375 f.
Knowledge, Plato's theory of, 44 ff., 47 f., 52, 66; Aristotle's, 56 f.; in Plotinus, 66 f.; in Augustine, 82, 89; in Aquinas, 98, 122; in Catholicism generally, 112 ff., 124 ff., 139; religious value of, 186 ff.,

INDEX 465

191 f., 193 f., 196, 331 f., 339, 344; in Kant, 241–258, 270; in Krutch, 362 ff.; critical discussion, 401–418, 451 f.
Krutch, J. W., 362 ff., 411, 417

Labor, problems of, in Catholic theory, 137 f.; in fundamentalism, 164 f.; in Adler, 274 ff.; as treated by Jesus, 336; in modernism and humanism, 354 ff.; in the new supernaturalism, 393 f.
Last judgment, doctrine of, 30, 38, 321
Leibniz, G. W., 238
Liberalism in religious thought, 280–358
Lippmann, W., 188, 193, 195
Locke, John, 176, 206 f.
Logos, doctrine of, in the Gospel of John, 40; in Stoicism, 63; in Philo, 65; in Christian orthodoxy, 74, 314
Lotze, Hermann, 267
Love as a religious virtue, 27 f., 31 ff., 38 ff., 53, 79, 81, 84, 86, 328, 337, 349 f., 357, 362 ff., 385 f., 390 f., 393 f.
Lowell, J. R., 317
Loyalty to a leader, problem of, in religion, 294 f., 326 ff., 333 ff.; critical discussion, 435 ff.
Luther, Martin, 146 f., 150, 153, 155 f., 159, 161 f., 164 f.
Lutherans, 146, 149, 153

Manichean dualism, 78
Marcus Aurelius, 63 f.
Mary the Virgin, 132
Mathematical conception of the world, 170 ff., 182 f., 190 f., 196; critical discussion, 425 ff.
Mathematics, nature of, 412 ff.; Kant's theory of, 243 f., 247, 257
Matter, Aristotle's theory of, 57 ff.; Plotinus', 67; in Catholic theory, 117 ff.
Mechanical conception of the world, 177 ff., 221, 299 f.; critical discussion, 425 ff.
Mendel, G., 135

Mercy as a religious virtue, 25, 28, 32
Messiah, doctrine of, 29 f.; applied to Jesus, 33 ff., 38, 40, 336
Metaphysics, role of, in religious philosophy, 71 ff., 79 f., 134 f., 139, 235, 236 ff., 241 f., 245, 252 ff., 257 f., 264 ff., 285 f., 288, 345 f., 419 ff., 424 ff., 452 f., 464, 469 f.; critical discussion, 419–431, 432–435
Method in religious philosophy, problem of, 135 f.; critical discussion, 448–457
Methodists, 146
Micah, 21, 25
Mill, John Stuart, 229 f., 233, 324
Milton, John, 148
Miracles, problem of, 294, 321 f., 328, 406; in Catholic theory, 126 ff., 140; in fundamentalism, 152, 160 f., 166; Hume's discussion of, 212–217
Modernism, religious standpoint of, 280, 326 ff., 349 ff., 359, 365 ff., 419, 435, 451, 455
Monistic religion of Haeckel, 192 f.
Moral argument for God's existence, 110, 150, 159 f., 166
Morals, in relation to religion, 10, 416 f.; for the Hebrew prophets, 20 ff., 23 ff.; for Jesus, 31 ff.; for Plato, 49, 53 ff.; for Stoicism, 64 f.; for Catholicism, 135 ff.; for Kant, 236 ff., 258–266; for Adler, 268 ff., 283; for modernism, 349 ff.; for humanism, 343 ff., 351 ff.; critical discussion, 432 ff.
Moses, 17 f., 21, 310
Mystery cults, 35 f., 41, 72
Mysticism, 8, 68, 72 ff., 79, 88, 428; critical disussion, 449 ff.

Natural religion, 319 f.
Natural selection, 109, 296 ff., 303 f.
Natural theology, 93, 95 f., 139, 147, 150, 159, 166, 169, 198, 455
Naturalism, in metaphysics, 301 f., 339 ff., 420 ff.
Naturalistic theism, 366 f.
Nebuchadrezzar, 311